GERMAN WORKERS
IN CHICAGO

GERMAN WORKERS IN CHICAGO

A Documentary History of Working-Class Culture from 1850 to World War I

Edited by
Hartmut Keil and John B. Jentz

with the assistance of
Klaus Ensslen, Hanns-Theodor Fuß,
Christiane Harzig, and Heinz Ickstadt

Documents translated by
Burt Weinshanker

UNIVERSITY OF ILLINOIS PRESS
Urbana and Chicago

Publication of this work was supported in part by a grant
from the National Endowment for the Humanities.

Library of Congress Cataloging-in-Publication Data

German workers in Chicago.

(The Working class in American history)
"This anthology of documents . . . resulting from the
work of the Chicago Project on the social history of
German workers from 1850 to 1910"—Pref.
  Bibliography: p.
  Includes index.
  1. German Americans—Employment—Illinois—Chicago—
History—Sources. 2. Labor and laboring classes—
Illinois—Chicago—History—Sources. 3. German Americans
—Illinois—Chicago—Social life and customs—Sources.
4. German Americans—Illinois—Chicago—Social conditions
—Sources. 5. German Americans—Illinois—Chicago—
History—Sources. I. Keil, Hartmut, 1942-   .
II. Jentz, John B., 1944-   . III. Chicago Project
(Universität München) IV. Series.
HD8081.GaG46   1988   331.6'2'43077311   87-10780
ISBN 0-252-01458-8 (alk. paper)

to the memory of Herbert G. Gutman

CONTENTS

ILLUSTRATIONS

PREFACE

This anthology of documents is one of several publications resulting from the work of the Chicago Project on the social history of German workers in Chicago from 1850 to 1910. Based at the America Institute of the University of Munich and funded by the Volkswagen Foundation from 1979 to 1983, the project was directed by Hartmut Keil with the assistance of John B. Jentz. Also participating in the project was a work group led by Heinz Ickstadt and Christiane Harzig at the John F. Kennedy Institute for North American Studies at the Free University Berlin. Dr. Hans Kolligs, chief librarian of the Kennedy Institute, lent the project substantial support by acquiring important source material. In addition, the project worked closely with the Newberry Library in Chicago, particularly with its Family and Community History Center. Publication of the German edition of the anthology was made possible by the Volkswagen Foundation. The American edition was jointly prepared by the America Institute of the University of Munich and the Family and Community History Center of the Newberry Library. The editing and translation of the German documents was funded by a grant from the Division of Research Programs of the National Endowment for the Humanities, an independent federal agency.

Many others aided in the success of this endeavor besides those noted on the title page. We want to mention especially the graduate assistants who contributed directly to the preparation of the anthology, Dagmar Ebert, Dona F. Geyer, Christine Heiß, and Ruth Seifert.

The project as a whole profited from a group of German and American social historians — Karl Bosl, David Brody, Werner Conze, Kathleen Neils Conzen, Herbert Gutman, and David Montgomery — who served as advisors. We would like to thank them all for their interest and their constructive criticism. However, since there would have been no Chicago Project without Herbert Gutman's enthusiasm and continuing encouragement, this book is dedicated to his memory.

Hartmut Keil
John B. Jentz

INTRODUCTION

This anthology seeks to illustrate the traditions of German working-class culture in America and its transformation in the context of a new social and cultural environment. Until recently immigration and labor historians have tended to ignore the fact that German immigration provided a steady stream of workers who moved into America's urban centers during the second half of the nineteenth century. Scholars approaching immigration history from a predominantly ethnic perspective and therefore less concerned with aspects of social position or class were inclined to perceive these immigrant workers solely as members of an ethnically coherent group. As a result, they showed little awareness of the many vital cultural traditions brought over and passed on by German workers, traditions which cannot simply be subsumed under the umbrella category of a national ethnic heritage.

Historians have therefore rarely noticed the extent to which early American labor organizations were founded and supported by German-American workers, especially in the period of rapid industrialization from the 1860s through the 1890s. It would be a serious mistake (and a repetition of the errors of the consensus school of history) if one regarded the efforts of German immigrant workers at organizing a heterogeneous American working class merely as the ineffective activities of a marginal group of radicals. Not only were German immigrant workers organized to an unusually high degree, they also helped establish the organizational structures later to be used by an emerging national and multi-ethnic labor movement. This anthology intends to recall one of the major foreign traditions contributing to that movement and to American working-class culture.

Focusing on one city can be justified on both thematic and methodological grounds. In the latter half of the nineteenth century, Chicago exemplified, like no other American city, the effects that industrialization and social change had on immigrant workers in the Gilded Age. Within a few decades Chicago expanded to become the commercial, trade, and industrial metropolis of the entire Midwest. It became not only the nation's second largest city, but also a center of German immigration. From 1850 to 1900, the German-born and their children accounted for between 25

1

and 30 percent of Chicago's population throughout the period, while the proportion of workers in the German-American community also remained high. As late as 1900, two-thirds of all German-Americans in the city lived in working-class households, providing a broad base for a viable German working-class culture.

Moreover, Chicago played a key role in the emerging American labor movement, which itself profited from an unusually high degree of German participation. From the 1860s onward Chicago's working class began to radically question Gilded Age American society, and in May, 1886, when more than 100,000 workers walked off the job, the city became the center of the eight-hour movement. Chicago is thus especially suited for an investigation of the organizational and radical traditions that German immigrant workers contributed to the Chicago — and to the American — labor movement.

A case study of this sort makes it possible to treat German working-class culture within the specific social and cultural context of urban America. It is a central assumption of this anthology that nineteenth-century working-class culture can only be adequately analyzed and understood if it is approached as an everyday culture that was lived and enacted by individuals as well as the community. Therefore we have tried to illuminate the context of the workers' everyday life, their self-perception, and their reaction to social change. Since this can only be accomplished by reconstructing a concrete social environment, we have sought to document not only the arrival and settlement of immigrant workers but also the conditions and ways of life in ethnic working-class neighborhoods as well as the forms and functions of working-class culture and literature. For an interrelated analysis of this kind, Chicago offered an ideal field of research. By focusing solely on Chicago and dealing with a wide range of material, this collection should, moreover, provide a basis for comparing the labor movements and working-class cultures in Germany and the United States. Thus we hope it will contribute to a better understanding of differing developments in both the country of origin and the receiving society.

Chicago's German Population and Working Class

When speaking of the more than twenty-seven million immigrants — mostly European — who entered the United States between 1820 and World War I, one can differentiate them in a general way not only as to national origin and tradition, but also as to their new place of settlement and position in the economy. The Irish, for example, tended to live predominantly in cities and to perform unskilled labor, in textile mills, for example, or in construction. By contrast, Norwegians were much more likely to settle as farmers or farm laborers in the upper Midwest. Such general characterizations can also be made for the more than five million German immigrants, though they tend to point in two different directions. On the one hand, Germans settled as farmers in rural areas, on the other, as artisans, skilled workers, and small businessmen in mid-Atlantic and midwestern cities. These distinct settlement and occupational patterns can be traced to a variety of causes, including the different economies of the regions of origin in Germany, the immigrants' social backgrounds, and the enormous time span covered by German immigration. Just as important are the continuing westward expansion and settlement of the United States, and the varying phases of economic and social development at any particular point in time.

Although the flow of German immigration continued at a high rate from the late 1830s to the 1890s, there were two peaks—one in the 1850s, when almost one million Germans arrived, the other in the 1880s, when 1.4 million entered the country. In both Germany and the United States changes occurred between these peaks which decisively influenced not only the immigrants' social composition but also their opportunities for advancement. In the 1850s, southwestern Germany represented the main region of emigration. Small farmers from this area commonly settled in rural America, while artisans tended to make their homes in the expanding cities, particularly of the Midwest where the economies and social structures had not yet solidified. By the 1880s, the main areas of emigration had shifted to the more rural Prussian provinces, especially those east of the Elbe River. Agricultural day laborers, accounting for an increasingly large percentage of the emigrant population, often did not have the means to acquire land in the United States, where this commodity had, in the meantime, become rarer and more expensive. Deprived of this possibility, they more commonly had to content themselves with positions as unskilled industrial workers in the cities. At the same time, large numbers of immigrant artisans and skilled workers found it increasingly difficult to save the considerable capital which would allow them to open their own shops and compete successfully with highly mechanized factories. In rural areas economic competition for all farmers had also become more fierce; droughts and high interest rates helped swell the numbers of indebted and disillusioned farmers moving away to urban areas. German immigrants who settled on farms in the 1870s and 1880s were sometimes confronted with a similar experience when failure forced them to move on to the towns and cities. Thus in 1890, a few years before mass immigration from Germany came to an end, two-thirds of all German immigrants were living in urban areas. At the same time, however, Germans still comprised the largest number of farmers of all immigrant groups.

Because of its advantageous geographic location, Chicago profited from both groups. Although the waterway via the Erie Canal and the Great Lakes had brought immigrants to the city at the southern tip of Lake Michigan from early on, it was railroad construction in the 1850s which provided the decisive boost. By the end of the decade the railroad had catapulted Chicago into the role of the leading transportation center of the Midwest, and later of the whole continent. As a result, not only were those people who recognized or anticipated its potential drawn to the city, but, as it had also become the center for population distribution throughout the Midwest, many immigrants who had originally intended to continue their journey to rural areas ended up settling in Chicago. In addition, toward the close of the century increasing numbers of people from the adjoining rural states of Indiana, Iowa, and Wisconsin, as well as from rural Illinois, moved to the city.

Chicago owed its original importance as a commercial and distribution center to the vast hinterland. Therefore trade in wheat and lumber were especially significant, while all those industries which made use of the region's natural resources and supplied its rural population were attracted practically from the outset: meat-packing (which became the largest industry in the city after 1870), agricultural implements and the production of household goods, building and construction, and furniture-making. In addition, the steel and metal industries, drawing upon the Lake Superior iron-ore range and the Illinois coal region for their raw materials, profited immensely from the need for rails, locomotives, and cars which accompanied railroad expansion, and the garment industry received an important boost from large army contracts during the Civil War.

These geographic and economic factors led to the rapid expansion of a city that only some twenty years earlier had been a sleepy and insignificant frontier town. Population figures offer telling testimony of the city's boom. In 1850 the United States census counted fewer than 30,000 inhabitants. By 1860, however, the figure had more than tripled, and from then on the population at least doubled each decade until it passed the one million mark in 1890. By 1910 Chicago had increased by another million inhabitants.

German immigrants and their children contributed significantly to this growth. In the mid-nineteenth century, prior to the first great wave of

German immigration to the United States, almost 5,000 Germans lived in Chicago. Growing faster than the overall increase in population, their numbers more than quadrupled in the next decade, and in 1860 the German-born accounted for 20 percent of Chicago's population, the highest proportion they would reach in the city's history. Although this percentage was reduced to half by the turn of the century, the absolute figures rose from some 22,000 in 1860 to over 170,000 in 1900. It must be noted, however, that a generational change was taking place in this period, and that the American-born children of German immigrants are not included in the above figures. By the 1870s the second generation accounted for more people than the immigrant generation, and this despite the fact that the constant stream of immigrants, rather than falling off, reached a new absolute record in the early 1880s. Thus in 1900 three-fifths of the 440,000 German-Americans living in Chicago were second generation, of whom over two-thirds were children and youths whose parents may have immigrated to the United States before marrying.

These figures are an indication of the characteristic heterogeneity of an immigrant group which cannot be defined adequately in national or ethnic terms alone. Even the rise of German neighborhoods was accompanied by important internal differentiation. The 1840s witnessed the emergence of the first large German neighborhood. Located on Chicago's North Side, it continued to grow rapidly throughout the remainder of the nineteenth century. Its dominant population of Bavarians and Württembergers soon dwindled to an insignificant minority when newcomers from the west, north, and northeast of Germany began immigrating in increasing numbers. In contrast, newly emerging German neighborhoods on Chicago's Northwest and Southwest sides reflected other regional origins from the outset. In 1880 there were blocks in the rapidly growing Northwest Side neighborhood settled exclusively by immigrants from the East Elbian provinces of Mecklenburg, Pomerania, West Prussia, and Brandenburg. At the same time, these neighborhoods were differentiated according to social status. There were more professionals, businessmen, and other middle-class members living on the German North Side than in the working-class neighborhoods of the Northwest and South sides, and it was primarily members of the upper classes who could afford homes closer to Lake Michigan or in plush Lake View. While artisans and skilled workers lived in the center of this North Side German neighborhood, unskilled workers had to settle for cheaper quarters bordering on the industrial belt along the polluted North Branch of the Chicago River.

The enormous size of Chicago's German population and its concentration in certain parts of the city made for an intricate network of social institutions which differed not only according to their functions, but increasingly according to class criteria as well. Thus gymnastic or Turner societies were founded, catering specifically to either middle-class or working-class members. And among the lodges, which basically served identical social purposes, there were those like the Order of Harugari or the Order of the Sons of Hermann whose memberships were drawn overwhelmingly from the working class, whereas the Free Masons and the United Order of Redmen catered primarily to the middle class. In this context, the enormous variety of church and associational activities among German immigrants can only be mentioned in passing.

Even in 1871, when Chicago's German community staged an impressive victory parade celebrating the unification of the German states into the German Reich following the Franco-Prussian War, one could hardly speak in terms of common ethnic interests. The celebration was so spectacularly successful only because it was so far removed from the reality of German-American life in Chicago, thus allowing for nostalgic identification with the country of origin. It is significant that this was the only demonstration of unity among Chicago's German population, and as such it signaled an end to rather than the beginning of a united German Chicago. Nor was it simply coincidental that the *Illinois Staats-Zeitung*, Chicago's German daily middle-class paper, referred only fleetingly to the participating workers' associations in its detailed report on the parade.

What impact did the German workers have on the city's diverse German community? First, they made up the great majority of its population, even though the proportion of the working class dropped from more than four-fifths in 1850 to roughly two-thirds in 1900. This decline reflects the process of social differentiation as described above. As a result, the middle class — especially small businessmen and employers, but also after 1880 more and more professionals — assumed greater significance. Whereas over 70 percent of the immigrant generation belonged to the working class, the American-born second generation was strongly drawn to the new middle-class occupations. Despite these tendencies German workers remained the largest ethnic group within Chicago's working class in the late nineteenth century — and this, in turn, had important consequences for its composition.

As in other midwestern cities, the proportion of unskilled German workers in Chicago was high. Even in 1900 over 25 percent of all German heads of households were unskilled, and although the percentage of unskilled workers was much higher among other ethnic groups—the Irish and Poles, for instance—Germans, because of their numerical strength in the city, still accounted for most of the unskilled laborers in absolute numbers.

Skilled workers played an even more important role among German immigrants. On the one hand, simply because so many of them belonged to the city's work force, they were represented in an unusually wide variety of trades. Thus Germans constituted the largest ethnic group in almost four-fifths of the seventy-five specific occupations listed in the Census of Population for the year 1900. On the other hand, occupational specialization led to significant concentrations of skilled German workers in certain industries. From the 1850s on, German workers were dominant in traditional crafts like shoemaking, tailoring, cabinetmaking, carpentry, blacksmithing, wagonmaking, butchering, baking, and brewing. These workers were especially affected by the advances of industrialization that increasingly threatened their status as independent artisans and often forced them into semiskilled factory work.

Just as in other manufacturing centers exposed to vast technical and social upheaval during the transition to industrial production, a vital labor movement also emerged in Chicago. That German workers played a key role in this movement is no coincidence, since they clearly represented the largest group in the trades that were among the first to be organized, such as tailoring, cabinetmaking, and—along with the Irish—building and construction. Considerably reinforced by continuing immigration from Germany, strong concentrations of skilled workers developed significant craft traditions by 1880 in the meat-packing, furniture-making, garment, tobacco, and building industries, in baking and brewing, and in the metal industry. In the early 1880s, for example, almost half the labor force employed by the McCormick Harvester Works had German names. When company efforts to fundamentally restructure the production process met with resistance, the Metal Workers Union—organized by German socialists—played a prominent role.

While continuities persisted, deriving from craft traditions adapted to the demands of industrialization and applied in the new context of large industrial production, the transition from one generation to the next could also result in breaks with tradition, especially when established crafts were no longer in demand and avenues to new occupations began to open up. If their fathers' trade was in a declining industry or was threatened by a cheap labor supply, sons of skilled German workers generally did not enter it. Instead—unless they opted for low white-collar occupations—they tried to find positions as highly specialized workers in new growth industries like the metal and electrical industries.

In its organizational endeavors this occupationally diverse German working class introduced various traditions into a labor movement reflecting a similar sort of heterogeneity. Along with radical thought originating in the prerevolutionary period of the Vormärz,[1] craftsmen immigrating after the failed revolution of 1848/49 also brought practical experience in organization and resistance, which they then used in the first craft associations and in the fight against slavery. Even communist ideas gained a foothold in Chicago as a result of Joseph Weydemeyer's brief activities in the early 1860s. The unlimited freedom of organization granted in the United States favored a strong trade-union movement, which gained weight after the Civil War under the influence of the Lassalleans and the Marxist Eisenachers.[2] Political organizations were also able to make themselves felt when sections of the First International and the Labor party of Illinois were founded. The Socialist Labor party (founded in 1876 as the Workingmen's party of the United States) as well as the International Working People's Association (which separated from that party in 1880) drew into their ranks immigrant workers who had been members, or at least sympathizers, of the German Social Democrats. They had left Germany after the Anti-Socialist Law of 1878 threatened their personal and political existence in the German Reich. Add to this the manifold efforts at political and union organization in which German immigrant workers participated—local workers' associations and craft unions, national trade-union bodies, the International Labor Union, the Knights of Labor, or the American Federation of Labor—and one is virtually forced to conclude that this diversity tended to weaken rather than strengthen the movement. Were there then no signs of an underlying continuity within the German-American working class?

We argue that there were indeed such continuities and that they were

1. The Vormärz refers to the period between Napoleon's defeat in 1815 and the thwarted revolution of March, 1848. In a literary context the term refers to a group of writers who helped prepare the intellectual climate for the Revolution of 1848, particularly Heinrich Heine, Ferdinand Freiligrath, Ludwig Börne, and Georg Herwegh. Even though they were radical liberals rather than socialists, their work greatly influenced the formation of working-class literature.

2. Lassalleans organized the General German Workers Association (ADAV) in 1863, while the Marxist-oriented German Social Democratic Labor party (SDAP) was sometimes labeled after the town of Eisenach, where it was founded in 1869 (under the leadership of August Bebel and Wilhelm Liebknecht). Both factions united at Gotha in 1875 to form the Socialist Labor party of Germany (SAPD).

primarily provided by working-class culture. Even during periods of rapid economic and social change, cultural norms and values do not shift immediately but tend rather to persist, thus offering a valid frame of reference which goes beyond specific political and union organizational structures and intentions. To a greater or lesser degree, labor organizations with thoroughly different political assumptions had to draw on this broader context of working-class culture, especially when occupying a marginal position—as did the immigrants—in a society inclined toward a Protestant work ethic. The analysis of persistent cultural structures and their gradual transformation can therefore help identify common traditions underlying—and surviving—short-lived political and union strategies and organizations. This approach will also help identify the common contributions made by German immigrant workers—entering the country over a period of more than fifty years—to the emerging multi-ethnic American labor movement and culture. But first we must attempt to arrive at an understanding of working-class culture.

German Working-Class Culture, Ethnicity, and the Dominant Society

Any effort to define the term *working-class culture* will result in complexity and dispute. The difficulty arises from a dual tendency inherent in any working definition of the term. It is expected to contain both common denominators for the concept of culture in general and more limited characteristics applying to a class-specific context only. Working-class culture can be defined as the material manifestations and enacted norms and values of the working class. This very general definition, however, tends less to clarify than to obscure the problems that arise when trying to analyze a specific working-class culture in a concrete social setting. German workers in Chicago comprised but one element within the city's heterogeneous working-class population, and the important ethnic differences embodied in this population indicate the absence of a common cultural tradition. The emergence of an American tradition was therefore accompanied by the more or less intense clash of various national backgrounds. Such instances of potential, and often open, conflict constitute an additional factor when we seek to determine the position of German working-class culture in Chicago (in contrast, for instance, to the situation in Germany). They add to the complexity of essential problems concerning the relationship not only to the dominant society, but also to the German-

American middle class, which viewed German cultural traditions in a different light. Thus it is also necessary to discuss the problems which arise when attempting to situate German working-class culture within a highly complex social order.

In its explicit restriction to one class, the term *working-class culture* implies alternative and even oppositional stances. Working-class culture is, for instance, inconceivable without the support of labor institutions, i.e., labor parties and/or trade unions. When—as was the case in Chicago— a new tradition had to be created, it was articulated in deliberate contrast to the values of the dominant culture. In this process, however, working-class culture was forced to orient itself within the framework of existing social structures and cultural forms—even while rejecting them. It therefore took advantage of social spaces which were not of central importance to, and not so tightly controlled by, the dominant society. In addition, it also incorporated lower-class traditions of feudal and early bourgeois origin by reinterpreting them for its own purposes. Hence working-class culture was embedded in lower-class lifestyles and in a folk culture from which it drew in many significant ways and with which it had much in common. It is therefore impossible to conceive of working-class culture except in relation to these other cultural traditions and ways of life: a rejection of them would have been equivalent to its own demise.

Thus a familiarity with German workers' everyday experience is imperative, since this very context nurtured German working-class culture in Chicago. One of the first hard facts confronting German immigrants upon arrival was the need to find the means of making a living: steady work, if possible, as well as a halfway decent place to live. But it also meant adapting to the hectic pace of an urban industrial world and to the ways of life in an ethnic working-class neighborhood. To cope better with these new circumstances, immigrant workers tried to maintain familiar habits. It was not so much material conditions and the work sphere, however, that provided emotional security, because workers were forced to adapt to new and changing factors there. Instead, this security was sought in the sphere of kin, family, and friends. Nikolaus Schwenck, a young coppersmith who immigrated to Chicago in 1855, relied on a large circle of relatives and friends from his home town in Württemberg for his first social contacts. This can be seen clearly in his correspondence—part of which is reproduced at the beginning of this anthology—and is typical of the experience many immigrants were to have. In much the same way, all German associations made up primarily of lower-middle- and working-class members—irrespective of their own specific goals—fell back on common forms of leisure and entertainment. Picnics were genuine family events for young and old alike, where dancing, drinking, games, and lotteries prevailed. Picnics held by labor associations characteristically offered additional features—a demonstration preceding the event, a tableau vivant of a revolutionary scene, or a political speech in order to use the celebration for presenting and enacting a specific political culture. By adopting folk cultural forms on such occasions, these picnics continued common German lower-class traditions and were thus able to relate to a larger public than the more limited labor movement. For this reason a larger crowd usually showed up at picnics than for purely political functions.

The relation between working-class culture and the everyday life of the lower classes also sheds light on the problem of the transfer of such popular traditions. Having grown up in working-class households in urban Chicago, the younger generation had no knowledge of the original cultural forms, only of their modifications. Different ways of life prevailed in Chicago, and the dominant society offered a different cultural tradition. One document in this anthology describes a dispute in the Schwabenverein in 1905 concerning the selection of a new park for the annual Cannstatter Volksfest. The conflict exemplifies the extent to which the second generation of German immigrants was already attracted to American culture. As far as the younger generation was concerned, profit-oriented events drawing on popular mass entertainment seemed thoroughly compatible with the festival; the older generation, in contrast, wanted to preserve the festival's traditional folk character. As in many other cases, we see here how changes in the everyday life of the German-American lower and middle classes reflect the fact that German working-class culture had to relate not only to a changed tradition but to a changing population as well.

Since German workers in Chicago used familiar German traditions, including, of course, the German language, they were part of a cultural heritage which went beyond class boundaries, and in which the German-American middle class participated as well. At the same time, the large percentage of German workers in Chicago played a significant role in shaping the city's working-class cultural traditions. Continually voicing their pride in classical German culture and their conviction that it was superior to other traditions, leaders of the German labor movement in Chicago were often attacked for their ethnic arrogance, especially by those who strove to overcome the ethnic fragmentation among the ranks of the working class. In this sense, the relation between working-class culture and ethnicity reflects two thoroughly different phenomena: on the one hand, a common cultural tradition tended to blur class antagonism within Chicago's German community; on the other hand, narrow self-interests of one national group within the working class threatened to retard solidarity among all workers.

There was in fact a consensus among the Germans of Chicago, but it was confined to efforts to preserve German instruction in the public schools, to fight temperance and blue laws, and to protect basic forms of the German way of life and German conviviality. Whenever an attempt was made to employ coalitions centered around these issues for larger political purposes they broke apart. Parochial schools, for example, offered a valuable service by promoting knowledge of the German language. Yet instead of being tolerated by the German labor movement for this reason, they were subjected to fierce attacks on ideological grounds. In the same way, the labor movement did not simply support all things German, but clearly judged German associations according to their specific functions and goals. It might be noted in passing that this attitude was not shared by leaders of the German-American middle class after 1900, who made concerted efforts to exploit ethnicity for political purposes and to stem the impending fossilization and disintegration of cultural traditions by forming an ethnic interest group. The labor movement regarded itself as the guardian of classical German culture, to which it claimed to add significant new impulses. In its view of the profit-oriented German-American middle class, the movement tended to emphasize potentially threatening Babbitt-like qualities.

The fact that Chicago's organized German workers valued and drew upon their country's cultural tradition should not be viewed as ethnic chauvinism. There was little else for them to fall back on. In the second half of the nineteenth century there was no generally established working-class culture in America into which German and other immigrants could have been readily integrated. After 1880 immigrants and their children made up more than 80 percent of the working-class population in Chicago. They contributed diverse cultural traditions to a working class which was continually being expanded and changed by the arrival of new national groups, and in this sense immigrants were themselves actively involved in the emergence of an "American" working-class culture. Thus it is not the question of ethnic fragmentation that should be of central importance here, but rather the question of how particular traditions were integrated into an emerging common tradition. In our case, the decisive test for the success or failure of such incorporation occurred during the transition from the immigrant culture to a second-generation German-American culture already changed by various influences in the adopted country.

This also raises the question of the relationship between German working-class culture and the dominant American culture. This relationship was characterized by a peculiar contradiction. On the one hand, German working-class culture fully accepted American political rights and liberties which were—in contrast to the situation in Germany—guaranteed by the Constitution as an inalienable part of the country's political culture. The Declaration of Independence, above all, was referred to as the symbol of the continuity between radical European and American republican traditions. Like other groups in American society, German workers were unconditionally committed to the preservation of these rights. This fact was illustrated during the Civil War when they joined the Union Army in disproportionate numbers, and during the Gilded Age, when they actively opposed an all-powerful plutocracy. In the same way the German-American labor movement defended the public school system as the guarantor of the liberal education of all citizens. And when this goal seemed to be threatened by church institutions pursuing their own particular interests, "free" Sunday schools were founded by German workers' clubs in Chicago in the late 1880s.

On the other hand, German working-class culture was faced with a double pressure to adapt German traditions to a specific Protestant way of life and to relinquish its class character as incommensurate with American reality. In the historical process this pressure varied. The culmination of an oppositional German working-class culture in Chicago clearly occurred in the 1870s and 1880s, when German workers—still at the center of Chicago's working class—were severely threatened by contemporary structural changes in industry and society. Later, when other immigrant groups had begun to displace German workers from their central place in production and in the working class itself, German working-class culture began to lose its predominant position and oppositional stance. These changes are usually seen as indications of social mobility and successful integration. And with the rise of the second generation, there can of course be no doubt that German working-class culture, like German immigrant culture in general, began to lose its most important medium, the German language. But it would be wrong to see this development as an indiscriminate immersion into the American melting pot. It must rather be seen within the context of larger economic and social changes, in the course of which integration into the dominant society was contingent upon thoroughly different criteria, including social and class position. Thus German working-class culture did not disappear without a trace into a homogeneous middle-class culture, but contributed to an American working-class culture which differed in significant ways from the norms and values of the dominant society.

The Structure of the Anthology

Since German-American working-class culture was situated within a complex social framework comprised of a dominant culture and a middle-class ethnic culture, as well as national folk cultures and ways of life, the categories used to select and organize the documents for this anthology are both broad and interconnected. Overlapping clearly occurs in some of the documents reproduced here. The main emphasis of our selection, however, is on those elements characteristic of working-class culture. Thus in the chapters that portray general experiences and ways of life we always focus on German workers, even though some of the examples of immigration and arrival or of everyday neighborhood life also apply to other social groups among German immigrants.

Thematic overlapping between chapters occurs whenever an important subject did not seem to lend itself to a separate chapter. This applies, for instance, to the role of women. Our decision not to devote a chapter to women resulted from the dearth of documents on the role of women in the family and household — a grave deficit since the overwhelming majority of married women worked at home. By contrast, there was a wealth of documents on women's work in industries and trades outside the home, where the workers were usually unmarried women and girls. In addition, we found valuable material on the role women played in needy families, as well as sporadic evidence of their activities in the labor movement. We decided to integrate these documents into the respective chapters on work, living conditions, and the culture of the labor movement. Similarly, leisure activities are dealt with in different ways in Chapters IV through VI.

A large variety of documents are reproduced in this volume: government investigations and reports, private correspondence and letters to the editor, poems and songs, reportage, editorials, and portrayals of personal experiences. They also represent a large range of literary forms. Even so, most of the documents are taken from the German-American labor press. This is not surprising, since the publications representing the dominant society barely took notice of the foreign immigrant workers. Occasions when these people became a matter of public interest in connection with workplace conditions, industrial production, or political unrest were rare. It is for this reason that such documents are concentrated in Chapters II and III, which deal with the work sphere and living conditions. In order to document the culture of Chicago's German workers, however, we had to turn to the labor press as its most important institution and mouthpiece. In many cases, the labor press represents the only source which continually furnished information about the workers' reaction to important events directly affecting them, and about their institutions and lived culture. Emphasis was placed on the 1880s, because this decade witnessed the flowering of German-American working-class culture in Chicago, and because later developments can be better understood on the basis of events which occurred at this time.

We would like to conclude this introduction with some brief remarks about our editorial practice. The opening chapter introductions explain the respective topic, while shorter introductions preface the documents themselves to set them in their relevant context. Sometimes, when they are thematically connected, several documents are introduced together. Further editorial remarks explaining words, places, and names are included in footnotes at the bottom of the respective page. The majority of documents are translations from the German originals, while only a few were written in English. Whenever English words were used in a German-language document, they are indicated by this distinct type, whereas Germanized versions of English words are given in special brackets behind the English translation; for example, "he had jumped ⟨gejumped⟩ over the fence." Obvious mistakes in the originals that either make for an ambiguous reading or make no sense at all were not corrected but designated with a [*sic*]. Omissions are indicated by ellipsis marks, additions by brackets.

PROLOGUE

Chicago as a Flourishing Commercial and Economic Center

In the 1850s Chicago stood at the threshold of its unparalleled economic development and population growth. By the turn of the century it had been propelled to second place among America's cities and become the undisputed transportation, trade, and industrial center of the Midwest. Early on, businessmen with a sure sense for profitable investment and speculation recognized the potential of the city on Lake Michigan, which expanded enormously almost from the beginning. It is thus small wonder that numerous German states wanted to see their commercial interests represented in Chicago and to set up consulates, as in the most important American ports and inland cities with sizable German populations. One of the first to offer his services as a consular official was the local lawyer and banker Francis A. Hoffmann. In 1854 he was entrusted with the consulate of Braunschweig-Lüneburg and later with the representation of other principalities. Even tiny Lippe-Detmold considered establishing a consulate in Chicago. By the middle of the nineteenth century Chicago had already established its reputation as a metropolis for trade and settlement, even in remote corners of Germany. Reports such as that sent by Hoffmann to the state ministry of Braunschweig-Lüneburg, excerpted here, contributed not only to burgeoning trade relations but also to the state of information in Germany about Chicago as well as to optimistic expectations about its future.

The name of the German-born Francis A. Hoffmann is inseparable from the early history of German settlement in Illinois and particularly in Chicago. At the early age of eighteen he was already a teacher and Lutheran minister in the village of Dunckley's Grove, which had been settled predominantly by Germans. Even though he quickly became well known in northern Illinois as a preacher, he gave up his position in 1851 and moved to Chicago, where his activities multiplied, somewhat like the population of the city. He speculated in real estate, founded a bank, trained himself as a lawyer, and took part in local politics. In 1853 he was elected alderman to the city council from an overwhelmingly German ward. A notable political career twice led him to the lieutenant governorship of Illinois, once at the end of the 1850s and again in the mid 1860s. Hoffmann worked closely with the liberal forty-eighters and promoted the abolitionist cause within the newly founded Republican party. In Chicago he participated extensively in the founding of German clubs and associations, which mushroomed amidst the wave of German immigration in the 1850s.

In the report reproduced here Hoffmann proves himself a typical booster of Chicago's business potential. Not only does he paint a fascinating picture of the advantageous geographical position of Chicago with her vast hinterland and ready access to raw materials, but he also uses a literary style common among the best-known English-speaking Chicago boosters — one saturated with rapturous optimism and an unshakeable belief in progress. Literary and bombastic, Hoffmann's German also shows signs of contamination with English words and phrases. Reports like this possibly influenced not only Braunschweig's commercial circles but German immigrants in general when they decided to settle in Chicago.

1. **Annual Report for 1855 from Francis A. Hoffmann, Consul of the Duchy of Braunschweig-Lüneburg in Chicago (Niedersächsisches Staatsarchiv Wolfenbüttel, 12 A Neu Fb. 5 Nr. 235, 184-192).**

To the High Ducal Ministry of Braunschweig-Lüneburg:

If, after having read my last report, the high Ducal Ministry still tends to doubt — not so much *Chicago's* gigantic destiny in general, but rather the geometric progression by which development here continues to leap forward — these last hesitancies will now — I am trusting to the strength of my columns of figures — gradually give way to the confident anticipation of a panorama which is ever more incredible, ever more wonderful. . . . We began to become unmistakably aware of the growing independence of the vast Northwest, not only from European affairs but even from the money market of our own East, and our pride and sense of victory began to swell. It is common knowledge that the center of the United States is gravitating westward, and accordingly, the consequences of this relocation must also be drawn for commercial and industrial developments. Just as our locomotive, thresher, plough, and other machine factories have emancipated themselves from *Lawrence, Lowell, Albany,* and *Rochester,* so too must our western credit system, regardless of *Wall* Street speculation, now be organized on a solid, unshakeable basis. To an eminent degree, this past year has testified to the fact that *Chicago* can indeed be independent. . . .

In regard to the expansion of commerce and production, the most important factor for *Chicago's* entrepreneurial spirit seems to be the opening of direct shipping lanes to the largest of America's inland seas, Lake Superior. By way of the *St. Mary River Canal,* Chicago has direct access to those inexhaustible iron and copper mines [on Lake Superior]. . . .

Able to grasp these metallic treasures with its sea-arm, and with the iron-arm of the *Illinois Central* Railroad reaching to the equally inexhaustible coal deposits of southern *Illinois,* Chicago is assured the conditions necessary for industrial development, thus lending the commercial sphere an indestructible basis and a guarantee of duration. The surveyor's chain has already marked areas in *Chicago* destined for the production of metal goods, centralized in such a way that they will be able to meet the rapidly growing needs of the back country along the immense tributaries running to the north and southwest of the metropolis. . . .

Whereas the causes precede the effects in European development, here the causes follow, as it were, the effects. Whereas the railroad generally follows a culture and a people, here the people and culture follow the railroads. Despite even the cheap congressional price ⟨Congreßpreises⟩ of $1.25 per acre for rich and easily cultivated land, without natural or artificial marketing avenues the vast tracts in mid and southern Illinois lay dormant for years, waiting in vain for buyers. And then, as though by a stroke of magic, the *Illinois Central* Railroad, trekking iron hoops across the length and breadth of the state, from *Galena* to *Cairo* and from *Chicago* to *Lasalle,* awakened cities with thousands of inhabitants, bestowed cultivation on vast tracts of fertile land and delivered substantial quantities of the virgin earth's first yield to the gigantic granaries ⟨Kornmagazine⟩ of the Queen of the Inland Seas. At the same time improvement was noticeable not only with respect to the quantity of the produce—the result of the enormous areas of newly cultivated lands— but also with respect to its quality. Nowhere is the general use of machinery more advantageous than on *Illinois's* expansive plains, and this, together with the progressive intelligence of our farmers—who have already recognized the necessity of land-grant colleges—explains the fact that a large portion of the grain sold as *Extra Genessee* (known as the best *New York* grain) should in fact be marked *Extra Illinois*.

And all of this is yet the beginning of the beginning. The state's land area totals 55,000 square miles; 80 percent of this is first-class grain-growing country. The state's total productive capability—44,000 square miles, or 28,260,000 acres ⟨Acker⟩ planted with corn averaging 50 bushels ⟨Buschel⟩ per acre—would thus yield the unbelievable sum total of 1,413,000,000 bushels ⟨Buschel⟩. If one also considers the facility with which the land is cultivated, one can imagine the amazing abundance accumulating here, and the powerful effect it must have on *Chicago,* abruptly elevating this city to the great commissioner of all these treasures.

Everywhere people are beginning to pay attention to *Chicago's* place in the international market; the first lustrous proof was the appearance of English and French government agents at our grain exchange. And *Chicago* was in fact the only place in the world where such million-bushel ⟨Buschel⟩ orders could be filled without further ado.

If, consequently, the production of the state and that of the surrounding back country has outdistanced the boldest expectations, it has also been accompanied by an increase in another important element for the creation of wealth. True to the great law which holds that capital is attracted to whatever generates the largest profit, considerable capital from bordering states to the south, from the East, and even from Europe has found its way here. Consider the multitude of our splendid stores in the most fashionable ⟨fashionablesten⟩ *New York* style; our colossal granaries, whose steam elevators remove the grain from railroad cars on the one side and deposit it on the other where schooners await; the amount of construction (2,700 new structures in one year), limited only by the lack of building material; in every single branch the complete outstripping of supply by demand—all this is characteristic, to an ever more grandiose degree, of this era of growing prosperity. Everywhere there is a doubling, a quadrupling. Take a look at the tonnage, at the number of our ships, everywhere there is the same miracle of multiplication. . . .

Thus it is that *Chicago,* shot forward on all sides by the generators of prosperity, stands on the threshold of this important year, 1856. However the dice may fall, *Chicago* will be the winner. *Chicago* beef and flour will not simply retain their first-rate standings on the international market, but will better them. The manufacturing industry in *Chicago,* stepping out of its short pants, will swiftly rush forward at a rate proportional to *Chicago* itself.

Is it yet necessary to enumerate in detail the advantages which go hand in hand with investment in any local undertaking? the incredible possibilities which lend themselves to reasonable speculation? Further growth in *Chicago's* trade is due to the *Canada* Reciprocity Treaty[1] by which Canadian imports have resulted in an augmentation of our lumber market. Thus, on the one hand, we send our railroads to the heart of *Wisconsin's* spruce forests; on the other hand, our fleet ventures to *Canada's* hickory forests[2] where we are easily able to pay for our building and fencing material with the abundant grain from our woodless prairies. And our penetration into yet unexplored regions has hardly begun. Despite the 500 miles of new rail laid in the past year, the *Chicago Fond du Lac* Railroad is forging into the northernmost extremities in the middle of winter in order to clasp the Father of Rivers, the Mississippi, at yet another place, this time *St. Paul,* far from content with having tapped it at *Dubuque, Burlington, Muscatine, Rock Island* and *Davenport.*

Finally, as far as the spirit of our citizens in general is concerned, this happy mixture of Americans and those born elsewhere is such that nativism has not been able to win a solid foothold: this spirit showed its liberal visage when, by an enormous majority, the hated *Maine* Law[3] was overturned. One consequence of this is the preference shown for *Chicago* by immigrants from Europe and from states tormented by legislation like the *Maine* Law, and the unparalleled increase in the city's population is just one area where it can be witnessed. . . .

The total picture of development to present is thus everywhere impressive and satisfying. Our expectations for the future are even greater. I have tried to discern the laws governing the stages of this wondrous development, and to escort the High Ducal Ministry to a majestic height from where a view, if only partial, of this great, vast panorama can be gained.

Chicago, January of the Year 1856

1. This was a bilateral treaty between the U.S. and Canada signed in 1854 that regulated fishing rights and duty-free importation of raw materials and agricultural products.

2. Hoffmann used the word *Fort* here although he probably meant *Forst,* or forest.

3. The state of Maine instituted prohibition in 1851, and its law served as a model for opponents of alcoholic drink around the country. Beginning in 1853 a temperance group advocated such a law in Illinois. Similar initiatives in 1855 by Chicago's nativist mayor Levi Boone led to the famous "Lager Beer Riots" in which both Germans and Irish participated. In June of the same year a referendum for a "Maine Law" was rejected at the polls by a clear majority.

I. THE ARRIVAL AND RECEPTION OF IMMIGRANTS

In the second half of the nineteenth century Chicago was as much a center for the arrival and transshipment of immigrants as any East Coast seaport, with the only difference that the immigrants arrived by land. In the early 1880s, at the high point of nineteenth-century immigration to the United States, thousands disembarked from the immigrant trains arriving from the East every month during the traveling season. The experience of both Germans and other immigrants on their arrival at Chicago's train stations remained substantially the same over decades: the immigrants were met either by relatives and friends or by agents of the railroads, the police, or the German Society, an immigrant-aid organization. There were also legions of "runners" trying to relieve the immigrants of their money by leading them to local restaurants and boardinghouses where they would be overcharged. Since the great majority of immigrants arriving in Chicago were merely passing through on their way to other places, a large number of them easily fell prey to such cheating practices.

The official representatives of the railroads, the police, and the German Society had functions other than simply providing information or looking for lost baggage. They were conduits in a local and regional labor market, channeling workers to businesses or employment agents. In 1870 the German Society even sent workers to Mississippi, and at the turn of the century German-speaking police directed unmarried German industrial workers to particular boardinghouses between the city center and the industrial belt, where they had ready access to the transportation network and job opportunities. The realities of this labor market often contradicted the overblown expectations of the newly arrived German workers.

While the experience of arriving at the train stations remained basically the same, the social composition of German immigrants as well as the character of the city itself changed decisively in the sixty-year period preceding World War I. The letters of Nikolaus Schwenck reprinted here show how an artisan arriving in Chicago with the first great wave of nineteenth-century immigration could realize the common dream of economic independence by setting up his own shop. His letters document the experience of many immigrants before 1870 who settled down in a booming but modest-sized city in which manufacturing was still largely based on skilled labor. The industrial metropolis that developed after 1870 offered other opportunities and problems; however, it also often contained bitter disappointments for German workers, who were confronted with fundamentally different economic and social factors than those encountered by Schwenck.

A Young Coppersmith from Württemberg Settles in Chicago

When Nikolaus Schwenck left his parents' house in the village of Langenau near Ulm in 1850, he was unmarried and not yet twenty years old. His comfortably situated family belonged to the established craftsmen and tradesmen of the village, where the Schwencks still occupy the same substantial house and run a hardware store today. Nikolaus spent several years as a wandering journeyman—a common experience for young artisans—traveling to the far corners of Germany and to the adjacent states to the east before he decided, after long hesitation, to emigrate to the United States. As he wrote his brother Christian in January, 1854, he wanted to "try [his] luck like so many thousands of others in that faraway land."

In March of the same year he sailed from Hamburg to New York and first found work for several months in a large pipe factory in Reading, Pennsylvania. Then he moved on to Philadelphia, where he stayed with a friend and sought work, unsuccessfully, in his trade. Disappointed, he traveled to the Midwest in order to try his luck in Milwaukee. Passing through Chicago Schwenck found friends from Langenau and decided to stay on. After a few attempts, he even managed to get work as a coppersmith. Quickly catching the speculative fever rampant in Chicago—which he came to condemn strongly during the financial crisis of 1857-58—Schwenck bought land in

Iowa, Indiana, and Chicago. His plans to become a farmer did not work out, however, and he settled in the city. There he met his wife, also a German immigrant from an artisan background. In the early 1860s Schwenck managed to open his own shop, first with a partner and then on his own. Tragically, in 1869 both he and his wife became gravely ill and died on the very same day. The local Mithra Lodge of the Free Masons, composed largely of Germans, took over responsibility for the Schwencks' four children. Before his early death, Nikolaus Schwenck had realized his goal of artisan independence, a dream that led so many other craftsmen to America.

Schwenck's life is an illuminating example from among the thousands of German immigrants who arrived in America in the late 1840s and early 1850s, when there was still a frontier and the industrial revolution was in an early phase. Although the German immigration of this period is commonly associated with the political refugees, especially intellectuals, fleeing after the failed Revolution of 1848, the great majority of immigrants were, in fact, farmers and artisans trying to escape the social dislocations brought on by the industrial revolution.

Schwenck was able to accustom himself to Chicago quickly, with the aid of friends and relatives. Even on his way to the Midwest he had relied on a network of personal relations, a common feature of the process of migration at this time. In Chicago his fellow countrymen from his home village—artisans like himself—helped him and others in the search for work. He was quickly integrated into Chicago's rapidly expanding German artisan and working-class community, where he found friends, a wife, business partners, and entry into the social world of clubs and associations. Nikolaus Schwenck spent his leisure time among the same people and sent along their greetings to family and friends in the letters he wrote home to Langenau. The economic crisis of the late 1850s threatened the livelihood of many workers, but Schwenck was largely spared its worst effects. Nevertheless, it made him an astute critic of America's economic and social life.

We would like to thank the Schwenck family of Langenau for permission to publish parts of Nikolaus Schwenck's correspondence, as well as Mr. James Edward Schwenck of Delray Beach, Florida, who called this correspondence to our attention.

2. **Excerpts from Four Letters from Nikolaus Schwenck to His Relatives in Langenau in Württemberg (Franz Christian Schwenck Family Archive, Langenau, Württemberg).**

Chicago, September 9, 1855 ⟨Septembr. 9. 1855⟩

My very dear brother & etc.!

I am finally in a position to give you some news about me. I received your kind letter in *Reading*, along with the few lines from S. Glocker, and as I traveled to *Philadelphia* soon thereafter I saw William Glocker and talked to him. Both of us were very happy about it as you can well imagine, and we both wished that we might be able to stay together for a while. But fate decreed differently! I stayed in *Philadelphia* some four weeks and took all imaginable pains to possibly find a position, kindly assisted in this endeavor by my friend Glocker. But all in vain, business was very poor last winter and this spring, with thousands out of work, and I could have stayed on, having means enough to allow it, but chances being hopeless anyway, I decided instead to go further inland, which is what I ended up doing. I headed *west* to the states of Pennsylvania, Ohio, Michigan and Illinois, thus coming to *Chicago* in the state of Illinois. Once arrived, I heard to my great surprise that a certain Bartholomäus Braun was here, and it was not very long before I had a second Langenau contact. Achim is Braun's son, and from him I now received more news, for example that Franz Paul is also here, together with his brother Christian. Likewise Ludwig Bischoff and Johannes Weiher, and after a while I came to meet all of them. (Also a certain Friedrich Schiehler, carpenter, and a Johannes Ernna, carpenter, who frequently stayed with his mother in Grüßbord in Ulm.) About three weeks ago Ulrich Braun also arrived here with his wife and daughter, because business was still bad in Buffalo. Their oldest son *Mattheus* is still in Buffalo, and will most likely stay there, since he is married. In addition, last week a certain Georg Strobel, shoemaker, arrived and has also found work here. So now we have gathered a nice little 'convention' of people from Langenau together, don't you see, dear brother! Oh well, you may feel like laughing, but I must say that so far they are quite well, everyone has work and therefore plenty to eat. The Binder and Braun people were very pleased to see me, as was I to see them, and we had a lot to chat about, one thing and another, such as all the things that have happened in our dear Langenau in the recent and not so recent past, etc. It moved something deep within me, causing me to think, yes, you would like to see Langenau again and talk with your people for a while (this a passing thought). I have seen quite a bit of the Brauns, and last Sunday they invited me to dinner, which was a special treat for me. And what do you think we had? Well, some of those very special Schwaben Knöpfle [dumplings] from Langenau, and I can tell you they were delicious.

To return to myself—so I was in *Chicago,* but did not feel at all like staying here, rather wanted to go to *Milwaukee,* a city in the state of Wisconsin. But man proposes, God disposes. After being here three or four weeks without work, I accepted a job, out of boredom, in a smith's workshop, and there I worked for two weeks as a helper. It was in the same shop ⟨Schopp⟩ where Franz Paul is still working today. They make only carriages and plows there, with 14 fire places in the workshop and about 30 smiths plus the same number of carriage makers, a nice big shop. So things were going quite well with me, but I heard of a place where they were looking for a *coppersmith* ⟨Koppersmit⟩. I went there right away and sure enough, I got the job. And I will stay there for as long as it lasts. My masters are two Americans *in partnership* ⟨in Compani⟩, a *coppersmith* ⟨Koppersmit⟩ and a *tinsmith* ⟨Tinsmitt⟩. We have six coppersmiths in the workshop, among them two Englishmen, three Swedes, and one German, namely my humble self. I like it quite well, only the English language is still a problem, but soon it will surely work out better. I already went to school and tried to force it along, but it just did not go any faster. With regard to the work, it is less than spectacular, we make nothing but pipes which go into locomotives for the railroad. In general, things are very poor in the coppersmith trade. And there can be no question yet about starting my own business.

I don't think I'll stay here very long, for I do *not* like it all that much. I want to travel south where things are supposed to be better for my trade, but this will not happen for a while. As far as other news of the usual kind is concerned, I don't want to get into that just now, but this much is certain: some are much more wretched here than in Germany, dear brother I am not referring directly to myself, as I can always get by in a tight situation, but if I were to write about what I myself have already seen, other letters that you receive would represent it as an untruth, and I do not want that. Let this suffice for now: so far I have been, thank God, sound and in good spirits, and I hope and wish the same for you, God willing. Many greetings from all the Langenau people to all of you, and also to their respective families, if they should happen to inquire. Franz Paul sends especial greetings to you and would like you to send his regards to his mother and brothers and sisters. He is quite well, as is his brother, *Christian,* who is presently not working here in *Chicago* but in

Freeport, some 100 miles, or about 30 hours, away from here, and they will write very soon. Also many greetings from Binder Braun's people, who have included a few lines which they ask you to forward to the address indicated.

To conclude, many warm greetings from me, especially to my dear good mother, my master and his family, Mr. Spengler, and to my dear B. Barthle and Brother Georg, as well as my sister, my brother- and my sister-in-law together. - Please accept, my dearest brother, for yourself and your dear wife and children, the warmest wishes from your ever devoted and loving brother,

Nikolaus Schwenck

Please write to me soon in reply.

My address is very simply

Mr. Nikolaus Schwenck Coppersmith ⟨Koppersmitt⟩
Chicago, Ill. (i.e. state of Illinois)
North America

Chicago, November 15, 1856 ⟨November 15.ten 1856⟩

My very dear brother Christian!

This letter, dear brother, contains more than all the others I have written, and my heart is already beating harder and warmer at the thought of telling you the news of so many interesting things. . . .

I have decided to take a wife by next spring. I am withholding further information, and a good honest word from your side is, as always, very welcome. — The How and the Who will likewise remain my secret. Just this one remark; I have carefully considered everything. I have considered all the possible troubles and misfortunes. And you, too, dear brother, will have to admit that I am capable of doing so. The seven years that have elapsed since first I took leave of the dear homeland should be proof enough; they will vouch for the fact that I am well able to go out into the world as a man and, even when far away, to make my way honorably, even if fate should tie me up from time to time more than it has till now. . . .

Though my circumstances, situation, and conditions are not exactly brilliant, I have nevertheless gotten to the point where I need not fear failure; and to take this step, which may be somewhat questionable, cannot be so bad, since it will be a joint venture.

As to my craft, dear brother — well, I was a coppersmith here, body and soul, but in America everything looks completely different. I have now decided to give up my craft for a while, and, if necessary, forever.

Though it is a very good craft, you first have to find a job. But you have to hunt for these—I mean a job where I could function as a master, because to work for others as a journeyman, dear brother don't blame me, but that's not really what I want. Yes, it has done so far and of course would continue to, but I would like to try something else, and finally to take a step which, if luck would have it, could lead to independence. I know this is something you least of all expected, but there is nothing dishonest about it.

Now dear brother, before I continue, let me take a look at the 18 months which have elapsed since I started working in *Chicago*. I haven't let this time pass without making use of it. No! I saved a respectable bit of capital and have bought land with it, good farm land. By next spring I hope to settle there and, furthermore, to try to feed myself from it. I liked being a coppersmith and had finally gotten to the point where I didn't have to take a second place to anyone else, and I was earning good wages because I am still at the same place, second among nine men. For a long time I was the only German, the others were Swedes and Englishmen, though recently there has been another German here at work (this only in passing).

Dear brother, I've been doing very well in the past several months, but this working around for *Others* does not make the future seem so bright. Hence my decision, and I am sure that, given the circumstances, you too will approve.—

And now dear brother, more still! As my decision to remain here in *America* and Never again to return to *Germany* is equally firm, I will allow myself, at the end of this letter, to very cordially request of you and all the other family members to send me what remains of my share of Father's fortune. . . .

Now you have, dear brother, all that seems necessary for me to write this time. I must confess that I am extremely light of heart! Oh, if only one of you were here now, it would make me happy beyond words! But fate doesn't want it so. And:—I am filled with the fullest contentment!!! . . .

My most cordial greetings to all, but especially to you, in heartfelt brotherly love, yours truly

Nikolaus

Chicago, March 20, 1857 ⟨März 20. 1857⟩

My very dear brother Christian! . . .

And now to continue, dear brother, my marriage plans, about which you already know, have been fully realized. Your letters, my marriage, all in one day—just think of our joy! I've been married now for two weeks and find myself well in every respect and together with my wife enjoy the greatest happiness. My wife is from Mecklenburg Schwerin, comes from a middling artisan class like myself, and has been here in *America* for 1½ years with her sister, brother, and her mother. Four other brothers and sisters are still in Germany, but all are also married. . . .

And now, dear brother, I want to briefly tell you how it is with the land business I spoke of before. It was my firm desire to buy a farm without having to pursue any other interest than my *Own*. So last year in July, along with another coppersmith—a Swede—I bought 160 acres ⟨Acker⟩ of land in the state of *Iowa* for the sum of 450 *dollars*. In the meantime I heard of another, somewhat more *cultivated* farm in the state of *Indiana* which borders *Illinois*. This seemed more suitable, and I and my brother-in-law, a tinsmith, traveled there and took a look at the land. We liked it and decided to think the whole thing over and then, if possible, to buy it. It was 100 acres ⟨Acker⟩ and 36 English miles from *Chicago*. They were asking 1,500 dollars, quite a good price, although it was still a little too expensive for us because my money was tied up in the land mentioned above and most of my *companion's* money was tied up in building sites and two houses that he owns here in the city. I then sold my land to my Swede, who took it all upon himself alone. I made quite a bit on it, as the value of land is constantly going up. . . . And that's the way it looks right now. I don't have any other land except two large building sites in the state of *Michigan* and a lot, or building site, here in *Chicago*. This last I bought for 755 dollars, but soon it will be worth 1,000, and in addition I'm still working for the same master. He was very much against my leaving, and for the first time raised my wages so that now, for 10 hours work, I earn a good 2 dollars. . . .

We send our warm greetings to you all, mother, brothers, sisters and sisters-in-law and remain, very loving if also partly unknown,

Nikolaus Schwenck - Coppersmith ⟨Koppersmitt⟩

Chicago, Novbr 17th 1857

Dear brother Christian & etc.! . . .

The worst of all bad times, this is what you hear everywhere, and it actually is! I don't need to read much in other newspapers, we have misery enough right here in *Chicago*. No work, and why?—because business is bad. Thousands of workers are unemployed and look with fearful hearts towards the approaching winter. And what is worst, most criminal of all, what little they had put aside with the sweat of their brows and invested in saving banks—is gone! Most banks are bankrupt, or at least have *suspended* their payments, and the worker who thought this well-invested money to be his only consolation and hope now finds himself without anything, more even, robbed of any prospect for earning money within the next six months. This, dear brother, is simply a truthful picture of the *present contemporary times* in general, for even the securest, the best, the largest businesses are declaring *bankruptcy,* and here again the workers are hit hardest, because not only like other big people do they lose what they have accumulated through *speculation,* no, they even lose their hard-earned wages! For you must know, dear brother, that things are arranged here in such a way that every week or every month the workingman gets only half his wages, or sometimes even less than half, the rest is left to be paid as a matter of course when conditions allow it. Now it may be true that wages here on the average are almost high enough to enable a man, even when he has a family, to get along on half his pay, so if the bosses are of good reputation and credit, who would ever think of taking precautions? Also, it cannot be said that *all* have been cheated in this way. But given the present enormous money crisis more than enough such cases are to be found, and truly often very sad ones. I myself have heard of enough of them from acquaintances here.

Now you will ask how this can happen in this blessed land of America, known for its golden times, where there is always enough money and work, and where someone can become a rich man in the course of a few years. All very well, that's how it was and how it will be again, and then later maybe these golden times will be more lasting, when things one day will not be so bad, with everything turning topsy turvy. This is liable to open people's eyes, because here everything has to work *under high steam,* i.e. either one day as rich as can be, or the next day a beggar, or the other way around, this is the rule in all branches of business, some blindly throw themselves into a highly recommended speculation, risk every penny and turn out to be lucky, which makes them even bolder, until eventually they fall and then others make their fortunes from this fall.—

But to return to our question, how does this come about? Well, it is these very overextended *speculations* which will often have their origin or conclusion in the word *swindle,* for the *main* cause is that all-engulfing flood of paper money, these *bills* or banknotes are valid today and as good as gold, and then the next day may not be worth a farthing *(no cent),* and the bank is broken, has gone *bankrupt,* and there is no insurance, no

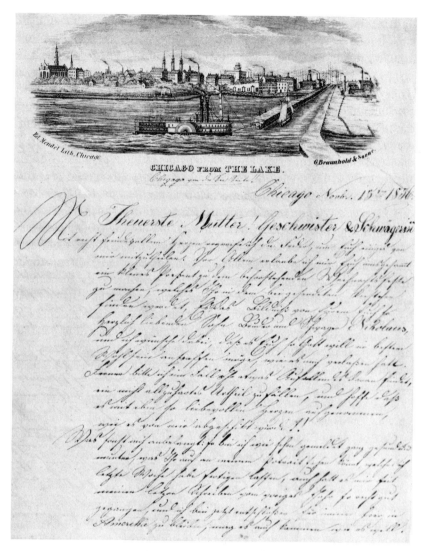

The first page of a letter by Nikolaus Schwenck to his relatives in Langenau. Apparently produced by a German firm in Chicago, the lithograph on the masthead shows the city from Lake Michigan with, among other things, McCormick's Reaper Works on the right and, in the background, smoking factory chimneys and the countless masts of ships docked in the Chicago River. (Family Archives of Franz Christian Schwenck, Langenau in Württemberg.)

Probably taken in 1863, both of these photos show the shop of the coppersmiths Müller and Schwenck at 65 North Wells Street on the North Side of the city. In the first photo the business partners are standing in the entrance to the shop with the older Müller on the left and Schwenck on the right. The group picture in the yard includes the six employees plus Schwenck's wife and child. (Family Archives of Franz Christian Schwenck, Langenau in Württemberg.)

compensation, oh no! Such a thing is not yet really known around here, or nobody wants to know about it, it takes too much time, or is too involved, in short, nobody gives a damn, or in plain English *Help yourself* is the only rule, and everybody has to accommodate himself to it. But if a businessman is really going strong, i.e. completely immersed in this bedouinlike life, this contented fellow will not worry about laws or the arts, about the police, taxation, religion, morality or health—none of this *exists* for him! The whole business world is one big battle in the open marketplace, everyone for himself, and nobody on anyone else's side. Principles are nothing, men are nothing, women are nothing, slavery is boring and freedom is boring, *patriotism* is humbug and virtue is humbug, untiring and painful diligence is contemptible, and twenty *percent* is the desirable profit, but not from our capital, which could easily be nonexistent, but rather from our deals. That is the primary goal of life.—

That the inclination for uncontrolled *speculation*, for fast, loveless and thoughtless risks (which *characterize* business life here in *America* more than on any other part of the globe), is the main reason for our present hard times, this, my dear brother, even you will not be able to doubt. But then, dear Christian, you will probably end up saying, what does brother Klaus want with all this stuff?—Well, actually no more than to tell you something new about *America,* but something that is true, I can see it with my own eyes, and talk about it from my own experience, and I only wish I were more inclined, or more adept, then I could tell you much more, and I am convinced it would interest you, too, but let it be enough for now, at least along these lines.—

I have still much more to write you about, oh a great deal more, especially about myself. In spite of bad times, illness, and money problems, you may believe your brother if I say that I am still happy and content! If it weren't so, I would not hesitate to tell you about it just as faithfully. But I have no reason to complain. It is true I am still not a master, and not a farmer either, but rather am still working at the same place as a coppersmith. Only just think, instead of 20 men we are now only three to four, which means that 16 workers have been laid off, which is a bit rough, don't you think? All the Swedish, English and American coppersmiths are gone, it is quite true, and this will give you an idea of how bad it is with other large factories, because this lack of employment extends into all *branches* (but now I have almost gotten away from myself again). So all my fellow workers are gone, and the only German in the place is still the only one there now, you understand, I alone still work there, and can go on working until the (shop) business either closes down or goes bankrupt.

Now, my beloved brother, let me turn to something else. First of all, I must humbly apologize for adding this appendix to my already very long letter. But I must still touch upon a little assortment of news items.— Well, the newest of my news is this: my dear wife has given me a little daughter whose name is *Anna Maria,* and in sharing this news with our dear *Mother,* could you kindly point out that we have permitted ourselves the honor of giving her worthy name *Anna* to our little *American world citizen;* and we, i.e. all three of us, standing before the inspiring prospect, Providence willing, of witnessing a branch of the *family a la Schwenck* prospering on this side of the *ocean* too, send our friendliest greetings.

As far as other news is concerned, I could write a lot more, but dear brother, I think I have to consider closing this letter. All the Langenau people, who are quite numerous here, are fine to the best of my knowledge. . . .

As you know, dear brother, I bought a lot last spring on a rather lively street here in Chicago, and in the course of this summer built a house on it, so I now live on my own land with a garden and house, and though the pilings of the latter are not yet quite solidly set, there is no lack of good will to have them finished very soon.

Now let this be enough for now, dear brother, and I hope that this letter will find you in the best health and comfort, also ask you to answer as soon as possible, and conclude with my best wishes to you, to *all of you.* We both, your brother & sister, send our warmest greetings and kisses to mother, brothers, sister, brother- & sister-in-law, other family & acquaintances. *All in all!* And we remain as always in love & friendship!!

Your brother and sister-in-law
Nikolaus & Marie

The German Society of Chicago Reports on Its Aid to German Immigrants

The following two documents are taken from the annual reports of the German Society (Deutsche Gesellschaft) of Chicago, an agency founded in 1854 to aid German immigrants. The German Society was one of the most significant charitable institutions of Chicago's German community well into the twentieth century; in fact it still exists. Founded by a small circle of German intellectuals and business people, many of whom were refugees after the defeat of the Revolution of 1848, it was supported throughout its history by the upper levels

*of Chicago's German population. There were models for the society
in other cities of the U.S., particularly in the ports on the East Coast,
as well as in midwestern cities with large German populations like
Cincinnati and St. Louis. These German immigrant aid societies
commonly maintained close mutual relations.*

*A printed annual report of the Chicago German Society appeared
for the first time for the year 1857-58. The passages selected here
describe the confusion of arrival in the train stations, as the newcomers sought lost baggage, other railroad stations, work, relatives,
food, and lodging. The scene from 1858 — including the varied and
difficult tasks of the agent of the society — could have taken place
practically any time before World War I. This report also illustrates
the pressures on the society during periodic economic crises when
the number of immigrants declined but when numerous local Germans, as well as unemployed men stopping over in Chicago during
their search for work, turned to the German Society for aid. The
founding of the German Workers Association (Arbeiterverein) and
the Workers Mutual Benefit Society (Arbeiter-Unterstützungsverein)
during the economic crisis of 1857-58 can serve as one indication
that the German Society was not designed, nor did it have the
resources, to meet the needs of Chicago's unemployed Germans.
Moreover, the society shared the current Victorian middle-class attitude that poverty and unemployment were the result of personal
defects of will and character, an attitude which did not exactly give
the society a good reputation among workers. The society, for example, was more preoccupied with the evil of begging than with
unemployment, advising strongly against giving alms. Instead, respectable people were supposed to refer beggars to the agents of the
German Society, who could more easily recognize practiced tramps,
assist in finding work for those seeking aid, or send people to the
officials of the established local relief societies. In this regard the
German Society was no different from the corresponding American
philanthropic organizations, except that as an ethnic institution it
felt the need to demonstrate its complete agreement with prevailing
American middle-class values.*

*Nevertheless the excerpts from the annual report of the agent of
the German Society for the year 1869-70 do not reflect this dominant
ideology. At this time the agent was Fritz Anneke, an old forty-eighter
who, in contrast to so many of his compatriots, had not slid from
engaged liberalism into complacent conservatism. (See the biograph-*

ical sketches at the end of this volume.) In his report he attempts to analyze the social roots of current problems, illuminating in the process the function of the society as an employment agency which often sent those seeking work into the countryside. Later this function of the society led to controversies with German labor organizations, which accused the society of providing firms with strikebreakers and criticized Anneke's solution for unemployment—directing German workers into rural areas—as inappropriate and ineffective. Yet at least Anneke was willing to confront such problems, concluding in the process that the society's distinction between recently arrived immigrants and the unemployed was artificial and therefore meaningless. People seeking work were a special problem for Chicago since it was the railroad hub of the country. Workers came to Chicago not only because of its reputation as an "El Dorado" but also because they had to stop over on their way to other destinations. Once in the city they often looked around for work, but according to Anneke few had the luck of the young coppersmith fifteen years before.

3. **Excerpts from the Annual Reports of the German Society from 1858 and 1870 (***Annual Reports of the German Society of Chicago for April, 1857-58, and April, 1869-70*** [Chicago: Chg. Sonne, 1858; and Chicago: Druck der *Illinois Volkszeitung*, 1870]).**

Annual Report of the Officials of the German Society in Chicago for the year from April, 1857 to April, 1858

Our attention has been focused on preventing the swindling of immigrants by innkeepers and their runners in and around the train stations. We had presented the city council with recommendations for laws to this effect and obtained their passage. One ordinance enacted in June requires that a licensed German innkeeper or runner present a business card when recommending his inn to arriving passengers. The card must give the following information in both English and German: name of the innkeeper, name of the inn and the street where it is located, the cost of meals per day, the cost of a room per night and per week, and whether he transports his guests with or without charge to and from his inn.

In order to see if and how the police were enforcing the new ordinances, the agent and I made an inspection of the various train stations, during which we were insulted by the runners ⟨Runnern⟩ in the most vile manner; the police captain was at a loss and could only suggest that we too be deputized. In this new capacity we brought about the arrests of several transgressors of the above-mentioned ordinance, and this had the desired effect.

Each day, however, we were unpleasantly reminded that our effectiveness would have to remain one-sided and insufficient as long as we did not have access to financial resources. Many families arriving from New York had been forced to ask for advances in Castle Garden[1] using their baggage as collateral, and they subsequently pestered us with requests to retrieve their baggage for them. But this could only be done by paying the freight and the outstanding debt in New York. Similarly, there were people who were still in possession of their baggage and wanted to continue on their way but had no more money to do so; many of them wanted to deposit their bags with us instead of with an immigrant innkeeper. Our means were unfortunately insufficient to aid each person in this manner, and it is possible that this led to frequent and considerable losses at the hands of the innkeepers. . . .

When continuing unemployment caused an unparalleled emergency situation last winter, the executive committee, believing it was acting on behalf of the society's constituency ⟨Constituenten⟩, extended aid—food, heating material, and clothing—to a l l G e r m a n i m m i g r a n t s. . . .

But the German Society was not the only organization which sought to alleviate the hardship of its fellow countrymen last winter. The efforts of the Workers Association, as well as The Workers Mutual Benefit Society, deserve the highest commendations. Together these societies accomplished what would have been impossible for either one of them alone due to their limited means. But because each association worked in i s o - l a t i o n through its own officials, it was unfortunately impossible to prevent one in the same family from receiving aid from both at the same time. Several such cases have come to my attention where unworthy people exploited this unfortunate situation to their own advantage.

It therefore seems imperative that only **one** German Society deal with the distribution of aid. I would thus recommend that our a i d t o G e r - m a n i m m i g r a n t s also be conducted according to the models furnished by the German Societies in New York and Cincinnati. . . .

As mentioned above, since last summer, together with the agent, I have taken over the surveillance of the train stations to see that the city ordinances are being enforced. But even if they had sufficient time, two officials would still be too few. I would therefore recommend that the president

1. Located in what is now Battery Park on the southern tip of Manhattan, Castle Garden served as the reception center for immigrants arriving in New York City from 1855 to 1892.

and agent be assigned to a committee of six to be elected for this purpose and to be called the Train Station Surveillance Committee.

These officials would likewise have to have police authorization. Their duty would not only entail being frequently present at the arrival of immigrant trains, but also at their departure. Here they would ask their departing countrymen whether they were satisfied with the food, living conditions, and treatment at the inn where they stayed; in the case of complaints or accusations, the officials would either take notes or detain the people until the case could be looked into by the proper legal authorities.

After having collected information of this kind for a few months, this committee would be in a position to draw up a list of those immigrant inns which are of good repute in our city. This list would then be sent to those German Societies in eastern port cities which could best make use of it. On the other hand, it would also be the duty of this committee to present the mayor with a list of those inns which have proven detrimental to the interests of immigrants, and to petition for the revocation of their licenses. Here, too, the character of our highest municipal authorities guarantees us the necessary support. . . .

Last winter some honest, upright craftsmen and their families, who were reluctant to ask strangers for help, were forced to bring beds, clothes, and household goods to the pawnbroker. For many, the payment or foreclosure date is at the door, and most of them still have neither work to earn the money nor friends from whom to borrow it. Several such families have turned to me in the past few days to advance them the interest ⟨Interessen⟩ for one or two months in order to put off the due date. They all hope to thus redeem their hard-earned possessions. I would like to recommend lending good families the interest ⟨Interessen⟩ needed to prolong foreclosure, while holding their pawn tickets as security. . . .

I still hear it said that the agent's wages are too high and that he has too little to do, that people would of course like to support the society, but that they don't want their entire contribution going to the preservation of the agent.

I am convinced that these people have not gone to the trouble to investigate what they maintain, and if they had, they would have found that the activities of this official fulfill the most important objectives of the German Society as it has existed to date. These people have not been to the society's office, they haven't seen the throngs—often uninterrupted—of people coming and going. The one asks the agent to find relatives or friends, the agent sees to the relevant

notice in the newspapers; the other has lost his baggage on the way from
New York to Chicago, the agent writes off to Detroit and Dunkirk;[2] a
third would like to send money—safely and without cost—to a relative
living somewhere or other, the agent takes care of this, too. Now immigrants come who want advances against their baggage so they can
continue their trip; the agent accompanies them to the train station or to
the inn, estimates the value of the baggage, pays the advances and has the
things brought back to the office. On the way he picks up five letters, all
addressed to the same person. The first is not very flattering; "Mr. Agent,
I've been waiting so long for my two suitcases, and you said you would
see to them immediately. Send the checks back to me so I'll know what's
going on!" The good man is of the opinion that the lost things must still
be where he last saw them on his trip. His bags, in the meantime, were
either pilfered by corrupt railroad officials or have been sent on a g r a n d
t o u r without their owner, but the latter suspects the agent of negligence
or even deceit. Next comes an entire family of immigrants, freshly arrived.
They have lost one of their suitcases in the train station or have been
cheated by an innkeeper; the agent goes along with them so that they,
too, will be content. A local citizen wants to bring over a relative from
his hometown in Germany. He requests a travel guide with exact directions
for getting from his hometown to Chicago, as well as sure means of alerting
the cousin of swindlers along the way; the agent, to the best of his ability,
also tries to satisfy this request. News is received from an immigrant inn
that the proprietor wants to throw out a sick immigrant. The agent goes
to see the sick person, gets medical assistance, calms the innkeeper or sees
to it that the sick person is brought to a hospital. The agent is once again
busy trying to finish a letter to somewhere or other when a man comes
in and interrupts him with the words: "Listen, the guy you sent me last
time was even worse than the others. I told him to go to the devil! Do
you have anyone good today?" Two years ago this same man with the
charming manners—always on the lookout for slave labor—was a dues-
paying member of the German Society; now, however, he'll not hear of
supporting the society because he had the misfortune of h a v i n g b e e n
d i s s a t i s f i e d with the workers r e f e r r e d t o h i m f r e e o f c h a r g e.

But what the agent has to suffer when he has evoked the righteous
anger of a patroness by having secured her a good-for-nothing maid—it
would be better if he told you himself. No one, in any case, would envy
him t h i s pleasure.

2. A railroad junction in western New York State.

I will not tax your patience any longer. But I would again like to strongly recommend that each member try to introduce at least one of his friends to the society; membership is so easily acquired, as the minimum annual contribution is only $1, and from then on up, absolutely no limits are imposed on generosity.

Annual Report of the Agent of the German Society of Chicago for the year from April 1, 1869 to April 1, 1870

The following numbers provide a general overview of some of the agent's most important areas of activity during the past administrative year.

Sought work, aid, and advice:	8022
Referred for work:	2067
Letters received:	385
Letters written:	592
Baggage traced:	67
Obtained support through the County Agent and the "Relief and Aid Society":	404
Referred to hospital:	103
Arranged free transportation:	192
Obtained free peddler's licenses:	38
Provided financial aid through the society to the total sum of:	$737.50

Employment

According to the statutes of the German Society, its primary function lies in furnishing aid to needy immigrants, while one of the duties of the agent is to "give preference to helping immigrants find employment." In the few months since I have assumed the post of agent of the German Society, the employment question has definitely become the most pressing. I will hence deal with this subject first and accord it as much space as can be permitted in a report of this kind.

As the above summary reveals, the number of applicants for work, aid, and advice has increased significantly over earlier years. While in the year 1867-68 such applicants amounted to 5051 and in the year 1868-69 to 6685, they totaled 8022 in the administrative year recently come to an end. This number would probably be considerably higher if the records had been more complete. By far, most of those included in that number were seeking work.

I am by no means saying anything new, rather only repeating something already said very often before, when I note here that the number of unemployed in the big cities is increasing from year to year and has reached alarming proportions in the northern cities during the long winter season. Chicago, one of the largest and at the same time northernmost of what could be called the major cities of the Union, suffers the most from this problem. On the one hand, its prominent reputation, not only in all parts of the United States but also in Europe, draws a mass of people who, expecting a new El Dorado, bring nothing along except their good will and their ability to work. On the other hand, during the endlessly long winter most of the businesses suffer a complete or partial shutdown, which has a more or less crippling effect in all areas of life.

The natural consequence of this is that the greater the demand becomes for labor in public and private works as a result of a recovery, the more extreme the setback must be in the long winter season — the time of unemployment, hunger, suffering and misery. The complaints in the course of the last winter, which is still not over, were countless. They came not only from those suddenly without work and any means of support, but also from those who, through years of hard work, had been successful in putting something aside for the future, in establishing some small, if only so modest, savings.

The only sweeping means of remedying such deplorable conditions is to be found in the complete restructuring of our social relations, in a better distribution of work and organization of workers. The work force and the will to work are there, but — deprived of job possibilities — cannot be taken advantage of. There is no lack of the products of labor, nor of all that which is part of a humane existence — shelter and housing, food and clothing of all kinds; on the contrary, there is an abundance of these. But all of these things are either completely inaccessible or available only in a thoroughly insufficient quantity to those who need them the most, since they don't have the means to obtain them; and even though the worker has the equivalent, namely the capacity and the desire to work, he is deprived of the opportunity to make products as payment for these goods.

A radical reorganization, which would make possible the continued realization of each person's abilities and would ensure him a corresponding portion of the social products, is for the time being unthinkable. Such a change will come only through progressive education, only through the correct understanding of the interests of the individual and of the community, the welfare of which is based on that of the individual. In the meantime, it is a matter of finding temporary remedies.

The most important of these remedies is a better distribution of the work force than that which presently prevails, and which is usually purely fortuitous. While the cities, particularly the big ones, have an excess of labor, the rural areas suffer from a labor shortage. Commerce, industry and the crafts are glutted with workers; more stream to them than can advantageously be accommodated; and there is no market for the excess products. In rural areas, however, in the production of raw materials, the raising of livestock in agriculture, and in the mining industry, a huge labor force could be accommodated in the United States over a long period of years, making products which would find a quick and profitable market.

The South, particularly the state of Mississippi, has made great efforts in the last year to obtain agricultural workers. In many counties in this state, immigrant organizations have been formed whose statutes call not merely for attracting immigrants but also for supporting them and protecting their rights once there. Through arrangement by the agent of the German Society during the last few months, between 300-400 German workers have resettled in various parts of the state of Mississippi — Oxford, Vaiden, Canton, Jackson, etc.; and of the many reports I have received, nearly all read very favorably. . . .

Not only unemployed and destitute workers went to Mississippi, but also many people with a little capital who intended to buy land there, should they like the conditions. From a few of these people I have already received the news that they bought property at a good price and are very satisfied.

Likewise, during the past weeks, the agent has received quite a few inquiries for agricultural workers from our own state and the neighboring states of Michigan and Indiana — partly for married workers, partly for unmarried. Only a few of these requests could be met, although some of the offers were quite favorable and numerous poor, unemployed people were always available. The reason why these job offers were not accepted lies essentially in the ever increasing preference, especially among younger people, for life in the city. All the pleasures that the city offers are either not available in the country, or are very hard to come by. Many of these people imagine they will quickly find work with a wage that will open to them all the pleasures of the city. They do not consider the coming winter when they are once again thrown back into a miserable existence without work and wages, an existence that can only be survived with the aid of so-called charity.

The heavy emigration to Mississippi, however, contradicts the lack of desire to remove to the country referred to above. The explanation for this seems to lie in the fact that people in the "sunny South" expect a splendid future, something those in the North never believed they could count on. These expectations led to the formation of a regular stream of southerly migration, sweeping along many who were as yet undecided. Such disorders[3] often determine the movements of large groups of people.

Aid

As already mentioned, the statutes of the German Society point out that its primary function lies in furnishing "aid to needy immigrants, and in special cases, other needy persons as well."

It is difficult to decide which people can be classified as immigrants. Strictly speaking, one can only count those who are still on their way from their old home on the other side of the ocean to a new one within the United States. Meanwhile, the definition has already been broadened through practice and repeated clarification so that all those who have lived no longer than six months in the United States should still be viewed as immigrants. But even this broader interpretation is not enough. The "s p e c i a l   c a s e s," in which "other needy persons" apply for support, are often counted among the regulars, particularly during the winter, so that it is absolutely impossible to hold strictly to the definition of "immigrant." The society must, according to its means, provide aid to e a c h p e r s o n who turns to it in desperation, and that includes not only Germans, but also Poles, Czechs, and members of other nationalities. Having no representation here, these people thus turn to the Germans in their need, the most closely related nation with whose language they are at least somewhat familiar.

The type of aid and manner of allotting it vary widely. I have already spoken in detail about providing aid through referrals to work. Assistance through advice and information, through support and care of all kinds, is the least obvious. It defies calculation and statistical tabulation, but is nevertheless the most meaningful and valuable aid which can be provided by the agent of the German Society. In order to be able to adequately appreciate this, one must himself either have occupied the position of agent or have observed his work uninterruptedly for some time.

The German Society can offer monetary aid only in the most urgent situations, its funds being so scarce that economization approaching parsimony is almost necessary to avoid falling into debt or bankruptcy. The agent is frequently impelled to turn away truly needy people or to be

3. Anneke has probably used the wrong word here. Having just referred to the "stream" [Strom] of migration, it is conceivable that the agent meant the word *Strömungen*, in which case the subject of the sentence would read "Such currents . . .".

extremely stingy in allotting aid, for the available funds are not sufficient. Most of the needy had to be referred to the County Relief Agency and to the well-endowed *Relief and Aid Society*. In the past year the latter had approximately forty thousand dollars at its disposal which it amassed through contributions, while the German Society barely had three thousand dollars. Almost all the needy families which I referred to the society were assisted in a suitable manner.

Several complaints were registered against the County Relief Agency, many of which, though not all, seemed to be legitimate. The majority of these complaints concerned the so called "visitors," whose job is to go to the living quarters of those registered as needy with the county agent, in order to evaluate the extent of deprivation and to determine or recommend the appropriate form of aid. In one of the last sessions of the "supervisory" ⟨Supervisoren⟩ board a number of cases were brought to attention in which the "visitors" had allotted aid to people who were not deserving of it, and who, on receipt of fuel and food, had proceeded to sell them. I have personally heard of other similar cases. On the other hand, I have received bitter complaints maintaining that, even in extremely urgent cases, the visitors in question never appeared, or only after fourteen days, and that they chose not to allot aid, regardless of the necessity. It is the responsibility of the supervisory ⟨Supervisoren⟩ board to remedy this abuse and see to it that only honest, able and reliable people are placed in the important position of "visitors". . . .

Immigration

In the past few weeks the number of immigrants has increased considerably. But it seems that few have remained here, that by far most have continued west, namely to the states of Iowa and Minnesota. I have come to this conclusion due to the fact that only a few newly arrived immigrants have sought the assistance of the agent of the German Society in Chicago, while a large number of those wanting to continue to the western states sought the assistance of their agents. It is generally a question of toting baggage and overcharging for excess weight. . . .

Finances

The funds of the German Society are so limited that the services of the society, and particularly of its agent, are curtailed in all respects. Were the means more significant, were they as they could and must be for a city like Chicago—a city which permits itself to boast of its scale, population, and wealth and the number and prosperity of its Germans—the German

Society would be in a position to at least come closer to the goals it has set. As things stand now, they remain far out of reach.

Chicago, 1st of April 1870   F r i t z   A n n e k e

The Chicago Labor Press Denounces the Practices of German Innkeepers

In this article from 1883 the Chicagoer Arbeiter-Zeitung *criticizes the long-existing abuses in the railroad stations. The problem was even more acute because this was historically one of the peak years of German immigration to Chicago and to America as a whole. In the preceding July alone, over 25,000 immigrants of all nationalities had arrived in Chicago's train stations. The* Arbeiter-Zeitung *accused both the German Society and the railroads of not dealing with the problem decisively enough. It denounced in particular the deceptions of the German innkeepers and their "runners," who did not hesitate to use the good reputation of the German Society among the immigrants to their own selfish advantage.*

A second article, taken from the Arbeiter-Zeitung's *Sunday edition, describes the desperate situation of a German immigrant family that fell victim to one of the "runners."*

4. "The Bloodsucking System of the German Immigrant Innkeepers" (*Chicagoer Arbeiter-Zeitung,* April 23, 1883).

H o w   a r r i v i n g   c o u n t r y m e n   a r e   a b u s e d.

In its last annual report the local "German Society" said that the railroads are always willing to cooperate in the transportation of immigrants. It went on to say that most of the boardinghouse keepers are honest people, about whom there are seldom complaints, and that they are concerned with the welfare of the immigrants. The first statement is correct. The railroad companies not only transport the immigrants efficiently—if not cheaply—but also attend to security within the train stations. Agents are employed by the railroads to see that hotel "runners" and other swindlers are kept out of the stations. But as soon as the immigrants have left the train station, they find themselves at the mercy of the "runners," the most vile and dangerous of all crooks, who with feigned goodness and humanitarian intent even warn the immigrants against the likes of themselves. It is impossible for the uninitiated to imagine the extent to which, and with what finesse and coldheartedness, the poor immigrants, especially the Germans, are bled of their last cent and then put out on the street with wife and child.

In Chicago there is no "Castle Garden" which protects immigrants arriving in New York. But there is, as perhaps a number of readers know, a "German Society" whose purpose it is to lend a helping hand to poor fellow countrymen, and especially to oversee the immigrants. One would think that this society would have made arrangements to meet the arriving immigrants at the train stations and to look out for them until they continue their journey. But the society is as little concerned with this as are the city police. As soon as an immigrant train arrives, the railroad agents are already standing on the platform, and in accordance with their regulations, the cars are emptied in a few minutes. Each takes his baggage and moves out onto the street.

The immigrants arrive exhausted by the long trip, confused by all the new impressions, with the sounds of a totally foreign language swirling around their heads, and full of the uneducated European's fear of the new-world wonders and swindlers. Given these conditions, the sound of their mother tongue coming from the mouth of the "runner" is like music to their ears. The "runner" exploits this first impression. With adroit tongue, he depicts all the dangers which threaten the "greenhorns" in America, especially those which lurk hidden behind each corner in the metropolis of the West. But above all he warns of boardinghouse keepers who bleed the poor immigrants and of rabble like himself who deliver the newly arrived into the hands of the bloodsuckers.

The immigrants have heard of all these dangers. They also know, what many Chicagoans do not know, that there is a German Consulate here; they have heard of the "German Society"; thus when all else fails, the "runner's" last trump is: "I am an official of the German Consulate" (or German Society). As a rule, he also wears a star on his chest or some other badge representing his alleged office. There is, for example, the "runner" for the boardinghouse "The German Empire," who with the most unmitigated gall refers to himself as an "Official of the German Empire."

The immigrants get in the carriage half voluntarily, half pushed by the "runner." Then the trip begins, to another train station from which they are to continue their journey. On the way, the "runner" stands on the running board and continues his exhortations and warnings. At the station everyone gets out and checks their bags. The people are naturally tired, hungry and thirsty. The "runner," to whom the group now clings as its savior in a dangerous situation, knows a good restaurant. The flock follows him, enters, and — is caught. They shyly sit down at the long tables decked with steaming bowls, and their hunger makes the food seem attractive.

They have scarcely made themselves comfortable when, so it goes, the train is about to pull out. Everyone starts to rush out. "Pay first!" the proprietor yells. The people slowly pass by the table, dejectedly counting out their last few dollars. Half of what remains them goes into the pocket of the innkeeper, $1 per head for the food they could not enjoy. They hurry over to the station, just barely making the train. Many even miss the train, and are thus forced to spend the night at the boardinghouse, where, as a rule, the last dollar is also eaten up.

How would it be if the "German Society" would finally abandon its wait-and-see attitude, and instead of calmly letting everything come to it, would pay officials under whose guidance the immigrants would be brought from one train station to another or to reputable boardinghouses? Certainly — the last Treasurer's Report being so favorable — a sum could be allocated for this purpose!

5. "Poor Immigrants" (*Fackel,* January 2, 1881).

The day before yesterday on the top floor of the wooden building on the corner of Wood and 13th Street, Adolph Scheßler, his wife and five children were found amidst the poorest conceivable conditions. They had neither stove, nor furniture, nor money. The family arrived here from Baden three weeks ago and fell into the hands of a "hotel runner" at the train station. They were brought to a boardinghouse on Canal Street. After having given the proprietor $20, Mr. Scheßler had to leave the establishment at the end of the second day.

Only around $12 remained to him, and from this sum he had to pay $9.50 rent in advance for the rooms where the family was found, so that he only had some $2 left. The family had been living off these $2 for the past three weeks. When the neighbors discovered them, they hadn't eaten for two days.

One of the small sons had his ears and his feet frozen, and the father, whose feet were also frozen, will probably lose a few toes. Most of the people living in this area are themselves poor, but when the family's horrible situation became known, the neighbors began to compete with one another, each trying to outdo the other with good deeds. One sent an old stove, another coal, a third something to eat, etc., so that the poor people presently have sufficient provisions for a few days. Mr. Scheßler stated that in his misery he had turned to the German Consul but was told that applicants who had not lived here a year are not eligible for any sort of aid.

Very nice. So a family has to starve and freeze for a whole year before anything can be done for them, i.e., they can die and rot. Why, after all, should it bother the gentlemen who themselves luxuriate in abundance?

The Attitude of the German-American Labor Movement to Immigration

The massive immigration of the 1880s not only overtaxed the German Society but had an impact upon all German institutions in Chicago. Between 1880 and 1890 over 5.2 million immigrants arrived on American shores, among them 1.5 million Germans. The American labor movement could not remain indifferent to this wave of immigration because the increased supply of labor threatened wages and made the control of the labor market more difficult for the unions. Analyzing these problems, the following article represents the attitude of the left wing of the German-American labor movement in Chicago. It rejects the argument that immigration inevitably depressed wages and speaks out against immigration restriction. Its author was probably Paul Grottkau, who before his emigration in 1878 was active as a union and party leader in Berlin. From 1879 to 1884 he served as editor of the Chicagoer Arbeiter-Zeitung *and the* Vorbote. *(See also the biographical sketches at the end of this volume.)*

6. "Immigration and the Unions" (*Chicagoer Arbeiter-Zeitung*, April 29, 1881).

It cannot have escaped the notice of local workers that the consequences of the tremendous wave of immigration have already begun to make themselves felt in the labor market. We are not enemies of immigration and hence cannot choose to fight it; but we must still raise the question: What should be done to lessen, or eliminate, the decrease in wages resulting from the huge labor supply? At present most of the immigrants are coming from Germany, and, as the majority of them are industrial workers, they consequently seek work and accommodations in the cities.

The last three weeks in Chicago have witnessed the recent arrival of another several thousand artisans, some with, some without their families. Already having had to accustom themselves to various sorts of deprivation, it is understandable that the first concern of each of these people is to find work. But it is commonly known that there is by no means a shortage of labor in Chicago, nor is there ever full employment among the native and foreign-born workers already here. What, then, can the new immigrants do save offer their labor below the established pay scale? Still unfamiliar with local labor practices, they will only get work in this way. As a consequence, other workers already established here will be forced to give way to the cheaper immigrant labor.

This also explains the enthusiasm with which the capitalist press welcomes immigration. The number of objects available for capitalist exploitation is multiplied, and the increased labor supply enables the exploiters to keep wages down and prevent wage increases. This obviously puts the resident workers at a disadvantage. How can it be overcome? Immigration restraints can neither be justified nor achieved by the workers. And it is simply inhuman to banish these immigrant artisans to the countryside, and to expect them to submit themselves to the degradation of rough treatment and the most unconscionable exploitation of their labor for a pitiful wage. Besides, such treatment of the immigrants would be of absolutely no value to the industrial worker. The general misery would only be augmented; it would be pushed to the side, but in no way overcome. At present the workers' one and only concern is to prevent their standard of living from being even further depressed; more, they must try to raise it. It is incorrect to assume that immigration must always have a negative effect on the wage scale because it increases the number of people looking for work. This is only true when the workers, and particularly the immigrants, remain unorganized; they are thus reduced to defenseless and irresolute objects of exploitation: working for starvation wages, they eke out a living in Chinese-like indifference.

If, on the other hand, the workers are well organized and use their organization to raise their standard of living, immigration cannot hurt them: the more people there are, the more needs there are to be met; and the more needs there are to be met, the more work there is to be done. Immigration should not rob the local workers of their jobs; rather it should, in proportion to its strength, make more jobs necessary through the needs it creates. When this happens—and it can be made to happen with the help of an effective labor organization—immigration does not hurt, but helps the local residents.

The advantages of this could be considerable and many-sided —which we will illustrate later—but this holds only under the precondition that there is a good labor organization in which, of course, the immigrants would have to take part. In the case of a lack of organization on the part of the workers, the inexperienced immigrants will become powerless wage slaves in the hands of the exploiters and an affliction for the resident workers. Their mere presence would be enough to prevent wage increases, but just the fact that they are seeking work would depress present wages.

Given such conditions, the labor unions must take a stand. If they fail to take action, they will be faced with a real danger. If, on the other hand, they are active and make an effort to enlist the immigrants—who are known to be among the most intelligent of their old fatherland, since the dumb ones stay home—they will enhance their own strength and prevent the entrepreneurs' despotic exploitation. In this way, they can take advantage of the increased production resulting from greater demand. By admitting the immigrants, the workers' organizations will gain the upper hand on the entrepreneurs, and consequently, not only will the depression of wages be hindered, but a reduction of work hours may also be attained.

The only effective regulator of the labor market is known to be a decrease in work hours. This can only be accomplished through an effective workers' organization, the creation of which is the task of the existing labor organizations. The Trades Assembly should not fail to establish a general employment bureau for all branches of industry. All the immigrants remaining here would of course go there first. The secretary would assign them to a labor union, and only when membership in the respective union was definite, and after adherence to the rules and regulations of the union had been sworn to, would they be referred to a job.

Only through such a procedure can the local workers as well as the new immigrants be protected from the insolent chicanery on the part of the employers. Therefore union comrades, do your duty!! If you are dilatory now, it will be your own fault if your situation worsens, for you have been warned!

The Disillusionment of an Immigrant Worker

In a letter to the Chicagoer Arbeiter-Zeitung *this disappointed meerschaum cutter warned his countrymen of the false promises of im-*

migrant agents in Germany and tried to show the realities of working-class life in America. Beyond describing the fate of this individual, the letter illuminates the international labor market of which Chicago was a part. Especially in the highly skilled trades, workers were purposefully sought out in Europe, a process in which the methods employed were sometimes, as in this case, deceitful. Information about employment opportunities in the U.S. which was more reliable than the testimony of profit-oriented immigration agents was available in many books and pamphlets written particularly for prospective emigrants, one of which is excerpted in this anthology as Document 12.

7. **"Voice from the People": A Letter to the Editor from an Immigrant Meerschaum and Amber Cutter (*Chicagoer Arbeiter-Zeitung*, February 6, 1883).**

To the editorial staff of the "Arbeiter-Zeitung"!

In November of the year 1881, I was urged to travel to America by the slave trader, Jaburek. He made me the most glittering promises. I am a meerschaum and amber worker by trade, and during my stay in Vienna I worked for four years in one of the largest Viennese factories, where I made a so-called good living.

Nevertheless, I let myself be deceived by the scoundrel and have been paying bitterly for it ever since. I was sent by the agent across the ocean on a steamship, and after a stormy twenty-two day trip, I arrived in New York where my distant fate awaited me. No one fetched me in New York, though Jaburek had promised me that someone would find me a job and a place to live as soon as I got there. But that was all part of the swindle. Jaburek just wanted to stick me with a 120 Mark ticket, and in this he succeeded. Like many of my comrades in suffering, I was lured here to compete with the other workers. After three weeks I finally found work with Karl Weiss in New York, where I was supposed to make $13.00 a week. But my problems had only begun. Weiss was going to deduct one dollar a week, so that, as he put it, he could give me the money at the end of the year. I wouldn't hear of it and was let go. Here and there I found part-time work with masters in small shops and in this way just managed to eke out a living.

I was informed by Mr. Benzinger in New York that a Mr. Metzler had written him; he and a Mr. Rothschild wanted him to send meerschaum and amber cutters to Chicago. Travel costs were to be reimbursed and the salary was said to be good. At that time I was completely out of work. A few people from Vienna took me into their care and got together the money necessary for me to buy a train ticket to Chicago. I had already been warned about Mssrs Metzler and Rothschild's foreman in New York. I didn't like him from the very start, and he acted hostilely toward me. He made trouble in order to get me to work for less and then offered me $10.00 a week. I demanded $12.00. He said the business turned little profit, which was new to me, since the owners were millionaires and the workers beggars. He finally gave me $12.00, but at the same time he wrote to New York for another worker. Eight days before Christmas I was let go. This clearly illustrates the capitalists' ruthlessness. I was thrown out on the pavement without a penny in my pocket, no friends, no relatives, starving and freezing. For eight full weeks I led a wretched existence. No work and no pay anywhere, and if I hadn't had so much endurance, I would long since have put an end to all my misery and suffering.

The foreman spread another outrageous lie about me in the firm. Kempelmacher, that's the fool's name, said I had wanted $14.00 and that I had left of my own accord. At that point I went directly to the owners in order to tell them the truth and ask for work. But they believed the foreman instead of me, and calling me a liar, showed me the door. I had conducted myself properly and that's why this action was even more disgraceful. Metzler recently went to New York to recruit new cheap labor but came back empty-handed. Now he is going to write off to Vienna to inflict the same fate as mine on those who don't know any better. Publish these lines for this reason, Mr. Editor, so that my countrymen will not be swindled and driven into the arms of poverty as have been I and so many others.

Johann Rosinger

II. WORK

The documents in this section help illuminate a distinct phase of the American industrial revolution during which production was systematically mechanized in practically all branches of industry. The early mechanization of the New England textile industry was exemplary, but also unique. Before the Civil War, industrialization more commonly meant the expansion and systematization of traditional craft production through the division of labor, the creation of larger production units, or the use of outworkers who made one small part of the final product in their homes. Machines played only a supplemental role, if any at all. The genuine industrial centers of antebellum America developed as smaller cities in the hinterland of the coastal states at the fall lines of streams where water power could be harnessed, such as Paterson, New Jersey, or the numerous manufacturing centers of New England. Nevertheless, the social and economic preconditions for industrial production were laid down prior to the 1870s, including both a national commodities market based on the expansion of the railroad network and a nationwide free labor market after the destruction or weakening of traditional bound labor, such as slavery and the apprenticeship system.

Beginning in the 1850s, but particularly after the depression of the 1870s, manufacturers in larger cities like Chicago began to change over to mechanized production using steam power. The larger cities had better transportation links and a labor supply fed by massive immigration since the middle of the century. The new method of production went far beyond the introduction of machines: the manufacturing process itself was reorganized to guarantee steady, continuous production, and work had to be routinized and subdivided in order for machines to be used efficiently and profitably. Skilled workers were replaced or assigned less important tasks, while foremen took over control of the production process. Instead of master artisans supervising journeymen and apprentices, foremen watched over unskilled and semiskilled workers who were easily replaceable and who in fact frequently changed jobs. The economists David M. Gordon, Richard Edwards, and Michael Reich have characterized the process of work reorganization in the late nineteenth and early twentieth centuries as the "homogenization of labor" and they single out the period from approximately 1870 to 1900—which is the focus of attention here—as a transitional era in which manufacturing based on crafts disintegrated while mechanized production was firmly established on a broad base.

The thrust of the new order was precisely captured in the contemporary term "drive system," which emphasized the new intensity and speedup of work. Previously work had been long and hard but also irregular, seasonal, and often paced by the tempo of the workers themselves. The new system did not change this traditional arrangement all at once—a surprising number of manufacturers in the Gilded Age did not operate all year round—but the trend was clearly in this direction. The new emphasis on time and mechanization resulted in a shift away from the traditional method of pay by the day to payment by the hour and by the piece, thereby facilitating control of a work force using machines. The fierce industrial competition of the era pushed wages further downward and led to the employment of women and children, who were paid drastically less than men. Yet the most salient characteristic of the "drive system" was the intensification of the tempo of work. It is thus small wonder that the emerging labor movement of the period put the eight-hour day at the center of its demands as it contested the employers' sweeping control over the work lives of their employees. The leaders of the labor movement were skilled workers, those most immediately affected by the new industrial order, and, since Germans made up a considerable portion of this stratum of the labor force, they played a prominent and active role in the contemporary labor movement.

Social historical studies of American cities in the nineteenth century have pointed out that Germans were overrepresented in skilled occupations, in contrast to the Irish, who constituted the only other ethnic group of comparable size. Between 1870 and 1890 in the cities of Detroit, Boston, and Pittsburgh, for example, the proportion of Germans in skilled trades averaged around 40 percent; the respective figure for the Irish was less than 25 percent. Chicago was no exception; in 1880 skilled workers made up 37.4 percent of all employed Germans.

Given the complex transformation of skilled labor, the experiences of skilled Germans were, nevertheless, considerably varied. In the documents in this chapter the woodworkers, particularly the cabinetmakers, best fit the standard pattern of the decline of a craft in the face of increasing industrialization. By way of contrast, the situation of the bakers was not so dramatically altered by mechanization, although they had already witnessed the degeneration of their craft in Germany as the apprenticeship system broke down and journeymen tramped around the country looking for work. While the German bakers found a similar situation in Chicago, conditions were different for the German sausagemakers in the city. Perhaps they had been butchers before they emigrated, but the highly specialized work they did in Chicago's meat-packing industry had never been incorporated into traditional craft labor. The changes they encountered were instead part of the ongoing restructuring of work in expanding mass production industry.

The cabinetmakers are just one example of a varied process in which work was reorganized, regimented, and speeded up. German immigrant workers were especially impressed by the increased tempo of work, while other social effects of industrialization, such as traveling in search of work, were already common phenomena in Europe. Nikolaus Schwenck, for example, already knew from his own experience that Chicago was part of an international labor market. In the final quarter of the nineteenth century this market increasingly attracted unskilled Germans from rural areas, for whom industrial Chicago may well have been a shockingly new social environment, whereas their fellow countrymen from Europe's industrial regions as well as longer-established Chicago residents were already familiar with urban industrial life. It was out of such a diversity of backgrounds that a vital labor movement emerged in Gilded Age America. The following documents illustrate the manifold transformation of trades and work that lay at the basis of this labor movement.

Homogenization of the Work Process

The following description of the work force in the carshops of the Illinois Central Railroad in 1883 clearly illustrates the transition in the process of production. Making and repairing railroad cars and locomotives, the car works employed large numbers of skilled workers who were subdivided into various and distinct shops, where they performed their tasks and supervised their numerous helpers. Even in this large and highly developed establishment skilled workers had a hand in the control of production, and that remained the case even after the early 1880s. Nevertheless, they trained practically no apprentices, while the helpers could replace skilled workers by tending machines that performed sophisticated tasks. The number and function of helpers was therefore a constant point of contention for the unions of this period. The editorial reprinted here points out the artificial subdivision of the work force by task and pay, a typical strategy used by employers to make union organization more difficult as the homogenization of labor increasingly united workers by lowering them to the same level.

The carshops of the Illinois Central Railroad were one of several similar establishments built by the various railroads in the city. Chicago's railroad carshops were centers of labor unrest throughout the late nineteenth century.

8. "How Wages Are Depressed" (*Chicagoer Arbeiter-Zeitung,* March 9, 1883).

Chicago's commercial zeal is vast and multifarious. With an amazingly extensive division of labor, big industry is predominant. In all conceivable industrial branches, big capital has taken the lead, employing the latest technology and imposing the division of labor which it both brings about and defines. Having unconditional supremacy over the labor market, big manufacturers can essentially determine the price of finished products and thus establish the wage level in any given industrial branch according to their whim.

The classification of workers within the same trade into various subordinate groups, sections, and branches resulting from the division of labor allows the capitalists to considerably depress the wages for the majority of the workers in any given trade. The division of labor in the big factories is by no means thus carried out to the nth degree simply because, as many believe, increasingly limited tasks for the individual worker necessarily lead to increasingly greater efficiency; this division of labor also serves the goal of splintering labor organizations and destroying feelings of solidarity within individual crafts. The artisan who is capable of producing a finished product is reduced to part of a whole worker who is now only required to execute some few, continually recurrent tasks.

Higher intelligence and general skill are no longer necessary for his work. The craftsman can therefore very easily be replaced by an unskilled worker. He has been relegated to the place of a day laborer in a factory and is also treated and paid accordingly. But because he might possibly move up to better-paying work with time, he is led to tolerate the situation. In order to clarify the above, we would like to point out that the 300 thoroughly distinct trades practiced in Chicago have been divided up into no fewer than 2,600 subtrades, or classifications of variously paid, segmented areas of work.

This segmentation of work, with its differing wage rates—advantageous for a few and disadvantageous for the overwhelming majority—is an immense hindrance to the unionization of workers. Afflicted by their egoism and in many cases completely contaminated by it, all the wage slaves still hope to be able to advance to the better-paying positions, and in this manner the interests of the majority of poorly paid workers are harmed and neglected in the most irresponsible way by the workers themselves. There reigns a spirit in the factories which can best be characterized by the words: Each man for himself, and the Devil take the hindmost. The minimal influence of unions in determining wages in the big factories is almost unbelievable, especially in cases where many different trades, which have been broken down or divided up into subgroups, work next to one another. Up until now, the lack of a feeling of solidarity and the self-centered striving among the workers in the big industries has led to the continued impoverishment of the whole class.

The big capitalists and their managers know the workers' weak spot and they know how to skillfully exploit it to their own advantage. We want to illustrate the way this occurs by way of an example.

In the Car Works of the Ill. Central R.R., located right here on the lakeshore between 25th and 26th streets, 682 men were working a ten-hour day in December, 1882. The company payroll for this month lists the following: one plant manager with a monthly salary of $175; 1 bookkeeper receiving $83.33 ($1,000 per year); 2 clerks together receiving $135 per month, or $67½ per man. 12 foremen receive $89.33 per man; 11 machinists receive $62 per man. These 11 machinists have 29 helpers who of course also have to be machinists, but who nevertheless receive only $1,043 together, or $36 per man per month.

These 40 men, 11 machinists and 29 helpers, have 2 apprentices who receive $22.50 per man per month.

Further, 35 smiths work in said Car Works, receiving $54 per man per month. These 35 smiths, though, have 51 helpers, naturally smiths themselves; the helpers receive only $36 per man per month. These 86 smiths have 1 apprentice who in turn receives $15 per month.

In the carpentry shop of the Car Works there are 172 carpenters who receive $51.60 per man per month; but they have 31 helpers who receive only $38 per man per month. These 203 men have 4 apprentices who receive $16.50 per man per month.

These same shops have 47 painters and varnishers who receive $51 per man per month; their 25 helpers get only $32 per man per month, the 1 apprentice a mere $6.50 per month.

3 tinsmiths receive $62 per man, their 4 helpers only $36.75 per month.

4 upholsterers receive $67 per man, their helpers only $47 per month.

In the iron foundry the situation isn't any better. 30 molders receive $73.40 per man per month, while their 33 helpers receive only $37.50. These 63 iron molders have 1 apprentice — his wages amount to $21 per month.

We could extend this list even further. But the above suffices to show how wages are arbitrarily scaled down through the artificial subdivision and segmentation of work into subordinate branches. We will later show in more detail that the same situation predominates in all other large factories. Apprentices, too, are no longer trained in sufficient numbers, and those that are employed receive but very one-sided instruction so that they will always remain the slaves of big capital. Will the workers soon realize that their labor organizations must assume an entirely different and better character if they are to defend their interests vis-à-vis big capital? There is no progress without solidarity, but rather an ever increasing degradation to the point of total enslavement.

Working Conditions of the Bakers

Baking was one of the trades in which Germans predominated, both in Chicago and nationwide. In 1880 Germans made up 41.8 percent of the city's bakers, while constituting only 24.4 percent of Chicago's entire manufacturing work force. Even in the early twentieth century, after the great period of German immigration had passed, the Immigration Commission found that Germans were the only ethnic group for which baking was among the top ten occupations. Notably, however, the commission also found that the immigrants' children did not follow their fathers into the trade. Baking was one of several traditional crafts such as cabinetmaking, cigarmaking, and tailoring in which Germans were strongly represented but which also suffered considerably from the effects of industrialization. The sons of craftsmen in these trades tended to look around for more lucrative positions in expanding industries.

The three following documents illustrate the situation of the German bakers in Chicago from various viewpoints—those of the union, of the Chicago Citizens Association, and of a socialist baker. Like the majority of their colleagues in the city, most German bakers worked making bread in the countless small bakeshops scattered throughout the ethnic neighborhoods. These bakeshops had to maintain themselves against competition from large baking firms that by the 1880s were already utilizing some machinery. Such establishments sold their bread wholesale to groceries, saloons, restaurants, and hotels. Bitter competition from these large bakeries, from other neighborhood bakers, and from housewives making bread at home made it extremely difficult for the small master baker to maintain his business. To cut production costs he paid low wages, provided his journeymen with poor-quality room and board, and set up shop in cheap rented quarters, often in dank and dingy cellars. The small master baker and his few journeymen did not experience mechanization directly, but like other craftsmen they suffered from the decline of their craft as a consequence of the restructuring of production during the industrial revolution.

The exploitation of journeymen bakers provided the instigation for union organization. Relying upon detailed information from a questionnaire distributed by the union, the first article—taken from the Chicagoer Arbeiter-Zeitung—*describes the living and working conditions in a declining craft where the journeymen still boarded with their masters. Despite repeated efforts by unions, city inspectors, and progressive reformers, these conditions changed very slowly.*

The report of the Citizens Association about one small bakeshop vividly underscores the complaints of the union organizers. Although this particular bakery was not owned by a German, the owners of other bakeries mentioned did have German names, and another report of the Citizens Association specifically said that many small German bakeries evidenced similar conditions.

Clearly written by a unionist baker, the poem was published in the Chicagoer Bäcker-Zeitung, *the short-lived organ of an independent, radical union of bakers. Like some German-American unions*

in other trades, the union had split off from the original bakers'
organization and fought on two fronts against more conservative
unionists and more traditional socialists. Note that the poem uses
the word "slave" to describe the bakery worker. At a time when
everyone still vividly remembered the Civil War, the word had a
particular rhetorical bite, pointing out the real danger of a new kind
of bondage created by industrialization. The designation of workers
as "wage slaves" was a common tradition in the nineteenth-century
American labor movement.

9. "Statistics on Chicago's Bakers" (*Chicagoer Arbeiter-Zeitung*, June 11, 1881).

We learned today from the statistical committee of the Bakers Union that so many of the questionnaires have already been filled out and returned that it is possible to draw some conclusions from the answers. The average workweek for the bakery hands in Chicago amounts to six days, the average workday to approximately 15¾ hours.

This workday, however, is stretched to 17 or 18 hours due to various short interruptions spread throughout the day. The two to three hours between the punching of the dough ⟨Teichspunchen⟩ and its rising are not taken into account in the above-mentioned 15¾ hours.

But on the other hand, anyone can see that such a break cannot be considered actual free time any more than it can be used to relax outside the shop. The final results of the statistics — representing all German bakeries throughout Chicago — can only slightly diverge from the picture of conditions described above, and this slight difference will most probably reflect even more unfavorably on the working conditions and thus justify to an even greater extent the striving on the part of the journeymen bakers to better their situation. From the responses already received, the following can be seen regarding the second most frequent grievance about which the journeymen bakers complain, namely the extremely poor boarding conditions with their employers: 75% of all the journeymen bakers are completely dissatisfied with their so-called living quarters. 30% are lodged above horse stalls; another 20% live in basements, in the bakeshop itself, or next to the bakeshop — but always within range of the bakeshop's heat. Still others have to camp in attics, or in various other little corners of the employers' houses.

The journeymen bakers' sleeping quarters are almost never whitewashed.

The sleeping quarters in the bakeries are never cleaned, scrubbed, or even free of bedbugs and other vermin, like rats, mice, etc., unless, that is, the bakery boss ⟨Bäckerboß⟩—not for the sake of the bakery hands, but rather to prevent his beams from completely rotting away—undertakes the most urgent, long overdue repairs in the house.

The workers also complain bitterly about the board ⟨boardingwesen⟩ they receive from the bakery bosses ⟨Bäckerbossen⟩. Though the quantity of the food is not insufficient, with few exceptions the quality is. . . .

The food placed in front of the hands in the morning and at night is unappetizing and almost always consists of warmed-up leftovers from the last midday meal. 80% of all the journeymen bakers complain about their board. Especially in the morning, exhausted after their 16-hour day, the hands have to wait several hours for their "breakfast" or go to bed hungry. This practice, and it is a general one, characterizes the callousness with which the bosses and their female help treat the workers. They are simply too lazy to have the meal ready when the bakers are finished with their work. Moreover, the married workers complain that under the present work system any type of family life is made absolutely impossible. With a little good will on the part of the bosses, this grievance could also be remedied without undue sacrifice.

10. "Unappetizing and Injurious to Health. What It's Like in a Few Bakeries on the West Side. Results of an Investigation by the Citizens Association" (*Chicagoer Arbeiter-Zeitung,* December 8, 1894).

A health official and Mrs. Paul, the representative of the Citizens Association, began their investigation on West 12th Street. A random choice, they went to the bakery at 149 West 12th Street owned by D. Barnett. Naturally he wanted to know by what right he was being harassed. That was about the extent of his English. He called someone over, and the visitors went into the bakeshop located on the ground floor. The foreman sleeps in the bakeshop, where, with all due respect, it stinks. As the foreman said, the place had not been cleaned for six months. He maintained that the many insects, spiders, flies, etc., were not his business. He was, he said, a baker, not an exterminator. There is old, dried-out dough everywhere, on the walls, on the windows, and in the kneading troughs. The walls are black, and the racks for the rising bread haven't been cleaned for two years. The entire six-member family sleeps on the ground floor, and their bedroom is separated from the bakeshop by only a wooden

A neighborhood bakery on the West Side of Chicago, No. 1118-1120 South Halsted Street. The photograph probably dates from around 1915. (Chicago Historical Society, ICHi-17538.)

Group portrait of the Chicago Bakers Mutual Benefit Society standing before the Cook County Building in 1883. (Chicago Historical Society, ICHi-17522.)

partition. The sewer and water pipes are in such bad condition that the odor streaming out of them gives one a headache. One of the workers has a suit that he wears day and night, at work and on the street.

It was about the same at Lazarus Silbermann's. A while ago the workers at Jakob Weishart's had to wear rubber boots because the bakery flooded when the sewer system backed up. Finally one of the poor devils punched a hole in the floor, and the sewage water drained out. The workers look miserable. Their eyes are cavernous, their chests caved in, they look at their surroundings, resigned and indifferent. They all look sickly. Everything in this bakery is dirty and foul smelling. D. Wagner at 104½ Desplaines Street, D. Jakobsohn at 153 West 12th Street, Wolf Wohlleber at 252 Maxwell Street and H. Bartelstein at 151 West 12th Street were then visited. These, too, were largely characterized by the presence of dirt, uncleanliness and misery.

11. "The Bakeshop Slave" by K. S. (*Chicagoer Bäcker-Zeitung*, June 1, 1889).

> 'Lone in cellars, dark and bleak,
> There where poisoned gases gather,
> Gasps the bakeshop slave, he sighs—
> Night for night and week for week.
> > Naught in life knows how to please,
> > Grief and languor steady merge:
> > From pale face, this grim dumb dirge,
> > To the X of trembling knees.
>
> Cats and rats his habitude,
> And sometimes a roach or two,
> Near his ear, mosquitos' songs,
> Jeering at his servitude.
> > Naught in life knows how to please,
> > Grief and languor steady merge:
> > From pale face, this grim dumb dirge,
> > To the X of trembling knees.
>
> > Ever thinner, bathed in sweat,
> > Coughing, weak, bent o'er the trough;
> > Dreaming, brooding, stupid musing,

Will he ne'er be out of debt!
Naught in life knows how to please,
Grief and languor steady merge:
From pale face, this grim dumb dirge,
To the X of trembling knees.

Want at home—his child and wife!
Quickly hands work on in vain—
And if he his wrath should show,
The slave driver bares his knife. . .
Naught in life knows how to please,
Grief and languor steady merge:
From pale face, this grim dumb dirge,
To the X of trembling knees.

Thus does he this cruel yoke wear,
Cow'ring, docile, he will bend
Like a lamb—and kneels, so crude,
In the filth and foul air.
Naught in life knows how to please,
Grief and languor steady merge:
From pale face, this grim dumb dirge,
To the X of trembling knees.

Mechanization and the Decline of Craft Traditions in the Woodworking Industry

German workers were also strongly represented in woodworking. In 1880 they made up 27.9 percent of Chicago's carpenters and joiners, 37 percent of the carriage- and wagonmakers, and 38.2 percent of the cabinetmakers and upholsterers. The significant craft traditions of these trades lent themselves to the founding of labor organizations: in the 1850s German woodworkers already had their own mutual benefit society; during the 1860s they organized several unions; and in the next decade Chicago's furniture workers played a leading role in the founding of the socialist party and the German-language labor press. In contrast to the bakers, woodworkers experienced the mechanization of production directly, particularly those working in the

manufacture of furniture, boxes, and musical instruments. The car-
penters in the building trades were less directly affected, but even
here the standardization of basic elements like sashes and doors
contributed to a fundamental restructuring of the construction in-
dustry.

The first three documents reproduced here underscore the strong
craft traditions in the woodworking industry up to the end of the
1870s. The personal ownership of tools was part of the very definition
of a wood craftsman, and the first two documents show the high
monetary and social value that tools had for German carpenters. The
price list for woodworking tools in America is taken from a guide
for immigrants published in Germany in 1850. The cost of a complete
set of tools constituted — by a conservative estimate — 20 percent of
a year's salary. The list also graphically illustrates the variety of tools
that a carpenter needed in order to pursue his trade. It is not surprising
that the furniture workers union set up a tool insurance fund for its
members, as the second document from the year 1877 shows, since
the loss of the tools could amount to a personal catastrophe. Even
in the larger furniture factories in the 1880s skilled workers still
owned their own tools. Significantly, the third document illustrates
that by the late 1880s the international furniture workers union was
campaigning against workers owning their own tools as an anach-
ronism in modern industrial plants. Craft traditions and craft forms
of production continued in Chicago up until the end of the century
in small custom shops and in firms making costly products on custom
order, but the significance of this form of production constantly
declined.

12. The Contents of a Carpenter's Tool Box (C. L. Fleischmann, *Er-*
werbszweige, Fabrikwesen und Handel der Vereinigten Staaten von
Nordamerika, mit besonderer Rücksicht auf deutsche Auswanderer
[Stuttgart, 1850]).

Here in this country every carpenter, journeyman or master, has his own
tools which he carries with him in a box, or "tool-chest" as it is called.

Such tool-chests, which can be found in all big city hardware-stores,
usually contain the following tools, the approximate prices of which are
listed here. The tools are made of the best steel and surpass their European
counterparts in practicality of design.

The prices listed here refer to tools of the best quality. Carpenters' wages range from $1.25 to $2.00 per day. Shipcarpenters and shipjoiners are paid more and get from $2.00 to $2.50 per day.

Jeder Carpenter, Geselle oder Meister, hat hier zu Lande seine eigenen Werkzeuge, welche er in einem Kasten, Tool-Chest, wie er genannt wird, mit sich führt.

Ein solcher Tool-Chest enthält gewöhnlich folgende Werkzeuge, die ungefähr die beigesetzten Preise kosten, und in allen großen Städten in den Hardware-stores zu finden sind. Sie sind aus dem besten Stahl angefertiget und übertreffen an Zweckmäßigkeit der Form die Europäischen.

Die hier angegebenen Preise sind für Werkzeuge erster Qualität. Der Lohn für Zimmerleute wechselt von D. 1. 25 C. bis D. 2 per Tag. Schiffszimmerleute und Schiffsbauschreiner werden höher bezahlt, und erhalten D. 2 bis D. 2. 50 per Tag.

Hobel und Hobel-Eisen.	Double Iron Jointer	D. 1. 75
	„ „ Fore Plane	„ 1. 38
	„ „ Jack „	„ 1. 00
	„ „ Smoothing Plane	„ 0. 94
	Single „ Jack „	„ 0. 88
	1 Set of 9 pair Hollows and Rounds, from $^1/_4$ to $1^1/_2$ in.	„ 6. 00
	1 Set of 9 Beads, from $^1/_8$ in. to 1 in., 56c ea.	„ 5. 00
	Rabbet Planes, $^3/_4$ in. 4s 6d, 1 in. 5s, $1^1/_2$ in. 6s, 2 in. 7s	„ 2. 81
	1 pair $1^1/_4$ in. Iron faced Match Planes, with handles	„ 2. 25
	1 pair 1 in. „ „ „ „ „ „	„ 1. 25
	1 pair $^1/_2$ in. „ „ „ „ „ „	„ 1. 13
	Sash Plane, to move	„ 1. 75
	Side Fillister	„ 2. 00
	1 ea. $^3/_8$ in. and $^7/_8$ in. Screw Stop Dado, at 11s	„ 2. 75
	1 ea. $^1/_2$ in. 5s, $^5/_8$ in. 5s 6d, $^3/_4$ in. 6s, Ovals and Square	„ 2. 06
	Screw Arm Plow and set of Bitts . .	„ 5. 50
Sägen.	Cast Steel Rip'g Saw, 28 in. . . .	„ 2. 00
	„ „ Pannel „ 26 in. . . .	„ 1. 75
	„ „ Blue Back Saw, 14 in. . . .	„ 1. 50
	„ „ „ „ „ 10 in. . . .	„ 1. 25
	„ „ Compass „ 16 in. . . .	„ 0. 50
	Keyhole Saw and Handle	„ 0. 63
Stemm-eisen.	Framing Chisel, ea. 2 in. 7s, $1^1/_2$ in. 6s, $1^1/_4$ in. 5s 6d, 1 in. 5s, $^3/_4$ in. 4s 6d . . .	„ 3. 50
	Mortice Chisel, ea. 3-16 3s, $^1/_4$ 3s, 5-16 3s 6d, $^3/_8$ 3s 6d, $^1/_2$ in. 4s	„ 2. 13
	1 doz. Firmer Chisels, ast'd, from $^1/_8$ in. to 2 in, with hickory handles	„ 2. 75
	1 doz. Firmer Gouges, ast'd to $1^1/_2$ in., handled	„ 2. 50

	Best Plated Brace, with 36 Straw bal'd Bitts .	„	7. 00
	Screw Drivers, 3½ in. 2s, 6 in. 3s, 16 in. 5s	„	1. 25
	Plated Squares, 4½ in. 4s, 9 in. 7s, 18 in. 14s	„	3. 12
	2 ft. Steel Square, 2 in. by 1½ in. . .	„	1. 25
	Best Cast Steel Claw Hammer	„	1. 00
Schrau=	Broad Axe	„	2. 50
benzieher,	Shingling Hatchet	„	0. 63
	20 in. Panel Gouge (Beach)	„	0. 75
Winkel=	„ Slitting „ „	„	1. 00
maße,	Screw Slide Mortice „	„	1. 00
	Cutting Gouge „	„	0. 31
Aexte,	Marking „ „ . . .	„	0. 15
Bohrer	4 Gimlets, 31 cents; Saw Sett, 37½ cents .	„	0. 69
u. f. w.[1]	2 Nail Punches, 6d each, 13 cents; Square Mal-		
	let, 50 c.	„	0. 63
	4 Brad Awls, handled, 31c; ½ doz. Saw Fifes,		
	ast'd, 60 c.	„	0. 91
	Augers, 1 each, 2 in., 1½, 1¼, 1, ¾, ½-28 qrs,		
	at 10 c. per qr.	„	2. 80
	6 Auger Handles, 6d each	„	0. 37
	Carpenter's Adze, D. 2. 00; Adze Handle, 25c	„	2. 25

13. The Furniture Workers Union Appeals for Support of Its Tool Insurance Fund (*Vorbote,* April 7, 1877).

The Furniture Workers Union

To all furniture workers and carpenters, to billiard, chair, staircase and piano makers, to carvers and turners of Chicago!

Fellow Workers! The fire this past week in Stotz and Woltz's Furniture Factory has once again proven to us how necessary it is to finally join together in a strong, determined organization. Is it not a disgrace for Chicago's furniture workers when even the capitalist press has to acknowledge that, among workers who have toiled diligently for decades, there are several who have not been able to save enough to buy new tools and now find themselves forced to revert to public charity?

For years the Furniture Workers Union of North America has been trying to improve the situation of it members and co-workers, but to no avail, as the majority of our comrades still keep their distance from the Union.

The Tool Insurance Fund is already more than sufficient for the im-

---

1. The German terms on the left margin read as follows: "Hobel und Hobel-Eisen" = planes and plane irons; "Sägen" = saws; "Stemmeisen" = caulking irons; "Schraubenzieher" = screwdrivers; "Winkelmaße" = squares; "Aexte" = axes; "Bohrer" = drills.

mediate reimbursement of each loss resulting from fire, water, explosion and building collapse.

The Fund is set up as follows:

Every member who uses his own tools can insure them, in accordance to their value, from 25 to 100 dollars. The guarantee fund is maintained through payments of 7 percent of the insured value of the tools (7 dollars for 100 or 7 cents for 1 dollar), but it is set up in such a way that, given the present low wages, payments can be made in 25-cent ⟨Centsweise⟩ installments. If one or more of the members loses his tools due to any of the above-mentioned circumstances, the loss will be replaced within four days in accordance with its insured value. This sum will then be made up by all members in order to replenish the fund.

This s i m p l e b e n e f i t f u n d, free from all capitalist humbug, h a s f u n c t i o n e d s u c c e s s f u l l y among the New York cabinetmakers f o r t h e l a s t f o u r t e e n y e a r s; since December 1 last year, it has been extended to the Furniture Workers Union of North America and will hopefully not fail in uniting Chicago's furniture workers in the near future.

Let no one think that it is unnecessary for him to insure his tools because there is no danger of his shop going up in flames.

Lulled into this false sense of security, the workers at Stotz and Woltz's were sure that there was no danger of fire in their shop and that they therefore didn't need insurance — and it is exactly this which makes their misfortune doubly hard.

14. The New York Union Thinks That It Is Outdated for Furniture Workers to Own Their Own Large Tools (*Möbel-Arbeiter-Journal,* March 10, 1888).

The cabinetmakers' grievance that they have to provide for their own tools has been cast into harsh relief by the massive fire at the Pottier & Stymus Factory. When disputes arise between employers and workers, the capitalist argument always makes much of the risks taken by factory owners in order to thus justify the profits they make. At the same time, the capitalists are affronted by the workers who have the impudence to want to set down guidelines for employers in their o w n shops, even if it is only a question of the most modest demands with respect to wages, working hours or shop regulations.

An incident such as this will cause some people who tended to consider these arguments justifiable to suddenly realize that this isn't quite right.

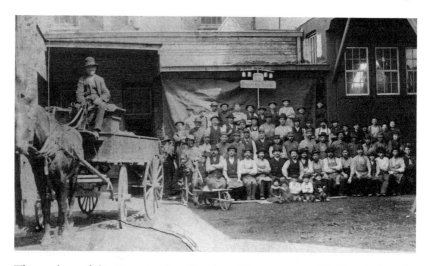

The workers of the Horn Brothers Furniture Company assembled just before the great eight-hour strike of May 1, 1886. Note the children in front and the woman in the upper right. The strike mobilized workers of all trades and levels of skill. (Chicago Historical Society, gift of Carol Hendrickson.)

Employees of the German-owned Tonk Manufacturing Company in 1893. The firm became the country's largest maker of piano stools. The men in the bowler hats are probably the proprietors and managerial staff. Children began to be employed in Chicago's furniture factories in the 1860s. (Chicago Historical Society, gift of Mr. and Mrs. Hampton E. Tonk and Family.)

The cabinetmakers employed in the various shops which were located in the burned-down factory had interests — invested in tools — amounting to at least $7,000. This represents, as the case in question illustrates, a very substantial risk, and it seems as though the time has come for the cabinetmakers to shift the load of this risk, a risk for which they — in comparison to other wage earners — receive absolutely no compensation.

Doing away with worker proprietorship of at least the larger tools, a notion which was already discussed in our organization years ago, has only just recently become more popular among a majority of the members. This is primarily the result of the decreasing stability of working conditions. The frequent change of the workers' place of employment results not only in large expenditures for transportation, but also in inconvenience and loss due to damaged tools. In addition, it infringes upon the worker's mobility while increasing his dependency.

The time has come to change this. The cabinetmaker, whose prospects of becoming independent are nonexistent, should free himself from this ball and chain — in the form of a wagon full of tools — and leave their procurement to the employers. This would also have the advantage of making it somewhat more difficult to open up new shops, which — while only increasing the existing competition — encourage employers to lower wages so as to be more competitive. Indeed, there are shops in the larger cities where the workers have invested more than the entrepreneurs, but where they are generally paid and treated most poorly of all.

Yet this goal, like others which would mean changes advantageous for the workers, can only be attained by organizing, and that is why the consolidation and expansion of our organization must receive primary consideration.

Here, too, it can once again be seen how necessary it is for cabinetmakers — as long as they are forced to provide their own tools — to protect themselves in the event of their sudden loss, and this can be done most advantageously and securely through the Union's Insurance Fund.

Slaughtering and Meat-Packing as Industrial Work

Slaughtering and meat-packing constituted Chicago's premier industry in the late nineteenth century. It employed the most workers, had the greatest value of product, and led the country in technological and marketing innovations. Giants of the trade such as Armour and

*Swift set new standards for the industry and reached out to control
the national and even international markets. The Chicago packers
not only introduced innovations like the refrigerated car that permitted the long-distance shipment of fresh meat, they also transformed
the process of production from the bottom up. To be sure, they could
not mechanize to the same degree as the furniture industry because
the nature of their raw material—living animals of various kinds,
sizes, and qualities—set limits on the introduction of machines.
Nevertheless, the tasks of slaughtering the animals and cutting up
the meat were subdivided into an incredible variety of minute tasks
so that hundreds of men were involved in the preparation of one
animal. In addition, a kind of "disassembly" line for the transport
of the carcasses was developed in order to speed up the whole process.
In this way, and without thorough mechanization of the individual
cutting tasks, the work in this branch of industry was standardized
or "homogenized," permitting the great majority of jobs to be performed by unskilled and semiskilled workers. Certainly there were
skilled workers, like the small elite of "splitters" who cut the animals
in half, but they, too, continually performed only this single task,
even if it did demand unusual skill and dexterity.*

    *Up until the turn of the century, Germans and the Irish were the
dominant groups of foreign-born workers in the Chicago packing
industry. The published census does not include, unfortunately, figures
on the exact character of this industry's work force, but in 1880 the
butchers in the whole city were 36 percent German, 14 percent Irish,
and 32 percent American-born; the latter included a high proportion
of sons of German and Irish immigrants. There is evidence that the
actual work force of the packinghouses included far fewer native-
born Americans and more Irish. As in other industrial branches, the
Germans were more strongly represented among the skilled workers
than the Irish, and therefore as a group the Germans were hit particularly hard by the displacement of skilled work and the homogenization of most tasks. The Germans also predominated in certain
sections of the industry, such as sausagemaking, where it was easier
to mechanize work, to introduce piecework, and to employ women
and children. According to the historian John R. Commons, the
Germans were able to maintain themselves in this part of the industry
until the turn of the century, when they were replaced by women
and children, particularly after their 1300-member union lost a strike
in 1903.*

The following documents all pertain to the experience of Germans in Chicago's sausagemaking plants. The short newspaper article from 1882 reports on the fight of casing cleaners against the installation of machines that practically eliminated their jobs. Two years later a worker in the sausage department of Fowler Brothers describes the strict work regimentation, introduced and enforced there by foremen. He also refers to measures the plant managers took against the union. This document reflects the state of organization among the workers in the packinghouses before the great labor upheavals of 1886, in which the men in the stockyards played a central role. As in 1879 and again in 1904, the disastrous defeat of the workers in 1886 was followed by a period of relative calm during which production was further mechanized and subdivided. In the sausage plants more machines were introduced and women and children were employed, beginning at the latest in the 1890s, as a letter from a sausagemaker written in 1895 makes clear. The proportion of women employed in the meat-packing industry rose in the 1890s from 2.2 to 4.3 percent.

15. "Occupational Extinction: 250 Casing Cleaners Replaced by Machines" (*Chicagoer Arbeiter-Zeitung*, July 8, 1882).

In the wake of its immense progress and the ruthlessness which accompanies it, big business has once again eliminated a whole occupation which until now had supported 250-300 workers alone, thereby multiplying the tremendous number of those fallen prey to occupational extinction.

Until just recently about 250 men were still employed in the local (stockyards), cleaning and preparing casings for sale to sausagemakers. A few days ago the "Turner Casing Co." let go all the workers employed at this job, about seventy-five men, with the comment that the work force had been replaced by a machine which was more efficient than all of them combined—that the men were superfluous insofar as modern technology had driven them from the arena and taken over their jobs.

Even if these exact words were not used when the "superfluous men" were informed of their discharge, this is still the long and the short of it.

Other firms also employing casing cleaners have already ordered similar machines. In a few days, having become superfluous, 250-300 men will thus be pushed aside, and just as many families will be left without means.

That is the way of all things, given the uncompromising tendency of ever-expanding big industry to relinquish to the arbitrariness of individuals what in itself should be a benefit for mankind. Big business has become a curse, a plague, promising want, destruction, and misery. Its merciless advance threatens to destroy the most revered basic principles and the noblest ideals of human society, once again leading humanity back to the original state of things, where the fight for existence in its most brutal and heinous form becomes the primary recurring motif.

The stranded casing cleaners insist in vain that the machines don't do the work as well as the human hand; that the cleaning process is a poor one since bits of refuse remain in the casings. We have no doubt that this is true. But how long will it be before improvements ensure that work done by machines will outshine that done by men? — Then these arguments will also be in vain. It is absolutely useless and senseless to resist the introduction of machines; the whole struggle and striving of working people should confine itself to bringing the means of production — raw products and machines — under their control, to apply them to the general good! - Only when the people have recognized this necessity will it be possible to make the benefits of economic development available to all; but until this happens, the worker is and will remain the slave of his products.

16. "The Fowler Brothers, Million-Dollar Thieves" (*Fackel*, November 23, 1884).

The following letter was forwarded to us for publication from a well-informed and reliable source:

Dear Editors,

Regarding the affair concerning the "Fowler Bros." and the "Journeymen Butchers Benefit Society," the writer of this letter would like to draw particular attention to the fact that several errors — which could perhaps be interpreted to the disadvantage of the workers — slipped into the discussion of said affair in the newspapers. In order to remedy this, I will herein present a true account of the facts.

The Fowler Bros. Packing ⟨Packinghaus⟩ and Sausage Factory, or as said men have rechristened it, "The Anglo-American Packing House Co.," is looked down upon by stockyard workers more than any other business of this type. The workers employed there are not only treated like slaves, they are treated like c o n v i c t s and c r i m i n a l s. At the factory entrance, in a little guardhouse built especially for this purpose, two policemen stand guard and watch over the free workers. No one is allowed to enter after 7:00 a.m. or after the lunch hour. Even the workers who are employed there are not allowed entry.

Sausagemakers in the Stockyards, 1902. Specializing in this branch of the meat-packing industry, Germans still constituted a large proportion of the workers in the sausage factories around 1900. (Chicago Historical Society, ICHi-14251.)

If they are just one minute late, they are not let in. These blue-coated creatures prowl around the work rooms too, spying, making sure that the sausagemakers don't take even the smallest bit of meat or sausage. The Fowler scoundrels, having swindled millions in the well-known lard scandal, probably think that one or another of their workers might get it into his head to follow the example of the million-dollar thieves—on a small scale, of course, taking maybe 5 or 10 cents worth of sausage—something which must be, in the opinion of these big-time swindlers and today's whole "normal" society, strictly punished.

The vileness of the Fowler Brothers became quickly apparent when Baier was injured. He was transported to Mercy Hospital at the order of the Fowlers. His co-workers immediately took up a collection and handed the proceeds over to Baier. Meanwhile, the hospital administration sent the bill to the Fowlers for payment. And what did they do? By way of the foreman, they ordered a collection, and with this money the hospital bill was paid. And it has even been rumored that the second collection amounted to more than the bill and that the company pocketed the difference.

When Baier was released from the hospital, he betook himself to Fowler Bros. and asked Mr. Fowler if he was willing to do something for him.

"Impudent!" Fowler snapped at him, referred him to the superintendent and slammed the door in his face. The superintendent offered him a position as a pig drover, where he might be able to earn $8.00 a week in the winter, but then nothing for most of the summer. That led to the lawsuit. The company immediately had an affidavit drawn up which stated that all the machinery had been in good working order. The workers who had been present at the accident were summoned to the office to attest to the company's affidavit. Most refused to perjure themselves. Only a few not in command of the English language let themselves be talked into this. The workers meanwhile, including the foreman, left the shop to look around for other work. And now for the very best. When the case came to court, the firm tried everything to win the witnesses over to its side. They promised them good, steady jobs with good pay in order to induce them to commit perjury.

Hermann Potell, a contemptuous figure, was chosen to direct most of this action.

In their ignorance, creatures like him don't realize that perjury is punishable by imprisonment. But everything proved in vain. John Baier's coworkers did not let themselves be led astray by promises, but rather testified according to the truth as befits honest and steadfast men. The outcome of the case is well known. With respect to the firing of the members of the Benefit Society, there is only one more thing to note. Though the miserable wretch Potell—who, incidentally, is also a society member— was unable to make himself useful to his Lord and Master by procuring witnesses, he still sought to prove his doglike servility in some other way. And that he did. He told the superintendent where Baier got the money for his court case, namely from the "Journeymen Butchers Benefit Society." Hence the call to the workers—either leave the society or the shop. Most left the shop. Only a few enslaved souls, with no feeling of solidarity, remained. The traitor Potell got his reward from the firm: he has been made "second" ⟨secondhändiger⟩ foreman. He will get his true reward— the one befitting a traitor—at a time or place when he least expects it.

Veritas.

17. "From the Stockyards": Letter from a Worker Who Was Displaced by a Child (*Chicagoer Arbeiter-Zeitung,* May 12, 1895).

A change of far-reaching consequence is stealthily taking place in the stockyards. Wherever possible, men are being let go and women and children are being put on in their stead. That's the way it was going in the department where I used to work as well. Sausage was produced in this department. The work is not difficult in and of itself, but it couldn't possibly be more unhealthy. All day long the floor is flooded with water. The electric lights burn all day to ensure sufficient light in case the room—as often happens—fills with smoke and steam. The smells are unbearable for a newcomer. And in this atmosphere—standing in water, inundated by the smells from the slaughterhouse—children toil ten hours a day filling sausages and cleaning casings. And the wages in the stockyards are miserable anyway. We received 16 cents an hour. Only the work was so irregular that for a long time we didn't earn more than $4.45 a week. Once we got it up to $6, but that was an exception. Yet even these scant earnings are being taken from family men and turned over to women and children who are mentally and physically destroyed by such work. Turned over? No, these unfortunate creatures receive only h a l f t h e p a y that men do for the same amount of work. The stockyard employers' tactic is to employ the workers for a very short time and to have as large a reserve army on hand as possible. Due to this and to the ever-increasing use of woman and child labor, the workers are becoming completely powerless. They cannot organize because their positions are too insecure and their wages too low. The exploiters can thus do what they want with them. Under such unheard-of exploitation, it is no wonder that some workers occasionally pocket a little meat. It is too tempting. To wallow in meat the whole day long and not get paid enough to buy any for oneself and one's family—that's too much. Cheated out of the rewards of his work, the slave takes what he should not. But in this way he only builds up the strength he has sold to the capitalists. And woe to the poor devil who is caught. Recently they caught someone who had about 16 cents worth of meat in his pocket. Naturally he was dragged off to the judge where he was relieved of an entire week's wages, for law and order must be maintained. And he got off easy! Maybe the judge was of the same mind as the poor sinner's lawyer who said in defense: "For a man paid such miserable wages, theft is all that is left."

When will the day finally come when the exploiters' pockets will be checked for the pennies they have stolen from the workers, when they will be held responsible for all the misery and despair that they have caused? When will the day arrive when they will be called to account for all the countless human beings that they have mentally and physically ruined?

Our foreman, O. L., understood how to be his employer's most dedicated servant. He made arbitrary deductions of up to 40 cents to the dollar. He had others begin work a quarter of an hour early. If all the shabby tricks this man has committed were to be disclosed, it would doubtless even excite the attention of his superiors. Or perhaps they already know about him and have made him foreman for exactly that reason? His predecessor was an honorable man who had to go because he opposed the introduction of child labor.

A worker, who was displaced by a child.

Child Labor

The employment of women and children in the sausage departments of the packinghouses was by no means an isolated case. Hiring children was not simply a result of the increasing use of machines, but rather part of the restructuring of work in the last third of the nineteenth century. Children frequently worked to supplement the family income, and, like women, they were employed at simple repetitive tasks irrespective of whether machines were involved or not. They pasted labels on cans in the packinghouses, put crackers in boxes for Nabisco, or sewed buttonholes for clothing contractors in the sweatshops that spread among the lofts and basements of working-class districts.

Since children worked for little pay and could hardly be organized, it is no surprise that the employment of children was heatedly debated as a grave social problem in the 1880s. Along with labor unions, progressive reformers also took up the question, particularly in the 1890s and afterwards, and their investigations provide us today with important sources for the documentation of this problem. Apparently the fight against child labor achieved a certain success, if one can believe the statistics, since the proportion of children in Chicago's industrial work force declined from 6 percent in 1880 to 3 percent in 1910.

Since labor activists and social reformers were trying to expose conditions and appeal to the public's sympathies, their reports on child and female labor often have a melodramatic, if not sentimental, tone. Both German-American labor leaders and social critics made use of this style, a convention of nineteenth-century reform literature, in order to cut through prejudices and class biases by appealing to

*the feelings of their audience. These conventions, which appear harm-
lessly melodramatic today, should not blind one to the realities they
were meant to confront.*

*The first document describes a cigar factory which employed chil-
dren. Although the cigarmaking industry was well organized by unions,
the workers could not prevent the introduction of machines or the
employment of children. The second document illustrates how powerless child laborers were in the face of their employers. These girls
produced candy, probably without the use of machines, performing
simple tasks with their hands such as dipping the candies in chocolate.
The employment of children in menial tasks ranged from cigar and
candy establishments to McCormick's Reaper Works (later the International Harvester Company), i.e., from the least to the most highly
developed industries.*

18. "How Girls Are Being Exploited in the Cigar Factories" (*Chicagoer Arbeiter-Zeitung,* November 2, 1883).

Women have already displaced men in various branches of industry.
This situation can be explained by the fact that, as a consequence of their
depressed social position, the standard of living for women is lower, and
their needs are fewer than those of men. They can therefore sell their
labor more cheaply.

All the preconditions are there for a change of this type to take hold
in the cigar factories, slowly but surely, over the course of the years. By
underbidding present wages, women will push men out of this branch of
industry. Whoever thinks this improbable may do well to consider that
the process has already begun.

Here, as in all other areas of industry, it is the machine which bridges
the differences in people's capabilities and establishes equivalence between
son and father, man and woman.

Girls already make up either all or a major part of the work force in
two sizable cigar factories in Chicago. One of these belongs to the well-
known slave driver Berryman on Kinzie Street, the other to Berry & Van
Fliet on Wabash Ave.

In these two factories, new machines—just recently invented—have
been introduced. They are run by boys and girls and are supposed to
produce as good a cigar as the most practiced cigarmaker. The machine's
productive capacity is also significantly greater than that of the craftsman.

And in this respect it should not be forgotten that the continual improvement of the machine will be accompanied by a steady increase in its efficiency.

Approximately one hundred girls are presently working in the two above-mentioned factories, and they earn, according to their skill, from 50 cents to $1.00 a d a y. Berryman stated that he intends to employ five times that number as soon as possible. For the most part, the girls are made up of Bohemians, Poles and also Germans. Naturally, the needs of these girls are also extremely modest, otherwise they wouldn't be able to get by on earnings of $3 to $5 per week.

The utilization of these machines and the small salaries of the girls make it possible to produce a thousand cigars for $5.00, or up to $8.00 for the best brands. The present wage costs for a thousand handmade cigars runs from $7.50 to $18.00. What a difference! Mechanization additionally results in a saving of tobacco. The retailer's profit — the plundering of labor — amounts to as much as 400 to 500 percent in this branch, and often considerably more.

About 500 young girls, aged twelve to fifteen, are employed in the tobacco factories. They "strip" ⟨"strippen"⟩ the tobacco and make from $2.50 to $6.00 a week. The majority of the poor things, children of the proletariat, are ruined by the work. Crowded together in poorly ventilated rooms, they inhale the harmful tobacco dust, causing consumption and other physical ailments.

One only has to go and observe the broken figures in these factories; they creep around, pale and feeble, drained of all life. They have to sacrifice their bodies, their blood, their health, and their lives so that a few bloodsuckers can luxuriate in excess and lust.

19. "In Bonde & Co.'s Candy Factory ⟨Candyfabrik⟩" (*Chicagoer Arbeiter-Zeitung,* December 23, 1884).

In Bonde & Co.'s Candy Factory ⟨Candyfabrik⟩ at Market and Washington, they are not only exploiting children to the full state of the art, but it also appears that the "good employer" is cheating the little ones to boot. About forty to fifty twelve- to fifteen-year-old girls work in the shop. With tears in her eyes, one of them told us the following, and it was corroborated by several of her little co-workers: "When we started several weeks ago, Mr. Bonde promised us $2.50 a week. But shortly afterwards he came and said that we had to do piecework. Then he set the prices so that even if we worked as hard as we could, we could barely earn $1.50. We complained and got a raise. We were then in a position to earn $2.00-$2.75 a week. But we didn't receive the money we had earned. Every week 40 cents to $1.00 was deducted so that we only got $1.50-$1.75 after all. We complained and were told that the situation would be looked into. The following week we got our full pay, but not the money that had been held back earlier. The next Monday we all went to Mr. Bonde and asked him to tell us if and when he intended to pay us that money, otherwise we were going to walk out. 'You cheeky little kid! You've stirred up all my girls. Get out of this shop on the double! and the rest of you get back to your work.' But my friends didn't go back to work; they came with me instead."

This a child's simple story. We have nothing to add.

Female Labor

Much of what has been said about child labor also applies to women's work. Traditionally women had performed unskilled labor like washing and ironing that had nothing to do with mechanization, but industrialization gave them new tasks. In contrast to children, the proportion of women in Chicago's manufacturing work force rose steadily, if slowly, from 15.3 percent in 1880 to 19.5 percent in 1910. German working women were typically in their teens and twenties, earning money to supplement their families' incomes before they married. In 1880, for example, dressmaking was the only female occupation among the top ten occupations for Germans in Chicago, and the median age of German dressmakers was 18.4 years. Both women and children worked in Chicago's apparel industry, which is the subject of two of the documents reproduced here.

Document 20 is an early form of investigative reporting that has a surprisingly contemporary ring. A young woman describes conditions in a pants factory that was located in unheated and poorly lighted rooms and in which workers were fined for mistakes. Another woman delineates similar circumstances in a letter to the editor of the Chicagoer Arbeiter-Zeitung; *she worked in a corset factory employing three hundred women. Her letter contains a detailed list of punishments and fines which were imposed if the strict rules of the firm were not observed. There follows a biting, satirical poem of a*

type common in the press of the German-American labor movement.
The author, Robert Seidel, was a Swiss labor leader and socialist.
(See the biographical sketches at the end of this volume.) He contrasts
the miserly pay of a shirtmaker with the actual social value of her
work. Taken from the reports of the Industrial Commission published
at the turn of the century, the last document provides examples of
two types of clothing firms, both of which were partly German-
owned and employed German men and women. One was a family-
run shop which employed only Germans; the other was larger, more
mechanized, and hired an ethnically mixed work force. The smaller
firm could not produce so efficiently as the larger and more modern
one.

Traditionally female occupations, such as those in the apparel
industry illustrated here, also underwent a leveling process in the
course of industrialization. More and more women found themselves
pushed into the role of tending machines that contributed to the
destruction of skilled trades in which men were employed.

20. "The Fate of Women Workers" (*Chicagoer Arbeiter-Zeitung*, January 16, 1882).

It was on January 13 in the year of our Lord 1882. She was wearing but a modest shawl, a short cotton dress, a straw hat, and slippers. In her thin arms she clasped a bundle that was twice the size of her upper body. She crossed a bridge leading to the western part of the city and, panting, mounted the creaking steps of a tenement house on Adams Street. Pressing her load against the wall and turning the key with her free right hand, she managed to open the door to a small, dark chamber. Inside were a cast iron stove, two chairs, and a sewing machine. Pale, yellow light filtered in through a single window. The girl threw the bundle on the table, which sagged under the weight, and blew into her hands. — A man entered and said that someone had spoken highly about the particularly accomplished shirtmaker who occupied the room.

"How much do you charge for a dozen?"

"Two dollars and 50 cents."

"You must have misunderstood. I wanted to know how much a dozen cost."

"Just as I said! And by the way, I'm asking a dollar more than the factories pay. Look, a friend of mine makes flannel shirts for a company downtown and only gets paid $1.75 a dozen, and even a good seamstress needs two full days for this work. Ha, if that were only all! But sometimes we even work for nothing. Last Thursday the foreman told Lizzie—that's my friend's name—that a bundle of her shirts was no good: the stitching in front was too close to the seam and it looked bad. He said she'd have to pull out the thread and stitch it over again, otherwise he couldn't pay her. And so she did it and had to be content with $3.00 for the week."

"Wouldn't you rather work in a factory?"

"No, never! I want to earn as much as I can, but for myself, and only for myself. In the factories they constantly make deductions on the flimsiest pretexts. For example, there's a company on Wabash Avenue. They employ '80 hands for overalls,' trousers made from stiff material. The machines are steam powered and most of them are old and on their last legs. Often, when you have to double-stitch, the needle breaks off, and at the same time, in eight out of ten cases, the 'throat plate' breaks too. One of these costs 50 cents, and the girls have to pay for it themselves whether it was their fault or not."

"That's not fair!"

"No, but that's just money. The worst is that the factories usually don't have light, and slowly but surely the women ruin their eyesight. It's as bad in the evening as it is during the day. The gasometer is turned down to half pressure, and the flame is barely as big as a match."

"Is it true that the girls are punished if they somehow damage the material?"

"Yes, in most places. For example, if they get a drop of oil on the front of the shirt, 10 cents are deducted from their wages."

"How much do the poor things make?"

"An *overall* seamstress makes $4 to $5 if she's good."

"And how much does it cost her to live?"

"Most live with their parents. But a lot of them have to 'board' ⟨'boarden'⟩, and the cheapest is $3 a week—if, that is, you share a room with another girl."

"Do those who work at home, like you, make out any better?"

"Yes and no! In any case, they're their own bosses. They have to come up with their own machine, but the factory provides the thread. It's a hard way to make a living. And then there's dragging the stuff back and forth! If the foreman refuses to accept the work, we have to take the bundle back without a murmur and then we've lost 3 hours for nothing. The worst is when you don't have a cent in the house and have to work just to get money for supper."

"How old are the factory girls on the average?"

"They range from 11 to 25. The youngest sew on buttons; the others work at the machines."

"Are they allowed to talk to each other?"

"If they do 'piecework,' they can prattle as much as they want; but if the boss pays them a weekly wage, they're not allowed to open their mouths. In some factories there's a rule that if a girl comes ten minutes late, she has to stay outside for an hour, and naturally her wages are cut for it.—But what are you doing?" she asked, cutting off the flow of conversation and turning directly to the visitor. "You're writing down what I'm telling you? O My! How stupid of me! not even to have realized I was talking to a reporter! If you tell the company on Wabash Avenue what I said—I won't be able to get any work in the whole city."

"But Miss," consoled the man with the pen, "you don't take me for a barbarian, do you? Wabash Avenue is long, and as for the names of the cursed guys who mistreat you girls so, why, I haven't even written them down. . . ."

21. "Voice from the People": Letter from a Seamstress (*Chicagoer Arbeiter-Zeitung*, May 8, 1882).

Honored Editors,

You have so often discussed the situation of us poor sewing girls that I wanted to help you along with more information. About 300 comrades of mine are employed in the corset factory at 250-252 Wabash Avenue, and we truly have to work for starvation wages. But this isn't the worst of it. Take a look at the following list of fines set for the girls, and tell me whether this robbery—an allegedly nonviolent and legal process— isn't just as bad as those things described by your police reporter:

Breaking a needle (at ¼ c ea.) or a stay (at ½ c ea.) 5c
Leaving the machine 5c
For each drop of oil on the work 5c
For cleaning the work of oil spots 20c
Slightly late in the morning 5c
Slightly late at midday (for ex., 31 minutes instead of 30) 5c
Breaking a "bobbin" 5c
For not coming to work, in addition to the loss of wages 20c

The highest price paid in the factory for a dozen corsets is 30 to 50c. Now just imagine what is left over for the poor girls after all the fines are deducted, especially with our "foremen," Jim Stone and Grace Murphy, running around arbitrarily imposing fines. Mr. Gustav Florsheim and D. H. Bal, members of the firm, endorse everything they say.

Besides which the water is almost undrinkable and sewer gases fill the house.

Respectfully,

A S e w i n g G i r l

E d i t o r ' s n o t e: Wouldn't one of the factory inspectors like to oblige and make a thorough investigation of this den of exploitation at 250-252 Wabash Avenue?

22. "One Hundred Shirts Your Weekly Quota," by Robert Seidel (*Fackel,* April 22, 1900).

"One hundred shirts your weekly quota!" -
Can it be? Have I gone blind?
No! It's here in all the papers:
"Let each seamstress we remind."

"One hundred shirts your weekly quota.
Plain and pleated, tapered, wide." -
Isn't this the greatest wonder,
Of today's amazing stride?

And these two quick female hands,
Aren't they like a magic wand?
Cov'ring scores of naked torsos
All through life (and then beyond!)

See this saintly magic grant
The enchantress bliss and pride,
As she struts along those paths,
Where the blessed all abide.

Stunning flowers she receives,
When the harvest fest takes place,
And all of the city's best
Seek her out and court her grace.

And when these hands skillful tire,
The rewards of years of work -
Twilight near - thus offer her,
Comforts where no shadows lurk.

Fools! from planets far away,
Is that how our world you see?
Do you think that justice reigns?
Do you deem all people free?

Do you think that those who sew
Clothes for all, themselves have bread?
Do you think that "Christian" means,
Human rights 'mongst all are spread?

One hundred shirts as weekly quota
Does not bring respect or food -
Only hunger, early death,
Endless suff'ring, wretched, rude.

'Midst the seamstress' darkened chamber,
Misery, complacent, creeps -
Drives her, screaming, "Hundred Shirts!"
Through the rich, cold city streets.

23. Description of Two Clothing Firms (this document represents the
    original English version; U.S. Industrial Commission, *Reports of the
    Industrial Commission on Immigration* [Washington, D.C., 1901] re-
    printed in the American Immigration Collection, Series II [New York,
    1970], pp. 360-63).

ESTABLISHMENT No. 8.

[Successor to family shop: Chicago; coat shop; gas power; contractor, German; employees German; 16 employees in one system; 75 coats per week; 60 hours per week.]

Contract price $1.75
Labor cost 1.47
Average wages per hour.. .115

	Hour.	Week.	Two-thirds year.	Average per week per year.
	Cents.			
Operator's wages..................................	9.7	$5.82	$201.76	$3.88
Baster's wages	14	8.40	291.20	5.60
Presser's wages	16.6	9.96	345.28	6.64

	Cents.
Cost of operating per coat	39.4
Cost of basting per coat	56
Cost of pressing per coat	27.8

	h.	m.
Time per coat	12	48
Operator's time per coat	4	41
Baster's time per coat	4	00
Presser's time per coat	1	36

Individual occupations, establishment No. 8.

Number.	Occupation.	Nationality.	Sex.	Week or piece.	Earnings.	Total earnings for the occupation.
1	Sewing sleeves	German	Female	Week	$9.00	$9.00
1	Stitching coats	do	do	do	8.00	8.00
1	Pocket maker	do	do	do	6.50	6.50
1	Inside pocket and lining	do	do	do	5.50	5.50
1	Stitching canvas, etc.	do	do	do	3.50	3.50
1	do	do	do	do	2.50	2.50
6						35.00
1	Head baster	do	Male	do	11.00	11.00
1	Second baster	Pole	do	do	10.00	10.00
1	Edge baster	German	Female	do	6.50	6.50
2	Sleeve baster, etc.	do	do	do	7.50	15.00
1	Seam presser	do	Male	do	9.00	9.00
1	Presser	do	do	do	11.00	11.00
7						62.50
1	Trimming, etc., by contractor	do	do	Piece	.06	4.50
1	Buttons and tacking	do	Female	Week	6.00	6.00
1	Felling	do	do	do	2.50	2.50
2						8.50
16						110.50

ESTABLISHMENT No. 9.

[Custom work on factory system: Chicago; coat shop; gas power; contractor, Jew; employees, Jews, German, and Polish women; 35 employees in one system; 300 coats per week; 60 hours per week.]

Contract price	$1.35
Labor cost	1.065
Average wages per hour	.152

	Hour.	Week.	Two-thirds year.	Average per week per year.
	Cents.			
Operator's wages	15.2	$9.12	$316.16	$6.08
Baster's wages	17.4	10.44	361.92	6.96
Presser's wages	22.5	13.50	468.00	9.00

	Cents.
Cost of operating per coat	30.4
Cost of basting per coat	34.8
Cost of pressing per coat	18

	h.	m.
Time per coat	7	0
Operator's time per coat	2	0
Baster's time per coat	2	0
Presser's time per coat		48

Individual occupations, establishment No. 9.

Number.	Occupation.	Nationality.	Sex.	Week or piece.	Earnings.	Total earnings for the occupation.
1	Sewing in sleeves..................	Jew	Male......	Week...	$16.00	$16.00
1	Making pockets	....do ...	....do	....do ...	13.00	13.00
2	...do ...	....do	....do	....do ...	12.00	12.00
1	Making linings	....do	....do	....do ...	8.00	8.00
1	....do ...	German....	Female ..	....do ...	9.00	9.00
1	....do ...	....do	....do	....do ...	8.50	8.50
1	Making sleeves....	Polish	....do	....do ...	5.00	5.00
1	Stitching under collar	....do	....do	....do ...	4.50	4.50
1	Stitching coat	German	....do	....do ...	11.00	11.00
1	General.................	....do	Male......	....do ...	14.00	14.00
10						101.00
1	Head baster	Jew	....do	....do ...	18.00	18.00
1	....do ...	....do	....do	....do ...	15.00	15.00
1	....do ...	... do	....do	....do ...	14.00	14.00
1	Second baster.................	German	....do	....do ...	9.00	9.00
1	....do ...	Polish	....do	....do ...	9.00	9.00
1	....do ...	....do	....do	....do ...	8.50	8.50
1	Edge baster	Jew	Female ...	....do ...	7.00	7.00
3	....do ...	Polish	....do	....do ...	8.00	24.00
1	Padding lapels	German	....do	....do ...	8.00	8.00
1	....do ...	....do	....do	....do ...	2.00	2.00
1	Pulling bastings, etc	....do	....do	....do ...	8.00	8.00
2	....do ...	....do	....do	....do ...	2.00	4.00
1	Under presser.................	....do	Male......	....do ...	8.00	8.00
1	....do ...	Hollander ..	....do	....do ...	11.00	11.00
17						135.50
4	Presser.................	Jew	....do	Piece ...	.18	54.00
1	Trimming and busheling	....do	....do	Week...	16.00	16.00
5						70.00
1	Felling armholes	....do	Female ...	....do ...	6.00	6.00
1	....do ...	German	....do	....do ...	8.00	8.00
1	....do ...	....do	....do	....do ...	4.00	4.00
3						13.00
35						319.50

Establishment No. 9 is run on the factory system, producing "special-order" coats at $1.35 per coat. This shop, compared with No. 8, clearly expresses the difference between the shop and factory. The time required on a $1.35 coat is 7 hours,

The Tempo and Subdivision of Work

The trend toward reducing work to a common unskilled and semiskilled level also led to an ethnically mixed work force in the factories. Work was directed more closely by foremen and the workers driven to greater productivity.

In the early 1880s this regimentation of work was still something of an innovation, as indicated by the indignation evident in the document on the American Cutlery Company. Operating with steam power, the firm was one of the larger plants in this branch of metal work, employing over ninety men, eight women, and twenty-seven children in 1880. Twenty years later, when the author of the last document, Alfred Kolb, worked in Chicago, the transformation of the process of production in the manufacture of bicycles, another branch of the metal industry, had proceeded much further. Located near the large concentration of Germans on the North Side, the plant described by Kolb represented the most advanced state of mechanization, the division of labor, and the homogenization of work. Having grown explosively in the preceding years, this industry lacked a tradition as a craft, and there was little resistance to the new methods of production. In contrast, Kolb also worked in a brewery, which represented an industry with a long craft tradition and a predominantly German work force. It is all the more striking that practically any other industry could have employed Kolb for the backbreaking physical labor he describes. Despite the fact that the plant where Kolb worked was modest in size, employing seventy workers, the unskilled workers there worked under constant pressure from a foreman.

24. "A Word of Warning to the German Unions" (*Chicagoer Arbeiter-Zeitung*, March 24, 1881).

The faithful translation of a list of factory regulations printed below will illustrate how absolutely necessary close union organization has become in Chicago. . . .

Only the lethargy of the workers could have emboldened the exploiters to go so far as to forbid the factory workers to speak, smoke, drink, swear and various other things which are absolutely none of their business; the exploiter can only demand the stipulated amount of work. What, then, is the difference between the freedom of the "free" worker in the factory and the convict in prison?

There is, in fact, one difference; it lies in the fact that the convict is not responsible for the tools he uses, while the so-called "free" worker is burdened with the responsibility for his tools and thus for their damage or loss. But the most obviously base aspect is the shameless one-sidedness of the working conditions.

The workers have to put down a deposit which they lose if they quit work without advance notice. The exploiters, on the other hand, not only don't put down a deposit, but do not in the least feel obliged to give their workers notice before letting them go.

The worker must give eight days' advance notice, otherwise he loses a week's wages. The exploiters can throw the workers out on the street any time they want for no reason at all!

This is a double standard. Should the unions tolerate such base contracts? Aren't they treated exactly like the convicts? We recommend that all workers study these representative factory regulations very carefully. The result of this study can only be: organize all workers to resist the baseness of the exploiters.

R e g u l a t i o n s   f o r   A l l   W o r k e r s at the *American Cutlery Company*
1. All workers must be ready to start work when the whistle blows in the morning and after lunch.
2. No one may stop work before the whistle blows.
3. Any worker found bringing intoxicating beverages into the factory will be dismissed immediately.
4. Smoking, swearing, and disorderly behavior are absolutely forbidden.
5. Visitors will not be admitted without a pass from the office.
6. Speaking or walking around (!) in the factory is forbidden, unless required by the job or, in specific cases, absolutely necessary.
7. If a worker wants to leave the job for a while, he should apply to his foreman in the form of a letter and turn the letter in to the office.
8. Each worker must see to the maintenance of the tools he uses and keep them in their proper place.
9. Our workers will be paid each Monday for the previous week.
10. If tools are damaged through negligence (through whose negligence and what won't they call negligence? the Editors), their value will be deducted from the wages of the worker who broke them or let them be broken.
11. If a worker wants to stop working for the Company, he must give a week's notice or lose the security deposit he was required to make.
12. Each worker must deposit a week's wages with the Company as security in case he violates Paragraph 8, 10 or 11.

Now all that is lacking is the whip to complete the uttermost and worst slavery. Workers take heed!

25. **Working Conditions in a Bicycle Factory and in a Brewery (Alfred Kolb,** *Als Arbeiter in Amerika. Unter deutsch-amerikanischen Großstadt-Proletariern* **[5th revised ed.; Berlin 1909], pp. 41-69, 74-79, 83-85).**

That morning it was like a railway station there [in the German Society]. The door was barely ever still. People of every age and appearance pushed their way in and asked about work. As everyone else had received a negative answer, I took out my letter of recommendation without much hope. But it worked. . . .

The assembly room was a huge hall twenty-seven windows long, its entire length traversed by wide work benches full of vises, tools, and miscellaneous equipment. The finished bicycle parts were carried here in a continuous stream on a rattling conveyor belt and then fitted together to make whole bicycles. The principle of the division of labor was thereby applied extensively, and the human hand was replaced by a machine wherever possible. Even the turning of screws was done mechanically by devices similar to that thin, whirring tube whose painful acquaintance we make when a tooth is filled.

The foreman led me to one of the long benches and instructed me in the work. It required neither skill nor much exertion, consisting of a few constantly repeated hand movements on the front wheels of the bicycles. The man to my left prepared the axles. I stuck them through the hub, and after I had checked the ball bearings, pulled a greased felt washer over it. The neighbor to my right put on nuts. The next ground down the ends of the spokes, slipped the rubber tires over, inflated them until they were firm, and so forth, until the wheel, all ready to go, arrived at the end of the table, where it was then inserted into the front fork of the frame.

I do not want to dwell here any longer on the details of our work. Suffice it to say that at the time it bored me beyond all measure. Through it, I gained an appreciation for certain accusations against the modern division of labor. Such division is of course indispensable. Today's entire technology would be unthinkable without it. But that is all the more reason why we may not close our eyes to the joyless, eternal monotony of an occupation which parches the senses and mind, which requires a few uniform muscular movements and so little thought that — to a certain degree — the process takes place beneath the threshold of consciousness. It would be difficult in such work to still find that measure of moral dignity that no occupation can forgo without, in the long run, ethically endangering those who practice it. Such work takes into consideration neither the individuality nor the talent of the person, but reduces him to a part of a machine, "a mere stopgap necessitated by human ingenuity." For me a further reason to hope for the curtailment of exactly this kind of industrial work.

The workday in the bicycle factories lasted the ten hours typical of the city; in the beginning there were also two to three hours overtime in the evening, but they were short-lived. The entire operation of the plants was cut up into seasonal work. At the beginning of winter, one worked day and night; that had already stopped when I began there. As summer approached, more than three-quarters of all the workers were gradually let go or else stayed away of their own accord because they found a more appealing job somewhere else. And those of us who remained still only got five days a week until finally that stopped, too, and the business shut down for weeks on end. But as far as I know, the daily wages were not reduced.

I repeatedly heard it expressed, and mainly from the mouths of newly arrived immigrants, that work was not so strenuous back home in Germany as here in America. There may be some truth to that; in America, in any case, one never stops hearing the warning, "Get going! Hurry up!" But no rules without exceptions. At first I had worked with all my might so as not to fall behind my comrades. Until one of them asked scornfully, "Hey, are you crazy? Working just like you're on piecework? Don't be a fool!" And when I answered that I didn't want to promote my dismissal, he laughed at me. "That's no reason to run yourself into the ground, greenhorn ⟨Grünhorn⟩. Look at me: am I knocking myself out? The main thing is to get in good with the foreman. His father runs a saloon. Whoever goes there and spends a bit doesn't have to worry about being thrown out."

This last tip was not completely unfounded. Despite the unrelenting pressure, there were several loafers among us who dawdled away the time without being punished for it, trusting in such behind the scene influences. The worst of the lot was a Bavarian, a true genius at doing nothing, and who on top of it all worked himself into a rage over the heavy labor. He worked near me, and I can still see him today, short and fat, alternately taking snuff and grumbling: "Holy Jesus, what a treadmill. Don't it never end? Holy Mother of Altötting!"[2]

The work began at seven in the morning and lasted until 5:30 in the evening. The half-hour lunch break was at noon. Sitting on the work benches, the married workers then ate the snack they had brought from home. We single workers hurried to the nearby cheap kitchens or saloons. At noon, as well as during overtime at night, we were allowed to get beer, for which most kept special tin containers. A half liter cost five cents. It was fetched by the errand boys working in the hall, who on payday got a few extra cents for it. Aside from these times, the consumption of

---

2. In the German text this quotation is in Bavarian dialect. Altötting is a Bavarian religious shrine.

alcohol was not permitted, and the rule was strictly observed. Whoever got thirsty during work drank from the bad tap water. . . .

Among my new fellow workers, I also made the acquaintance of a few teetotalers. None of them spoke German. That may have been purely coincidental, but the fact is that the great majority of our fellow countrymen over there want to hear nothing of temperance. That is perhaps the only question about which they agree, and nothing was more loathsome to them about McKinley's colonial policies than the tax on spirits. It is further true that comparatively more alcohol is drunk in Germany than in the United States. . . . Yet for all that, it seems to me as though I saw more real drunks over there; more people who go the limit, and who, once they have started, don't stop drinking until they are under the table. . . .

When I began there, the bicycle factory employed about 2,500 workers, lots of them German. The number of trained machinists was remarkably small; after all, everything was done by machine. Among the masses of unskilled were people of the most varied backgrounds who, whether permanently or merely temporarily, had fallen into the midsts of the industrial proletariat. In motley rows stood merchant and farmhand, teacher and craftsman, musician and who knows what else, all together at the vise. We had educated people in the assembly hall, too. A theologian, a philologist, and three lawyers: all Germans. As I found out later, the fallen schoolteacher indulged in Socratic love, which was doubtless also the reason for his having had to leave his homeland. The theologian had found the beer in Erlangen too good to resist until finally his money ran out, and instead of stepping up to the pulpit, he stepped onto an immigrant ship. That was probably about twenty years ago—o n e long chain of disappointment, recklessness and misery. As a factory worker he merely scraped through the winter, while in the summer he ran around soliciting advertisements during the day, and at night, for free beer, sat at the ticket window of a honky-tonk. . . .

Standing before me, the man betrayed no sign, either inwardly or outwardly, of better days. It was apparent that he had long since buried whatever hope and courage may once have swelled in his breast. His theology had been extinguished along with his religious conviction in order to make room for that superficial materialism which hypnotizes the masses of the German-American proletariat. Idealism and spiritualism cast aside, all intellectual content in life evaporates, leaving but hopeless resignation: eat, drink, and be merry, dear soul, for tomorrow you'll be dead.

. . . .

Although Chicago is an industrial city with some 200,000 workers, it does not have industrial districts in the true sense of the term. Its innumerable shops are spread throughout its various quarters; tall smoking chimneys can even be found in the inner city. The T. brewery is located on the South Side, a German mile from the city center. . . .

Right next to the entrance gate in a low wing was the bottling department. Such an operation is not quite so simple as one might think. The beer is pushed out of the vats by compressed air into the filling machines which do the bottling by themselves. Filled in this manner and thereupon corked, the bottles are sterilized in a steam bath, and the better brands are then decorated with labels, wires, and tinfoil caps. The washing, brushing, rinsing, bottling, corking, wiring, and labeling was done by machines which were operated by young or female workers.

Besides this, there were many considerably more strenuous tasks which were done by men. A greenhorn, I found them doubly difficult. Even today I remember with misgiving handling wet barrels and heavy beer cases. Among these cases were many old ones studded with glass splinters, splints, and nails. Within eight days my hands were covered with bloody cuts and cracks. My back had become stiff, my gait and carriage clumsy and heavy. I like to think that as a rule I'm not unusually awkward; at least not to such a degree as one might be tempted to take for granted of a bureaucrat. Once, however, shortly before quitting time, a heavy case full of empty bottles which I was to bring into the basement slipped out of my tired arms. Of course, the foreman really told me off, and a small office penpusher with a four-inch stand-up collar who happened to be passing by turned up his nose and said: "That guy's probably soused!"

Now and then, when there wasn't anything to be toted, the men were temporarily put to easier work too—nailing cases, stacking bottles, washing the floor, cleaning up, etc. We took weekly turns at other such chores—for example, cleaning the toilets. These were water closets with enamel bowls and lifting seats, neat and clean—and by the way characteristic of

---

On facing page

Metal workers in the McCormick Reaper Works on Blue Island and Western Avenues circa 1900. McCormick's was one of the largest metal-working plants in Chicago. (State Historical Society of Wisconsin, International Harvester Collection, 1276.)

Closing time at the McCormick Reaper Works circa 1900. (State Historical Society of Wisconsin, International Harvester Collection, 808.)

the standard of living. When I did the cleaning, they were even outstand-
ingly clean.

My fellow workers, some seventy in number, were without exception
unskilled, younger people, mainly of German origin. And German was also
the language spoken among us. We addressed each other—even the foreman—by first names.[3] An occasional "you silly ass!" was taken as inof-
fensively as it was meant. In the beginning I sometimes had difficulty
suppressing a smile when some fresh youngster shouted at me: "Alfred,
come here and pick up the case!" But not for long; hard work makes one
dull. And our work was certainly hard and heavy enough. This I can state
from experience, because later on I had a much easier time elsewhere.
Probably a calmer pace prevailed at other times in the brewery. But just
at that time—so the rumor went—there was a huge order in from Havana,
and therefore whatever strength and energy we had was squeezed out of
us. Small wonder that we were completely winded. If for once someone
actually paused to catch his breath, the foreman appeared immediately to
drive him on. I noticed a look of dull sullenness stamped on the men's
faces about the roots of the nose and the corners of the mouth. My own
face probably didn't look any different.

It need hardly be mentioned that under such conditions any exchange
of ideas during work was out of the question. During the one-hour lunch
break, too, everybody silently squatted or lay in some corner. At best,
something like a conversation started after quitting time, when we had a
drink together before going home. But nothing much came of it. Most
pressed for home, and a recurring saying was: "Glad the grind is over for
today!" . . . .

To protect our clothes during work we used an outfit made of strong
blue linen which, as the name *overall* indicates, is worn like a cover over
the clothes. Since my return home I have looked around for such overalls
in German factories. Of course they are also known here, but not nearly
so commonly used. This may also be a reason why the workers in the
streets of Chicago appeared to be cleaner than in Germany. With exceptions, naturally. My comrades in the brewery, particularly, were usually
unclean and in rags. . . .

The regular workday in the brewery lasted from 6 to 12 and from 1
to 5, i.e. ten hours. There was no coffee or late afternoon break. But beer
was handed out at 9 and at 3 o'clock. Admittedly, everyone drank at other
times also, whenever we got thirsty. As long as you didn't lay your hands

3. The original text refers to the use of both first names and the familiar form of the
pronoun *you* in German.

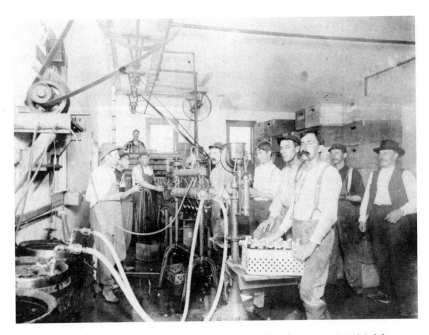

The bottling room at the Siebel Institute of Technology, 1422-1424 Montana Street. Founded in 1872 to train brewers and bakers, the Institute broadened its program after 1893. (Chicago Historical Society, ICHi-17537.)

on stout or other good brands, the foreman looked in the other direction. By the way, this license was not at all abused. It is true that cheese was preferred at breakfast, "because it makes you so pleasantly thirsty." But I hardly ever saw anyone tipsy; except maybe during overtime, when the men restored their vanishing strength with alcohol. Overtime night work was almost routine; usually until 9, sometimes 10 in the evening. In that case a half-hour break was taken at 6 o'clock, which would have been very nice if the lunch break had not been shortened accordingly. Thus the total length of work was from 14 to 15 hours. In addition, we worked on Sunday mornings from 6 to 12 o'clock.

Most of the workers usually hurried home for lunch. Those who lived farther away brought along a cold snack or ate in a saloon. The snack consisted of bread, eggs, ham, sausage, and roast. Tartar with the long mild American onions seemed very popular. There was always meat, and always plenty of it. Also, I never saw the bread, fine wheat bread, without butter or jam. Along with the others who lived there, I ate at my landlord's. I must concede that his old battle-ax of a wife was a very good cook. Each of the three daily meals cost 15 cents, but was much better than in the 15-cent restaurants ⟨Fünfzehncentrestaurants⟩ of the inner city. There was no menu from which to select; you just helped yourself to everything — and to as much of it as you wished — that was put on the table. Even the empty meat dishes were promptly refilled. In the morning at 5:30 we received coffee, bread and butter, cheese, fried eggs, fried potatoes, and a warm meat dish, usually pork ribs. For lunch — soup, vegetables, potatoes, and always three different meat dishes; not infrequently goose giblets and delicious hasenpfeffer. In the evening at 6 o'clock the same was offered as at lunchtime. Though the place was a saloon, we almost always had coffee with meals. Only the boarders had breakfast there. But at noon and in the evening numerous diners showed up — maltsters, brewers, black-smiths, firemen, beer draymen. There was such a great rush that people ate in shifts. While some were eating, others were impatiently waiting behind their chairs.

Thus there was little time for talk. Also, most men were too dull and rough for any half-reasonable conversation. Only crude teasing and coarse answers came of it, and one evening these even came to blows. Two deserters were involved — onetime corporals from the province of Baden — two incredibly rude customers. One, suspecting me a former comrade, once asked me why I had "cut out." Addressing people with "you scoun-drel," "you heel," emphasized by dirty adjectives, was nothing unusual. Equally common were expressions like dumb Swabian, blind Hessian, horned bull of Baden, Bavarian swine, Prussian beggar — a microcosmic reproduction of the regional antagonisms which the German doesn't give up even on the other side of the ocean....

If incidents at work were mentioned — at best only every now and then — they were skimmed over rather than discussed.... In such confined circles conversation crept along, at lunch and at night in the boarding-houses, not even faintly touched by matters of political, religious, or social interest — with ever-dwindling exceptions. One day the machine attendant was caught by the driving belt of the big steam engine and torn to pieces — no wonder, by the way, given the lack of any safety equipment. Returning on the night of the funeral, his acquaintances talked about the deceased. "Too bad for him," someone said, "he was a good guy! Now he's had it!" Whereupon someone else said: "Eat and drink, guys; because soon we'll all have had it, and that's that." The others were silent; they seemed to agree....

If I mention the idle chatter I had to listen to in the boardinghouse where a few older people who spent ⟨spenden⟩ a good share of their weekly wages at the bar bored us with sanctimonious talk about an impending hunger riot . . . then I believe that I have pretty well recounted the social and political subjects which came up. But I believe it would be a mistake to infer quietism and contentment from the lack of more general topics for conversation going beyond daily events. These people were simply too dumb and worn out; they also had too little sense of community and solidarity to explain to themselves and others the vague sentiments that brooded in them. There was some indication—more felt than observed—that beneath the layer of dull apathy there glowed and smoldered the spark of gnawing, though yet confused, discontent. . . .

We received the standard wages for Chicago's unskilled manual labor—for boys 50 cents, for women 75, for young men 1 dollar, for adults 1¼ dollars per day. Overtime was paid separately, but not higher. A carpenter, my landlord received 60 dollars a month. Brewers and maltsters earned 17 dollars a week and up. After a failed walkout, their *union* and the brewery administration agreed upon this sum as the minimum wage; non-union members may not be hired.

The most I earned in a week was 10 dollars. Forty-two Marks, a tidy little sum. But bitterly earned with 2 0   h o u r s   o v e r t i m e. Only those who have been through it themselves can understand what so much overtime at hard labor means. The question as to long hours and their consequences has been discussed countless times. I had read and heard enough about it. But I didn't think seriously about it until I felt these consequences in my own body. He who feels no weight has a light load.

Day after day, ten long hours of standing, toting, bending, lifting—it's no trifle. To say nothing of fourteen and fifteen hours. Evenings at 9 or 10, when I dragged back to my room which I'd left that morning at 5:30, ready to collapse from fatigue, I had only one wish: to fall into bed. And yet still, at the beginning, the thought of lying down as filthy as I was was so offensive that I preferred to sacrifice a portion of my meager time in bed and—it was in the middle of winter with freezing temperatures down to minus 20 degrees R.[4]—first lit the oven to warm water. But these heroics didn't last long. When we began to have to work even on Sundays and weren't let off till it was impossible to bathe anyway, the need for cleanliness also began to gradually and gently fade away. It was like getting used to staying at a series of bivouacs during a rainy maneuver. First you

4. "R" stands for Réaumur, a temperature scale which registers the boiling point of water at 80 degrees and the freezing point at 0.

think you'll suffocate in the filth and begin to disgust yourself, and then finally—inevitably—you notice with amazement how little soap a person needs to get by.

Of course I don't mean to imply that each and every one of my fellow workers didn't wash. . . .

Even when I just started working at the brewery, I thought I perceived that the people—especially the single workers—were much more poorly clothed than the workers I'd seen at the boardinghouse and on the streets.

The friendly young man who saw to it that I didn't oversleep on the first morning wore a suit which obviously hadn't been cleaned for a long time. Only the worst holes had been mended. Beneath it a brown woolen shirt as well as undergarments and stockings just like it. Like almost everyone there, he kept his underthings on at night so that he simply had to slip into his boots and clothes in the morning and then he was all ready. As long as I knew him I don't believe he once changed his undergarments. Otherwise an honest soul, though life had treated him hard. His father died on him when he was still young; his mother had remarried, and when he was 15, his stepfather showed him the door.

This I learned later. On that first morning, sitting across from him under the light at the breakfast table, I was secretly shocked by so much dirt and disorderliness. But wrongly so. It didn't take long before I was on my way to resembling him. Working with cases as we did, it was impossible to avoid getting holes and rips. If I returned home from work on into the evening it was too late to run off to a tailor. I had to turn to the needle myself; and what my exhausted hand was able to patch together looked just as disorderly as that which had originally so offended me on that poor devil. It was also too late to take my dirty things out to be washed; too late to buy anything. I couldn't even ask my landlord and his wife. They were already in bed by the time I got home. But leave was most difficult to obtain. If one also considers the incredible fatigue—and that general indifference toward everything awaiting one in the next hour which comes from it—one can perhaps imagine the way I looked. At the beginning I felt this life to be absolutely unbearable. Ultimately I did as my comrades: I took things as they came.

I had to force myself to take notes. I hardly wrote any letters. I looked at newspapers just as infrequently as the others. I had no desire to seek out the reading rooms in the magnificent Public Library. I was most content to sit around home and smoke in dull apathy. At best, certain spontaneous desires would flare up and I'd recall that statistical problem which a

Frenchman had so drastically formulated with the phrase: *Les enfants poussent dans la misère comme les champignons sur le fumier.*[5]

It needn't be pointed out that the unaccustomed work weighed three times as heavily upon me, the greenhorn. I'm aware of that myself. But this I know just as well: my comrades suffered too. Yes, in a certain sense even more. The knowledge that I merely had to go to a hotel and change my clothes to change the person, that at any time I could remove myself from all the misery—this knowledge lent me a spark of resiliency which the pressing weight of the situation had long since extinguished in these poor creatures. And if, at close quarters, they represented that which they appeared to, then the reason for it could also be traced to this situation.

5. Children sprout up amidst misery like mushrooms on a dung heap. (Footnote in the original text.)

III. LIVING CONDITIONS

The resolution of the Civil War and the abolition of slavery nourished the optimistic nineteenth-century American belief in progress, particularly the assumption that all parts of the nation would share in an ever-increasing prosperity. This optimism was fundamentally shaken, however, by the economic depression of the 1870s and the accompanying social unrest culminating in the great railroad strike of 1877. Initiated by a reduction in wages that exacerbated an already desperate situation among workers, the strike took on unprecedented national scope, leading to violent confrontations, especially in Maryland, Pennsylvania, and Chicago. It even provided the occasion for a short-lived seizure of power by the workers of St. Louis that evoked nostalgic memories—or nightmares—of the revolutionary Paris Commune of 1871. These events aroused the country and confronted it with the social consequences of the rapid industrialization that had been going on in its midst.

Developments in Chicago accentuated what was happening in other urban centers. The Great Fire of 1871 had already marked the end of "old Chicago," as most of the central city was consumed in one of the great calamities of the century. Although the fire became a metaphor for the shifting eras, economic and social changes did as much to define a new order. The scale of industrial enterprise that developed after 1871 was substantially larger than before, as was the influx of workers, both of which added to the divisions and tensions in the city. When the great depression hit, mass marches and conflicts between the unemployed and city authorities—some of them over the distribution of fire-relief funds—brought the reality of class conflict home to Gilded-Age Chicagoans. To the surprise and consternation of local and national politicians and businessmen, social unrest and labor conflict did not disappear with the end of the 1877 railroad strike and the return of better times. In fact, they took on even starker form during the 1880s, when American workers were able for the first time to organize permanent national unions and labor organizations.

*The severity of the depression and the newly aroused labor move-
ment forced a broad range of the country's leadership, from reformers
and socialists to senators and business magnates, to evaluate the new
social situation and propose remedies that would prevent another
economic and social crisis. Friendly to labor, Henry George published
what was to become one of the classics of American reform literature
in 1879. Its very title —* Progress and Poverty: An Inquiry into the
Cause of Industrial Depressions, and of Increase of Want with
Increase of Wealth *— expressed a broadly felt doubt about the ability
of the new industrial economy to satisfy all the material needs of
American citizens. Legislative and congressional committees took up
the same issues, investigating "Relations between Labour and Capital" and the "Causes of the General Depression in Labor and Business." They sought testimony from entrepreneurs, bankers, journalists, politicians, labor leaders, and ordinary workers. In some states
like Illinois these hearings did lead to concessions on particular issues,
such as the creation of labor bureaus to watch over and document
industrial conditions, although these agencies lacked substantial power
to change them.*

*One of the most telling testimonies about the conditions of workers
in Chicago was the questioning by a Senate committee in 1883 of
P. H. McLogan, a representative of the Chicago printers union.*[1] *With
thoroughness and numerous statistics, McLogan described the pre-
dominance of the foreign-born among Chicago's workers, child labor,
dilapidated tenements, the limited extent of home ownership, low
wages, and the high cost of living for Chicago's work force. He also
outlined the considerable alienation of workers from religious institutions and the appeal that socialism had for them. A year later the
Illinois Bureau of Labor Statistics presented a similar report on the
living conditions of Chicago's workers.*

*Both hearings point to an increasing awareness of a fundamental
social crisis within America's industrializing society. No longer could
the country's leadership ignore that basic institutions of the social
order like the churches were not reaching broad sections of the foreign-
born work force, that old ideals like individual upward mobility in
a classless society were being turned into myths by a harsher social
reality, and that class conflict was dividing a country that prided
itself on its distinction from the Old World and felt that its social*

1. U.S. Congress, Senate, Committee on Education and Labor, *Relations between Labour
and Capital*, 47th Congress, 1st Sess., 1881, pp. 566-85.

*order was based on consent to common political and social ideals.
This general sense of threat was heightened by the fact that so many
workers were foreign-born.*

*The documents in this chapter were part of the same effort to
understand, and change, the rapidly emerging new order in American
society. Since they contain such rich material, we have included some
excerpts from legislative and congressional hearings, as well as from
an Illinois Bureau of Labor report. But given the goals of this anthology, we have relied primarily on the German labor press and the
records of the German Society to illuminate the standard of living,
the housing conditions, and the social situation of Chicago's German
workers, particularly the transient, the single, and the poorest among
them. These latter groups were often dealt with separately by contemporary reformers and government authorities under various rubrics such as "the poor," the "tramp menace," and the "boarding
house problem." Scholars commonly treat them under similar categories. Yet tramping and poverty were among the realities of working-
class life in Chicago, realities too seldom connected with Germans
in historical accounts.*

Wages and the Standard of Living

*Evaluating the economic and social position of workers in American
industrial cities was one of the most controversial undertakings in
the late nineteenth century, and it remains so among historians today.
Almost always included in such an effort was an attempt to compare
the condition of workers in America and Europe. Both state and
federal agencies repeatedly tried to establish that America had a higher
level of wages and real income. Even the most fundamental and
comprehensive comparative study to date—Peter R. Shergold's recent*
Working-Class Life: The "American Standard" in Comparative Perspective, 1899-1913—*has not been able to lay the issue to rest.
Several problems make such a comparison particularly difficult. Differences between trades, regions, and ethnic groups almost preclude
reliable generalizations. Also the purchasing power of wages and the
actual daily needs of the work force are exceedingly difficult to
determine. Most important, given the seasonality of work in so many
branches of industry and the intermittent character of employment*

generally, one must attempt to calculate the real yearly income instead of relying on daily or weekly wages projected for what is too often a fictional full year's employment. And yet comparisons of the conditions of labor in America and Europe have rarely been based on real annual income.

German-American labor unions early recognized the necessity for reliable statistics on wages and cost of living in order to back up their demands for higher pay, a shorter workday, and improved living conditions. As early as 1878 an article in the Chicago Vorbote *recommended that local furniture workers unions imitate an exemplary statistical survey of their trade, excerpts of which are reprinted here. The* Vorbote *was at the time the official organ of the national furniture workers union, and the article was written by Carl Speyer, a former member of the First International. Shortly afterwards the rapidly growing Knights of Labor instituted the position of official statistician, and it is probably no accident that another former member of the First International, Theodor Cuno, was its first occupant.*

Chicago's unions were also active in this field. Both the socialists and the city's Trade and Labor Council took the initiative, prompted in 1879 by impending investigations of the condition of Chicago's workers by committees of the Illinois legislature and the United States Congress. They were thus able to present the first results of statistical surveys undertaken by individual unions. The committee of the Illinois legislature was set up under the initiative of the representatives elected by Chicago's Socialist Labor party, and one of their number, Charles Ehrhardt, was among its five members. The second document reprinted here includes excerpts from the evidence presented both to this committee and to the similar congressional committee meeting during the same year. Descriptions of the state of particular Chicago trades organized in unions have been reproduced, rather than the detailed statistical material.

The question of prison labor stands out among the grievances discussed at these hearings. Heatedly debated in the 1870s and 1880s, prison labor had developed to such an extent that it threatened the existence of trades like shoemaking and coopering. It was no accident that the spokesman for the coopers was George Schilling, probably the best-known German-American labor leader in Chicago during the nineteenth and early twentieth centuries. Among his many activities, he took a decisive part in the election of John Peter Altgeld as governor of the State of Illinois in 1892. Altgeld in turn appointed him director of the Illinois Bureau of Labor Statistics. Schilling was also influential in Altgeld's controversial pardoning of those Haymarket anarchists who had been sent to prison instead of being executed. Overall German-Americans were strongly represented among the unions whose spokesmen testified before the investigative committees. Although at this time there were no reliable figures on union membership, the federal population census for 1880 does break down whole trades in the city by ethnic groups. The cigarmakers, for example, were more than 40 percent German, the shoemakers about 33 percent, the coopers 37 percent, the unskilled workers almost 30 percent, the cabinetmakers and upholsterers 38 percent, and the leather workers (including tanners) over 40 percent.

Thanks in part to the significant vote obtained by the Socialist Labor party in the local elections of 1879, the organized workers in Chicago were able to initiate the formation of the Illinois Bureau of Labor. It carried out basic investigations into industrial conditions that were of primary importance to the state's workers. In 1884 the bureau published a detailed report on the living conditions of working-class families in Illinois. Document 28 consists of nine cases from this report that exemplify the situation of German working-class families in Chicago. The families can be roughly subdivided into two groups. Those headed by the carpenter and the trunkmaker represent the relatively narrow stratum of the "labor aristocracy." Comparatively small, the carpenter's family could afford a modest-sized house with a garden. They were well situated compared to the baker's family, which had to get by on about the same income but with five persons in the household. Despite its large size, the family of the trunkmaker achieved a modest material prosperity because he earned an unusually high income. In contrast, all other families lived in much worse circumstances. Either the annual income of the fathers was much less than that of the carpenter, who was regularly employed throughout the year, or the head of household had to support a much larger family, as did the streetcar conductor. Temporary unemployment, as in the case of the cigarmaker, or considerably lower wages, as in the case of the baker, made these families dependent on the earnings of the sons or the wives.

The standard of living of these families is most clearly revealed by their housing conditions. Generally, they lived in crowded districts, and their homes were poorly furnished. Although five of the seven families occupied single family homes, most of these obviously were *cheaply built and run-down frame houses. Not even one family owned its own house; they all rented instead. Only a few of Chicago's German workers in the 1880s could realize the ideal of the skilled craftsman who, through industry and hard work, improved himself and bought his own home. Finally, in only three of nine cases— among them notably the families of the carpenter and the trunk- maker—was the family income higher than the expenses. The third family, the baker's, managed to end the year with $20, but certainly at the cost of their standard of living. This family of five spent less than half as much for clothing and household goods as the family of the trunkmaker, which was exactly the same size; also $3 versus $30 went for books and newspapers; and $10 compared to $25 was given out for miscellaneous items.*

In the next document, a letter to the Chicagoer Arbeiter-Zeitung, *a carpenter explains how he must maintain his household in order to get by on his wages. His figures are close to those of the official report of the Illinois Bureau of Labor. Like the baker's family, he too ended the year with some $27, even when he was unemployed for two months, yet he emphasized that 1881 had been a good year. In his letter, as in some of the cases cited in the Bureau of Labor report, one can sense a feeling of deep dissatisfaction, as, for example, when this carpenter describes himself as an "upright man" but "never- theless a poor devil," or when the family of the blacksmith is noted in the report as "not satisfied with their condition," or when the streetcar conductor complains that "the company is grinding him and all the others down to the starvation point."*

26. Statistical Survey of the Furniture Workers Union of North America (*Vorbote*, February 16, 1878).

Central Committee of the Furniture Workers Union of North America to the Local Unions.

Esteemed Comrades!

The following is a statistical directive prepared by our specialist, Com- rade C. Speyer. We ask you to make the most extensive use of it and, if possible, to report to the Central Committee at the end of each quarter.

For the Central Committee:

Henry Stahl,
corresp. Secr.

Directive

for the preparation and calculation of the following statistics for the Furniture Workers Union of North America.

Foreword.

During the past few decades, the two major social classes in Europe's modern civilized countries have been paying the closest attention to labor statistics. The class of owners, because the bare statistical figures uncontestably expose the refined and brutal manner by which this class absorbs all of the workers' physical and mental strength, while giving them over to poverty and deprivation. On the other hand, organized labor in these countries sees statistics as an unrivaled weapon to be utilized to the fullest degree in the struggle for liberation. The class of owners fears statistics about working conditions for the same reasons workers strive to attain them.

To the extent that workers yet unaware of their situation are presented with a true picture and made conscious of their class interests, labor statistics have also proved useful as an agitational strategy. And when studied and tended to by the workers themselves, statistics serve to educate, and to elucidate the views gained by those who—having already occupied themselves with labor statistics—oppose the existing economic order.

In general, the workers often either do not recognize, or underestimate the value of statistics, because the information is not conveyed in rousing language which excites the imagination, and because the worker, mentally and physically exhausted, sees a considerable difficulty in following the data and tables. But—despite the fact that one can generally assume only common, elementary knowledge—serious occupation with and inspection of the statistics on the part of the worker prove this difficulty to be illusory. What the worker lacks in scholarly knowledge, he makes up in practical experience and interest, which is closely related to the matter.

It is therefore the obligation of all labor organizations in America to direct their members' attention to labor statistics, and to see that they are attended to.

––––––––––

When treating the material produced by the statistical questions posed by the Furniture Workers Union, the following points should be taken into consideration . . . :

1. The model printed here should be copied into a book for the data resulting from a given quarter, and the completed questionnaires received

from the members are to be recorded under the appropriate rubrics. The statistical secretaries, however, should pay attention to the following:

a. that for the question: average weekly wage?, the members do not give the weekly wage as stipulated by their contracts, but rather their **real quarterly earnings** calculated week by week;

b. that for the question: cost of living per week?, they take into account board, lodging and clothing costs, in short, all expenditures which have to do with the cost of living, and that they only deduct from their wages the sum that they have really been able to put aside;

c. that for the question: shop?, they give only the number of people employed on one floor and the area of this one floor;

d. that for the question: lodging?, they don't count the space rented to relatives or other people.

2. The compilation of the quarterly and semiannual results should be arranged alphabetically and should be comprised of the following, separate paragraphs. Given the time, however, the eager researcher will always be able to use them as new sources in order to arrive at further interesting results. In the same way, a comparison of the quarterly and semiannual data over a period of several years offers much of interest. . . .

Statistics about the Members

for the months of October, November and December, 1876, and in February and March, 1877.

In the first 3 months, 47 members turned in statistical information, in the last months, 35.

A. Furniture Branch:

The statistics during the months given above show that 81% of the members are cabinetmakers, 15% chairmakers, and 4% pianomakers.

B. Common Workday in October, November and December, 1876:

During these months, 80% worked 10 hours, 12% 9½ hours, and 8% 9 hours a day.

January, February and March, 1877.

In these three months, 81% worked 10 hours, 12% 9½ hours and 9% worked 9 hours a day.

C. Average Weekly Earnings:

In the first three months, average earnings amounted to $10.97, and in January, February and March, 1877, they amounted to $11.3½.

D. Average Weekly Cost of Living:

57% of the members exhausted their earnings for living expenses, 11%

saved from $1 to $3.50 a week, and 33% of the members suffered a weekly deficit of 75 cents to $5.50.

E. Steadiness and Unsteadiness of Work:

October, November and December, 1876.

In these months, work for 32% of the members was steady and for 69% unsteady.

In January, February and March, 1877, work for 28% of the members was steady, for 72% unsteady.

F. Fluctuation in Wages:

Wages for 67% of the members decreased. For 33%, wages remained the same. In no case was a rise in wages reported.

G. Unable to Work due to Illness:

In October, November and December, 1876, 7% of the members lost an average of 1 day and 9½ hours due to illness. In the latter three months referred to above, 5% were unable to work an average of 5 days due to illness.

H. Shop:

1. During the above six months, the number of workers employed on an average floor in an average shop was 17. The maximum number was 180, the minimum was 2.

2. The average area for one worker in an average shop was 211.1 square feet and the volume was 2317½ cubic feet.

3. 2% of the members work on the ground floor, 11% on the second floor, 26% on the third, 45% on the fourth, 10% on the fifth, and 8% of the members work on the sixth floor.

I. Lodging:

1. 3% of the members average 4 heads and live in 4 rooms; on the average, all four rooms are exposed to the light, but are found outside the city. 16% live in three rooms and average 5 heads; as a rule, only one of these rooms is exposed to the light. 55.5% live with an average family of three in two rooms of which one is exposed to the light. 25.5% of the members are unmarried and live either in one room or a half room. In these cases, the rooms are generally exposed to light.

2. 13% of the members live on the second floor, 26% on the third, 41% on the fourth, 11% on the fifth, and 9% on the sixth.

C. S p e y e r, statistical secretary.

We recommend that the above be carefully studied by all union members, and especially by the various central bodies.

27. **The Condition of Workers in Various Trades (this document represents the original English version; U.S. Congress, House of Representatives,** *Report of the Select Committee Investigating the Causes of the General Depression in Labor and Business,* **46th Cong., 2d Sess., 1879; Illinois State Legislature, Assembly,** *Report of the Special Committee on Labor,* **31st Assembly, 1879).**

[Hearing of July 29, 1879]

Remarks on the condition of the various trades.

Wood Carvers.

There are cabinet-makers employed in our shops that receive not more than $3 and $4 for six days hard work; most of them have large families to support, and their condition is most deplorable; yet, should they quit work, plenty of others would willingly take their places. Boys are replacing adult labor and reducing the wages of those still employed.

Upholsterers.

Wages are good in busy times (about five months in the year), but as soon as the rash [*sic*] is over the men are at the employers' mercy; short time, discharges and reductions are then the order of the day. Boys are employed at from $2 to $5 per week, performing work that, if paid for at the regular rates, would cost three or four times as much; these boys are always kept at work. The trade is very unhealthy, a perpetual cloud of dust fills the shops, causing catarrh, consumption, and death among the workers. This could be prevented, if the almighty dollar was not of the greatest importance and the health and lives of the workers of no value.

Silver Gilders.

The introduction of child labor into this trade has been very injurious to the workers, in some instances displacing 50 per cent of the adult labor. The sanitary condition of the workshops is a disgrace to the employers, and a sad commentary upon the industrial system that holds the lives of the workers so cheap. In winter the shops are insufficiently warmed. In summer our work requires that all the windows shall be closed. No means of ventilation being provided, the shops are constantly filled with tainted and poisonous air, the inhaling of which produces consumption.

Shoemakers.

In this trade, among many other evils, convict labor is the most injurious. There are five boot and shoe manufacturing firms in Chicago that have ceased to employ any but convict labor, thus forcing 250 men to seek work elsewhere, or beg, borrow, or steal the means of life. Failing to find employment, these honest mechanics must become paupers or criminals, and eventually be employed either by their former masters or other employers of convict labor. The present convict labor system suits our employers very well, as it gives them the advantage of getting good mechanics cheap, and if we (so-called) free mechanics complain about low wages, we receive the following consoling answer: We employers of free labor must compete with convict labor, and to do this successfully we must reduce wages as near as possible to the rate paid to the convicts.

Tanners.

This trade for wages [*sic*] laborers has arrived at the point of evolution. Wages have been reduced every year, until, in some branches, tanners are compelled to work for six and seven dollars per week. One-third of the tanners only work two-third time, and either have to leave the city or linger around, Micawber-like, waiting for something to turn up.

Tinners.

At this trade the remuneration for labor is so small that it is impossible to support a wife and family. While a man is able to work, he can hardly make his living; when disabled, there is no prospect but the poor-house. Labor-saving machinery is a benefit only to those who own it and get the profits.

Planing-Mill Lumber Shavers.

Men are employed at this laborious work at 50 cents and 75 cents per day; and in addition to giving so much hard work for such small pay, the men are cursed and abused by the foreman in a manner that would have disgraced a Southern plantation in the palmy days of chattel slavery.

Laborers.

In this work muscle is the thing required. In a few years we become old and our muscles stiff and weak. We are not able to work like young men, and hence are discharged. Not being able to save anything from our small pay, no matter how we try, we become paupers. This is our encouragement. But we cannot murmur at our hard lot, because that is wicked, and for doing so we shall go to hell, and if we are not afraid of hell, they have the militia to keep us quiet.

[Hearing of March 1, 1879]

Cigar-Makers' Trade.

Mr. Goldwater [on behalf of the Trades Council] . . . proceeded to explain how manufacturers paid their employes [*sic*] in cigars, and the evil effects of the system upon the cigar-makers. He stated that the latter had to peddle the cigars received in payment for wages around town, and sell them for what they could get. As a rule they got very little, became destitute and desperate, and in consequence, frequently resorted to drink, committed crimes themselves, and their poverty often drove their wives, sisters and daughters to lives of shame. He showed the evil effects of the contract convict system not only upon his own trade but upon others in forcing all wage-labor, through competition to the level paid for the labor of convicts. On being questioned as to what remedy should be had for the evils of the convict labor system he replied that, in his opinion, under no circumstances should convict labor be allowed to compete with and thereby reduce to a common level all other laborers engaged in the same kind of work. . . .

Coopers' Trade.

Mr. George A. Schilling, on behalf of the Coopers' Union, stated that the coopers' trade was about ruined by convict labor, that it was not the quantity or quality of the work which produced the result, but the manner in which this kind of work was thrown upon the market. Men were forced to compete with convict labor, and that to do so their wages were lowered to conform to the penitentiary rates. His trade desired a law to prevent the competition of convict labor with honest labor; also a law reducing the hours of labor.

28. **The Condition of German Working-Class Families in the 1880s: Examples from the Illinois Bureau of Labor Statistics (this document represents the original English version; Illinois Bureau of Labor, *Third Biennial Report* [Springfield, 1884]).**

(See pp. 112-14.)

No. 4.   BAKER.   *German.*

EARNINGS—Of father... $450
    Of son, aged sixteen...   150
          Total... $600

CONDITION—Family numbers 5—father, mother and three children, all boys, aged
sixteen, eleven and thirteen years. Two of them attend public school. They
live in three small rooms in rear part of a large house, which are very dark
and dirty, and for which they pay $11 per month. The whole family seem
to be very ignorant, and are unable to speak any English. Father works
fifty weeks in the year, at an average of $1.50 per day. He does not belong
to any union and carries no life insurance. If it were not for the assistance rendered by the oldest son, their expenses would exceed their earnings.

FOOD—*Breakfast*—Bread, coffee and crackers.
    Dinner—Soup, meat and potatoes.

COST OF LIVING—
  Rent... $132
  Fuel...   15
  Meat and groceries...   300
  Clothing, boots and shoes and dry goods...   100
  Books, papers, etc...   3
  Sickness...   20
  Sundries...   10
    Total... $560

No. 6.   BLACKSMITH.   *German.*

EARNINGS—Of father... $450

CONDITION—Family numbers 7—parents and five children; three boys and two
girls, aged from one to seven years. Occupy 4
rooms in tenement block, and pay $12 per month for same. The surroundings
are only fair. The rooms are carpeted, and family appear comparatively comfortable, but are not satisfied with their condition. Father belongs to the
Labor organization and considers himself somewhat benefited thereby. He,
however, is only able to secure work twenty-five weeks in the year, and receives $3 per day for his work.

FOOD—*Breakfast*—Bread, meat, butter and coffee.
    Dinner—Lunch at work; family at home, bread, tea, etc.
    Supper—Bread, butter, meat and coffee or tea.

COST OF LIVING—
  Rent... $144
  Fuel...   40
  Meat and groceries...   160
  Clothing, boots, shoes and dry goods...   80
  Books, papers, etc...   10
  Trades unions...   5
  Sickness...   10
  Sundries...   25
    Total... $474

No. 20.   CARPENTER.   *German.*

EARNINGS—Of father... $624

CONDITION—Family numbers 2—husband and wife. They live in a house containing 2 rooms, located in a good, pleasant and healthy part of the city. Have a
nice garden, from which they get vegetables in season. They pay $15 per
month for the house, which is seemingly large rent for a house of 2 rooms,
but the large yard and garden accounts for it. Husband works fifty-two
weeks of the year, and receives an average of $2 per day for his labor. He,
belongs to no trades organization, and carries no life insurance.

FOOD—*Breakfast*—Coffee, sausages, bread, etc.
    Dinner—Lunches.
    Supper—Tea, meat, potatoes, etc.

COST OF LIVING—
  Rent... $180
  Fuel...   30
  Meat and groceries...   250
  Clothing...   40
  Boots and shoes...   10
  Dry goods...   15
  Books, papers, etc...   5
  Sundries...   70
    Total... $600

No. 22.   CIGAR MAKER.   *German.*

EARNINGS—Of father $240
       Of son, aged sixteen... 200
            Total.. —— $440

CONDITION—Family numbers 8—parents and six children, four boys, aged sixteen, fifteen, nine and six, and two girls, thirteen and two. Occupy house of 3 rooms, for which rent is paid at the rate of $20 per month. House is scantily and poorly furnished, no carpets, and the furniture being of the cheapest kind. Wife attends to news stand and candy store, and, with the proceeds of this business added to what earnings father and son make, they manage barely to keep out of debt. House is in an unhealthy location and kept in a filthy condition, consequently children are sick at all times. Three children attending school. Father belongs to trades union, and says he is unable to procure steady work, and only works at "piece-work."

FOOD—*Breakfast*—Bread and plain coffee.
      Dinner—Lunch.
      Supper—Bread, meat and potato soup.

COST OF LIVING—
   Rent $240
   Fuel.. 20
   Meat and groceries 364
   Clothing, boots and shoes and dry goods 150
   Trades unions... 11
   Sickness... 100
   Sundries 300
     Total.. —— $1,185

No. 49.   LABORER.   *German.*

EARNINGS—Of father $375

CONDITION—Family numbers 4—parents and two children, boy aged one year, girl three. They pay a rental of $9 per month for a house containing 4 rooms, which is in a filthy condition, it being in a block of miserable frame tenements. The family are in want; they are only about half clothed and fed, look sickly, and are exceedingly illiterate.

FOOD—*Breakfast*—Salt meat, bread and coffee.
      Dinner—Coffee and toast.
      Supper—Bread, butter, meat and tea.

COST OF LIVING—
   Rent... $108
   Fuel... 25
   Meat... 40
   Groceries 100
   Clothing... 10
   Boots and shoes.. 6
   Dry goods.. 25
   Sickness... 25
   Sundries... 36
     Total.. —— $375

No. 80.   STREET-CAR CONDUCTOR.   *German.*

EARNINGS—Of father......... $728

CONDITION—Family numbers 7—parents and five children, three girls, aged one, two and three years, and two boys, five and eight. Four of the children attend school. Live in a house containing 4 rooms, and pay rent for same at the rate of $12 per month. House is in unhealthy location, and furnished poorly. Father says he was compelled to run in debt, and that fact keeps him behind in his expenses. He works sixteen hours every day in the year; never gets time to read the papers. Says the company is grinding him and all the others down to the starvation point. The only time he has when not at work is occupied in sleeping.

FOOD—*Breakfast*—Coffee, bread, butter and cakes.
      Dinner—Lunches.
      Supper—Bread, butter, tea, steak, etc.

COST OF LIVING—
   Rent... $144
   Fuel... 24
   Meat... 70
   Groceries 190
   Clothing, boots and shoes, dry goods, books, papers, etc 150
   Sickness... 30
   Sundries... 150
     Total.. —— $758

No. 92.   TEAMSTER.   German.

EARNINGS—Of father $378

CONDITION—Family numbers 6—parents and four children, one boy and three
girls, ages not stated. The children all attend school, and after school they
pick up rags and coal. They rent a house of 4 rooms for $8 per month. The
rooms are miserable affairs, dirty, inconvenient and consequently unhealthy and furnished very poorly. Family is dependent upon charity for
most everything they have. Father works forty-five weeks a year, and receives on an average of $1.50 per day of from twelve to fourteen hours. The
cost of living far exceeds their earnings. Had considerable sickness during
past year.

FOOD—Breakfast—Bread, butter and coffee.
       Dinner—Meat, bread and potatoes.
       Supper—Bread and tea.

COST OF LIVING—
   Rent.. $96
   Fuel..   12
   Meat and groceries..   200
   Clothing, boots and shoes and dry goods.................................   100
   Books, papers, etc..   ·5
   Sickness   50
   Sundries   10
      Total ....   —— $473

No. 95.   TRUNK MAKER.   German.

EARNINGS—Of father.. $900

CONDITION—Family numbers 5—father, mother and three girls, one, three and six
years old. Two of them attend public school, and the entire family are church
members. The house they occupy contains 3 rooms, and pay rent for same at
the rate of $15 per month. The house is one of a good brick block, in a very
healthy location. Family dress well, seem to be intelligent, and among their
other possessions they have an organ. They manage to save about $100 per
year. Father belongs to trades union, but does not carry any life insurance.

FOOD—Breakfast—Bread, meat and coffee.
       Dinner—Meat, bread, vegetables and coffee.
       Supper—Cold meat, bread and coffee.

COST OF LIVING—
   Rent $180
   Fuel..   40
   Meat and groceries...   300
   Clothing, boots and shoes and dry goods.................................   210
   Books, papers, etc...   30
   Trades unions..   10
   Sundries..   25
      Total..   —— $795

No. 98.   UPHOLSTERER.   German.

EARNINGS—Of father.. $480

CONDITION—Family numbers 5—father, mother and three children, one boy aged
seven, and two girls five and two years old. The house they occupy contains
four cozy rooms, all nicely carpeted. Family comparatively healthy. Wife
quite intelligent, and children neat and well dressed. Father belongs to
trades union, and carries some life insurance. He states that he has run in
debt during the past year somewhat, but principally for groceries. Father
works but about forty weeks during the year, and receives $2 per day, for
seven hours work in winter and ten in summer. If he had work the entire
year he would not now be in debt.

FOOD—Breakfast—Coffee, meat, bread and butter.
       Dinner—Lunches.
       Supper—Coffee, bread, potatoes and meat.

COST OF LIVING—
   Rent... $120
   Fuel..   15
   Meat and groceries...   260
   Clothing, boots and shoes and dry goods.................................   100
   Books, papers, etc   4
   Life insurance...   8
   Trades union..   7
   Sickness   20
   Sundries   50
      Total..   —— $584

29. "A Worker's Financial Report" (*Chicagoer Arbeiter-Zeitung,* July 19, 1882).

A carpenter writes: Almost every day the worker is reproached for n o t h a v i n g s a v e d e n o u g h. If someone could solve the problem and tell me how a worker can save anything, I would be extremely grateful. For years I have been working—and working hard—whenever work is available. And because I am nevertheless a poor wretch—though I am not at all wasteful—I kept records of my income and of my expenditures throughout 1881. Without a doubt, this was the best year we've had for business in a long time. My results are as follows. I was employed for ten months and was out of work for only two.

E x p e n d i t u r e s

Rent ⟨Rente⟩	$144
Foodstuffs, etc.	260
Clothes for myself and my wife	75
Fuel	30
Light	5
"Carfare"	24
Leisure	10
Illness	10
Household appliances	10
Tobacco	5
	$573
Earnings over 10 months at $60 a month	600
thus remain to cover extras.	$27

I am a thoroughly steady person and my family is small. Now I ask you: Given the present situation, how can the worker possibly put anything aside?

X.

Needy Families

The German working-class families selected from the report of the Illinois Bureau of Labor represented "normal" households, in that no unforeseen crises had disturbed the routine of their lives. Yet such families had to rely on themselves when problems arose, even when their income was the bare minimum necessary to keep things going. What happened when unexpected events disturbed their precarious financial equilibrium, when, for example, someone in the family became seriously ill, or when the breadwinner was laid off or died in an industrial accident? The insurance available to workers' families through private companies, unions, or fraternal orders was typically meager and of short duration, even when a family was lucky enough to have it. The only remaining option was to turn to religious or private charity organizations, or to the inadequate relief offered by public welfare institutions. The experience of approaching these was often bitter and demeaning. Before taking such a step families usually tried to help themselves by sending wives and children to work, or they sought aid from relatives and friends.

The following cases represent households who in fact had to turn to a philanthropic organization for help. They have been selected from the large files of the German Society of Chicago. According to the report of the society's agent taken from the Chicagoer Arbeiter-Zeitung, *there was theoretically a clear division of tasks between the German Society and the Chicago Relief & Aid Society, which was responsible for aiding people of all national groups in the city. While the German Society was to aid the newly arriving Germans, the Relief & Aid Society was to help the resident poor. Thus it was common practice for the German Society to deny aid, or stop it after a while, and send an applicant to its sister agency, and vice versa. As the years passed the accumulated cases of both societies amounted to a massive documentation of poverty and need in the city. Between 1883 and 1910, when the German Society conscientiously registered each case on a printed form, it recorded over 10,000 requests for aid, and many others were not even considered serious enough to record. The Chicago Relief & Aid Society treated considerably more.*

Applicants for aid either went to the German Society directly or through the recommendation of a member of the society; to come with a reference clearly increased one's chances for help. The society certainly did not blindly distribute its resources but rather sought information from neighbors or sent officers to investigate the situation of the applicant. The initiation of the specially printed forms in 1883, as well as their conscientious use, indicates the further professionalization and bureaucratization of the society's philanthropic activities. The society's agents sought to determine if the applicants were truly worthy persons. When filling out the detailed forms, the agents' very choice of words often betrayed the symptomatic nineteenth-century distinction between the deserving and the undeserving poor.

The overwhelming majority of applicants for support were working-class families, mostly with children, and requests increased during economic slumps. During the depression of the 1890s the rising number of families from the Polish provinces of Germany is also striking. Often recently arrived, these people were severely hit by unemployment. The German Society apparently felt responsible for these families because, although ethnically Polish, they had left from the German Empire and in most cases could understand and perhaps speak German.

The society distributed many different kinds of aid—some applicants received money, but only for very specific purposes; others were referred to jobs; still others got tickets entitling them to anything from room, board, or medical attention to clothes, coal for the winter, or seats on the train. The German Society tried to limit the duration of support for a family, but nevertheless it sometimes ended up helping an individual or family repeatedly for years. In one case reprinted here the society aided a family intermittently from 1893 to 1908.

The official forms reproduced below reveal more than the mere daily bureaucratic routine of the agent: they illuminate the everyday life of three poor German families in Chicago. The report of the agent shows how he was personally affected by the cases placed before him.

30. Report by the Agent of the German Society concerning Needy German Families (*Chicagoer Arbeiter-Zeitung,* **September 6, 1884).**

Aside from those [who are just passing through], the local inhabitants truly in need of support are either unattached, sick people, who are unable to earn their livings without the support of others, or families, whose breadwinners have either been long bound to the sickbed due to chronic physical ailments or whose untimely deaths have left wife and children in extremely difficult situations. This group of unfortunates demand our most urgent attention, even if they have been here for a longer period of time. This view, however, contradicts the actual objective of our society, which primarily seeks to alleviate the immediate difficulties confronting newly arrived immigrants. But it seems that these other unfortunates must nevertheless be given special consideration, since national, county or municipal institutions set up for this purpose are completely inadequate.

Permit me to clarify this by way of an example.

On July 11, the German Society was requested by a wife and mother of four children—aged 14, 11, 6 and 2½ years—to lend assistance, as her husband, who had been making $12 a week, was laid up with rheumatic fever. On the same day the woman received $3.

On the 19th of the same month the woman came again to complain of her suffering and to ask for help. She had paid the doctor and apothecary, and had exhausted all means to assure her husband the aid he so needed to get well again. The family was living in a basement and this was the primary cause of the man's illness, as his craft (tailor) didn't expose him to the rigors of dampness and the like. She was urgently advised to rent other rooms, and she was recommended to Doctor Raymond Ulrich and to Apothecary Schroll. In addition, she received financial support from the German Society. On the 30th of the month the good woman returned and, with warm appreciation, reported that the change of lodging, coupled with Dr. Ulrich's advice and assistance, had led to an improvement in her husband's condition, and that she was now optimistic that he would soon be back on his feet. But the doctor had instructed her to feed her husband better, to give him a glass of wine, too—how, though, was she to comply? The G. S. gladly accorded the good woman the means to do so. Neither the state, the county, nor the city gives out cash. The county does have a hospital as well as an almshouse, but the prejudice against these is so great that a family would prefer to suffer the most extreme privations rather than send one of its members there. The unattached person, of course, has no choice.

Let's look at another case, where a family was deprived of its bread-winner through sudden death. While crossing a railroad track, the husband was run over and died immediately. He was survived by a sickly wife, unfit for hard work, and four small children, the oldest among them 6, the youngest only a few weeks. The latter was born after the death of its father. What are the state, county or city willing to do for these unfortunates? The county contributes some foodstuffs, insufficient for the needs of a mother with four small children. How will expenses for lodging, clothes, etc. be paid? Do they want to send the children to the orphanage, the mother to the almshouse? It would then be necessary to triple the number of employees there.

For criminals—who often enough bring about the ruin of whole families—the state and county provide more than enough, while their victims can perish in hunger and misery.—The much-praised Christian charity doesn't concern itself with them. So be it! According to the last census,

Chicago's German population presently amounts to 210,000 souls, only eight hundred of which belong to the German Society. A disproportion which, in contrast to other nationalities, casts us into the shadows—so deep into the shadows that one is overcome by a smoldering feeling of shame. Is there no way to multiply this continually decreasing number of members by at least five?!

The rush of applicants for aid is growing with the increase in the city's population; but our means to assist them are not growing at the same rate—forgive me if I have dedicated too much time and space to reflection. But the situation is too serious to simply touch upon in passing. . . .

W i l h. C. A. T h i e l e p a p e, Agent.

31. Three Cases of Families Receiving Aid from the German Society in Chicago (German Aid Society Records, the Library of the University of Illinois at Chicago).

No.[2]   *Chicago,* Oct. 16, 1893
                              Feb. 20, 1902

Name of husband and wife: J. & F. S.
Age: 43 & 51
Number of children: 2 B/22 G/14 in 1898 when 22 son married; has 4 children
Age:
Address:
(39 Frankfurt St.) 17 Coblenz St. April 9/98
Nr. 45 Upton St. . . . (900 No. Lincoln St.)
(150 Coblenz St., Oakley Ave) 98 No. Park Ave . . .128 Mohawk St. (224 Hudson Ave . . . 528 Sedgwick St. Nov. 3/99, backhouse, April 1904 93 Mohawk St. Sept. 28/04 173 North Ave. 1st fl. rear, Jan. 1905 751 No. Halsted St.
Occupation: Worker   *Earnings:*
Nationality: West Prussian
How long in the country: 2 years   *in the city:* 2 years
Aid received, and from whom? —
To which congregation, lodge or club do you belong? —
Recommended by whom? County Agt.—Provisions see card of Nov. 16/98
Do you pay rent? how much? $6 $5.—

---

2. In order to protect the anonymity of the applicants in the following cases the form numbers have been eliminated, and the full names have not been used.

Applicant requests: financial support for rent.

Report:

The whole family has been out of work for months, and now they can't pay the rent. The people aren't suited for the city and should actually move to the country.

Allocated Oct. 16, 93 $5.00

"   Oct. 21, 93 $1.70 for transportation to a farmer in Naperville. As the farmer, John Stenger, wrote on 18 [*sic*] Oct. 93, even though these people received free tickets, they didn't go. —

Given Jan. 21, 1897 to wife one pair of shoes (=men's shoes) and old clothes.

Allocated Apr. 1, 1898 $2.— for foodstuffs and one pair of men's shoes. On Apr. 18, 1898 referred to work, didn't go. . . .

May 10, 98: Mrs. S. is again in need and asks for some short-term aid, just until her husband receives his pension from Holland next month. She needs money for foodstuffs and promised for certain that she would regard the money as a loan and would repay it in June.

Allocated May 10, 1898 $3.—. . . .

"   Oct. 12, 98 1 pair of shoes, the husband was in Ia., where he'd found four days' work on the RR. Came back today empty-handed. Because he had to walk all the way back, his shoes were in tatters. —

Allocated Oct. 15, 1898 $3.—for foodstuffs; the husband is still out of work.

Given on Oct. 31, 98 1 pair of shoes for the son, who hasn't earned anything for a while. . . .

Allocated Nov. 15, 98 ½ ton of Ohio River Coal, $3, the husband is sick and thoroughly unable to work.— . . .

March 28, 1899: allocated, 1 pair of men's shoes and 9 x [times]
⟨März 28, 1899⟩   work for the husband, Bk. 32/451

Apr. 1, 1899	"	$4.— for subsistence stuffs and some old men's clothes
Apr. 10, 1899	"	$3.— have received notice to move out and the people still need $3.— to move into new lodgings
May 2, 1899 ⟨Mai 2tn 1899⟩	"	$2.— in place of the coal which wasn't delivered
May 29, 1899 ⟨Mai 29 1899⟩	"	$1.— for shoes for the wife

No. 5

Chicago, _Oct. 16_____ 189_7_

FEB 20 1902

Name des Mannes und der Frau: Alter: _____ _____

Zahl der Kinder: _2_   Alter: _____

Wohnung: _____

Geschäft: _____ Einnahme: _____

Nationalität: _____

Wie lange im Lande: _2 Jahr_____ in der Stadt: _2 Jahr_

Unterstützung erhalten, und von wem? _____

Zu welcher Gemeinde, Loge oder Verein gehören Sie? _____

Von wem empfohlen? _____

Bezahlen Sie Miethe und wie viel? _$6 $5.—_

Applikant wünscht: _____

Bericht: _____

The form used by the German Society of Chicago for people seeking assistance. This one has been transcribed here as the case of J. and F. S. The complete names as well as the case number have been omitted to preserve the anonymity of the persons involved. (German Aid Society Records, the Library of the University of Illinois at Chicago.)

June 10, 1899   " $3.— for rent and etc. The husband is sick
⟨Juni 10 1899⟩   and not in a position to earn. . . .
Nov. 4, 1899   " $3.— for rent. Mrs. S. promises not to apply
                                  for any more aid.
Allocated Dec. 6, 1899 $3.— Mrs. S. asks o n c e again for aid. . . .
May 7, 1900: Mrs. S. is sick and instructions were given to the German Hospital to issue her free medication. . . .
Sept. 11, 1900, $1 allocated. Wife is sick and could therefore not earn anything washing.
Oct. 10, 1900, allocated in cash: $2.— The husband is still sick and can only earn a bit here and there.
Nov. 8, 1900, allocated for rent ⟨Rente⟩: $3.— plus ½ ton hard coal.
Nov. 30, 1900, allocated for medicine and foodstuffs: $1. According to the wife, the husband is very sick and has almost completely lost his hearing.

...1901, instructions for Anton Frank, 65 Washington St., to give J. S. 1 hernia support; according to a certificate from the German Hospital, he needs one.— ...

...1901 request for aid refused, referred to the CR & A.S. and the Co. Agt.[3] The people have n o children to feed; all are grown. The husband belongs in the almshouse, as he allegedly cannot work; the wife is healthy and vigorous and very well able to work and feed herself.

Jan. 29, 1902. Today Mrs. S. came again and said that they'd have to leave their lodging today if they can't make a $3 payment as the rent ⟨Rente⟩ is overdue. The husband is home sick and for months has been without work and pay. She asked us to help her again. Allocated: $3.—

Feb. 15, 1902. According to the husband, the wife is very sick, bedridden, and they don't have a penny in the house for medicine and foodstuffs. The family's request for aid is once again granted. Allocated: ½ ton of soft coal, $3.—

Feb. 20, 1902. Mrs. S. has been taken ill with St. Anthony's Fire[4] and is in need of medicine and etc. Allocated: $2.25.

Nov. 13, 1902. The husband is in the Alex Bros. Hosp.:[5] $2.50. ...

Apr. 15, 1903, allocated: $3.50. Both husband and wife are sick, and because the daughter has to stay home and care for the mother, she, too, is now earning nothing. ...

June 13, 1904, allocated for funeral costs: $5.—The husband died on June 12, 1904. ...

Sept. 5, 1908, allocated for rent and foodstuffs: $2.10

Oct. 13, 1908,   "   "   "   "   "   and medicine, is very sick. $3.25.

No.   *Chicago*, Nov. 5, 1894.
Name of husband and wife: A. L.   *Age:* 42
Number of children: K̶. [crossed out in the original] 5 G/15 sick B/14 B/11 K̶/K̶ [crossed out in the original] died G/4 B/2
Age:
Address: (11 Commercial St. L. V.) 860 Dudley
Occupation: Widow   *Earnings:*
Nationality: West Prussian

3. Chicago Relief & Aid Society and County Agent.
4. Erysipelas, an acute and infectious skin disease accompanied by fever.
5. The Alexian Brothers Hospital was the German Catholic hospital in Chicago.

How long in country: 11 years   *in the city:* 11 years
Aid received, and from whom? County Agent Chic. Rel & Aid Soc. Nov. $10.—
To which congregation, lodge or club do you belong?—
Recommended by whom? Through the newspapers.
Do you pay rent and how much? $6—
Applicant requests:
Report: The newspapers reported that the husband took his life because of a lack of work and trouble feeding his family. The investigation undertaken due to these reports revealed the truth. The man, Ferd., a laborer, seems to have been an unvital person and hanged himself because he saw no other way out. The wife is small and weak, as is the oldest girl. The situation is urgent.
Allocated on Nov. 5, 94 $5.00
     "   Dec. 13, 94 $5.00
     "   Nov. 15, 95 $5.00
     "   Mar. 26, 96 $5.00
Jan. 11, 1896. The oldest boy is without work, the oldest girl is bedridden in the Elisabeth Hospital.
Allocated on Jan. 11, 96: $5.00
On Feb. 3, 97, 1 portion of old clothes and an allocation of $4.—The Chic Rel & Aid Soc. refused to help.

No.   October 8, 1900
Name of husband: H. C.   *Age:* 36
Name of wife: W.   42
Number and age of children: X̶ X̶ [both crossed out in the original] 4 G/ 12 B/9 G/7 B/5 (G/1 week old, died July 23 1901 ⟨Juli 23 1901⟩) All the children were born in Germany.
Address: 970 W. 21st Place Basement (1033. W. 20 St. basement) 1033 W. 22nd St.
Occupation: Laborer
Nationality: Danzig, West Prussian
In country: Husband 5-6 years, wife 1½ yrs.   *in city:* same
Recommended by:
Rent: $6.—
Impression made by person making request? orderly
How does the household appear? very simple

Relief received and from whom? —
What is especially desired? general aid
Cause of predicament: without work or means
Name and address of relatives living here. The husband is the son of Mrs.
M. C., Relief Case Bk - p. -.
Investigator's Report: The husband hasn't had steady work since last July,
and it isn't possible for the people to get by on the $2.- to $2.50 the wife
earns each week sewing trousers. The husband worked till July for Simon
& Halske, but was laid off because business was slow. He was earning
$1.50 a day. The wife makes a sickly impression and is working beyond
her strength.
Allocated on Oct. 8, 1900: $3.00
Allocated on Dec. 1, 1900: $3.00
Allocated on Jan. 5, 1901: $4.—The husband has been sick for almost a
whole month but hopes to resume work at Simon & Halske when he's
better.
March 27, 1901: According to Mrs. C's attached letter, the family is in a
desperate situation due to the wife's illness and husband's unemployment.
Mrs. C. gave birth to a daughter last week. Dr. Weiss is asking $15.—
for his services. Allocated and turned over to daughter Frida: $5.—
July 23, 1901: Allocated and turned over to daughter Frida: $5. The baby
died this morning, and in addition, the family is in desperate straits.
Feb. 24, 1902: Allocated for foodstuffs: $5.—
Mar. 13, 1903: The husband hasn't had work for 16 wks., and the family
has recently been beset by sickness. Given: $5.
Dec. 14, 1903: Allocated due to husband's unemployment and other pressing
matters: $5.— The 15 year old daughter lost her job because she's only
15 years old.
Jan. 30, 1904: Allocated, $5.—
Mar. 11, 1904: The above family's situation is generally unchanged and a
further $5.10 in aid is therefore being allocated.

Chicago March 27, 1901
Distinguished German Society!
Because I find myself in a terrible situation I am turning to you through
this letter with a large request if there would be some kind of aid left
over for me as my husband hasn't had much work and now it's unsteady
and I am in childbed where I've needed 2 doctors and now after 8 days

I had to have a relapse with bleeding and the 5 little children and in my illness I'm turning to you distinguished German Society.

W. C.

1033 W 20 St.

Dr. Weiss Mch 10 1901

Receipt for $15.—medical attendance

Chicago July 23, 1901

Distinguished German Society!

As I'm in a terrible situation, my child died yesterday after a long illness and I can't walk because of my illness and my husband has also been sickly for the past few weeks, I'm turning to the distinguished German Society with a large favor to ask in the hopes that you can afford me a bit of assistance. I would also like to thank you most warmly for the assistance you gave me in March.

Thank you so very much W. C.

1033 W 20 St.

Rehabilitating the Poor and Needy

The German Society, in association with the Chicago Relief & Aid Society, not only sought to limit its support to deserving people: both societies also attempted to develop a system of philanthropy that would support itself in part at least. To this end they established a woodyard on the North Side of the city where they sent some petitioners, primarily single unemployed men, to cut wood in order to earn their room and board. The willingness of applicants to work in this yard was used as a test for their worthiness to receive help. One repeatedly finds in the records of the society a notation that another man had snuck away from the woodyard.

The following two documents taken from the Chicago Vorbote come up with another explanation for the woodyard and the reaction of the men to it. The paper saw the yard as another example of the ruthless exploitation of workers who were neither accustomed to, nor suited for, this kind of work. Worked to exhaustion, they were paid starvation wages which they received, not in money, but in tickets for food and lodging.

32. "The Tramps' Lumber Yard" (*Vorbote,* February 13, 1884).

The Tramps' Lumber Yard, that "charity institution" on Maple and Clark so lauded in every way by t h e l o c a l R e p t i l e,[6] is now open. It does the 19th century spirit of charity a great honor! — Each "tramp" who saws and splits a quarter cord of wood is allotted a meal worth 10-15 cents; to earn three meals and the luxury of not very enviable lodging for the night, one cord of wood has to be sawed and split. But only a very skillful and experienced lumberjack could accomplish this in one day. The latter, a n d o n l y t h e l a t t e r—working ten strenuous hours— would thus be in a position to earn three poor meals and an even worse night's lodging, amounting to a value of about 40-50 cents. — Chopping up a cord of wood generally pays from $2.50-$3.00; the new charity institution has this work done for 40-50 cents. The enterprise will undoubtedly pay for itself. We would like to pose one question: Do "charity institutions," abounding in the spirit of charity, have the indisputable right t o m u r d e r their beneficiaries? — If they don't have this right, we would urgently like to request the public authorities—in the name of humanity— to suspend work at the Tramps' Lumber Yard immediately— i t i s m u r d e r! If hunger drives an unemployed tailor, shoemaker, goldsmith, bookkeeper, etc. to said "charity institution" to earn a meal through so-called "honest" work, he has to "chop up" a quarter cord of wood— more than what unexperienced hands could accomplish in ten hours. It is not unlikely that such a poor devil will then be completely incapable of work, sick, for 3-4 days. The strength thus expended is considerably more than the "compensation" — a poor meal. — This is murder, nothing more, nothing less!

33. Relief Society's Circular about the Lumber Yard (*Vorbote,* February 20, 1884).

The Relief Society, acting out of pure humanitarian sentiment, has set up an area where homeless and hungry tramps can chop up wood. A circular was distributed yesterday, in which the following is explained:

1. The lumber yard is a **touchstone**, to find out whether the masses of capable men loitering about our streets really w a n t t o w o r k o r n o t.

2. This *touchstone* will enable the Relief Society to identify all those

6. Almost certainly a reference to Richard Michaelis, editor of the *Freie Presse,* with whom the Chicago German socialists had repeated polemical battles. See also Chap. IV, the introduction to "Neighborhood Solidarity I," as well as Document 52.

who do not want to work, and to turn them over to the p o l i c e as professional tramps and beggars.

3. The yard is open from 7 A.M. to 4 P.M. Those capable of and willing to work can earn (?) themselves a meal or a night's lodging right there on the premises.

4. Reimbursement is n o t made in the form of money, as it is by no means our intention to employ all "tramps" or to pay them in **full** for their work.

5. We ask the public to support us by purchasing firewood from our charity yard, so that our enterprise can *"pay"* its way.

6. Citizens are urgently requested not to give any more when approached by "tramps" and the like, but rather to first refer them to the t o u c h - s t o n e.

It shouldn't surprise us if—despite this clarification—there are still people who cast the charitable spirit of the touchstone's founders into question.—Such people are simply beyond help!

Housing Conditions

Given its rapidly growing population—300,000 in 1870, over 500,000 a decade later, and more than one million in 1890—Chicago had a constant housing shortage in the second half of the nineteenth century. The need for housing was met primarily with small frame houses built out of lumber that was shipped to Chicago from the forests along the upper Great Lakes. This relatively inexpensive building material combined with ample land on the low-lying plains around the city made such wooden homes more economical to build than multiple family dwellings made of stone and brick. After the Great Fire of 1871 destroyed one-third of Chicago's housing, the city council drew legal "fire limits" around the center of the city and required that only stone and brick buildings be erected within them. It hoped to prevent a similar catastrophe in the future while giving insurance companies on the East Coast the assurance that it was safe to sell fire policies in the city again. This new ordinance, and even more the increasing value of real estate in the core of the city, led to the construction of multistoried residential buildings in the city center. They typically were operated as boardinghouses. At the same time the ethnic neighborhoods were more thickly settled as immigrants continued to pour into the city. Two-story wooden apartment houses were commonly built in these areas, while the older frame houses were pushed to the back of the lots along the alleys and rented out. Since the normal lot was 25 by 100 feet, this concentration of buildings all but eliminated the small gardens and severely reduced the light and space between the dwellings.

Conditions had become so bad by the beginning of the 1880s that the Citizens Association initiated an investigation of housing in the city's working-class districts and issued a report. The Chicagoer Arbeiter-Zeitung *summarized the findings of this report in an article that has been excerpted here. The association's report describes the different housing conditions of the groups making up Chicago's work force — single men, families, various ethnic groups, skilled and unskilled workers. Among the association's recommendations was the construction of more apartment buildings near the center of the city, since Chicago's geographical expansion was creating an increasingly long distance between home and workplace.*

The worst living conditions were to be found in the working-class districts near the branches of the Chicago River. Short sketches of these areas have been taken from the weekly reports of the Tenement House Inspectors. Italians and Poles were not the only ones who lived under such conditions, as the report of the Citizens Association implies. The seven houses described here were packed closely together in a district on the Northwest Side, not far from the North Branch of the Chicago River and the large factories located along it. Here amidst cramped and dirty conditions lived Poles, Irish, Scandinavians, and Germans. The names of the owners also point to this ethnic mixture, even though the landlords probably lived somewhere else. The description of living through a severe Chicago winter taken from the Vorbote *provides a glimpse of what it was like to live under such conditions.*

It is thus all the more understandable that people wanted to flee such districts. This was possible if one could scrape together the savings to buy or rent a small house in the new residential areas developing on the city's periphery. The better-paid skilled workers were the ones most capable of achieving this goal, which meant that a considerable number of Germans were among the potential customers of the city's real estate developers. Illustrating this fact is an advertisement in English and German from one of Chicago's biggest home builders, S. E. Gross, himself a German-American. A com-

*parison of the monthly cost for one of these advertised homes—
$15—with the rents listed in the 1884 Illinois Bureau of Labor
report shows that only members of the "labor aristocracy" were in
a position to afford them. The house in the ad measured approximately 18 by 30 feet, and the interior plan illustrates its simple layout.
Gross advertised a brick house, which was by no means typical. His
ad also does not show how small the lots were or how closely together
the houses were built; the following photograph does. It pictures a
typical Chicago working-class neighborhood constructed of standard
wooden frame houses.*

34. "Workers' Lodgings: A Report by the Citizens Association" (*Chicagoer Arbeiter-Zeitung,* September 3, 1883).

As we have referred to repeatedly, a committee from the Citizens
Association has been investigating the lodgings among the poorer classes
of Chicago's population for the past several months. The committee intends
to discover shortcomings and grievances, and to make recommendations
for their alleviation. Accompanied by a tenement house inspector, the
committee has made frequent tours through the workers' quarters in the
city, and has written up an extensive report. We haven't space enough
here to reproduce the report in full, but we do want to pick out the most
important points.

After a general introduction, the report continues along the following
lines: in relation to their wages, rents paid by workers are excessively high.
This is the result of the limited number of more or less livable tenement
houses. Thousands of married and unmarried people live in boardinghouses, hotels, etc., because they can't afford the high rents. Several thousands live on the city's outermost periphery, in quarters without sewer
systems, while large areas in the city's center lie nearly, or completely,
unused. Within a radius of 15 minutes from the city's business district,
high tenement barracks should be constructed, so that time and transportation costs could be saved. Property in the city is too valuable to be
turned over to Bohemians, Poles, Irish, etc., for the purpose of constructing
small huts where people herd together like sheep in a fold.

Overcrowded Tenement Houses.

That part of the population presently living in tenement houses has not
been so crowded together since 1873, because its size has increased con-

siderably, while only a few new tenement houses have been built. During this past hard winter, at least 200,000 workers lived in tenement houses inside the city, whereby a lot with several small houses inhabited by several families is considered a tenement house. Poles and others do not build high, roomy tenement houses with free court space, but rather cover the lot with small huts, which frequently house three to four families in two rooms. If one views such a lot as a tenement house, and if one further includes all those houses inhabited by three or more families, the number of workers cited above — with their families — are forced to lodge in 15,000 tenement houses.

After a brief review of the workers' situation in general — of little interest to us here — there follows a discussion of the prevalent, scandalous

Boardinghouse System.

According to the committee's opinion, this system is a disgrace to Chicago. The boardinghouse proprietors supply herds of voters, hundreds of them, who vote in the officials, often the proprietors themselves. Some of those sitting in the city council are the boardinghouse proprietors' stooges. Elected by the lodgers — whose votes are often illegal — some members of the city council are in the proprietors' employ. The committee had no time to look into the moral, or rather immoral influence of the boardinghouses. But this can't be criticized too strongly, nor are there measures which could be too quickly taken or too stringently enforced. The children who grow up in this kind of environment are largely bootblacks, paper boys, errand boys and factory workers. As they get older, they join the ranks of criminals. Our public schools cannot accommodate thousands of children who should be going to school instead of loitering about or causing trouble. Their parents would be happy to send them off to school, but of course they cannot afford private institutions.

The Immigrant Population.

Our immigrants are primarily German, English, and Irish. They — especially the first and last — are very prolific, while the Americans practice the (shockingly immoral) technique of aborting the embryo to an ever greater degree. In this way, the immigrant element in Chicago is slowly but surely winning the upper hand. Among the immigrants, there are many who were bound to the countryside in Europe, and hence are not good factory workers. They came primarily from regions where people live with the cattle under the same roof, where sewer systems are unknown, where there can be no question of sanitary measures. Should cholera find its way here from abroad, there are 70,000 tenement houses in Chicago which would be completely vulnerable. Above all, Chicago should keep its houses and their surrounding areas clean. The unhealthy condition of many places makes them

Breeding Grounds for Epidemics.

We need but recall the smallpox epidemic which, thanks to the disgraceful condition of the tenement houses, lasted for several years. It cost the (so-called) Board of Public Health huge sums in its efforts to fight (in reality to further) the epidemic through vaccination and other measures. One-third of all those stricken with smallpox succumbed to the disease. Of the 6,600 reported cases, 2,200 people died.—Scarlet fever, diphtheria, tuberculosis and other contagious diseases can be attributed to the conditions in the houses, and the house proprietors are responsible for the occurrences. These gentlemen should be indicted as *"public nuisances."* The committee visited more than 20 dilapidated barracks all belonging to the same man. They were inhabited by Italians. There were frequently as many as six families in one single room; their "rooms" separated only by wooden panels. The floors were rotten and full of holes, the walls covered with excrement, the chimneys didn't draw, the roofs leaked, stagnant water welled under the houses, the toilets overflowed, the sewer pipes were clogged, a horrible stench permanently hovered throughout the whole house. Each house belonging to this profiteer had been afflicted by smallpox: in each house, one human life was claimed by the epidemic.

Boardinghouses for Single People.

The rooming and boardinghouses for single people are generally wretched, overcrowded, and frequently dirty and gloomy; in short, they are to a large degree unhealthy. When possible, the better-paid worker boards with a family. Many only rent a room and eat in restaurants. But the overwhelming majority is crammed into houses which barely offer room enough to sleep. The normal, good worker, to whom cleanliness and good health are important, would rather quit the city than rent space here. That is why it is so hard to keep really good workers in Chicago. Almost all of these boardinghouses are connected to a saloon which also functions as dining room. After work and on free days, the people loaf around these saloons. The consequences of this can well be imagined. . . .

The Workers' Financial Situations According to Nationality.

The report states the following about the workers' financial situations: the best off are married Americans, English-speaking Germans and Scandinavians. The most skilled workers naturally earn the most. More than the others, the nationalities mentioned above aspire to decent, clean, healthy places to live. With few exceptions, the Italians and Poles seem to be content with the worst and dirtiest houses and areas. They show but little desire to improve their situation.

Single workers of each sex fall into the same pattern. If they can, they live with families of relatives or fellow countrymen. But they are often pushed into the unhealthy holes described above because of the lack of decent boardinghouses. Here they gradually submit to the influence of disease and vice. Many of these people could be saved, because they still wish to better themselves, though this is unfortunately unrealizable given the present situation. Others, granted, sink so low that they wouldn't take advantage of it even if a possibility presented itself. "In large part, the reason for the existence of 4,000 saloons in Chicago," — here the committee touches upon the Citizens Association's sore spot — "lies in the fact that the people who frequent them have no place else to go after work."

35. "Tenement Houses Hazardous to Health: Tenement House ⟨Tenementhaus⟩ Inspector's Weekly Report " (*Fackel*, October 2, 1881 and *Chicagoer Arbeiter-Zeitung*, September 4, 1881).

Fourteenth Ward.

No. 21 Fox Place, owned by Anton Nasilk, inhabited by four families totaling 16 people; sewer pipes defective, toilets flooded and in miserable condition, local sanitary facilities very poor.

No. 33 Fox Place, owned by H. Schultze, inhabited by nine families totaling 39 people; sewer pipes defective, local sanitary facilities very poor. . . .

No. 746 Noble St., owned by Michael Leran, inhabited by five families totaling 20 people; sewer pipes defective, local sanitary conditions poor.

No. 702 Noble St., owned by Jakob Lartheck, inhabited by six families totaling 32 people; sewer pipes defective, local sanitary conditions poor, the gutter in front of the house is clogged with dirt.

No. 734 Noble St., owned by W. Rosenthal, inhabited by three families totaling 18 people; toilets flooded and in miserable condition, the gutter in front of the house is clogged with dirt.

No. 718 Noble St., owned by Johanna Leran, inhabited by three families totaling 12 people; sewer pipes defective, toilets flooded and in miserable condition, the gutter in front of the house is clogged with dirt.

No. 560 Noble St., owned by Peter Bjuhm, inhabited by four families totaling 20 people; sewer pipes defective, local sanitary conditions poor.

36. "The Worker's Winter" (*Vorbote,* January 6, 1886).

We know that the privileged and rich are never in want of comfort and luxury, whether in summer or winter. Winter—be it as hard as in Siberia—poses no threat for these people. If it is cold, then they warm themselves with precious furs. If it snows, then they have themselves driven through the streets in coaches and carriages. With their balls, concerts, various pleasures and entertainment, winter offers as much distraction as does summer, with the open spaces, beaches, country houses, the trips and picnics. . . .

For the worker, however, winter is not at all charming. The cold weather means extra expenses for firewood, coal, clothing, etc. And even for those with jobs, these expenses make themselves felt. During the warmer seasons it's hard for a worker to make his way; during the winter, it's impossible in most cases. And then how easy to catch cold! Maybe the boots are torn and don't keep the water out; a warm overcoat is very often not to be had. The cold gets worse, becomes a serious illness, the worker collapses, has to give up his job. How horrible the misery which immediately moves in! And how he has to wrack his brain to try and come up with bread for his family! The united enemies—cold, hunger and want—quickly congregate in the unfortunate's lodging and destroy him and his family.

Let's take a look at this lodging, explore this breeding ground for rheumatism, stomach and abdominal troubles, childhood illnesses of all kinds. The reader need only pay a visit to Chicago's South Side to examine such lodgings, though they can also be found aplenty on the North, Northwest, and Southwest sides. These so-called houses are so miserably built that, despite the efforts to seal all the openings and holes, each change in weather has a considerable effect. In these lodgings, one is protected neither from the rain nor from the cold, and even the hardiest people will soon capitulate. The actual living space, which is supposed to serve as living room and—perhaps more important—as bedroom, is absolutely unsuited for this purpose. The dampness here covers every object with mold, and is responsible for a permanent musty smell which couldn't have

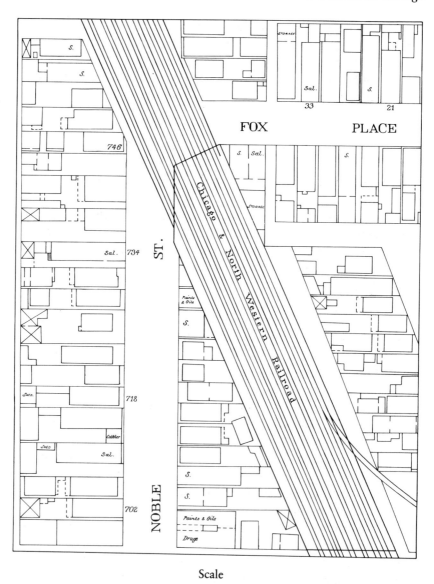

Scale

The city blocks on the Northwest Side including the houses visited by the tenement house inspectors whose reports are included in Document 35. The numbers in the streets by some buildings are those visited. Buildings marked with an "S" include a store: those noted with "Sal." include saloons. (Map drawn by Karin Kunkel on the basis of *Robinson's Atlas of the City of Chicago, Illinois*, vol. 4, plate 22 [New York, 1886].)

been worse in the most oppressive of medieval dungeons. The furniture has to be pushed away from the walls and is nevertheless falling to pieces. The lodger, once a man brimming over with strength and health, soon finds himself a half-invalid whose last vestige of earning power finally falls victim to rheumatism. And his wife, too, suffers the inevitable consequences of having stayed in this "boudoir."

Lodging in this modern paradise is hazardous to one's health —even fatally so—due to yet another grievance: it so happens that this paradise is heated with an iron stove whose stovepipe is attached to a chimney. This same chimney conveys the smoke from the "flat" below. Besides the various vapors, the people in the rooms above also have to reckon with smoke and the steam from washing, all of which enter through the chimney. To complete this idyllic picture, there is the water closet. It is found next to the living room, ensuring the satisfaction—with respect to dampness, smoke, steam, and . . . odor—of even the most coddled taste; all the more so as the courtyard lies between the high neighboring houses and is about as large as a fair-sized living room. If one wracks one's brains enough, and stands straight and tall, one might even be able to sight the summer sun, and at night—given extremely favorable conditions—the moon and some of its glittering companions. —And here are housed Chicago's workers, as is the case in all of America's big cities.

37. The Real Estate Firm of S. E. Gross & Co. Advertises Houses for Workers.

(See p. 136.)

This advertisement from 1883 offers solidly built brick homes to readers of both English and German. Better-paid skilled workers could afford such homes. (Chicago Historical Society, ICHi-06577.)

(See p. 137.)

Chicago's largest real estate firm dramatically advertised a new German neighborhood on the rapidly expanding Northwest Side. (Courtesy of the Newberry Library, Chicago, *Fackel*, August 11, 1889.)

(See p. 138.)

Taken between 1910 and 1920, this photo shows a typical working-class neighborhood composed of frame houses with an industrial plant in the background. (Chicago Historical Society, ICHi-00855.)

Housing for Single Men and Women

One of Chicago's most severe social problems in the late nineteenth century was lodging for single people. They arrived in masses from abroad and the city's own hinterland, staying sometimes but more often just passing through. The housing for such people was constantly discussed and investigated by social reformers, city inspectors, the labor movement, and various self-appointed defenders of morality. Located between the core of the city and the outlying residential neighborhoods, boardinghouses were situated near public transportation and large concentrations of industry. There were several grades of boardinghouses, from those catering to particular trades or recommended by unions to barracks where tramps slept packed together in huge halls. The unemployed usually ended up in the latter places, as did the farm laborers who flocked into the city during the winter.

Taken from the Vorbote, *the first document is an investigative report on one of these boardinghouses and the experiences of its "guests." Aside from the miserable quarters, the article describes the strict regulations imposed in such establishments as well as the general degradation of the masses of single men. Those who could not muster the 5 cents needed to sleep in one of these boardinghouses had an even more miserable time of it: if they did not want to freeze during the winter they had to sleep in the police stations, where they filled the cells and sometimes covered the floors. The writer of a letter to the editor of the* Arbeiter-Zeitung *knew from personal experience what it was like to sleep in the police stations. He did not exactly give the police high marks for humanitarian treatment of their fellowmen, but he also let it be known that the precinct stations were the last refuge in the dead of winter. This document makes clear the ambiguity of the popular word* tramp. *Those who actually "tramped" as a way of life made up a small minority of the people to whom the term was applied; the overwhelming majority were unemployed workers, members of the industrial "reserve army" who had not been absorbed by the labor market. During economic depressions the numbers of such "tramps" swelled. The use of the word functioned more to morally distance the middle class from the men involved than to describe their actual situation.*

Single young women faced an especially hard and precarious situation. They often came to the city from the rural hinterland and sought jobs as seamstresses, saleswomen, or servants. It was not simply that there were fewer places for them to live; staying in a boardinghouse also raised questions about their moral rectitude. On the other hand, philanthropic institutions like the Working Women's Industrial Home appeared to be at least as interested in the women's labor as in their integrity. A reporter from the Arbeiter-Zeitung *found out just that when he interviewed a young woman who had worked in the Industrial Home. The women in it were exploited as much as the men sent to the woodyard set up by the aid societies.*

38. "Nocturnal Infernos. Refuge for the Homeless" (*Vorbote*, November 27, 1893).

The harsh seasons double the misery of the poor. While the nights are warm, the poor camp out of doors. The shelter of a byway, some old planks, an empty case and God knows what else — these provide protection from the summer winds and showers. But as the days get shorter, the nights get cooler, until the icy north wind, the cold rain, finally snow and frost set in. Gone are the nights spent out of doors.

The poor devil has to find someplace to spend the night, so he scrapes together 10 cents for lodging in a cheap boardinghouse. At this time of year, the nocturnal refuges are overflowing with poverty. Mostly one finds upright, but unfortunate workers. Once in a while there may be a thief amongst them, or someone having arrived at the point where a dissipated existence casts off honesty. But the true robber doesn't linger in places such as cheap boardinghouses, which are so frequently under police surveillance. Brigands and burglars generally take rooms someplace where they can hide their spoils, and in this sense, these refuges for the wretched are not suited to their purpose. The "Liberty Bell" on Desplaines Street is one of the largest among the city's cheap boardinghouses. In the office located in no. 47, one finds down-and-out figures sitting around in the chairs, waiting for the clock to strike 2 A.M. Then those present either have to purchase a "bed," or leave the premises. In the middle of the room there is a sort of wire cage; a clerk inside enters the guests' names. Half of the cage is used as a sort of security locker. One night not so long ago, there were a bunch of dirty bundles stacked there. Above them were the words: "We can only guarantee the safety of valuables if they are deposited here."

Two reporters approached the cage and asked for permission to take a look around upstairs.

"What for? Do you want a bed?" the clerk snapped at them.

"No, we want to tell our readers how you can sleep for 10 cents."

"You and your readers can go to the devil," was the angry reply. "If you want a bed you can have it, if not, go to hell!"

20 cents were paid for two people.

"Jim, take these two-bit boys ⟨Zehncentleute⟩ upstairs."

Jim took the keys and climbed the steps. The reporters followed. The stairway was dirty and narrow. Two people couldn't walk side by side. It was dark and they had to feel their way. Their feet slipped in the dirt lying on the stairs. The air was stagnant; there was a foul, annoyingly musty odor.

Having reached the top, the nocturnal visitors once again found themselves in front of a door.

"Open up, Jack. Got some two-bits ⟨zwei Zehncenter⟩ here." The door flew open. Jim pushed his two people inside and then slammed the door shut. Jack, who maintained the order upstairs, didn't look exactly trustworthy. He was dressed scantily, as the atmosphere here was hot and oppressive; it was permeated with all imaginable odors offensive to one's sense of smell. His wardrobe was comprised of a grimy flannel shirt ⟨Flannel-Hemd⟩ which opened at the back, old trousers and a pair of worn slippers. Jack hadn't shaved for about two weeks. Grey stubble disfigured his face. Raising a lantern reeking of petrol, he shone the pale light on the faces of the newcomers. He was of solid build and his large, dirty hands indicated that he could really get the job done if necessary.

"Ugh," he growled, "couldn't be later. Get on inside."

"Inside" was a room about ten feet by twelve feet. Plank beds had been set up along the walls, four in all, one above the other. There doubtless would have been more if the ceiling hadn't been so low. Two rows of "beds" were set up in the middle of the room. There was just enough room between the rows to enable one to squeeze through.

No windows were to be seen. The walls had assumed that undefinable color brought about by years of neglect. Two of the plank beds were empty. The others were occupied by sleeping figures.

A long, narrow corridor traversed the whole building. On each end there was a stove. Along the walls were lockers for clothing. There were about 20 feet separating the entrances to the bedrooms. Three meager, sadly flickering gas flames produced a sort of twilight. There was no trace of ventilation, as all the windows along the corridor were closed.

"Come on, let's go," growled Jack. "Get into bed and don't wake the others."

"Do you think we could be awakened in the morning?"

"Wake you? Think this's a Palmer House?[7] You'll be thrown out!"

In the bedroom there was nothing to be seen save the nearby berths just below the ceiling. These were about two feet wide and were comprised of the plank base, a straw mattress and a blanket. The bed things looked as though they had been dragged around a stockyards and then washed in the Chicago River. Rodents also made their home there, something which could be quickly ascertained.

People had to get undressed in the hall. Those already asleep had rid themselves of all their clothes. This is done to keep the latter free of vermin. But it doesn't always work.

Again someone knocked, and a beggar with a wooden leg clumped in. A wilderness of red hair sprawled around his forehead, eyes, and nose. The guard measured him with a scornful look. Whoever enters a boardinghouse has to abandon all thoughts of human dignity, because he's treated as though he belonged to some four-legged species. But the thick-skinned devils who seek refuge from the night there are not proud, either. Destiny has long since snuffed out their pride and pretension.

The one-legged man could not tip-toe very well. Jack didn't like this.

"Hey, peg leg! Keep it down," he said angrily.

The beggar said he couldn't help it.

"So, you can't, can't you? No way, huh? Well, let's just see if there's a way or not!"

Jack fell upon him and grabbed the rebel, against his will, by the collar. Despite the latter's efforts to defend himself, the next instant he was tumbling down the stairs. His wooden leg clattered and banged. The second

7. The Palmer House was Chicago's most fashionable hotel.

guard awaited him below. Without further ado he was ordered out onto the street. From above, the sound of his wooden leg could be heard clumping along the pavement.

Jack stared vacantly into the dark which had swallowed up his victim, his face a picture of self-satisfaction. "I took care'a him, all right," he said to himself. But then he turned around; he wanted to see what kind of impression he had made on his audience.

"The same'll happen to you gents if ya don't crawl into bed in a hurry."

The artist—one of the reporters did drawings—said as naturally as possible:

"I left my toothbrush downstairs; may I fetch it?"

"Ugh," growled this Cerberus, "whoever goes down, stays down!"

"Will my money be reimbursed downstairs?"

"Reimbursed? Ha, not bad!"

"I've got to get something else."

"Then go to the devil," snapped Jack. And with this he conducted the artist and the other reporter to the door.

The nocturnal wanderers gulped deep breaths of the clean night air. Behind them, like a bad dream, lay the experiences of the past half hour. Before them, with its 500 inmates, with its harshness and foul vapors, rose the poorhouse, like a huge monument to the shame of our civilization.

It was even worse in the late-night saloon at no. 44. The floor was covered with sawdust, tobacco juice, filth from the street and an assortment of other wonderful things. The air was thick enough to cut with a knife, filled with tobacco smoke, and the vapors of bad schnaps and beer. It was crowded with people who occupy the lowest rung on the social ladder.

In the so-called "Workers' Exchange," a saloon of the worst sort, there were about 200 people. Some were standing about, some had dropped onto the few available chairs. Leaning against the wall, holding a bundle which didn't look very clean, was the red-bearded beggar with the wooden leg. He appeared to have survived Jack's rough treatment without any harm to his person. Next to him was a man who looked like what our imaginations conjure up when we think of a brigand; but he could still have been an upright man, if not somewhat down on his luck. This latter was talking to a boy of about 16, who had been driven here by some cruel fate.

On the west wall, in large letters, were the words: "No loans made here."

The poor devil with the wooden leg was asked if he'd gotten his money back.

"No. And that's pretty bad for me. These days, ten cents is a real fortune. Today I had bad luck. The whole day long I only got three 'shots' and ten cents that a sympathetic person gave me on his way out of the theater. Then I was thrown out. I can't hang out on the street, either, or I'll be pulled in by the cops."

"That's pretty rough."

"Sure is. I'll stay here till I'm chased out again. I can't buy anything, 'cause I don't have any dough. Won't be long till they notice it and then it's out of the temple with me."

"And then?"

"If I can keep out of the cops' way, I'll go to some other saloon till I'm chased out again," said the philosophical beggar with the wooden leg.

"And how do you earn your keep? Do you have a trade?"

"Sure! I'm a fencing instructor. It's a lot of work."

"And for food?"

"Oh—'free lunches' ⟨Freilunch⟩ and 'please, dear lady, can't you help a cripple.' Sometimes I come up with 50 cents. I've even ended up with a dollar at the end of the day. But once in a while I don't get a single cent. Today was especially bad." And with these words, the poor devil approached a group of men drinking beer, in the hopes that they'd give him some, too.

There are a number of such boardinghouses and late-night saloons in Chicago. And just as one rotten egg resembles another, so too do they.

Wretched are the poor who frequent them. But they are not the very worst off. To find these, you have to go to the police stations ⟨Polizeistationen⟩.

39. "Voice from the People": Letter from a Homeless and Unemployed Worker (*Chicagoer Arbeiter-Zeitung,* December 23, 1884).

To the Editors of the "Arbeiter-Zeitung"

> When you've hit rock bottom,
> Well, you may as well rot,
> 'Cause the right to live, Pal,
> Is for those who've got.

No one understands the truth of these lines more bitterly than one who is without work and without shelter in these United States of America, so richly blessed by nature.

Yesterday the newspapers published a report about the sheltering of the unemployed and homeless in the police stations ⟨Polizeistationen⟩; it closed with the words: "These unfortunates were provided with warm food before leaving the station house ⟨Stationshaus⟩."

Reading these words, I could once again taste this alleged "breakfast," because in reality, neither I—who for weeks have been forced to spend my nights at the police stations ⟨Polizeistationen⟩—nor any of my companions in misfortune, have ever received anything edible at the station houses ⟨Polizeistationen⟩. With the exception perhaps of those few lucky enough to rise early, who are permitted to clean up, polish the boots of the policemen—for their services they are given something to eat.

Permit me to take this opportunity to paint a small portrait of the above-mentioned lodging rooms ⟨Logirrooms⟩.

When requesting the favor of being allowed to spend the night at a police station ⟨Polizeistation⟩, a gruff voice usually replies: "Just one night, after that we'll send you to the workhouse." Upon which the turnkey— whose callousness usually far exceeds that of the policeman—locks one into a cell.

But I specifically want to describe last night.

The station house ⟨Polizeistation⟩ on Chicago Avenue was last night's hotel for me and twenty companions in misery. After the office had approved our request, we were locked ten men to a cell, accompanied by the turnkey's usual unflattering remarks. This place is about five feet wide and seven feet long; pressed tightly together, eight men could lay their weary bodies on the cold stones. The remaining two had to spend the night standing, as there was simply not enough room for ten sturdy men to lie down. Besides which, we were forced to share this space with a number of rats and mice.

Oh, how I envied these animals. They enjoyed the privilege of entering and leaving, and of satisfying their hunger just as they pleased. After repeated requests, our turnkey consented to provide us with water, accompanied by the usual curses. Our pleas to transfer some of the men to another space, since it was impossible to sleep ten men in such an area, were answered with: "Captain's orders: 'ten men to a cell.'" Whoever wasn't satisfied would immediately be put out onto the street, and anyone who still had anything to say would be sent to the workhouse. It is easy to imagine what it's like to spend a night there when I add that these ten men were also forced to exercise their bodily functions in this cell, which naturally fouled the air. Early, at about six o'clock, the door is unlocked, and one is immediately chased out, without being given enough time to wash up. So it goes in most police stations ⟨Polizeistationen⟩, though in some of them there's more room. The only exception is the Larrabee station house ⟨Stationshaus⟩. They don't mistreat you there, or lock you up. You have the opportunity to clean and wash up, but you can only go there once, or twice at most. There are many who can attest to the truth of what I have written here.

And yet those who read this will hardly believe it when I say that nonetheless, the police station ⟨Polizeistation⟩ is our El Dorado, and one often yearns for it when, shivering with cold and fatigue, one slinks through the streets.

I assure the reader, that those who spend their nights at station houses ⟨Polizei-Stationen⟩ comprise the best elements among the so-called tramps: most still possess a sense of honor and shame, which prevents them from begging money for "lodging." For months I have been leading the sorry existence of a tramp, and would like to separate my experience of these people into three categories. The first category is that of the drinkers. Most of these are still very willing to work, but drink prevents them from keeping one job for very long and quickly drags them under. To the second category I assign those who shirk work. Drinkers are seldom found among this group: they are professional beggars, and understand and exercise this existence as their trade. They are mostly "well off," live relatively well, and know how to manipulate the public's pity. You will not find this type in the police stations ⟨Polizei-Stationen⟩; they always have enough money for "lodging," and yet they are pitiable, contemptible creatures. The third and by far largest category of tramps is made up of poor devils reduced to this state through no fault of their own. The mass of night lodgers at the station houses ⟨Polizei-Stationen⟩ derive from their ranks. They are also those who are most frequently sent to the workhouse, since the police operate under the rule that he who most frequently begs for shelter is the biggest rascal. I should probably stop here, if I still want this to appear in print. I could write volumes about so rousing a topic. Is there then no one in Chicago who will tear me away from this fate and return me to the world? I have learned things here and there in the course of my life, and am prepared to perform any work for modest wages. Most recently I was engaged in kitchen and housework. Out of consideration to my family in Germany I have borne my life here thus far; should it continue like this, I fear I will lose my mind. Should someone wish to give me work, he can obtain my address from the editors of the "Arbeiter-Zeitung."

H. B.

40. "Helpless and Deserted" (*Chicagoer Arbeiter-Zeitung,* October 17 and
    20, 1881).

Single women and girls are helpless and deserted in a large metropolis
like Chicago, slaves in the hands of the capitalists, contemptible goods to
the lechers. There is no society of good people to protect them, to feed
them, to offer them a helping hand when an inexorable fate, brought about
by the monopoly, has forced them to their knees. There is not even a
group of preachers who would welcome their souls in exchange for protection from bodily harm. The salaries paid for women's work are miserable, more than that, they are criminal. . . .

One of these poor slaves told a reporter for the "Arbeiterzeitung": I
pay $3.50 a week for room and board, fifty cents for "carfare," fifty cents
for laundry; I earn $6. The other day I had to buy some underwear, and
consequently couldn't pay my landlady. On Monday I received a card
from her in which she said: "I must insist that you pay your rent regularly,
otherwise you will be required to move out."

A few months ago a reporter visited the "Armory Police Station" ⟨Poli-
zeistation⟩ late one night. Near the station he met a policeman who was
holding a pretty, sobbing young girl by the arm.

Tom—who do you have there? asked the man of the pen.

A poor girl. She has no money for a room. I thought it best to lock
her up.

Well, we ought to be able to come up with fifty cents! And the reporter
went into the station ⟨Polizeistation⟩ waiting room, where he bantered a
professional bailsman for such a long time that the latter finally made an
offering of 75 cents to the Altar of Virtue. The reporter then accompanied
the girl to a reputable hotel on the North Side. On the way, they had the
following conversation.

Reporter: You're up and about rather late.

Girl: Yes, unfortunately. I was waiting on the corner of Lake and Clark
Streets for a girlfriend who was going to bring me fifty cents to pay for
tonight's lodging. But she didn't show up. The police picked me up instead.

What do you do?

I sew buttonholes for a German tailor on the North Side.

How many can you finish in a day?

Maybe twenty. I'm paid two cents a piece.

Don't you have a place to live?

I used to live with another girl on Sangamon St.; we paid $3 a month.

But then the slack season came along, we didn't earn anything, and the landlady threw us out.

Where did you work before that?

For a seamstress on the West Side. She gave me $5 a month plus board. When she ran out of work for me—that was in July—she gave me $10. I bought myself a shawl for $4, a pair of shoes for $2.50, and a dress for $2.

Where do you sleep?

Once, when I had no money at all, in a grocery wagon ⟨Grocery Wagen⟩ that was standing in an alley behind LaSalle St.; it rained the whole night and I got totally soaked. The next morning I went to the ladies room at the "Atheneum"[8] to get washed up, but they immediately turned me away. They told me I was getting their towels wet. Usually I sleep in one of the lodging houses ⟨Lodging Häuser⟩ on Halsted St.

Where does your family live?

In Bulinton, Wisconsin.

Why don't you go there?

My brother showed me the door as soon as I was old enough—or seemed to be—to fend for myself.

Don't you have anyone else?

Father, mother—they're all dead. I wish I were, too. We girls don't stand a chance.

Why don't you go to some institution, until you have some work again?

They won't take me in a reputable place, and I'd rather sleep on the street than together with bad women.

Have you tried the Home for the Friendless?

Yes, but they only take in old people and children . . . !

More tomorrow!

II.

In Monday's article we gave a few examples of how women are generally paid, and which dangers single female workers are exposed to in the "Christian" city of Chicago.

Surely the reader asked himself if there isn't some institution which provides shelter for the poor.

Well—yes and no! Let's read about the experiences of a girl who was forced to fall back onto such an institution.

"I came here and found a job as a clerk in a fancy goods shop for $3

8. A philanthropic institution supported by Chicago's elite, the Atheneum grew out of the Chicago Christian Union. It was known above all for its training programs and lecture series.

a week. I was living in the 'Good Samaritan Home,' where I paid $2.50 a week. I had a clean bed and was allowed to wash my things there. But in time I began to regret my lack of clothes; the other girls I worked with and the shop owner said I'd have to make more of myself. So I decided to look for a cheaper place which would allow me to spend a larger part of my salary for dress. First I turned to the 'Home for the Friendless.' But I wasn't admitted: 'You're earning a salary, you can pay for your food.'

"Then someone told me I could live at the Woman's Industrial Home on Fulton St. without having to pay much if I were prepared to work there in my free time. So I knocked on their door and was informed that I could room and board there for nothing if I wanted to help with breakfast and with washing up at night. That first night I slept on a mattress in one of the corridors; around me lay drunken women and prostitutes. There didn't seem to be any pillows or blankets.

"The next morning I had to get up at five to set two tables, wait upon the children at breakfast and sweep out the parlor. When I came back that night, I helped the maids with their ironing and couldn't retire to 'my bed' until ten. With another woman and a child, I was sent to a very dirty room; the pillow was so filthy I had to cover it with my slip. At midnight a drunken Fury entered our room, and pounced upon my spot. I abandoned it to her and spent the rest of the night sitting on a chair next to the window.

"I didn't return to the 'Home'; a bench in Lincoln Park served as my bed for the next thirty nights. — "

It was on the eighth of this past month that a young girl rang the bell at the "Christian Home."

She said to the woman at the door: "I'm a stranger here; I have neither money nor friends, and need someplace to spend the night. Could you take me in? I'll be happy to help out with the work, or pay back whatever I owe for board once I've found a job."

"We're not running a poorhouse," was the friendly reply. "You should go to the 'Working Woman's Industrial Home' instead."

"I was already there, and I have too much self-respect to stay there."

"Go to the Home for the Friendless."

"I was there, but I was told that they only take in children and the aged."

"Sorry, but we can't accommodate you."

"But you can see that it's raining; I don't have a shawl, I don't have an umbrella. Can't I just spend the night?"

"It's against our policy." —
Did you hear? It's against the principles of this institution—an institution bearing the name of charity's most noble friend—to perform charitable, Samaritan acts! Women push away members of their own sex, like mangy dogs—on principle; women put a poor, soaked girl out on the street, hungry, miserable, without money, discouraged.

Is it any wonder that this city has six official prostitutes per thousand inhabitants? People say that there is no prostitution where there are no pimps.

Just the right word! The factory owners, the rich, the legions of loafers, the instigators of child labor,—what an army of pimps—and the C h r i s - t i a n d i r e c t o r e s s e s o f C h r i s t i a n o r g a n i z a t i o n s, what a powerful confederate!

A country girl, having come to the Garden City to find work, was directed to the "Working Woman's Industrial Home"; there she was supposedly to find cheap board. We will recount the experiences she amassed during an eight-day stay there:

Board amounted to $2.50 a week, which could either be paid in cash or made up in work around the house. In the house rules there is a paragraph which reads: "Wholesome meals will be served at regular hours."

This promise wasn't kept. The cook was a woman who worked for her board; at the same time she had to care for two sick children. The quality of the meals was poor. On further inquiry, it was revealed that $1 a day was set aside for meals; that $1 was to feed ten female workers and seven children. Our female readers can well imagine how the cuisine turned out. . . .

One must not forget that this "Industrial Home" is a kind of charity institution, founded for the purpose of furnishing single working women and girls with a place to live. In the past year—besides substantial amounts of food, clothing, beds, etc.—the institution received between $2,000 and $3,000 in cash. Where is this money? Who is receiving all these foodstuffs?

We can't undertake a detailed investigation; time and space necessitate that we limit ourselves to conveying the facts. We have shown that there is ultimately no place in this large city where single women and girls can take refuge. We can only leave it up to good people to decide whether this situation should be allowed to continue permanently or not.

In New York there are numerous homes for women; there—even if seeking shelter only for one night—they don't have to worry about being heaped together with the scum of their sex, or of having to relinquish their last cent to the administration—for an act of charity! A place to sleep and breakfast cost 7 cents. Each girl receives a small locker for her belongings; there are baths and libraries.

Similar institutions are urgently needed in Chicago; a quick and definitive end should be put to the old routine slackness which prevails here. Every cent spent on the existing institutions is a cent spent in vain; and while perhaps abetting human baseness, will never find itself in the service of virtue!

As they exist today, "Homes for Single Women" are only able to produce an aversion to poorly paid work and honest endeavor.

IV. NEIGHBORHOOD AND
SOCIAL LIFE

Ethnic neighborhoods have decisively shaped the image of Chicago up to the present day. Today's immigrants come predominantly from Latin America, and to some extent from Russia, Eastern Europe, and Asia; like groups before them they congregate in neighborhoods defined most obviously by each group's characteristic stores, restaurants, and cultural institutions. During the nineteenth century Irish, German, Scandinavian, Bohemian, and Polish neighborhoods developed, into which southern and eastern Europeans moved after the turn of the century. Even when they lived dispersed in other parts of the city, members of a national group were attracted to their own distinctive ethnic neighborhoods because these areas came to represent their cultural identity and contained the institutions that made it possible to maintain at least parts of their traditional way of life. The nature and function of neighborhoods have changed significantly, however, for in the nineteenth century they were more densely populated by one group and played a greater role in everyday life than they do today.

In the second half of the nineteenth century, urban residential areas were more clearly shaped by the character of the nearby industries in which the population worked. The streetcar lines that made up the main form of public transportation permitted some geographic mobility, but not over considerable distances; and for ordinary people they were relatively costly, particularly for daily commuting. A study of Philadelphia found, for example, that in 1880 the "vast majority" of residents lived within one and a half miles of their places of work. Workers lived even closer, and the great majority of them walked to their jobs. In the last decades of the century the expansion of the mass transportation system may have contributed to a greater ethnic concentration by giving people more freedom to choose to live among their countrymen at a greater distance from work. Nevertheless the separation of work and residence so characteristic of the twentieth century was by no means so common in the nineteenth. Thus neighborhoods usually provided the geographical context in which the workers of the rapidly industrializing city acted publicly and politically, as in strikes or boycotts in which the whole neighborhood took part.

Just as important for the significance of neighborhoods, the commercial popular culture that defines the use of leisure time in the twentieth century was only in its infancy in the last third of the nineteenth. To be sure there were famous entertainment institutions with national reputations, such as the circus of P. T. Barnum; when he came to Chicago in 1884 he had to put on two performances each day to meet the demand, even though 20,000 could be seated at a time. But such events lasted only a week. The rest of the time people were left to locally based forms of leisure offered by saloonkeepers, managers of small theaters, owners of beer gardens, or more frequently by groups and associations. Thus, leisure and social activities usually took place in the neighborhoods.

This was particularly true for the Germans, who organized themselves in countless associations in the districts where they lived. The most important German neighborhoods toward the end of the nineteenth century were on the North, Northwest, and Southwest sides, located near the industrial districts that stretched along the two branches of the Chicago River. The German neighborhood on the North Side had developed since the 1840s and maintained its German character well into the twentieth century through its groceries, specialty shops, saloons, restaurants, beer gardens, churches, and Turner halls, even after it was pushed northward by the expanding city and newly arriving immigrant groups. In contrast, the Northwest and Southwest sides were more predominantly working-class districts in which there were more points of contact among the diverse ethnic groups residing in them, whether it was on the job or on the large commercial streets where stores and shops catered specifically to their working-class customers. These large commercial arteries, particularly Blue Island and Milwaukee avenues, were almost as important in determining the structure of the neighborhoods as the nearby industries or the local working-class organizations.

In this chapter we concentrate primarily on the German neighborhoods on the Northwest and North sides in order to better relate *exemplary institutions and activities to their local context. The ad-joining map is meant to provide orientation to the reader. Places of importance for some of the following documents are marked on it. The documents on social life and entertainment are not limited to these two neighborhoods, although they also illustrate how leisure activities were closely embedded in neighborhood life.*

Church and Turnverein—Two Contrasting Neighborhood Institutions

The following excerpts from the histories of the Roman Catholic Church of St. Boniface and the Aurora Turnverein document the origins and transformation of the German neighborhood on the Northwest Side. Both institutions were established in the 1860s, when the area west of the Chicago River around Milwaukee Avenue was increasingly settled by Germans. In contrast to their physical proximity—their buildings were less than a mile apart—they maintained what amounted to mutually exclusive cultural and value systems that made participation in both almost impossible, although neither was able nor wanted to prevent its members from joining other institutions as long as they supplemented its own goals. Yet certainly the claim of the church was broader than that of the Turnverein. In addition to its religious tasks, the church sought to determine the whole social life of its members and the education of their children. Like other Roman Catholic churches, as well as Lutheran parishes, St. Boniface maintained a parochial school that at the turn of the century had over 1,000 students. A thick network of social organizations were also sponsored, such as youth clubs, singing societies, and mutual benefit associations.

In contrast to St. Boniface, the Aurora Turnverein combined a regimen of physical training with the German Turner movement's traditions of political liberty, republicanism, and democracy. But while the German Turner movement as a whole became more conservative and nationalistic, a process accelerated by the founding of the German Empire in 1871, the Aurora Turnverein developed into an institution of workers and small businessmen and promoted a socialist and free-thought culture. The Aurora Turner Hall became

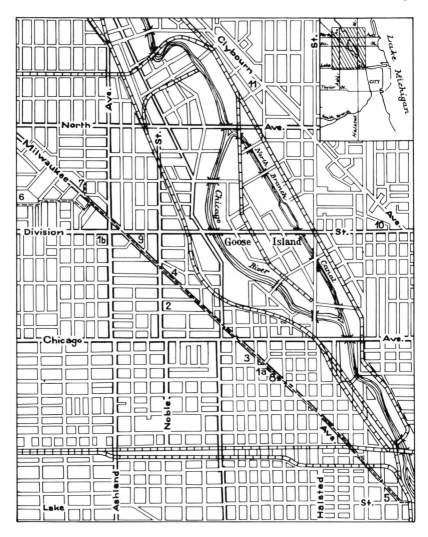

The Northwest Side and parts of the North Side, with reference to the important buildings, places, and institutions mentioned in the documents of this chapter. The key map in the upper righthand corner situates the neighborhood in the larger city. (Drawing by Karin Kunkel on the basis of A. M. Askevold's *New Guide Map of Chicago* from 1878.)

Legend:

1a. The old Aurora Turner Hall
1b. The new Aurora Turner Hall
2. St. Boniface Church
3. Odd Fellows and Masonic Hall
4. Thalia Hall
5. Greif's Hall

6. Home of August Spies
7. Home of Adolph Fischer
8. Home of George Engel
9. Home of Lucy Parsons
10. Bruschke and Co.
11. Ogden's Grove

in fact a much frequented center for the German-American left, particularly after the end of the 1870s when the Lehr- und Wehr-Verein, a self-defense organization based among Chicago's German workers, began to use the hall for its meetings. (On the Lehr- und Wehr-Verein see Chapter V, "Armed Organizations.") Moreover, meetings and performances of numerous other organizations took place in Aurora Turner Hall, whether they be lodges, singing societies, or mutual benefit associations. For years this large hall, its stage, and numerous smaller rooms provided the best quarters in the area for a multitude of functions.

Although at a different pace, the Aurora Turnverein and St. Boniface were transformed along with the area's population. By 1896 the Turnverein sought a new hall over a mile to the northwest, since the center of German settlement had shifted in that direction as increasing numbers of Poles and southern Europeans moved into the old neighborhood. St. Boniface stayed where it was, but the character of its congregation changed to reflect the new inhabitants of the parish.

41. From the History of St. Boniface Church (this document represents the original English version; Rev. F. L. Kalvelage, *The Annals of St. Boniface Parish 1862-1926* [Chicago: Schmidt Printing Co., n.d.]).

From the western bank of the Chicago River, to the city limits marked by the present Ashland Avenue there was [in the early 1860s] a vast expanse of territory sparingly covered by small frame buildings. In this area were found twenty to twenty-five families of Catholic faith. These families had migrated into this country from Germany. Their friends and relatives were arriving in this country, but only few at a time, so they had to make new associations and acquaintances. . . .

The sparsely settled district west of the Chicago River was, in the early days, a veritable swamp. The neighborhood today is marked by the elevation of the streets some ten to fifteen feet above the ground floor of homes. Sidewalks in time became level with the streets, but early in the history of this section the acclivous and declivous construction of boardwalks was indeed very evident and made walking a difficult and strenuous exercise. . . .

Elevation of the streets caused many a flood. Then, too, the growth of the neighborhood caused the sewerage system to become quickly incompatible with conditions. The pipes strung beneath the ground to take care of the overflow from rains were only half the size they should have been, and consequently floods would be the outcome.

The streets were for a time, only dirt roads. Later, we had the plank roads, such as Milwaukee Avenue, and that, planked on one side of the street only. A toll gate was to be found on Elston at Milwaukee Avenue. . . .

Owing to the hardship of travel, the Benedictine Fathers of St. Joseph's Church [located on the North Side], as an accommodation to their parishioners on the western banks of the Chicago River, established in the year sixty-two a small frame building. This one-story frame structure was really a combination building. It was because of its rolling partitions or Venetian blinds, which were a marvelous convenience easily operated, a church and school. The people of those days referred to it as the "little white school house" because it was the only seat of learning in the western section of the city. . . . The West Side district of Chicago had become in two years [after 1862] quite a settlement due unmistakably to the establishing of the mission. Now because of their growth they must expand. . . .

Of course, you recollect that the "little white school house" was located on the corner of Carpenter and Chicago Avenue and so, naturally, the tendency was to build a church near the old stamping ground and even, somewhat east of the "little white school house." The West Siders certainly were well acquainted with this portion of the city. It was very well settled, but the question arose as to the advisability of building in the midst of such a well-settled community. Experience seems to point out that the people move in the vicinity of the church and in that way give birth to a new neighborhood.

Father Kalvelage did not favor the eastward trend of a few of the committee, from Chicago Avenue and Carpenter Street and did not favor the central location either, fearing that growth might bring too much business activity and crowd out the tenants. After some consideration the committee finally agreed to erect the church on the northeast corner of Cornell and Noble Streets, the site of the present St. Boniface Church. At that time, in 1864, the city limits were Ashland Avenue which made the boundary on the west rather narrow, but it was the hope of the committee that this would surely adjust itself in later years. It was not long and the city limits stretched beyond Ashland Avenue to Western and farther as time went on and growth of this section continued. . . .

Father Phillip Albrecht [the first appointed priest] was a congenial man.

He worked up social activity in the parish. Several picnics were held under his regime. The famed old stamping ground for these festivities were the "Elston Gardens" located at Augusta and Racine Avenues. "Dieden's Garden" figures quite prominently also, as a social gathering park for the early parishioners of St. Boniface Church. The latter place of amusement was located at Elston and Division Streets.

Whenever any festivities were conducted in either of these two gardens, it meant a fifteen-hour day of gaiety. Early in the morning the children would gather about the school so as to be in readiness for the march to the park by nine o'clock. Almost to the minute, when the hands of the clock covered its numerals nine and twelve, the band would play the famed old selection: "O Susanna, wie ist das Leben doch so schoen!" which, at that time, was akin to the later-day college selection: "Hail, hail, the gang is here!"

The line of march was always led by a horseman. In Father Albrecht's time, this distinction usually came to a Mr. Anton Buettgen. His task of marshal on these occasions was taken as a serious matter and he rode his steed in true German fashion which always reflected his cavalry training in the forces of the Kaiser. Mr. Anton Buettgen was a good mixer, but when in command of his forces and under the instruction to besiege the picnic grove and destroy all that was found within that arsenal of pleasure, he acted almost like the local prohibition enforcers in a cleanup with half the agitation and publicity and a great deal more genuine satisfaction which made him beloved by all. . . .

In the first week of July, the year 1867, appears the name of Reverend James Marshall [the second pastor of St. Boniface Church]. During the remainder of that year the baptismal register points out very explicitly to the baptism of ninety-one children. This is a fair indication of how St. Boniface parish was growing. By leaps and bounds, it had increased its membership from about twenty-seven families in 1864 to at least four times that many in less than four years. . . .

Few of the outstanding qualities of Father Marshall can herewith be mentioned. He was a learned man. He spoke English, German and Polish fluently. Occasionally, he even conducted devotions in the Polish language. For at that time, the Poles were beginning to make entrance in the settlement. He was concerned about all the people of the vicinity and being a linguist was surely able to give them his personal and undivided attention. It must be remembered that St. Boniface Church was the first church in this vicinity; where now, there exists [*sic*] within an area of a square mile seven Catholic churches. . . .

[During the pastorate of Father Clement Venn, who took over as the third priest of St. Boniface in 1869 and remained for twenty-six years] . . . the people of the diocese were . . . infected by the spirit of the times and were always causing trouble for their priests. This was especially true in the German and Polish parishes, and St. Boniface was no exception. The first occasion for this strife between the new pastor and his people was as follows: A very disreputable character, a drunkard and very lax morally, having left his wife in Europe, was a member of the choir. With perfect justice Father Venn dismissed him without consulting the trustees or the officers of the St. Bonifacius Unterstuetzungs-Verein[1] which organization was especially active in opposition to Father Venn. His "high-handed" manner immediately aroused the opposition of the Unterstuetzungs-Verein, only too glad to find any pretext, and really constituted the source of all succeeding troubles. The Unterstuetzungs-Verein used to conduct many picnics, which were attended with drunkenness and excesses of every kind. In order to curb their power, Father Venn organized the St. Bonifacius Liebesbund[2] in 1874. . . . Shortly after the Liebesbund had been founded Father Venn refused to permit the old Unterstuetzungs-Verein to receive Holy Communion in a body as a Catholic society at Easter time. The reason for this action was not only because they were the source of all opposition in the parish, that their picnics and other entertainments were a scandal to the rest, but also because a great many of them came totally unprepared, some of them having failed to go to confession, or to receive absolution, others being drunk, etc. But they were determined upon their rights. One Sunday morning they formed ranks outside and started to march down the middle aisle in all their regalia. Father Venn, however, had also determined upon a showdown. He knew that he had to fight the battle here and now. So in his vestments supported by the Liebesbund and the faithful members of the parish, he marched against them. He was at the head of his army, his faithful lieutenant John Reisel with the staff of authority at his side. The clash came about the middle of the church. In the battle that followed, the Unterstuetzungs-Verein was routed, regalia, banners and all were thrown out, and from that time they started to dwindle, and never asserted themselves again. . . .

On account of his experience with the picnics of the Unterstuetzungs-Verein, Father Venn never favored picnics as a source of parish revenue. But he did have many Bazaars, which were generally held in the Northwest

1. St. Bonifacius Mutual Benefit Society.
2. St. Bonifacius Association of Love.

Hall, corner Cornell and Rose Streets, the Aurora Turner Hall, Milwaukee and Huron; one even was held downtown in the Metropolitan Block....

Father Venn was a scholar.... Unlike many other immigrant priests he immediately set himself to master the English language, and acquired great fluency in it. On account of this, he was accused by some of his parishioners of attempting to make the parish Irish. On one occasion when he read a letter from the bishop in English, some of the kickers walked out of the church saying: "Das darf man sich nicht gefallen lassen."[3]

[The Great Fire of 1871] started a new era in the growth of St. Boniface Parish. Many of those who had come over as refugees bought property and made their permanent residence here. Many of the old frame buildings still in evidence on our alleys and streets date from that time. It also meant a new era of building for the parish itself....

In 1891 the parish had increased to more than 600 families; besides his own people Father Venn took care of a great many of the parishioners of Holy Trinity Polish Church, which in consequence of the old trouble between the clergy and the laity had been closed for 18 years....

There is but one reason for the decline of St. Boniface. It was the fact that one by one with the ever-increasing impetus, the old German families were leaving the neighborhood for the more attractive outskirts of the city. The appalling rapidity of this calamity can best be visualized from the attendance in our school. In 1901 and 1902 when our school was at its best, it numbered almost 1,200 children; in 1916 there were less than 200 in spite of the fact that almost half of these 200 were children from the neighboring Slovak parish, which just then was building its own school. The exodus of the Germans was caused by successive waves of migration. The new arrivals were a mixture of Jew and Polish. The Jewish migration, however, which was so strong for a few years, that almost 80% of the public school attendance was of Jewish children, passed its peak in 1913 and 1915. After that the neighborhood became almost purely Catholic Polish. In his efforts to keep his own people clustered about the church, Father Evers used every promising means to make this neighborhood attractive. He worked for pavement of the streets and alleys, for proper lighting of the streets, for sewers and the best sanitation, and finally he was chiefly instrumental in having the ten acres now composing Eckert Park, which really should be called Evers Park, condemned for park purposes. For years property ads were run in every issue of the Pfarrbote; but all these efforts well directed as they were, were in vain.

3. "We don't have to put up with this."

42. "The Aurora Turnverein" (*Der Westen: Frauen-Zeitung,* November 15 and 22, 1896).

The "A u r o r a   T u r n v e r e i n," situated on the Northwest Side, is the second-oldest existing Turnverein in Chicago. Today it is looking back on a varied and eventful thirty-two-year past. . . .

In the fall of 1863 several members of Chicago's Turner community tried to create a new Turnverein on the Northwest Side. The members of the "Aurora" social club, which was in the process of being dissolved, furnished a welcome base for their plan. Following successful agitation, the "A u r o r a   T u r n v e r e i n" was founded on February 22 (Washington's birthday), 1864. . . .

At the beginning, the Aurora Turnverein was lodged in N i e m e y e r ' s H a l l, No. 113 Milwaukee Avenue, where the Concordia Hall is today. . . . Originally there were 28 members, all but two of whom were active Turners. . . .

Due to the Verein's rapid progress, the hall soon proved too small, and the Verein was thus forced to look around for another location. Since it couldn't readily find anything suitable, the members decided, on May 13, 1867, to build their o w n   h a l l, an undertaking which the Verein would later often regret. Non-interest-bearing shares were issued at $25 each, and every member was obligated to buy at least one share. Then the people living on the Northwest Side were approached, and they in turn became very interested in the project, as every section of the city desired a large hall. Thus by August, 1867, $9,000 had been pledged. The Verein's capital at that time came to $4,000; there were 93 members; and 34 pupils were attending the Turner school. With this base the Verein felt it could dare undertake construction and purchased property on Milwaukee Avenue and Second — Huron Street — valued at $7,500. . . . On October 10, 1867, with the appropriate festivities, all Chicago's Turner societies as well as many other clubs and lodges participated in laying the h a l l ' s   c o r n e r - s t o n e. . . .

On June 1, 1868, the Verein moved to the new hall, where, in the meantime, only the Turn area was ready for use. Although construction was not completely finished, the d e d i c a t i o n   c e r e m o n i e s — preceded by an imposing parade — took place on June 29. Among the enthusiastic participants were the Turner societies, singing societies and social clubs, lodges and local residents — a festival the likes of which had never been seen on the Northwest Side. The program was made up of Turn exhibitions, presentations by guest singing societies, speeches, etc. . . .

The Verein was soon in a position to rent out the new hall to other societies on days when it wasn't being used by "Aurora" members, for instance to the newly founded "Norwegian Turnverein," with which the "Aurora" is on the best of terms to this very day. . . .

By the time they had moved in on June 1, the a d m i n i s t r a t i o n of the new hall had already been entrusted to Turner Lang. The executive management, however, lay in the hands of the administrative council, comprised of 25 members, half of them Turners, half local residents. . . .

On March 28, 1869, the Aurora Turnverein was legally incorporated. . . .

In March, 1875, the dramatic section began presenting regular German theater performances in the Aurora Turner Hall, and for a time these drew large audiences. The m a s k e d b a l l s which the Aurora Turnverein had been organizing for several years, as well as the so-called shareholders balls, used to be the events of the season on the Northwest Side, drawing many people from other parts of the city as well. But most of the profits from these delightful festivities were consumed by the hall. That the Verein, despite the costly administration, was able to stay above water at all was primarily thanks to the active Turners. These Turners, aside from being responsible for most committee obligations, threw themselves into the breach at every occasion to make the hall popular. At festivities sponsored by other societies, they set up human pyramids, tableaux vivants, marble statues, etc. . . .

But the crisis was not to be held at bay. The hall's income became ever smaller. . . .

When finally the Verein's debts had climbed to $22,905, there was no way out save transferring all its possessions — with the exception of the Turn equipment, its library, flags and pictures — to the banker Bühler against the above sum. The members had abandoned the Verein like rats on a sinking ship. There remained but 28 Turners, not counting the honorary members. . . .

In July, 1877, a delegation from the Furniture Workers Union called on the Verein and asked for financial and moral support in their case against the Chicago police. . . . The facts are as follows: in July, 1877, the Furniture Workers Union called a mass meeting in the Vorwärts Turner Hall to organize workers; it was at the time of the so-called July strike. The meeting had already been adjourned, only the elected union delegates ⟨Unionleute⟩ were still present, when several of the policemen stationed outside the hall were stoned by a group of juveniles. The police pursued the fleeing boys into the meeting room, and, using their clubs, brutally attacked the union people ⟨Unionleute⟩. They drove them from the hall, despite the fact that it had been rented by the union. This act of violence ended in the death of one of the furniture workers, a certain Teßmann, who was shot by Officer Householder. As is known, Judge McAllister stated in his decision that the men would have had the right to kill the police.

The "Aurora" elected not only to declare itself in full sympathy with the ideas of the Furniture Workers Union, but to ensure its moral support, and further, to take up a collection on the union's behalf.

At a meeting held on September 12, 1877, the Verein elected to scratch all of the so-called "honorary members" from the list, as the Verein had received no support from them in times of need. Since that time, "prominent" members have found it very difficult to establish roots in the Aurora T.V. . . . In addition, this meeting saw membership fees lowered from $5 to $2. Turner Fritz Leusch assumed direction of the boys' and girls' classes which were set up anew; and on December 5, 1877, in the General Assembly, it was decided to reintroduce benefits for the sick, primarily in order to attract new members. The "Lehr- und Wehr-Verein,"[4] already established some time before, rented the lower rooms for several days a week and from the outset had its headquarters in the Aurora Turner Hall. In addition, the Turn area was once again put at the disposal of the "Norwegian Turnverein" for single days of the week.

Though the evening festivities held on the occasion of the Verein's reorganization only yielded $30, the subsequent masked ball in February 1878 resulted in profits of $227, proof that the residents of the Northwest Side sympathized with the Verein. . . .

It was also at this time that the Verein elected to make Marine blue the color of the Turners' outfits, as well as to discontinue the "Zukunft"[5] which had been the Verein's journal to that point, and instead to make available subscription lists for the "Freidenker."[6] . . .

On November 6, 1878, a women's section was established which bore the name, "A u r o r a   W o m e n ' s   V e r e i n." The excellent services provided by the women's section greatly contributed to the expansion of the Turn School as well as to the success of the festivities. Especially when it came to distributing gifts to the pupils at Christmas, the women's section soon proved indispensable. . . . At the first joint meeting on December 31, 1878, Turner Fritz Leusch held a lecture on the "Eight Hour Law" and Turner Peter Ellert on "Women's Suffrage." Among the well-known men

4. See the introduction to Documents 70 and 71.
5. Future.
6. Freethinker.

admitted to the Verein around this time were Paul Grottkau,[7] Frank A. Stauber,[8] and Hermann Knoke. The Aurora Turnverein also took active part in the Commune Festival of the Socialist Labor party held on March 22, 1879, in the Exhibition Building. . . .

On January 6, 1880, the "Aurora" held — as did other Turner societies — a Turn show on behalf of the linen weavers suffering in Silesia and Thuringia. The festival yielded a net profit of $250, which was turned over to the Relief Committee of the German Turners.

On May 19, 1880, the P u p i l s   V e r e i n, comprised of boys ranging from 14 to 18 years old, was founded. It was conceived as a sort of preschool for the Verein. Each year a number of its members, having reached their eighteenth year, are in the habit of joining the Turnverein. The Pupils Verein serves to familiarize young German-Americans with the Turnverein and in this way preserve the German language and German customs. The head of the Pupils Verein is an able and reliable Turner who is appointed by the Verein's president. The founding of the Pupils Verein was followed in October by the establishment of a W o m e n s   T u r n   C l a s s which, although initially hindered by all sorts of petty and prudish "moral misgivings," soon overcame these prejudices and made encouraging progress, receiving third prize at the District Turners Festival in Elgin.

On September 29, 1880, the Verein elected to reinstate a d r a m a t i c   s e c t i o n. Various members took part, but after the presentation of a few plays the project petered out due to a lack of interest. The considerable effort invested in the library in 1880 can primarily be attributed to the administrative capabilities of former librarian, Turner H. K n o k e. A d e b a t i n g   s e c t i o n was also formed in this year, meeting once a week in the rooms of one of the members. When his turn came, each member was required to hold a lecture, which was subsequently opened for debate; the number of members reached 25. . . .

At the national conventions of the N o r t h   A m e r i c a n   T u r n e r   B u n d, the delegates ⟨Delegaten⟩ of the Aurora T.V. were always on the "extreme left," with the exception of the Pittsburgh convention where, as instructed, they worked against the introduction of women's suffrage. Especially with respect to labor questions, the Verein was almost always strictly radical. It was on friendly terms with workers' organizations, and received so many invitations to picnics, balls and other festivities that it finally decided not to take part in any more non-Turner marches. There

7. See the biographical sketches at the end of this volume.
8. See the biographical sketches at the end of this volume.

were also Turner outings each year—in the Pupils Verein, too—and these always offered an abundance of entertainment. . . .

On January 15, 1883, the Aurora T.V. organized a Turn show for the benefit of the R h i n e f l o o d v i c t i m s and made a notable profit of $300. To this sum another $100 was added from the Verein treasury, and the total was then sent to Wilhelm Liebknecht,[9] a member of the German Reichstag, for distribution.

As had already been the case earlier, when it interceded for the preservation of G e r m a n c l a s s e s in the public schools by calling a mass rally, the Verein decided, on May 10, 1883, to agitate for the introduction of T u r n c l a s s e s in the curriculum. And as is now well known, the Turners of the district—through meetings, petitions, etc.—succeeded in attaining their goal.

After 1877, members of the Aurora T.V. were mostly workers or liberal-minded small businessmen who sought to further the l a b o r m o v e - m e n t to whatever extent possible. They took the part of their struggling brothers at shutdowns, lockouts, etc., and barred nonunion products from festivities. Each member was obligated to support organized labor as much as possible, a stance which was subsequently adopted as one of the principles of the North American Turner Bund.

In 1881, Mssrs. F r i t z s c h e and V i e r e c k[10] were sent to the United States by a Congress of the German Social Democracy, and while in Chicago they held lectures. The Aurora T.V. elected to help further their endeavors to the greatest possible extent by participating in corpore at the mass meeting which took place on March 17. For its informal educational get-togethers, the Verein showed a preference for freethinking or otherwise progressively inclined speakers. . . .

At this time the Aurora T.V. enrolled in the T u r n e r L i f e I n s u r - a n c e P l a n, which had just been founded in Milwaukee. . . .

The Turners showed extreme interest in the informal educational get-togethers and regularly scheduled evening debates. Attendance was high, and members generally acquainted themselves with books from the library pertaining to the topics under discussion so as to be able to join in the debates. The singing society also played a large role in bringing fresh life

9. Wilhelm Liebknecht was one of the most important leaders of the German Socialist Labor party.

10. Fritzsche and Viereck were members of the German Reichstag for the Socialist Labor party. They came to America primarily to solicit financial support for the Reichstag elections. In the same year Fritzsche emigrated to Philadelphia. Viereck emigrated to the U.S. several years later.

Opened in 1868, the Aurora Turner Hall on Milwaukee Avenue was the center for meetings and performances in the German neighborhood on the Northwest Side into the 1890s. (*Der Westen,* November 15, 1896.)

to club meetings. The Education Committee was comprised of Turners August Spies,[11] Wilhelm Legner and Hermann Knoke, the best representatives of those different viewpoints found in the Verein. The liveliness of this period was reflected in the Verein's numerous picnics, entertainment evenings, Turn exhibitions, parties for the pupils, and the masked balls which once again regained the importance they had formerly had. Socially, these years thus represented the high point in the history of the Aurora Turnverein. On January 1, 1884, membership had reached 240, and 360 children — 100 girls among them — were attending the Turn school. . . .

11. See the biographical sketches at the end of this volume.

A Turn class at a German Turnverein in the mid 1880s. (Chicago Historical Society, ICHi-14858.)

Because of the large run on the library, the Verein determined, on April 21, 1884, to rent and furnish two rooms to be used as l i b r a r y   a n d r e a d i n g   r o o m s. A library for Turn pupils was founded on September 20; suitable books and other reading material were acquired, and this not only attracted young people, but also helped in furthering the German language. In order to ensure that unmarried members were cared for in times of illness, an agreement was reached on January 1, 1885, with the Alexian Brothers Hospital whereby sick members would be cared for in a suitable manner for $5 a week. . . .

The years 1886 and 1887 brought on a battle for the Aurora Turnverein which, threatening its very survival, called forth all the Verein's latent powers. T h e   l a b o r   m o v e m e n t, fighting for the eight-hour day, called upon all the different groups in the population. As already stated, the Aurora Turnverein had always sympathized strongly with workers' organizations, and it now reacted to the situation accordingly. Following the large number of strikes and lockouts on May 1, 1886, and the subsequent shooting of several workers at McCormick's Harvesting Machine Plant on May 3, agitation among the workers reached its peak. . . . Numerous mass protest rallies were called. At one of these, which took place at the "Haymarket" on the evening of May 4, 1886, several Turners held speeches, among them A u g u s t S p i e s, a prominent member of the Aurora Turnverein. Later during the meeting, a police division from the Desplaines Street Station appeared on the scene to disperse the rally, and that was when the fateful b o m b w a s t h r o w n, causing death and destruction.

Charged with inciting to murder, Turner August Spies was arrested the following day. Since he didn't even have the means to pay for his defense, his friends organized a collection. Many members of the Aurora Turnverein also expressed the desire that the Verein allocate a sum for the d e f e n s e f u n d, because Turner Spies, especially at the informal educational get-togethers, had done the Verein a great service, winning the love of those who shared his opinions and the respect of his opponents. The question was brought to the floor at a meeting on May 19, and after the majority had voted to allocate $100 for the defense fund, 28 members who had opposed the decision resigned their membership. Among them were several able members who had worked for the Verein with enthusiasm and love. But the majority felt themselves bound by honor to stand by a member in need of support. With banners waving, the 28 recently resigned members marched off to the accompaniment of band music. They later founded the C e n t r a l T u r n v e r e i n. . . .

Within the Verein itself, all these events created a considerable stir, inciting a heated discussion as to whether or not the Verein a s s u c h — even if the individual members disapproved of the charges brought against Turner Spies — should be involved in raising money for a defense fund. The meetings were always very well attended, both sides giving their best efforts. The "reds" finally got hold of the field, and thereafter Verein meetings were placed under police surveillance. Thanks to the skill of the Verein's leaders and the political training the members had had, the Turners managed to refrain from reacting to this provocation; cool heads prevailed despite the fact that the Verein had to put up with this unrequested "police protection" until well into 1888. . . .

When on November 11, 1887, despite all endeavors to save him, August Spies was executed, the Aurora Turnverein — upon request of Spies's relatives — assumed responsibility for the f u n e r a l c e r e m o n i e s. On November 13, in the presence of a large part of the Turner community, the body was sent to Waldheim [Cemetery]. The A.T.V. was represented in the procession by 250 Turners. On November 23, 1887, the Verein determined to send the mother of the deceased a letter of condolence. And where the Turners had previously raised a considerable sum of money for the defense fund, the "Aurora" now joined with the "P i o n e e r A i d a n d S u p p o r t A s s o c i a t i o n" in its commitment to look after the survivors who had been robbed of their breadwinners through the executions. . . .

Just as it had collected a considerable sum for its erection by way of fund-raising lists, the Verein also participated "in corpore" at the u n - v e i l i n g o f t h e m o n u m e n t in honor of the executed anarchists in Waldheim. . . .

Toward the end of the year, the members' desire to move out of the old hall was once again expressed with so much vehemence that something decisive had to be done. But as the means to build its own hall were lacking, there was no other alternative than r e n t i n g a n e w h a l l. . . . A committee was then formed to contact the owners of the A s h l a n d H a l l on Ashland Avenue and Division Street. . . . The i n a u g u r a t i o n o f t h e n e w h a l l occurred on May 10 of that year. With few exceptions, all of the district Turner societies took part, not only in the inaugural ceremony but also in the accompanying parade and in the Turn exhibition in Schönhofen's large hall, which was rented for the occasion because of its space. . . .

After having reached 527 in June 1890, membership in the Verein, for various reasons, began to decrease again. One of the most decisive factors had to do with the generally hard times, the unemployment among many of the members, who, no longer able to live up to all of their obligations, resigned. This was also the case in other Turner societies. . . .

When in 1891 the n a t i v i s t s tried to force the public schools to do away with G e r m a n c l a s s e s—and instead to introduce the Bible as a textbook—Chicago's Turners made a stand against this venture by holding protest rallies and by petition actions which resulted in 70,000 signatures. Whenever it was a question of striking back at the nativists and bigoted pietists for their attacks on personal freedom, the Aurora T.V. was seen to stand at the head of the liberal-minded on the Northwest Side. Turner Landau, representative of the Aurora T.V. in the district committee, worked with all his might to see that the authorized petition was successful with the school committee. The A.T.V. alone wasted no time in amassing 4,000 signatures. . . .

Aside from participating in the sorts of festivities mentioned above, each year in October and May the Aurora Turnverein organizes a Turn exhibition, as well as annual Christmas Turn exhibitions with gifts for the pupils, trips in the summer, basket picnics, glee club concerts, carnivals, and masked balls, parties for the Turn pupils, etc. The Verein is always happy to have the active support of the residents of the Northwest Side.

The Verein sent resolutions to the appropriate officials in favor of the so-called "C h i l d   L a b o r   B i l l" in April 1895, after Mrs. Florence Kelley, the Factory Inspector, spoke at the convention of the Chicago Turner district, and explained the bill and its consequences. . . .

The Verein soon became more lively following its move into the new hall. Instead of decreasing from month to month, the Verein can now confirm an increase in membership. Attendance at meetings is better, and—as is proper—the Turner hall has once again become the Turners' headquarters.

Milwaukee Avenue as a Center for Transportation, Business, and Entertainment on the Northwest Side

The First Public Transportation

Originally providing the only access to the city from the northwest, Milwaukee Avenue developed early into the main street of the rapidly expanding Northwest Side. Cutting diagonally through the area, the street became its commercial and transportation artery, as well as its entertainment center. Local businessmen promoted the advantages of their thoroughfare in order to attract new stores and customers: in 1875 they published a street guide which in addition to including advertisements described important stores and firms and contained a list of the street's inhabitants. The guide announced with pride that the new private omnibus line was "one of the institutions of the avenue." Later these horse-drawn cars were replaced by cable cars, which in turn gave way to an electric street railway; in the process the whole system was extended into a dense transportation network. Privately owned and primarily run for profit rather than for meeting the citizens' needs, the mass transportation system was associated throughout the era with corruption and political patronage. The expansion of the system, the quality of service, and the amount of the fare appeared repeatedly as volatile issues in city politics.

43. Advertisement for the Citizens' Omnibus Line (this document represents the original English version; *Holland's Directory of Milwaukee Avenue* [Chicago, 1875]; photo Chicago Historical Society, ICHi-17612).

(*See p. 171.*)

This omnibus line is one of the *institutions* of the avenue and can boast of being one of the largest bus lines in the city. Mr. A. Steinhaus, its founder and present able general superintendent, is determined to spare no pains or expense to make it the BEST LINE in Chicago. They have an immense barn and buildings contiguous, which are used as harness shop, blacksmith shop, coach factory &c. They make all their own buses, do all repairing, horseshoeing, &c., on the premises; have 26 buses and over 200 head of good horses. Mr. S assures us buses and horses shall be increased from time to time as necessity demands. Everyone should patronize the Citizen's Omnibus Line. General offices room 40, Metropolitan Block, corner LaSalle and Randolph sts. Hon. E. F. Runyan, Secretary and Treasurer. Barn and factories Nos. 1053 to 1059 Milwaukee Avenue. A. Steinhaus, general superintendent, office 1055 Milwaukee Avenue.

Stores and Businesses

By the 1870s a multitude of businesses, stores, meeting halls, artisan shops, and saloons had been established along Milwaukee Avenue. The nature, number, and variety of these establishments is apparent from the following list based on Holland's Directory of Milwaukee Avenue *of 1875:*

Saloons	110	*Dress Makers*	7
Grocers	40	*Harness Makers*	7
Boots & Shoes	36	*Hotels*	7
Butchers	24	*Photographers*	7
Clothiers	24	*Tinsmiths*	7
Tobacconists	21	*Notaries Public*	6
Dry Goods	19	*Stationers*	6
Physicians	18	*Billiard Halls*	5
Bakeries	15	*Plumbers*	5
Barbers	15	*Shirt Manufacturers*	5
Flour & Feed	15	*Tailors*	5
Notions	14	*Dentists*	4
Druggists	13	*Midwives*	4
Crockery	12	*News Depots*	4

Furniture	12	Restaurants	4
Hardware	12	Shoemakers	4
Milliners	11	Undertakers	4
Jewelers	10	Wagonmakers	4
Coal Yards	8	Banks	3
Coppersmiths	8	Boarding Houses	3
Real Estate Dealers	8	Painters	3
Blacksmiths	7		

Businesses that appeared only one or two times were not included in this list. The great majority of these establishments were packed along only one mile of the street.

Among the illustrations included here, A. C. Lausten's three-story brick building represents the more prosperous businesses on Milwaukee Avenue which in the 1870s stood out over the more numerous frame buildings depicted by Thalia Hall. Containing numerous Americanisms, the Co-operative Department Store's ad from 1903 possibly reminded the neighborhood's numerous working-class consumers of European models of consumer cooperatives.

Women were of course most involved in the daily routine of shopping. The butchers, bakers, and milk dealers along Milwaukee Avenue not only provided for their families' material needs but also formed a central meeting ground where friendships were kept up and information exchanged. The commercial street thus contributed to a communications network that helped define the neighborhood as a community.

44. Advertisement for A. C. Lausten & Co. (*Holland's Directory of Milwaukee Avenue* [Chicago, 1875]; photo Chicago Historical Society, ICHi-17611).

(See p. 173.)

45. Advertisement for the Milwaukee Avenue Co-operative Store (*Chicagoer Arbeiter-Zeitung*, March 27, 1903).

(See p. 174.)

Meeting Halls and Working-Class Saloons

The public halls on Milwaukee Avenue were centers of social life and meeting places for the clubs and lodges of the whole district. The Odd Fellows and Masonic Hall, like the Aurora Turner Hall, had an imposing appearance that visually expressed the relatively high status enjoyed by the members of the two fraternal orders that built it. Well into the twentieth century such fraternal orders — as well as mutual benefit societies organized along ethnic, trade, and sometimes class lines — provided both insurance against sickness and death as well as, in some cases, support in old age. This primary function of fraternal orders is illustrated by the excerpts from the constitution and bylaws of the Robert Blum Lodge of the Odd Fellows, which was organized as early as 1849. It was mainly because they provided some kind of social insurance that such lodges spread rapidly among German immigrants.

Although by no means outwardly as impressive, Thalia Hall, a saloon with meeting rooms, was just as frequently used by groups and organizations. It served as the regular meeting place of other lodges of the Northwest Side, like the Harugari and Sons of Hermann, whose memberships were composed largely of workers and small businessmen. In addition, the section of the Socialist Labor party on the Northwest Side and later the groups of the International Working People's Association chose Thalia Hall for their meetings.

The manifold uses of such halls are illustrated by the interior plan of Greif's Hall and the interior view of Neff's Hall. Located near the center of the transportation network and in the heart of the industrial district on the Near West Side, Greif's Hall was the most important meeting place for German workers from the late 1870s to the end of the century. Numerous German unions met there, as did their citywide organization, the Central Labor Union. Greif's Hall was also the scene of attacks by the police on two labor meetings in 1891, an incident that is described in Document 123 in Chapter VII. This document mentions the meetings of two labor organizations taking place at the same time in the hall and contains references to how the hall was set up. A sketch of the interior of Neff's Hall on the North Side gives more vivid detail. Groups regularly meeting in these halls often stored their business records in them, and their rooms were decorated with symbols of the German labor movement and working-class life.

46. Odd Fellows and Masonic Hall on Milwaukee Avenue (*Holland's Directory of Milwaukee Avenue* [Chicago, 1875]; photo Chicago Historical Society, ICHi-17613).

(*See p. 177.*)

47. Constitution and Bylaws of the Robert Blum Lodge, No. 58 of the Order of the Odd Fellows (*Constitution und Nebengesetze der Robert-Blum-Loge No. 58 des unabhängigen Ordens der Sonderbaren Brüder des Staates Illinois, welche ihren Sitz in der Stadt Chicago hat, und im Oktober 1849 von der Groß-Loge des Staates Illinois verbrieft wurde.* [Chicago, Ill.: Gedruckt bei Kriege u. Höffgen, 1849]).

Preamble.

The Odd Fellows are . . . a society united in a holy and indivisible bond, comprised of true friends and brothers who are bound—to the extent that honor, duty and conscience allow—to stand by one another in good times as in bad times, to support those in need, to rush to the aid of the sick, to care for the widows and orphans of their deceased brothers, and to do everything in their power to give these latter advice and protection.

To do good deeds may be considered to be and should be recognized as the sole intention of the Odd Fellows, and Friendship, Love and Fidelity their motto. . . .

Constitution.

. . . .

Article 2: Concerning the Members.

§1. The candidate is to believe in an Absolute Being, in a Creator, Preserver and Governor of the Universe; he is to have reached his twenty-first year; he is to be a white male of sturdy moral character; he is to be industrious, able to prove an honorable means of earning his livelihood, and free of all shortcomings which could hinder him from earning his living.

. . . .

Article 5: Concerning Contributions and Support.

§1. No one is to be admitted to the Lodge for a sum of less than five dollars.

§2. No rank is to be awarded for a sum of less than two dollars.

§3. Regular contributions to the Lodge Fund are to amount to no less than 6¼ cents per week and to be determined by the bylaws.

§4. By means of bylaws, the Lodge may call for further contributions

for an educational fund, a widows and orphans fund, for burials—either for all of these purposes or individually, as prescribed by the Lodge.

§5. In the case of sickness or poor health, each member who is so entitled according to the bylaws is to receive a weekly allowance from the Lodge Fund, the sum of which is to be determined by the bylaws and not to be less than three dollars if the scarlet degree has been reached or less than two if it has not.

§6. In the case of the death of a Brother entitled to support, the Lodge is to pay a sum of not less than twenty dollars in the form of a burial allowance, which is to be used as determined by the Lodge.

§7. At the death of the wife of a Brother entitled to support, the latter is to receive a sum of not less than ten dollars to help cover burial fees.

....

Bylaws.
Article 1: Language.
All of the Lodge's business and proceedings are to be transacted in the German language, and no proposals to change the business language are to be considered as long as there are five members in this Lodge who still possess a good knowledge of the German language and who desire to retain it.

....

Article 5: Committees ⟨Committeen⟩.
§1. The permanent committees ⟨Committeen⟩ consist of an Administrative Committee (Trustees), a Finance Committee, a Committee for the Sick, a Committee for Widows and Orphans, and a Correspondence Committee.

....

§4. The Committee for the Sick is to be comprised of the president, the vice-president, the treasurer, and four Brothers whose names are to follow alphabetically. It is their duty to visit sick Lodge members living in the city of Chicago at least once a week and to report to the Lodge on their condition at each of the regularly scheduled meetings. . . .

§5. Each year at the first meeting in July, the president is to appoint a Committee for Widows and Orphans made up of three members to serve for one year. It is their duty to visit the widows and orphans of deceased Brothers of this Lodge from time to time and to report to the Lodge on their findings.

....

Article 7: Benefit Recipients.
§1. Any Brother who has been a member of this Lodge for three months and who, due to sickness or accident, becomes unable to earn his living, is to receive a weekly allowance amounting to $4, and should he have

reached the scarlet degree, is entitled to $5 for the duration of his sickness or inability, provided that this sickness or inability has not been brought about by his own immoral actions, and that the Brother has not forfeited his claim by having violated any of these bylaws.

....

§3. In the case of the death of any Brother who is no more than four months behind in payments, a sum of thirty dollars is to be allotted for burial costs and paid to his widow or next of kin living anywhere in the United States.

§4. Should a Brother die in the city of Chicago, the president and vice-president are responsible for extending the last worldly tributes in a proper and solemn manner, and the secretary is responsible for inviting all the members to the funeral ceremony.

§5. Should the deceased not be survived by family or relatives in the city, a committee comprised of three members is to ensure that his effects, or an equivalent sum, be sent to the proper heirs, and to give an exact account to the Lodge.

§6. In the case of the demise of a wife of a Brother who is entitled to benefits, this latter is to receive a sum of fifteen dollars from the Lodge to cover burial costs.

§7. Should a Brother from this or another Lodge, finding himself in necessitous circumstances, apply for assistance, a committee of three is to be appointed to make inquiries into his situation and to report their findings to the Lodge; should the Lodge find the applicant worthy of assistance, the latter will be accorded a sum from the relief fund as deemed appropriate by the Lodge and in keeeping with its financial resources; in no case, however, will it surpass four dollars.

§8. Widows and orphans surviving Brothers of this Lodge who find themselves in need and who qualify according to the laws, are entitled to assistance appropriate to the circumstances as determined by the Lodge.

48. **Exterior View of Thalia Hall, Interior Plan of Greif's Hall, and Inner View of Neff's Hall (Michael J. Schaack, *Anarchy and Anarchists* [Chicago, 1889]).**

(*See pp. 180-82.*)

Together these different views of three German taverns give one a good impression of typical working-class saloons and meeting halls.

THALIA HALL.
From a Photograph.

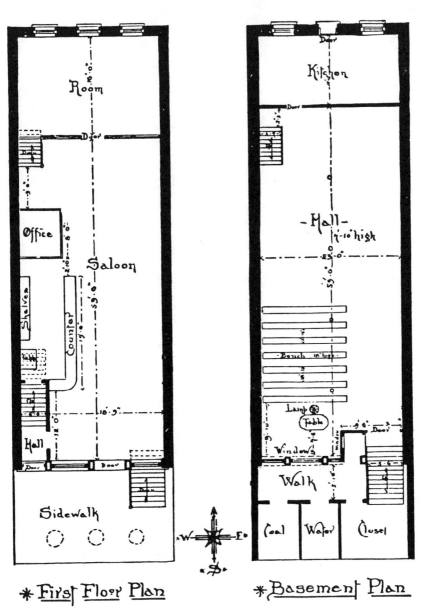

INTERIOR PLAN OF GREIF'S HALL.

INTERIOR VIEW OF NEFF'S HALL.

Neighborhood Solidarity I: A Collection for the Victims of a Flood Disaster in Germany

Special occasions are required to illustrate neighborhood solidarity, since it was so much a part of everyday life that it was taken for granted and seldom documented. A disastrous flood on the Rhine and Danube in the winter of 1882-83 led to a massive collection of funds among the Germans of Chicago. Initiated by the Chicago Turngemeinde, volunteers with subscription lists were sent to all parts of the city asking for money. The socialists took part in this collection, although they offered people the option of giving to a fund organized by the Chicagoer Arbeiter-Zeitung. *This fund would go to Wilhelm Liebknecht, one of the major leaders of the German Social Democratic party, since the socialists trusted him more than the official authorities* to get the money directly and quickly to the people who needed it most. The Northwest Side was the center of this special socialist collection.

Excerpts from reports about the effort, which lasted for several weeks, are reprinted here. The Arbeiter-Zeitung *noted with special pride how many clubs and associations preferred to trust it with their money. It saw in their activities proof of the predominantly working-class character of their memberships, of their confidence in Chicago's socialists, and of their sympathy for the German Social Democrats. The Aurora Turnverein gave the largest sum—the proceeds of a special masked ball held for the purpose supplemented by some of the association's own funds.*

The success of the separate socialist effort aroused the ire of the editor of the Chicagoer Freie Presse, *Richard Michaelis, who initiated a smear campaign against the socialists and the chief organizer of their collection on the Northwest Side, Frank Stauber. Michaelis accused Stauber, who had served as the socialist alderman from the Fourteenth Ward in the late 1870s and early 1880s, of putting all the money he collected in the socialist fund without the knowledge and against the will of the contributors, although the socialists were supposed to give people a choice. Despite the fact that several businessmen, like the well-established baker Voltz, refused to contribute to the socialists' list, the reaction to Michaelis's attack revealed substantial support for the socialists among the local businessmen. Their sympathy cannot be seen as simply an opportunistic bow to the politics of their customers. Rather this support is an example of how closely entwined were the institutions, culture, and politics of the local working and lower middle classes. Stauber himself owned a hardware store, and other businessmen on Milwaukee Avenue had most likely once been skilled workers themselves who frequently still maintained radical-democratic and free-thought traditions, which made them more open to Social Democratic demands.*

49. "Over $2,000 for the Proletariat Living in Flooded Districts" (*Chicagoer Arbeiter-Zeitung*, January 28, 1883).

Over $2,000 has already been turned in to the office of the "Arbeiter-Zeitung" on behalf of the proletariat living in flooded districts in Germany. Of this sum, $1,632, or 6,800 German Reichsmark, have already been dispatched telegraphically to the socialist member of the Reichstag, W. Liebknecht, for distribution among the distressed proletariat in the flooded districts. . . .

Dispatched Funds.

By way of the banking house of Mssrs. Felsenthal & Kozminski, the "Arbeiter-Zeitung" has telegraphically dispatched the following sums to Mr. Wm. Liebknecht:

On January 11, $192 =   800 Marks
On January 17, $240 = 1,000 Marks
On January 23, $480 = 2,000 Marks
On January 25, $720 = 3,000 Marks

    Total   **$1,632 = 6,800** Marks

Other collections, initiated by the Turner societies, have amounted to almost $25,000. From this sum, 80,000 Marks have already been dispatched to Mr. Kapp in Berlin.

It is noteworthy that no fewer than **22 German societies and lodges** have entrusted the "A r b e i t e r - Z e i t u n g" with contributions of $10 to $100 to be sent to Mr. Liebknecht. Proof that most of Chicago's societies and lodges are inspired with a progressive and liberal-minded spirit.

By giving their contributions to the "Arbeiter-Zeitung" to send to a socialist in Germany, **twenty-two** German societies and lodges, which, estimated conservatively, represent members totaling 5,000 men, have thus declared that they place more trust in a socialist than in the whole government and priestly clique in Germany. Three cheers for these societies and lodges!

50. List of Lodges and Societies Contributing to the Flood Victims (*Chicagoer Arbeiter-Zeitung*, February 11, 1883).

The following is a list of those lodges and societies which have entrusted the "Arbeiter-Zeitung" to forward their contributions to Mr. Liebknecht:

Aurora Turnverein 431.40
Harmonia Grove U.A.O.D.[12] 20.00
Central Committee S.L.P.[13] 10.00
North Side Social Club 10.00

12. United Ancient Order of Druids.
13. Socialist Labor party.

William Tell Lodge No. 194 D.O.H.[14] 25.00
West Chicago Grove No. 18 U.A.O.D.............................50.00
Jägerverein[15]...10.00
North Side Socialist Mens' Singing Society 20.00
"Vorwärts"[16] Singing Society 25.00
United Brothers Grove No. 41 U.A.O.D. 25.00
Columbia Lodge No. 178 D.O.H.................................25.00
Peace Lodge No. 61 D.O.H. 10.00
"Red Men" Singing Society 25.00
Hod Carriers Union 25.00
Carpenters and Joiners Branch 7 ....10.00
Schiller Lodge 347 D.O.H. 20.00
Lasalle[17] Lodge No. 446 D.O.H. 25.00
Tecumseh Branch No. 109 U.O.R.M.[18] 25.00
Southwestern Lodge No. 484 I.O.O.F.[19] 10.00
Main Lodge of the United Order of Red Men......................50.00
Walhalla Branch No. 93 U.O.R.M.................................25.00
Garfield Lodge No. 2619 K. of H.[20] 25.00
Concordia Lodge No. 19 O.D.H.S.[21]...............................25.00
Thusnelda Lodge No. 21 O.D.H.S. 15.00
Socialist Group, Salineville, Ohio...................................25.55
Bakers Union 50.00
Bakers Mutual Benefit Society of Chicago.........................50.00
German Brickmasons Benefit Society...............................25.00
Hermann Lodge No. 17 O.D.H.S. 15.00
North Chicago Grove No. 23 U.A.O.D. 25.00
Carpenters Union Branch 2...25.00
Social-Political Workers Association Cincinnati, Ohio..............50.70
Social-Political Mutual Health and Benefit Society 50.00
Thüringer Verein..25.00
Socialist Men's Singing Society, Detroit, Mich......................20.00
Socialist Group, San Francisco, Cal.................................25.00
Court Halsatia, Independent Order of Foresters....................25.00

14. German Order of Harugari.
15. Hunters Society.
16. Forward.
17. Lassalle is spelled differently in these lists and in other documents in this volume.
18. United Order of Red Men.
19. Independent Order of Odd Fellows.
20. Knights of Honor.
21. Order of the Sons of Hermann.

Workers Mutual Benefit Society A.U.B.O.[22]........................25.00
These are thus the 38 German Societies and Lodges.

51. List of Businesses on Milwaukee Avenue Contributing to the Flood Victims (*Chicagoer Arbeiter-Zeitung,* January 31, 1883).

We, the undersigned, herewith declare that, on the occasion of the collection for the distressed people in the flooded districts in Germany undertaken by Mr. Stauber in the company of Mr. Steinbock, o n e collection sheet entitled "For the flooded, distressed proletariat," and o n e collection book issued by the "North Side Committee" were presented. It was left up to us to sign one or the other list; we signed our names in full awareness that the money will be sent to Mr. Liebknecht and distributed among those most in need:

G. Engel, 280 Milwaukee Ave	*Toy Store*[23]
John Schultz, 602 Milwaukee Ave	*Saloon*
August Grosch, 817 Milwaukee Ave	*Saloon*
G. D. Nutzhorn, 636 Milwaukee Ave	*Saloon*
Leon & Freitag, 828 Milwaukee Ave	*Hardware*
Marcus Clark, 720 Milwaukee Ave	*Saloon*
M. Cohn, 740 Milwaukee Ave	*Clothing Store*
Aug. Moeller, Milwaukee Ave	*Tailor Shop*
Oswald Fulde, 728 Milwaukee Ave	*Watchmaker*
Ignatz Deimel, 719 Milwaukee Ave	*Saloon*
Ignatz Gottlieb, 801 Milwaukee Ave	*Grain and Feed*
Chas. Rixon, 701 Milwaukee Ave	*Hardware*
Fred. Voltz, 680 Milwaukee Ave	*Bakery*
L. Wreden, 661 Milwaukee Ave	*Furniture Store*
F. Damert, 627 Milwaukee Ave	*Tailor Shop*
Louis Klein, 657 Milwaukee Ave	*Saloon*
Aug. Behrens, 644 Milwaukee Ave	*Cigar Production and Sale*
Stephan Klein, 642 Milwaukee Ave	*Plumber*
Boese & Kloeckner, 640 Milwaukee Ave	*Cloth and Haberdashery*
Carl F. Maaß, 640 Milwaukee Ave	*Office Employee*
Elizabeth Kling, 355 Milwaukee Ave	*Sewing Machines*
L. N. Schmidt, 302 Milwaukee Ave	*Photographer*
Ahlswede & Kaese, 712 & 714 Milwaukee Ave	*Clothing Store*

22. Order of the Workingmen's Relief Society.
23. The information on the kind of store or business was taken from the 1883 Chicago City Directory.

View towards the northwest along Milwaukee Avenue from the intersection with Ashland Avenue, 1906. (Chicago Historical Society, DN 55,533.)

52. "The Collection on Behalf of the Unpropertied People in the Flooded Districts" (*Chicagoer Arbeiter-Zeitung*, Februrary 1, 1883).

The alleged reason for Mr. Michaelis's . . . brutal and slanderous attack on Mr. Franz A. Stauber was the collection the latter initiated on behalf of the unpropertied people in the flooded districts along the Rhine. It is well known that the reactionary German government and all those organs dependent upon it are not impartial when it comes to allotting charitable gifts. These are not distributed to the helpless according to their needs, but rather primarily in a way which favors the propertied classes and reactionaries.

These facts are beyond any doubt. They have been illuminated in the crassest and most outrageous manner during earlier floods along the Elbe, the Oder and the Vistula rivers, as well as during the famines in the Silesian Eulen Mountains and in East Prussia. In view of these experiences, Chicago's socialists have organized collections through the "Chicagoer Arbeiter-Zeitung," the proceeds of which will definitely flow to the poor and poorest among those people in the flooded districts so cruelly penalized by the organs of the German government. These collections are thus unmistakably motivated by human interest, and as a result of this they have been extremely successful. With special zeal, Mr. Franz A. Stauber has honorably dedicated himself to this work of love and justice. In the company of Mr. Steinbock, he has collected several hundred dollars.

The agent of the brutally reactionary, misanthropic Prussian government in Chicago, "Herr" Richard Michaelis, flew into a rage about it. This same man, whose mouth is fed by secret Prussian funds, had made a motion in the General Collection Committee — into which he had himself voted — that all the money collected in Chicago be sent to his Lord and Master Bismarck. Yet with the exception of the reptile referred to above, the members of the General Collection Committee were honorable enough to decline this motion. Instead, they sent the money to a private person of whose honesty they were convinced. But Chicago's socialists said: We'll send our money to a representative of the proletariat in the flooded districts. It is obvious that the member of the Reichstag, Mr. Liebknecht (who is an enemy of the reactionary Prussian government), is the socialists' surest guarantee that their money will find its way to the hands of the poor and poorest among those in the flooded districts.

Mr. Liebknecht need simply hand the money over to the workers' organizations in the flooded districts, and the leaders of these organizations, knowing exactly who is most in need, will distribute relief accordingly. This cannot be maintained in the case of Mr. Kapp, who is receiving the rest of the money, because he is not in direct contact with the workers' organizations.

Suffice it to say that a portion of the money collected in Chicago will be dispatched to Mr. Liebknecht; this in itself is a cruel blow to the Prussian government, so hostile to people, and reason enough for its local agent to slander all those working on behalf of the poor and poorest. . . . Just how mean and base the reptile's attacks against Stauber were can be gathered by the fact that yesterday the General Collection Committee returned Mr. Stauber's collection book with the request that he take up his activities again. And this happened despite the fact that the committee knows that Mr. Stauber is also in possession of a socialist collection list. By this action, the General Collection Committee has b r a n d e d Michaelis's slander for just what it is!

53. The Aurora Turnverein Holds a Carnival Ball on Behalf of the Flood Victims (*Chicagoer Arbeiter-Zeitung,* February 11, 1883).

Yesterday the Aurora Turnverein celebrated Carnival in its Turner hall. As in previous years, last night the friends of the Verein were so numerous that the hall proved far too small. . . . The hall was decorated tastefully, the impression enhanced by the colorful throngs of costumed men and women. Several crazy exhibitions by the merry Turners added to the tableau, already so varied and lively, which offered itself to the more sedate spectators. Especially noteworthy was a large painting by Mr. Fritz Hundt portraying the distribution of relief amongst the people in the flooded districts in Germany. On the one hand, it showed how the needy proletariat was pushed aside by the clergy and by government officials. And on the other hand, it symbolized the solidarity among working people, showing the American proletariat, under a rippling red banner, rushing to the aid of their German brothers. It was all a huge success.

54. Telegram of Appreciation from Wilhelm Liebknecht (*Chicagoer Arbeiter-Zeitung,* February 9, 1883).

"Arbeiter-Zeitung," Chicago

W o r t h y C o m r a d e s !

While confirming receipt of the 800 Marks for the workers in the flooded districts, I would like to express, in the name of all of us, our warmest thanks, and to assure you that we will be most conscientious in using the sum as was intended by the donors.

Help is indeed urgently needed!

With greetings from the Social Democratic Party,

W. L i e b k n e c h t.
Hamburg, January 17, '83

Neighborhood Solidarity II: The Funeral Procession for the Haymarket Victims

Chicago was the center of the powerful national movement to institute an eight-hour working day that culminated in the spring of 1886. A few days after the massive demonstrations of May 1, a meeting was held in Haymarket Square to protest the shooting by the police of demonstrators at the McCormick Reaper Works the preceding day. As the meeting was breaking up a bomb was thrown, allegedly by an "anarchist," and seven policemen were killed. Eight anarchists were tried and found guilty for instigating the incident, among them

*five of Chicago's German-American left. Four of the eight were exe-
cuted on November 11, 1887 — another had committed suicide the
day before — and two days later an imposing procession preceded
their funeral at Waldheim Cemetery.*

*Since four of the five dead had lived on the Northwest Side the
procession was centered there. It began at the homes of August Spies,
former editor of the* Chicagoer Arbeiter-Zeitung *and member of the
Aurora Turnverein, and Adolph Fischer, who had been a printer for
the paper. (See the neighborhood map at the beginning of this chapter.)
Accompanied by numerous local associations, lodges, unions, and
singing societies, the procession then went down Milwaukee Avenue,
stopping amidst throngs of people along the way to be joined by the
hearses bearing the bodies of the other victims. It was an imposing
demonstration of the bitter solidarity of both the Northwest Side
and the Chicago labor movement. The procession also shows how
Milwaukee Avenue functioned as a public space for the Northwest
Side where symbolic rituals were acted out.*

55. "Final Salutations. The Five Victims of Their Humanity Are Accompanied on Their Final Journey" (*Chicagoer Arbeiter-Zeitung*, November 14, 1887).

The sun rose bright and clear yesterday morning to illuminate the final
act of the most infamous drama the century has witnessed. In the early
morning hours the streets of the Northwest Side were already filling up
with people, who, in deep mourning, were making the final preparations
for the burial of those men whose legalized murder has occupied the whole
world for the past several days.

The sidewalks leading to the houses of mourning were already occupied
by mourners, and the crowd increased so quickly that finally all other
kinds of traffic were brought to a standstill. The women from the Societies
Lassalle 1 and 2 and Fortschritt gathered in Thalia Hall before proceeding
to the house of mourning where Fischer used to live. Typographia No.
9, Fischer's union, had already lined up, and countless numbers of other
mourners squeezed their ways to the windows of the modest apartment
to take a last look at that man who, although a worker, had subordinated
his own interests to those of humanity at large, and whose name is certain
to go down in the annals of history in ineffaceable print. Although everyone
was crowded together, there reigned the most solemn quiet around the

little house which held the precious remains. A few minutes before noon the coffin was closed and, as people in the crowd respectfully bared their heads, brought to the funeral coach. Within minutes the coffin was covered with magnificent, in part costly, floral tributes. Some of these were brought by the Typographia No. 9, the personnel of the "Arbeiter-Zeitung," the Typographia No. 7 from New York, [the Typographia] from Indianapolis with the inscription, "From Friends in Indianapolis," a wreath from the local Central Labor Union with the inscription, "To those martyred for worker emancipation," and from the women's societies. The Southwest Side Men's Singing Society reinforced by the International Men's Singing Society sang "Good Night" in plaintive accord, whereby the female mourners broke into tears. After the murdered man's tender wife had been led, or practically carried, to the waiting team, the procession assembled and set off to Milwaukee Avenue.

At 12:30, having reached the corner of Milwaukee Avenue and Paulina Street, the procession accompanying Fischer's corpse came to a stop and awaited the funeral coach bearing Spies's earthly remains. Along the sidewalk the people in the crowd stood with bared heads. No pushing, not a sound broke the silence. It was clear that the crowd knew what was going on. A muffled stillness hovered over the masses. From far off, first faintly, then louder and louder, could be heard the sounds of a funeral march, and then the musicians' shiny helmets, reflecting the sun's rays, became visible. Playing Gounod's "Funeral March," they slowly proceeded down Milwaukee Avenue. Behind them came Spies's funeral coach, which then joined Fischer's. The people along the sidewalks pushed forward, formed columns and also joined the procession.

Wherever the procession went, people bared their heads. Not a word was spoken, but the only feelings, clearly recognizable, were those of resentful grief, bitter anguish, and a fury for the murderers of the five. It was as though the quiet before the storm was gathering over the crowd. Men and women followed the funeral coach with tears in their eyes, and whenever a policeman was seen, he was confronted with unmistakable looks which said, "You share the guilt for this murder." Without being stopped, the procession marched on, past Parsons's house to the Aurora Turner Hall, where Parsons's corpse was waiting. Here, too, was an enormous crowd which occupied the whole width of the street, and it almost seemed as though the procession would be forced to halt. But the throngs of people made way, forming a passage through which the march continued until coming to a standstill in front of Engel's house.

The funeral of the anarchists was a major neighborhood event on the North Side during which Milwaukee Avenue changed from a commercial thoroughfare into a public space. (*Leslie's Illustrated Weekly,* November 26, 1887; photo Chicago Historical Society.)

Here the Lassalle Music Band played the "Marseillaise." The strains of this revolutionary song had hardly sounded when, as though on cue, everyone removed their hats and joined in enthusiastically. In mighty accord, the sounds filled the air, and the thousand-strong crowd yelled "Hurrah!" The police stood there, looking on in terror. Faced with this huge crowd which expressed its sympathy with the murdered men in such a demonstrable manner, they didn't dare intervene. They stood there with horrified looks on their faces and watched as the procession reformed and set out once again. The procession marched across Milwaukee Avenue to Desplaines Street, then down Lake Street to Fifth Avenue, and from there to Polk Street and the Wisconsin Central Train Station.

When the procession reached the corner of Desplaines and Lake streets, a man in a veteran's uniform separated himself from the crowd of onlookers and, removing an American flag bordered by black crepe from beneath his coat, proceeded to the front of the marchers. Shouting, "The procession marches under this banner," he began to wave it over his head. A policeman swinging a billy club grabbed him by the shoulder and tried to pull him out of the procession. But several powerful fists struck out at the policeman, and before he knew what had happened, he was flying headfirst into the crowd of onlookers. Shouting again, this time: "A rip in this banner is a rip in my heart," Trogden — that was the veteran's name — reassumed his position at the front of the marchers and continued unhindered. When the procession passed Marshall Field's[24] house on Lake Street, the crowd, as if on command, broke out in oaths directed against the capitalists.

Trogden shouted, "Three cheers for the murdered victims!" and "cheers" thundered from thousands of voices in unison. The people crowding along the sidewalk bared their heads, waved their hats and joined in. The procession reached the train station without further demonstrations. The crowd pushed into the waiting cars. The procession order was as follows:

Marshal: Chas. Hepp.

Adjutants: Stante, Becht and Braun.

Howell Trogden, with the American flag bordered in black crepe.

Meinkens' Band.

Turner Societies: Aurora, Germania, Fortschritt, Garfield, Joliet and Pullman.

Spies's funeral coach.

Carriages with the relatives and the members of the Socialistic Publishing Soc.

Members of the Arrangement Committee.

Fischer's funeral coach.

Typographia No. 9.

Carriages with Fischer's relatives.

Unorganized workers.

Fischer's music band.

Parsons's funeral coach.

Carriages with Parsons's relatives.

Knights of Labor 1037 Assembly, District Assembly K. of L. 24 and 57.

Various local assemblies of the K. of L.

Section of the Central Labor Union.

Engel's funeral coach.

Lingg's funeral coach.

Carriages with Engel's and Lingg's relatives.

The Socialist Men's Singing Society of the North and Southwest Sides,

24. Marshall Field, owner of Chicago's largest department store and an influential member of the Citizens Association, had opposed commuting the death sentences to life imprisonment at the beginning of the same month.

International Men's Singing Society, Aurora Turnverein Singing Society, Swiss Men's Singing Society, Bakers Singing Society, Herwegh's Men's Singing Society, Lassalle Men's Singing Society, Pullman Men's Singing Society, Rhineland Choral Assn., Plattdeutsch Guild Men's Singing Society, Schleswig-Holstein Men's Singing Society, Concordia Men's Singing Society, Harugari Men's Singing Society, and others.

Unorganized workers.

Lassalle Band.

Section of the Central Labor Union.

Carpenter Unions 291, 244 and 243.

Bakers Unions 49 and 1.

Swedish Bakers Union.

German Saddlers Union.

Wagonmakers Union.

Coopers.

Brewers.

Furniture workers.

Carriages with flowers.

Section of the Central Labor Union.

Music band.

Women's Societies Lassalle 1 and 2.

Women's Mutual Benefit Society.

Women's Verein Fortschritt.

Carriages with the members of these societies.

Local assemblies K. of L.

Section of the Central Labor Union.

Unorganized workers.

Carriages with acquaintances.

At the train station there was a terrific rush to the waiting cars, and in no time these were filled with people overflowing onto the platforms ⟨Platformen⟩.

The coffins and flowers were brought to a baggage car and the train steamed off to Waldheim [Cemetery]. The track was lined with thousands and thousands of people who raised their hats as the train approached. Three additional trains were sent out, but the Railway Company showed itself in all its grandeur: for hours it kept the people waiting for the trains' departure. These last three were also completely packed. More than 100 cars, crammed to the brim, departed for Waldheim.

Neighborhood Solidarity III: A Strike in a Furniture Factory

The mixture of industries and residences in cities like Chicago during the late nineteenth century had advantages for the organizers of unions, because they could mobilize entire neighborhoods for the support of strikes and boycotts. The following example of a furniture workers' strike in 1886 documents how a German neighborhood united against a local German entrepreneur named Bruschke.

A considerable part of Chicago's substantial furniture industry was concentrated on the North Side and around Chicago Avenue on the Northwest Side in a district that included the Aurora Turner Hall. Bruschke's firm lay on Vedder Street in the heart of the large North Side German neighborhood. (See the neighborhood map at the beginning of this chapter.) His company was one of the largest in the city, employing about one hundred men in 1880 and utilizing steam power to drive its machines. However, his skilled workers still brought their own tools to the factory in 1886, an indication that the mechanization of production had not yet developed to the point where craft skills were completely eliminated from the production process.

Taking place amidst the eight-hour movement of 1886, the strike illustrates many themes that historians have found to be characteristic of labor unrest in both England and America during the early phase of industrialization in the first half of the nineteenth century—a violated sense of popular justice, the use of folk traditions to support the cause, and crowd action to enforce the popular will. Yet this strike took place during the peak of the industrial revolution, and the participants were German immigrants in an American big city. This is one indication of how decisively people's lives in this neighborhood were shaped by traditions of popular protest and a common German popular culture as well as by common work experiences.

56. "Labor Affairs: Bruschke" (*Vorbote*, March 31, 1886).

The rumor that Charles J. Bruschke had sold his factory to one of his foremen made its rounds through the Clybourn Avenue-Division Street area yesterday. The strikers were of the opinion that Bruschke had only done this nominally, in order to be able to smuggle scabs into the factory. Bruschke is also said to have stated that he would no longer put up with

One of Chicago's countless German working-class saloons, No. 239 West 12th Street. The photograph was taken about 1895. Free lunches were available at numerous saloons, paid for by the beer consumed. (Chicago Historical Society, Northwestern Store Repair Co.)

German workers in his factory, and that he was only going to hire Poles. Bruschke, the music lover, is thus boycotting ⟨boycottet⟩ the Germans. There is naturally a great deal of anger among Bruschke's German neighbors. They are on the verge of organizing a parade with music and signs in Mr. Bruschke's honor.

Bruschke has very few friends. Everybody knows him and can tell quite interesting stories about his conduct. If ever a strike was justified, it is the Bruschke strike. The striking workers simply requested that they be paid their wages regularly. Not they, but rather Bruschke himself provoked the battle. Bruschke's neighbors know this very well, and all the city's workers must also learn of it so that they will actively support the strikers and the Furniture Workers Union which has adopted their cause.

Mr. Bruschke is apparently very desperate, otherwise — being a very small man, as everyone who knows him would admit — he would not have undertaken such Herculean steps. Mr. Bruschke felt himself deeply offended by the story about the striking workers' meeting which appeared

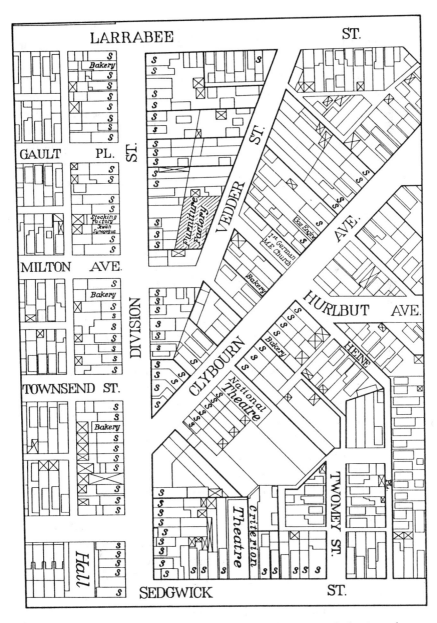

The neighborhood in the vicinity of Bruschke and Co.'s struck furniture factory on the North Side. The presence of two theaters nearby reveals how close Bruschke's plant was to the center of German community life in this area. (Drawing by Marlise Kunkel on the basis of *Robinson's Atlas of the City of Chicago, Illinois*, vol. 3, plates 16 and 19 [New York, 1886].)

last Saturday in the "Arbeiter-Zeitung." Because he didn't like the report, he brought suit against the "Arbeiter-Zeitung," demanding $25,000 for damages.

But Bruschke isn't stopping there. He wants to completely eliminate the Furniture Workers Union No. 1 in Chicago, i.e., 1,500 men at one stroke, and especially its organizer, Wm. Stallknecht. Bruschke called in a lawyer, A. C. Story, for deliberations, and decided to request an injunction against the Furniture Workers Union, Stallknecht, and the strikers. In this way, the accused would be prevented from frequenting the neighborhood around the factory, especially Division Street, allegedly so they won't prevent the scabs from bringing their tools into the factory and carrying out their work. . . .

In his indictment, Bruschke begins by telling the story of his life: in 1873, the firm of Bruschke & Ricke was created from the firm of Ricke & Olm which had just gone bankrupt. Prior to 1873, Bruschke had been employed in the bankrupt firm. He had saved $1,500. With this sum and additional money borrowed from friends, he had become a shareholder in the business. From 1873 until 1884 business had been good. The workers had been content with payment every three weeks. Only a few months ago, the situation changed, and for the following reasons: a certain August Limbach, who had only been in the country for four months and spoke no English, found work with him, Bruschke. This Limbach, and with him Stallknecht, Braunling and Seehafer, had been appointed by the Furniture Workers Union to agitate in Bruschke's factory. This Furniture Workers Union itself had been formed by the above-mentioned people for the purpose of forcing him, Bruschke, and the other shareholders in his firm, as well as all furniture manufacturers in Chicago, to raise wages and to pay common day laborers the same wages as the specialized and experienced craftsmen. A further purpose of this union was to dictate to the owners who they were to hire, how the employees were to be treated, which machinery and tools were to be used, and what kinds of furniture they, the owners, were to manufacture. Should the owners of the furniture factories refuse to meet these requirements, it is the principle of the above-mentioned Furniture Workers Union to ruin these factory owners, and to use all means to punish the disobedient business people.

Bruschke further enumerated all he has had to suffer since the beginning of the strike. The strikers ⟨Streiker⟩ have kept his factory under surveillance, he has been threatened, his workers have been stopped and prevented from carrying out their work, etc. That was why, he wrote, he was requesting the courts to issue an injunction against the people referred to above. . . .

Mr. Bruschke stated that in the future he would be sure to keep any groups planning boycotts or bands of conspirators from entering his factory.

Mr. Bruschke, you will yet come to the boycott authorities and to the conspirators on your own!

. . . .

The strikers are receiving cigars, lunch, beer, etc. from Bruschke's neighbors free of charge. In addition, the beer breweries nearby Bruschke's factory sent the strikers several free kegs of beer. All of Bruschke's neighbors are announcing their sympathy for the strikers ⟨Streiker⟩ in one way or another. Despite all his recently acquired fame, Mr. Bruschke himself is said to be in poor spirits. All morning yesterday he sat in his office and studied his organ, Meik's Paper.[25]

57. "Bruschke's Lament," by F. Fischer (*Vorbote,* April 7, 1886).

Melody roughly that of Dr. Eisenbarth[26]

I am the sire of blusters wild,
Sheddy weddy witt pompom.
As Bruschke knows me every child,
Sheddy weddy witt pompom.
And each who comes to hear my name,
Sheddy weddy witt whoopbetrassa,
Has long since known toward what I aim.
:,: Scheddy weddy witt pompom.:,:

Throughout my fact'ry, rich reward
Is offered to the toiling horde.
To saving they cannot be led,
And thus they have not got ahead.

The saving art I tried to teach,
But vain my efforts this to preach.
The fools can't see - blind every man!
How useful is my savings plan.

25. The reference is probably to the *Chicagoer Freie Presse* edited by Richard Michaelis.
26. "Dr. Eisenbarth" was a popular German satirical song about a physician who applied cures to his patients that were worse than their diseases.

By force I sought to have my way,
For weeks on end they got no pay.
And with their bank notes neatly curled,
I struck out for the business world.

And then they shouted with elan,
We do not want this savings plan!
And more there was, like S.O.B.
Like bone masher and misery!

"Exploiter," cries this motley brood,
Simply because my means are shrewd.
When nought they have, it's nought they eat,
And then they lay it at my feet!

And beer they drink, oh - that's just swell,
Go binge on water and stay well!
"Shut up," they say, "you lazy jerk,
Please spare us your old water-cure quirk!"

To thus insist I have no right,
I wish them to hell with all my might.
And now they strike, the toiling herd,
The Devil take you's my last word.

For oh so long, the papers claim,
Rebellion is the people's aim;
That reds are here, I need not say,
By whom the worker's led astray.

In my own shop, there is no doubt,
There is just such a riotous rout:
The horde of reds is active still,
And telling all to plunder, kill.

Oh heavenly beaut'ful, maiden dear,
From your art I take cour'ge and cheer;
And should this evil my peace prick,
Console you will - oh my music.

A nobler maid there's never been,
Me cleansing of this horrid spleen;
Now in the storm, I sense a lapse —
Let's see who'll be the first to collapse!

But what a shock he was to get,
When by that coxcomb he was met:
"Hey, stay a while, t'won't be for nought,
And pass some time with Brother Boycott!"

"I'm stopping here, and what is worse
Will leave with you the workers' curse.
A lesson hard is yet in store,
For soon your workers will be no more!"

58. "A Little Stand" (*Vorbote,* April 14, 1886).

Gay throngs of people swarmed around Bruschke's factory throughout the whole of yesterday afternoon. The factory is located right on the border of the 16th and 17th wards, and the sovereign voters of these wards, made cheerful by the beer and whiskey lavishly handed out by office seekers, honored each other with visits, thus enlivening the otherwise quiet area. Wandering musical bands gave themselves great pains to increase the citizens' gay moods. Shouts of *"Three Cheers!"* or *"Down with the gang! Down with the scoundrel!"* were heard from all sides. *"Down with Smith!"* shouted a fanatical Democrat. "He's an enemy to the workers. The Central Labor Union is boycotting ⟨boycottet⟩ him!" "Hurrah for Smith!" was the response from another side. *"Down with Bruschke!"* someone suddenly shouted. And all those present joined in the call. *"Down with the scabs! Long live the strikers ⟨Streiker⟩!"* someone else shouted, and in no time the 300-strong crowd of sovereign voters and neighbors of Bruschke proceeded down Division Street and stopped in front of Bruschke's factory. . . . It is well known that the love reserved by the voters and tax payers of these wards for their neighbor and fellow citizen Bruschke is not the tenderest. On several occasions it has been proven that their relations with Bruschke are very tense. When a collection was taken on Bruschke's behalf, there were only three contributions: 1 cent, 5 cents, and 10 cents. It was these same citizens who some time ago staged a rally to express their indignation and who were once on the verge of organizing an anti-Bruschke demonstration. . . .

When the crowd reached the factory, the scabs were standing around, just about to leave. As soon as they showed themselves at the gate, they were met by the howls of the huge crowd. "Rats! Scabs! Long live the strikers ⟨Streiker⟩! Down with Bruschke!" were the words from hundreds of people. Three of the scabs dared pass through the gate and into the street. They will not soon forget the reception which met them there. They were thrown to the ground, beaten terribly and chased for several blocks. Their fellow workers lost heart and stood by the gate like terrified sheep who, their escape having suddenly been cut off, could no longer move. In no time two citizens had planted themselves next to the gate and began to throw the poor devils into the crowd like inanimate objects. There they were gathered up with horrible cries, tossed around like balls and beaten. The two citizens did their work so quickly that, within three minutes, 15 scabs had received the same baptism.

Deputy Sheriff Stecker, who had the building under his surveillance, stood there helplessly, in total despair. He was pushed, knocked into the wall, shouted at. It finally got a little too lively for him and he drew his revolver. This just increased the crowd's fury. Once again the shouts rang out. "Down with the scabs! Long live the strikers ⟨Streiker⟩!" And a storm of rotten eggs poured down on the sheriff, the scabs, Bruschke's foremen and his factory. The sheriff and the scabs hurriedly fled behind the factory, pursued by the crowd's rotten eggs and stones. Then they really began to bombard the building; a number of windows were broken. And all the while the crowd grew larger and larger. Each successful throw—each time breaking glass was heard—was accompanied by the crowd's "Bravo! Hurrah!"

Suddenly two bluecoats appeared in the distance. They ran forward, flushed, out of breath, billy clubs raised. Behind them were two patrol wagons ⟨Patrolwagen⟩ and an additional twelve constables. The gang was received with repressed laughter. They had come too late. Everything was over. Amazed and furious, they stood there in front of the mocking crowd, not knowing who to take first. The spectators applauded—Bravo! Finally they selected three men from the crowd, hustled them into a patrol wagon ⟨Patrolwagen⟩, frisked them and drove off. The crowd on the street and the men and women watching from nearby windows accompanied the "victorious" policemen with the flattering cries of "Rats! Scabs!"

A few minutes later not a trace of the huge crowd was to be seen on Division Street, and complete quiet reigned in the area surrounding the Bruschke "établissements." The three men taken into custody were brought to the Chicago Avenue Police Station ⟨Polizeistation⟩, where they identified themselves as Anton Jagdfeldt, Gustav Timmer and Gottfried Waller. Jadgfeldt and Timmer are cobblers. The former is said to be an intimate friend of Bruschke's. It was in fact he who refused to sign the famous statement Bruschke's neighbors sent to the Superior Court ⟨Superiorgericht⟩. Waller is a furniture worker, but not one of the strikers.

The strikers ⟨Streiker⟩ refrained from taking even the least part in the rotten egg demonstration, remaining far from the scene of the action throughout. Only Meik's, Bruschke's organ, claimed this morning that t h e   s t r i k e r s ⟨Streiker⟩ organized the "attack." The same "paper" ⟨Päper⟩ maintains that Waller is one of the strikers ⟨Streikern⟩.

Those taken into police custody were booked ⟨gebucht⟩ for disorderly conduct and released last night on the promise that they appear before Judge Kersten this morning at 9 o'clock.

Picnics

Legitimate possibilities for public amusement were narrowly limited in a country like nineteenth-century America whose dominant culture was so strongly shaped by puritanical and evangelical religious values. The problem was made more difficult by the fact that Sunday was still the only complete day of free time available to most working people. Like their fellow immigrants in other American cities, the Germans of Chicago had fought hard and repeated battles since the 1850s against ministers, temperance advocates, and Sabbatarians, who found German forms of public leisure offensive and sought to repress them. Yet the Germans of Chicago were a group large enough to oppose such efforts successfully, often in alliance with the Irish, who were under similar pressure.

The picnic was a popular form of leisure frequently sponsored by German associations. On summer Sundays their picnics also attracted people of other nationalities to Chicago's beer gardens. Particularly for workers these outings were a welcome opportunity to escape from the confines of their homes and the congestion of the neighborhood, and the fact that the whole family took part made them even more attractive. No German association could forego having at least one picnic a year, and German-American unions, political parties, and other labor organizations also used them to entertain their memberships, raise funds, and attract new followers. The author of the first document reprinted here explains the German-American picnic as the result of the appropriation and transformation of a Puritan tradition. Whatever the validity of his historical generalizations, he at least throws light on the cultural self-perception of German immigrants in America. The second document describes the music, dancing, drinking, and good-natured mood during the picnic of the

Desplaines Hall Workers Club in Ogden's Grove in 1869. In addition to Germans from all regions of the mother country, other nationalities including young Americans also took part. In the opinion of the author, again only the Germans really knew how to have a good time.

The Cannstatter Folk Festival (Cannstatter Volksfest) was the annual festival of the Swabian Society. Like the picnic of the Desplaines Hall Workers Club, the festival usually took place in Odgen's Grove, a beer garden and meeting ground near the North Branch of the Chicago River much frequented by German organizations at that time. The Cannstatter Volksfest, however, had more the character of a large fair open to all Chicagoans, and apparently it received broad popular support. (In fact, it still takes place today.) Twenty-five years later in 1903, the Swabian Society was in the midst of a conflict between the generations over how the festival should be celebrated. The site that they had been using for the festival up to then, the North Side Sharpshooters Park, had been invaded by new forms of popular commercial amusement which contradicted older Swabian ideas of leisure. More open to things American, the younger generation thought the new amusements were not only fun but, even better, more profitable. The older generation recognized a genuine threat, however, for the commercial amusements it rejected were from a world external to the neighborhood and its local institutions where the old ethnic culture had thrived. By a narrow vote the Cannstatter Volksfest was moved to more appropriate surroundings. This disagreement within the Swabian Society illustrates a conflict that touched all German associations around the turn of the century. People had to choose between maintaining old values and customs and run the danger of isolating themselves from both the younger generation and American society at large, or they had to somehow accommodate their cultural forms and expressions to a changing city and new needs.

59. "The Origin of Picnics" (*Chicagoer Arbeiter-Zeitung*, June 27, 1883).

Anyone who has been in America long enough to have acquainted himself with the character of picnics knows what they are today. With few exceptions, they represent festivities where the participants find an abundance of entertainment, where families, far from the four walls of their lodgings, can find a few hours of distraction, where the women can take a break from the relentless commotion of the household, where the children can pursue their games unmolested—in a word, they offer an agreeable opportunity to get away from the toil, problems and strains of day-to-day life. In this sense, it can well be said that German societies have played an enormous role in civilizing the practice. Many a father, the family's animal of burden, will not be able to muster much enthusiasm when he hears the call to a picnic, because he sees his comfort threatened for a few hours. But just ask the women and the children, ask the young people: despite many a small problem and the numerous inconveniences leaving the house entail, their enthusiastic response can be summarized in the shouts of "three cheers for the picnic!"

But where do picnics come from? History is silent as far as the actual inventor is concerned, which is just one more proof of the poet's words, that "the great name of the inventor is so often lost in the night's obscurity." Of course Klopstock[27] is speaking here of the inventor of ice skates, but his words are just as fitting for the first organizer of a picnic. The picnic has its actual origin in Puritan England, where friends and their families were in the habit of getting together in one of the participant's houses. Everyone brought all sorts of choice morsels which made their way to the table in the course of the evening. At the beginning, a constrained tone dominated these festivities, the participants yearning tensely for the moment when they could devour the morsels which had been brought along. But the Puritan stiffness, tough as pigskin, didn't last long in a society made up of the most varied elements; the Eternally Feminine[28] especially, in its earlier years, didn't particularly favor this atmosphere.

As is the case now, so too was it then impossible to force the young people into the philistine mold of the lethargic bourgeoisie without encountering all sorts of protest. The picnic's original organizers probably intended to sing from hymn books, to recite from the Bible, to talk about this or that Bible passage and pursue other sorts of pious activities. Spirits were strictly prohibited and music was completely out of the question. Whoever would have suggested organizing a dance would have encountered the twice-distilled wrath of all the local saints. Gradually, though, the young people figured out how to get the better of these festivities, and the latter slowly took on a more liberal character. The old philistine with stern look and deliberate movements vanished from the scene and the town's young men and girls began to determine the picnic's atmosphere.

27. Friedrich Gottlieb Klopstock, German poet, 1724-1803.
28. A phrase taken from Goethe, *Faust II.*

It is then supposed to have become less serious than had been the get-togethers under the regime of the virtuous elders. In the course of time these festivities were also held out-of-doors, and if one can believe the old chronicles, these outings had nothing less than a religious character. The philistines prophesied a second flood and other events by which heaven would punish the abandon of the picnic youth.

And strangely enough, in a way this prophecy has come true: the terrible punishment which the narrow-minded Puritans invoked in their anger survives in the form of frequent rain visited upon modern picnics. But otherwise picnics are a very pleasant institution. What we understand by picnic today, however,—an out-of-door festivity—is not so much a remnant of the tradition brought over from England, but rather much more something preserved by the Germans, and especially by the German societies.

In Germany, people hang up the day-to-day mask of constraint and depression and take part in out-of-door excursions, to thoroughly enjoy that untranslatable something: Gemütlichkeit. Each participant is overcome by feelings of sociality and togetherness, and everyone instinctively seeks, in a free and easy manner, to contribute to the general diversion. Before German societies had begun to develop in the United States, the so-called picnics here were completely accommodated to an essence of philistinism. The participants bore themselves as though they were being sentenced to death in criminal court instead of relaxing and having fun out-of-doors.

60. "The Desplaines Hall Workers Club Picnics in Ogden's Grove" (*Der Westen,* July 22, 1869).

Ogden's Grove. - Coffee and Topfkuchen.[29] - Over a glass. -
Music and musicians.—Oh, I'm so tired etc.—Women and men dancing.
—Young America is also dancing, and how! . . .

"You go down North Avenue ⟨Nordavenue⟩, all the way till you get to Halsted Street ⟨Halstedstreet⟩; follow this street along your right till you get to Willow Street ⟨Willowstreet⟩; there you turn to face the setting sun, lift your eyes and you'll see the tips of green trees; you head toward them till you get to the entrance; step cheerfully past the gate—and find yourself in the middle of the woods' cool shade." - That's the way a friend told me how to get to Ogden's Grove.

29. *Topfkuchen* is a kind of sweet bread made with yeasted dough that is similar to coffee cake.

"Woodland shade!" Who could possibly resist this promise? I started off to Ogden's Grove; not yet having left Halsted Street ⟨Halstedstreet⟩ behind me, I heard the exultant sound of horns. I hurried my pace. Yes, the call of the horns is coming from the woods! -

Sunshine, woodland green and woodland shade, the sound of horns! on a Sunday afternoon, what more could a German heart possibly wish for?! - A good mug of beer! -

"Fellow countryman," I asked the cashier as he accepted my 15 cents, "would you have a drop of beer, too?"

"Oh, plenty!" answered the man from Holstein . . . "not to mention spirited company!"

The Desplaines Hall Workers Club was having a picnic under the oak columns at Ogden's Grove. There was a large group with many women and children and there were so many other people there that all of the tables and benches were taken.

Cheerful groups everywhere, families and their friends taking of Sunday afternoon nectar, extra-strong coffee, and the ambrosia without which it wouldn't be complete in the form of "Stippels" — Topfkuchen and buttered almond cake. There, in all the different dialects of the dear German homeland, chatting and blabbering . . . and groups of young and old men and boys drinking beer. . . . That there was no lack of "hopping and jumping boys and girls" . . . is self-evident; . . . But American boys and girls were also "jumping" ⟨"jumpten"⟩ around under the trees.

There was a break in the music; the musicians . . . were partaking of the beer industriously . . . but then they climbed cheerfully . . . back onto the old and rickety bandstand and the sound of horn, flute and fiddle once again resounded through the woods. . . . Everyone raced to the dance floor. . . . Slim, strong youthful figures; the young girls in their Sunday best, simple, tasteful, elegant, according to their means and fantasy, though not at all conspicuously attired. The few young women who wore their hair short and curly with Grecian-style ribbons were apparently Celtic or Anglo-American offspring, but were none the less pretty for it; taste varies. . . . All of Germany was dancing together . . . from the "ocean extremities" to the heights of Switzerland . . . young America was also there; but the tall young Americans, with their long, narrow steps, were not at ease here on the dance floor . . . clinging self-consciously to one another . . . awkward and stiff . . . as though dancing were a terrible punishment for them . . . delicacy

ter Abstimmung das Land mit Schrecken zu erfüllen; und um der Heuchelei und Lüge die Krone aufzusetzen, in seinem Berichte an den Kaiser behufs Einberufung des Staatsgerichtshofes erklären: „Wir hätten gehofft, daß Geduld und Sanftmuth genügen würden, die Leidenschaften zu besiegen, aber unsere Geduld wurde für Zaghaftigkeit, unsere Sanftmuth für Schwäche gehalten..... Die Revolution wurde durch den legalen Waffenstillstand, den wir ihr bewilligten, nicht aufgehalten. Die Revolutionäre wollten durch ein Verbrechen den Souverän untertreten (den Kaiser tödten), in dem Augenblick, wo eine Constitution aufgegeben und eine andere noch nicht votirt ist..... Unter solchen Umständen ist es unsere Pflicht, die Justiz öffentlich zum Einschreiten aufzufordern".— Nein, so etwas ist noch nicht dagewesen!

Aber freilich, die Verzweiflung verdoppelt die Kräfte des Betrobten. Die Verräther Ollivier sah den Abgrund vor sich, alle Klassen der französischen Gesellschaft, mit Ausnahme der Räuber, die sich im Budget und in Börsenspekulationen mästen, kehrten ihm den Rücken; das Plebiscit drohte die neue Ollivier'sche Constitution des Empire's zu verwerfen; die gemäßigten Republikaner, die friedseligsten Liberalen wendeten sich von ihrem toll gewordenen Ollivier mit Abscheu ab; trotz aller Drohungen mit dem rothen Gespenst ging die antiplebiscitisch- Agitation ihren Gang ruhig fort. Da mußte ein großer Schlag gewagt werden. An die Gefahr hin, die Komplottcomite hinterher als ein eigenes Polizeimachwerk ausgespielt zu sehen, mußte sie am Vorabend der Abstimmung in Scene gesetzt werden. Wenn auch ihre Wirkung, wie lästig ihre nächste augenblickliche, nicht von großer Bedeutung sein kann, so werden sich doch vielleicht eine bal e Million Furchtsamer zu einem günstigen Votum für die Regierung dadurch bestimmen lassen; und das genügt dem Verzweifelnden. Vor allem Dingen mußte dafür gesorgt werden, daß das Empire nicht in der Minorität bleibe. Statt vier bis fünf Millionen, sagen jetzt vielleicht fünf bis sechs Millionen ihr Ja zu der neuen Verfassung.

Um so heftiger wird die Krisis nach der Abstimmung werden. Die cynischen Manöver der Regierung, die vor keinem Mittel zurückbebt, um das Land zu betrügen, werden entlarvt, die Regierung wird zu stets willkürlicheren und gewaltsameren Maßregeln schreiten müssen. So wird die Revolution von Tag zu Tag reifer und unvermeidlicher.

Sie werden den Bericht des Generalprokurators Grantperret, diesen anticipirten Anklageakt der Republikaner der Internationalen, verfaßt von derselben Hand, die dem Anklageakt gegen den Mörder Pierre Bonaparte in einen Entschuldigungsakt umwandelte, in den Zeitungen lesen; ich habe daher nicht nöthig, dieses confusen Machwerk hier zu analysiren (zerlegen). Nur darauf will ich aufmerksam machen, wie aus diesem Meisterstuck von Unehrlichkeit hervorgeht, daß weder die Mitglieder der internationalen Arbeiterverbindung, noch des französischen Gewerksgenossenschafts-Verbandes sich von den Agents-provocateurs haben verführen lassen, an deren

Fest-Programm
— des —
Arbeiterverbrüderungsfest's
— in —
Ogden's Grove.

Sammelplatz: Ecke Lasalle- und Lake-Straße.

Abmarsch: 9½ Uhr Morgens:

Der Zug bewegt sich in folgender Reihenfolge:

Musik.
Arbeiter Central-Verein.
Union Trades Assembly
Labor Union.
Musik.
Bauschreiner-Verein.
Silverleger-Verein.
Schuhmacher-Verein.
Musik.
Allgemeiner Deutscher Arbeiter-Verein.
Social republikanischer Französischer Verein.
Musik.
Schmiede Verein.
Teutonia Männer-Chor.
Bricklayer Union.
Musik.
Bäcker Verein.
Nord Chicago Männer Chor.
Böhmischer Arbeiter Verein.
Musik.
Schneider Verein.
Allgemeiner Holzarbeiter-Verein.

Und geht am Sonntag durch Clark-Straße bis Divisionstraße nördlich, Divisionstraße westlich bis Clybourne Avenue, dann Clybourne Ave. entlang bis zum Festplatz.

Am Montag Wellestraße nördlich bis Divisionstraße und von dort wie Tags vorher nach dem Festplatz.

Bekanntmachung.

☞ Das Fest-Comite des „Deutscher Arbeiters" versammelt sich von jetzt an jeden Dienstag Abend 8 Uhr, 46 Süd-Well-Straße, eine Treppe hoch.

E. Witte, Vorsitzender.

der Ver. Staaten, und eintreffen.

Vereins-Anzeigen.

Das Arrangementscomite versammelt sich am Freitag den 3., Samstag den 4. und Dienstag den 7. Juni Abends 8 Uhr, 46 S. Wellestraße.

Wittig, Secretär.

Schneider heraus!!

Sonntag den 5. Juni, Morgens 8 Uhr, 77 Dearbornstraße, Zimmer No. 17 Sammelplatz zum Auszug zum Arbeiterverbrüderungsfest nach Ogden's Grove. Es wird erwartet, daß sämmtliche Berufsgenossen am Auszug Theil nehmen werden.

Das Comite.

Bäcker - Unterstützungs-Verein.

Die Mitglieder obigen Vereins werden alle ersucht sich am Sonntag den 5. Juni präcis 8 Uhr in der Vereins-Halle zu erscheinen um sich am Fest-Zug zu betheiligen.

Franz Elldaf, Präs.
August Junge, Secr.

Bekanntmachung.

Zum Ausmarsch nach dem Arbeiterfest sind folgende Anordnungen für den allgemeinen deutschen Arbeiterfest getroffen. Der 7. Ward-Verein versammelt sich Morgens ½8 Uhr 104 Canalport No. Von dort bewegt sich der Zug nach 381 Blue Island Av., wo sich der 8. und 9. Ward Verein versammelt.

Von dort wird sich der Zug der Blue Island Ave. entlang, durch Halstedstraße bis nach Randolphstraße; derselben östlich folgend bis Lasalestraße, — dem Sammelplatz sämmtlicher Vereine — hinbewegen.

Sämmtliche Mitglieder sind ersucht pünktlich zu erscheinen. Ebenso werden die Mitglieder anderer Vereine, welche auf der Süd- und Südwestseite wohnen, ersucht sich anzuschließen, indem sie dann noch noch früh genug eintreffen, um sich am Hauptsammelplatz zu ihren eigenen Vereinen zu begeben.

Das Arrangementscomite.

and measure seem to be totally missing in the ears and feet of young America. The most recent friend I made today, a chap from Hannover, knew how to use his legs much better. . . .

Ha! The Germans like nothing better than a party under the oaks! The life our forefathers had in the woods still clings to us. . . . I forgot that I was participating in a party so far away from the homeland in a foreign country. I exchanged many a cheerful word with many a cheerful person, was happy among happy people. It wasn't long however, before I was

---

On facing page

The program of the "Labor Brotherhood Festival" in Ogden's Grove. (*Der Deutsche Arbeiter,* June 4, 1870.) The text reads:

Program of Events
———— for the ————
Labor Brotherhood Festival
———— in ————
Ogden's Grove

Meeting place: corner of LaSalle and Lake streets.
Start: 9:30 in the morning
The parade order will be as follows:
Music
Workers Central Verein.
Union Trades Assembly
Labor Union
Music.
Building Carpenters Verein.
Silversmiths Verein.
Shoemakers Verein.
Music.
General German Workers Verein.
French Social Republican Verein.
Music.
Blacksmiths Verein.
Teutonia Men's Choir.
Bricklayers ⟨Brickleger⟩ Union
Music.
Bakers Verein.
North Chicago Men's Choir.
Bohemian Workers Verein.
Music.
Tailors Verein.
Associated Woodworkers Verein.
And on Sunday goes north down Clark St. to Division St., then west on Division to Clybourne Ave. along Clybourne Ave. to the festival site. On Monday, north on Wells St. to Division St., and from there just like the day before to the festival site.

unfortunately called back to reality, remembered that I was a stranger here; oh why am I so ponderous in my attempts to reconcile myself with the local conditions!

61. "The Cannstatter Volksfest" (*Chicagoer Arbeiter-Zeitung,* August 21, 1879).

Yesterday's questionable weather, which was quite threatening for a while, couldn't prevent hoards of Chicago's merry Germans from going to Ogden's Grove on Clybourn Ave. for the annual Swabian fall festival. A cloud of dust hovered over the fest site itself, and even from far away it was evident that a huge crowd had gathered there. This was confirmed again upon entering the "garden," or grove, where one caught sight of the thousands of visitors being swept along by the maelstrom, helplessly tottering back and forth amidst the powerful human current. The conglomeration of folk culture which was developing here was, as always, of an extremely interesting and enjoyable nature. The carefree observer was offered a tableau of such earthy and exciting activity that it was a pure pleasure simply to be in the middle of the flow. The usual platitudes about the success of the festival cannot be applied to this occasion, as it poses an exception to the rule. And although this reporter is used to a lot, he nevertheless always finds new material here for original comparisons.

The arrangement of the stands, booths, tents for eating and drinking, the carousels, theater, and other attractions are generally the same as they have always been, but this is the very least. The main attractions are the stage presentations, the performances by amateurs and artists, the outstanding promenade music, folk dances, illuminations and fireworks, shadowgraphs, etc., and finally the faithful rush to the various booths, the most popular of which is the wine bar, the social center for the cheerful Swabians. This is also where the magnificent "pillar of the vine," under which the 1873 Riesling from the royal caves in Stuttgart is sold, has been set up.

Yesterday's Cannstatter Volksfest was wonderful, and as today is yet another day promising good times under the "pillar of the vine," it will presumably be no less so. All of yesterday's performances will be repeated today, so whoever wants to participate in the last day's activities, just come along to Ogden's Grove. You won't regret it.

This lithograph shows the seventh Turn Festival of the North American Turner Bund in 1869 held at Wrights Grove in Chicago. The illustration gives one a sense of the social atmosphere at picnics and beer gardens that characterized the Cannstatter Folk Festival and similar events organized by German associations. (*Leslie's Illustrated Weekly*, August 28, 1869; photo courtesy of the Newberry Library, Chicago.)

62. "Cannstatter Volksfest. A Move to Brand's Park. - Lively Debate between Representatives of the Older and Younger Generations in the Schwaben-Verein" (*Chicagoer Arbeiter-Zeitung*, January 19, 1905).

At yesterday's quarterly meeting of the Swabian Verein in the North Side Turner Hall, presided over by Ernst Hummel in the presence of 231 of the some 900 enfranchised members, there was a lively debate between representatives of the older and younger generations over the choice of a picnic area ⟨Picnicplatzes⟩ for the annual Cannstatter Volksfest. Attorney Henry Kraft, representing the conservative elements, was heard first. He spoke at length about how it was time for a change, claiming that the North Side ⟨Northseite⟩ Schützenpark is no longer what it was when the Swabian Verein decided to hold the Cannstatter Volksfest there. At that time it had been considered important to have a simple, attractive field with trees for shade, someplace where everything could be arranged according to the good old homeland tradition. All that, Mr. Kraft continued, has changed. In keeping with American business practices, the park has been turned into a general amusement park, full of so-called novelties and attractions, which, like other American exhibitions, are a far cry from the idea of the old homeland. Mr. Kraft felt that it would be proper and in keeping with the former tradition of the festival to relocate. All that would be needed would be a pavilion offering sufficient elbowroom for dancing, and open fields where traditional games could be played and where the participants could romp about.

Then it was the other side's turn. They maintained that there was nothing offensive about the "Pike" or the Little Codaly [*sic*] Island in the park, all the less so in that these were appealing and tended to bring in money, as was evidenced by the large profits the Verein had to show last time.

Nevertheless, the secret vote that followed upheld the decision to relocate to Brand's Park on Elston and Belmont Avenues, with 125 in favor, 106 opposed.

Theater and Entertainment

In the second half of the nineteenth century social life and entertainment for Chicago's Germans were inseparably bound to the activities of their associations. Even the annual celebration of carnival was popular in Chicago among practically all German organizations including workers' associations and unions. The first document printed here shows how at its masked ball in 1897 the Socialer Turnverein took advantage of the carnival tradition of frivolity and license to criticize and satirize the distribution of wealth and power in American capitalist society. It used tableaux vivants or "living pictures," which came out of a long European theatrical tradition and were frequently and effectively used on political occasions. (See Chapter V, Documents 85 and 86.)

The German theater tried to establish itself on various levels in Chicago. Although an establishment with high pretensions like the Schiller Theater was able to maintain itself for a while in the center of the city, the smaller popular theaters located in the German neighborhoods were more numerous and apparently attracted a larger audience. Various theaters were established on Milwaukee Avenue,

*for example, and during the 1890s they began to move farther away
from the inner city and toward the northwest along with the German
population.*

*The second article reprinted here describes yet another form of
popular theatrical entertainment, vaudeville and melodrama, as performed on weekends by amateur companies in saloons and halls.
They offered skits, farces, and other melodramatic fare in order to
attract patrons for their employers' beer and food. Although the article
from the* Illinois Staats-Zeitung *describes such occasions well, the
author is too interested in judging them by high bourgeois literary
standards to appreciate how such entertainment helped meet the
public's real need for diversion and conviviality. These forms of
theater were thus embedded in the rich and diverse culture of the
saloon and meeting hall. Typically entire families went to see such
productions which were followed by eating, drinking, and dancing,
even in the more respectable popular theaters. Such theatrical performances in the saloons and halls, combined with the plays presented
in the popular neighborhood theaters, were the most common form
of commercially sponsored entertainment available to the German
population in the late nineteenth century.*

*The situation changed dramatically after 1900 when nickelodeons,
penny arcades, and film theaters seemed to spring up everywhere
throughout Chicago's ethnic neighborhoods. The older forms of popular theater offered scant competition. Symbolic of the transformation
of popular entertainment was the conversion into a movie theater of
the old Aurora Turner Hall, which had for decades also been used
for German theater productions. The last document describes the
new commercial entertainment and its special attraction to young
people, most of whom were probably the children of immigrants.*

63. "The Social Turnverein's Masked Ball" (*Chicagoer Arbeiter-Zeitung*, February 27, 1897).

The above-mentioned Turnverein will hold its eleventh gala masked ball
on Saturday, February 27, in its two halls on the corner of Belmont Ave.
and Paulina St. And as the Social Turnverein is the master with respect
to this sort of thing, an extraordinary degree of splendor and pomp can
be expected. The Party Committee more or less hopes to have outdone

itself this time, and its announcements are of such a promising nature that young and old alike, among both the Turn enthusiasts and carnival enthusiasts, are looking forward to this affair with a great deal of excitement. The feature attraction is the stage presentation which "has never been seen here before and won't be for a while," namely "Confidence" and "Prosperity," a sensational "you can't-trust-anybody" comedy presented by the greatest political comical acrobats of the times, Mssrs. McHannes and Company. This certainly sounds very encouraging with respect to the present conditions of "Malheuritas."[30] The four tableaux comprising the two-part harlequinade also seem to be very fitting. We can't deny ourselves the pleasure of giving a brief sketch of them:

Part 1: "Confidence" in 2 tableaux:

Tableau 1: "Banks in Floribus."[31] To the accompaniment of the "Confidence" march, humanity brings its money to Dreyer and Sechser,[32] Schneider[33] and son-in-law, etc.

Tableau 2: "An out and out crash." "And then they wanted to have their money back but then they couldn't have it back." Choir of the Duped: "Oh du lieber Augustin,"[34] etc.

Part 2: "Prosperity" in 2 tableaux:

Tableau 1: "Prosperity" and the rich. The Seeley dinner. Extravagant ballet. "Little Egypt" in her original dance, "in the altogether." The showoffs close their eyes (not on your life), the champagne flows.

Tableau 2: "Prosperity" and the poor. Factories closed, money none, a *ring-a-lievio* of hunger and cold. Grand finale: thrown out on the street in zero-degree weather.

Moral: "When you've hit rock bottom, well then, you may as well rot / 'Cause the right to live, Pal, is for those who've got."

Whoever wants to participate in the fun need only drop off 25 cents per person per ticket with a Verein member in advance, otherwise you'll have to pay twice that at the door. For misanthropes and pessimists, this is the perfect opportunity to really change their natures.

30. A self-coined word using the French root for *misfortune*.

31. Banks in full bloom.

32. Edward S. Dreyer was a millionaire banker in Chicago; his name is a homonym of *Dreier*. *Dreier* and *Sechser* both allude to the game of dice as well as to older German coin designations.

33. Georg Schneider, also a banker and millionaire, was president of the National Bank of Illinois.

34. A German round, the refrain of which is "All is lost."

64. "Back Alley German Theaters in Chicago" (*Der Westen: Frauen-Zeitung*, October 23, 1892).

Up till now, there were always several hundred theatergoers who had to be turned away from the door of the Schiller Theater on Sunday evenings when performances took place. Although the theater seats 1,300 people—including the gallery—it was always sold out. Weekly performances, on the other hand, were always very poorly attended. . . .

The "popular theaters" and the few erudite stages cannot be held responsible for the drop in attendance. It is much rather the fault of the well-to-do Germans in this city who are apparently not yet ready to appreciate the artistic pleasure offered by a competent German Theater Company and its able director. In a city where there are over 400,000 Germans, and where, in addition, there are no blue laws limiting Sunday activities, several more popular theaters could easily exist alongside a permanent German theater without hurting the latter. Yes, we will even go further and maintain that our "municipal theater" would benefit from the better of these smaller theaters, as they would prepare their audiences, comprised of small business people and workers, to appreciate the more noble pleasures of theater. Whoever has seen a performance of "William Tell" in a small theater—where it is evident that a distinctive performance cannot be offered—will surely not miss the opportunity to see the same play being performed in the municipal theater. He will want to experience the work as it unfolds in its formal and artistic totality. In this sense the well-managed small theaters not only pose no threat to the permanent German theater, but rather help it along. . . .

Just about all of the "five" popular theaters . . . offer reasonably well polished performances, not at all sloppy. The troupes are comprised of average-quality actors with only a few amateurs. Granted, in perhaps more than fifteen of the other small theaters . . . the ratio of hapless actors to most hapless amateurs is just the opposite. But the managers of these small theaters choose to renounce support by the press. By giving out generous numbers of free tickets—the manager often sees to it himself—to small merchants and businessmen, the theater can count on these recipients to encourage their customers to attend performances. Good beer consumers will not have to pay for the whole season. But tickets are so cheap that even workers with large families and not so much money can afford to attend performances, frequently "with Mother and all the little children."

The people don't know that they're being "taken" by the sham manager after all.

The temperature is oppressive in the poorly ventilated and low, narrow halls, where art and beer are on tap. And this fits so well into the scheme of the sham theater manager. By the end of the first act the audience has developed a burning thirst. Naturally, the intermissions are at least a quarter of an hour long, sometimes longer. More or less—mostly less—friendly waiters hurriedly pass out beer in glasses—not much larger than the water containers for pet birds—for the going rate of 5 cents a glass. Along with "Herr Direktor's" favorites—namely the "nonpaying guests"—the spectators, tormented by thirst, gather in the taproom which is directly adjacent to the theater; here the beer glasses are of the same "smallness" as inside. A quarter, a half dollar, and when a lot of people are being "treated"—for there will surely be much of this sort of horrid round-drinking which encourages excess—a whole dollar or even more has soon been spent. After the performance there is some "leg shaking," for to write that the "ball takes place"—as the program claims—would be doing the greatest injustice to the real pleasure dancing can give. And once again money is taken in on beer and other beverages, this time primarily from the young people eager to dance. The next morning the people who took part in this event where "art and beer are on tap" awake with heavy heads and depressed, empty purses. They weren't exposed to even a trace of an artistic treat for their money, and instead of the kind of cheerful dance the German societies offer, they ended up with rough leg shaking and carousing. For perhaps one-fifth of that which they spent, they could have had highly polished artistic entertainment at the German Theater, could have improved their minds, and by getting into bed early and getting enough sleep, their bodies, too. On the other hand, the "sham manager" chuckles into his fist the next morning when the "barkeeper" tells him how many kegs of beer, bottles of wine and boxes of cigars are empty; after all, that's his game and that's why he's content to fill his theater with "nonpaying guests."

This is the way a disproportionate number of small German theaters support themselves in Chicago. This situation could perhaps be rectified—as has been the case with private swindlers—if the city council were to grant beer and wine licenses only to societies, not to the managers of popular theaters or to individual persons. More about other swindles—like the organization of balls, especially around the carnival time, of concerts followed by balls, frequently under the guise of charity, etc.—another time.

65. Theatrical Performance in the Workers Hall (*Chicagoer Arbeiter-Zeitung,* September 13, 1886).

By seven o'clock, when the box office was to open, there was already a certain sense of excitement in the "Workers Hall." The people who didn't want to miss the first performance of the season in this Temple of Art were afraid that they wouldn't get seats. The cheap tickets, the good beer which is on tap in this popular theater, the funny music-hall songs and burlesques, and especially the chance to swing a leg, all these factors ensured that the hall was completely sold out. There was additionally a coffee klatsch on stage which the ladies couldn't resist. The representatives of the tender sex were amazed by—and envious of —the sharp tongues of their "sisters," laughed and applauded so thunderously that it could be heard on the street, and nobody was happier than the proprietor and the director. Favorable auspices thus accompanied the opening of the winter season in the Hall. . . .

Upon entering the Apollo Theater, our patron of the arts witnessed the cobbler's son, August, receive a resounding slap which marked him as a journeyman. But at the same time it turned out that this same August was a changeling, in reality a baron. But this symbolic fellow, now removed to a castle, has such wild escapades and gets so sick of living a constant spree that he begins to yearn for his pitched cobbler's thread. The audience, believing that nothing is better than an honest trade, warmed to the representative of these ideas to such an extent that the action was accompanied by permanent applause. At 10:30 the Muses' Temple was turned into a dance hall, and in place of their hands, the people now gave rein to their feet.

66. The "Musicians' Songs," by Kneisel (*Chicagoer Arbeiter-Zeitung,* September 6, 1886).

The "Musicians' Songs" is a play by Kneisel which, despite its having been performed for years and years, is still always well received. Reason and feeling are present in the play. The struggles between capital and idealism, between a dizzying desire for money and a love of art are portrayed in a gripping manner via the experiences of the traveling musician, Lebrecht[35] Winter. This family story reflects the contemporary class system, with its rich blockhead scoundrels, and its poor but honest wretches, and

---

35. His name literally means "live right."

naturally ends in marriage. The spectators—who, by the way, though they weren't sitting squeezed next to each other like sardines in a tin, nevertheless filled the hall—used their handkerchiefs more often to wipe away the tears from their eyes than the sweat from their brows. Warm-hearted Lebrecht, his beautiful and sacrificing daughter, her droll sweetheart who, though an "enfant terrible" for his parents, remains true to the lover's oath, even when the old man is "thrice beside himself"—all the characters quickly won the hearts of the spectators. That's the way it is, the play is a popular play, the Apollo Theater is a popular theater. Whoever hopes to find not so much a temple of classical drama but rather a place where tear ducts and diaphragm can be exercised, that person will have come to the right spot. *Vivat sequence!*[36]

67. "The Penny Arcade and the Cheap Theatre," by Sherman C. Kingsley, Superintendent Chicago Relief and Aid Society (this document represents the original English version; *Charities and The Commons*, June 8, 1907).

The rapid increase of five cent theaters and penny arcades in Chicago and other cities large and small, is a matter of common observation. Evil consequences have demanded the attention of juvenile and municipal courts, probation officers and social service workers along all lines. Aroused by hold-up scenes, shoplifting episodes, or fascinated by stage life and the influence of unscrupulous actors and actresses, children get into trouble. Even more frequently the desire to witness these shows leads boys and girls to steal. An investigation of these conditions was recently made by the committee on charitable and correctional institutions of the Chicago City Club.

The Moving Picture World for April 20, 1907, contains a letter written by a representative of the Kline Optical Company of Chicago. This statement is made with reference to five cent theaters. "Our estimate is that the attendance at all of the Chicago places combined averages 100,000 daily." If true, this means an attendance of 700,000 a week or 36,500,000 a year. The percentage of children is not stated but those who are familiar with cheap amusement places know that it is large. . . .

Cheap amusement places seem to divide themselves into four groups more or less distinct, viz.: Penny arcades, five cent theaters, theaters charg-

36. Let there be more!

ing ten cents and over, appealing to the young, and those of higher price appealing to older boys and young men and offering lewd and suggestive plays.

The penny arcade is a place fitted with slot machines where by dropping a penny and turning a crank, pictures of various kinds and musical selections may be seen and heard. There are usually other features connected with these arcades. Sometimes a shooting gallery, knife stands, photograph galleries and frequently a section marked "For Men Only." The objectionable exhibits ranged from thirty to sixty per cent of the whole number. They were much worse in some localities than in others.

The entertainment in the five cent theaters usually centers around a little play lasting less than half an hour. It is carried on through moving pictures, instrumental music, clog dancing jokes, and sometimes a play with more or less of a plot. One strong impression left by visits to these places, especially in the residential portions of the city, is that they answer, imperfectly to be sure, a real need of the community. This impression was borne out by the character of the audience. Father and mother, the baby, the older children, the grand parents — all were there. Objectionable features are sometimes introduced, such features as robberies, suggestive jokes, hold-up scenes, but in the main the performances were not objectionable.

In the theaters of the second class that attract children, admission can be gained to the "nigger heaven" for ten or fifteen cents. Here young boys are found in large numbers. In one place the visitor counted thirty boys who were not over twelve and about one hundred that were under sixteen. They were unattended and did not leave the theater until half past ten. All these boys were in the gallery; there were small boys all through the audience. This particular play was called The Eye Witness. On Sunday afternoon the visitor went again to the same theater. As he walked down the gallery three little fellows called: "Here's a seat, mister. Oh, mister, it's fine! There's a guy that steals the old woman's pocketbook." The visitor later discovered that he was nine years old and his two companions were both eleven.

"Do you come to the theater often?"

"Yes, we come every Sunday. All the boys do. Sometimes we come week nights but not often."

"Do you go to any other theater?"

"Oh, yes, we go to them all, the Haymarket and the Bijou, too."

"What about the five cent theaters?"

"Yes, we go to them but we like the real theaters best."

"Of all the plays you have seen what was the one you liked best?"

The nine-year-old did not hesitate — "it was the one we saw last winter, The Way of the Transgressor."

There were in this theater fifty unattended boys under twelve and one hundred not over fourteen. In this class of theaters the plays are often sensational, depicting hold-ups, robberies and similar scenes. These boys and girls soon outgrow the five cent theaters and desire something more thrilling.

The fourth class of theaters is still higher priced and draw particularly the older boys and young men. There was usually a scattering of small boys in the audience. Here the limit of indecency is reached. Bills differ widely different weeks, but there is usually something that, it would seem, would satisfy even the most depraved taste. On one occasion the visitor counted fifteen policemen in uniform. . . .

It is interesting to know that Hull House is opening a five cent theater. It is to be strictly up to date and the experiment will run for three months. A Catholic church in Chicago is introducing moving pictures and entertainments for its people. A sub-committee of this group appointed to cooperate with Chief Shippy is making a study of the larger use of Chicago's unsurpassed field houses and playgrounds. It is gratifying to know of these efforts along the line of Dr. Patten's suggestion, that to release virtues is better than to suppress vices.

V. CULTURE OF THE LABOR MOVEMENT

The cultural expressions of Chicago's German population far exceed what one might expect of a foreign group living in an English-speaking country. Comprising immigrants from various European nations, as well as from the Americas and from Asia, Chicago's population has exhibited an enormous cultural diversity. Only with the second generation did English establish itself as the language of everyday life. In the latter half of the nineteenth century when Germans composed such a large proportion of the population, German was the second language of the city. Beginning in the 1850s, an intellectual elite developed within Chicago's German population that contributed enormously to the advancement of German cultural traditions in the city, one example of which was its critical support for the founding of the Chicago Symphony Orchestra. Nevertheless, the great majority of German immigrants belonged to the working class. Around the turn of the century about two-thirds of Chicago's Germans still lived in working-class households. There was therefore a real potential for the formation of a German working-class culture in Chicago, but the forms and contents of this culture were often distinctive in a social context that was in many ways fundamentally different from Germany.

Obviously, the emerging culture of Chicago's German workers remained indebted to German traditions and models. This is no surprise when one considers that German-born craftsmen and skilled workers were at the very core of Chicago's growing labor movement, the institutions of which were the precondition for an emerging working-class culture. Building a new culture in a foreign land, these immigrant workers began with the organizational and social forms familiar to them—the more so since they settled early in the city when there was little else for them to fall back upon. Since immigration from Germany continued almost undiminished until the turn of the century, the emergence of German Social Democracy in the 1870s

and 1880s had an immediate impact upon the German labor movement in Chicago. This intimate connection is most obvious with
respect to the editors of Chicago's German labor press. Experienced
German journalists appeared as editors of even the very earliest
attempts to found a German labor paper in Chicago—men like Joseph
Weydemeyer, Karl Klings, Gustav Lyser, Paul Grottkau, Joseph Dietz-
gen, and Julius Vahlteich, all of whom had already edited labor papers
in Germany.

The German labor press was only one of the institutions that were
copied in an effort to build as complete a network of alternative
working-class institutions as possible. Such an undertaking encountered narrower and different limits than in Germany, since the definition and articulation of working-class culture in America was often
submerged in the necessity of asserting ethnic identity in an unfamiliar
dominant culture. Thus the institutions and forms of German working-class culture in Chicago were under pressure from two sources:
On the one hand, American society demanded cultural integration,
on the other hand the local German population as a whole expected
ethnic solidarity. The latter impetus promoted the perception that
working-class culture was the legitimate heir of the German classical
tradition, a self-concept that was shared by the labor movement in
Germany. This sense of cultural mission was closely tied to the labor
movement's resistance to the increasing "embourgeoisement" of the
German-American population. At the same time, the German labor
movement strove to establish both political and cultural connections
with the numerous ethnic groups in the city by constantly stressing
the movement's international character. Both of these concerns decisively shaped the forms of German working-class culture in Chicago.

This culture was embedded in the neighborhood life of the German
residential districts and had much in common with both middle-
class and religious cultures. Irrespective of differences in politics and
world view, a vigorous associational life spread throughout the German population; and all groups drew on traditions and practices of
a vital German popular culture—such as celebrating with music,
theater, and dance in local meeting halls or holding picnics attended
by the whole family in neighborhood beer gardens or in picnic grounds
located outside the city limits. Nevertheless the culture of the labor
movement distinguished itself from that of other groups when it used
these cultural forms for the promotion of its own particular tradition.
Thus the movement established its own festivals and celebrated its

*own heroes, such as the annual commemorations of the Paris Com-
mune or of the executed Haymarket martyrs. Labor singing societies
sang songs by German "worker" poets from the Vormärz or by
authors among their own ranks, and even the German theater was
used for agitational purposes. In these efforts, outstanding talents
among radical German-American writers were as rare as in Germany.*

*German working-class culture is most appropriately evaluated as
the lived culture of the German-American labor movement. Embedded
in Chicago's union and political movements, this culture formulated
an alternative to the existing order, as well as symbolically presented
this alternative during the movement's regular rituals and celebrations.
Public performance and communal experience were thus decisive
parts of this culture, and they help explain the preference for forms
of expression suited to promoting working-class solidarity. Since it
was a living culture, its contents and forms were also adapted to the
new conditions of life in America and Chicago—a process that was
most complete in its written expressions. For good reason, therefore,
a separate chapter is devoted here to literature (see Chapter VI). The
effort to take up and incorporate American traditions is also evident
in the contents of poems and theater pieces, in the occasions for
celebrations and commemorations, such as those around Haymarket,
as well as in the reinterpretation of Christian traditions and in the
adoption of the ideals of the American Revolution. Finally, one must
also appreciate the intensive effort to transcend ethnic boundaries by
giving celebrations and commemorations an international character
in both theme and audience, just as in the efforts to organize unions
and political initiatives. In this way German working-class traditions
did not simply remain the exclusive domain of Germans, but were
introduced into the ethnically diverse Chicago labor movement.*

The History of Chicago's German-American
Labor Movement

*A year after the great eight-hour movement of 1886 that reached its
peak in Chicago on the May 1 demonstrations and the bomb explosion in Haymarket Square a few days later, the* Vorbote *published
a series of articles that evaluated the historical development of Chicago's labor movement. Excerpts from this series, which was written*

under the influence of these recent events, appear at the beginning of this section. They are included not to present new historical details but rather because the articles express the movement's historical understanding of itself and because they represent its effort to evaluate the experience of the past fifteen years and make it usable for the future. Their very title—"The First of May: the Birthday of the Labor Movement"—radiates this optimistic orientation toward the future, and the account itself sought to make the first of May into a symbol for labor's sense of identity. Two years later in Paris the International Socialist Congress adopted it as Labor Day for the international labor movement. The articles claim an epochal and heroic character for the labor movement, calling—with some irony— on the myths of ancient Greece and asserting that a new age had begun that might even justify the introduction of a new calendar.

The Vorbote's history also contributed to defining an anarcho-syndicalist tradition for the Chicago labor movement that lasted well into the twentieth century. The events singled out in the texts selected here—the demonstration of the hungry and unemployed workers in the winter of 1873, the attacks of the police and militia during the great railroad strike of 1877, the unpunished election swindles against the socialists in 1880—all reinforced the bitter feeling of the politically organized workers that they were systematically excluded from the exercise of basic civil and political rights as well as subject to the arbitrary power and manipulation of industrialists and governmental institutions like the police. The mistrust of official power and authority led to the founding of self-defense groups (see the section on "Armed Organizations" in this chapter) as well as labor institutions that were designed to guarantee local autonomy.

This interpretation of recent historical experience also had an impact on particular developments in the subsequent history of the Chicago labor movement. The events of 1877 and 1880 presented in these texts helped justify the pardoning by Governor Altgeld in 1893 of the three remaining Haymarket anarchists, who were in Joliet prison. George Schilling, the most prominent German-American labor leader in Chicago, was instrumental in the pardoning of the three men. As director of the Illinois Bureau of Labor, Schilling was responsible for the collection of court records and affidavits that were quoted in Altgeld's detailed judicial pardon. Having himself taken part in all these events, Schilling also wrote an introduction to the writings of Albert R. Parsons, one of the Haymarket victims, in which he accepted the Vorbote's *historical point of view. (August Spies, also a victim of Haymarket, probably contributed to the articles.) The anarcho-syndicalist tradition continued up to the founding in 1905 of the Industrial Workers of the World in Chicago. This syndicalist industrial union represented, among other things, an alternative to the political co-optation of the exclusive craft unions and their domination by opportunistic functionaries.*

68. "The First of May. The Anniversary of the Labor Movement. The History of the Development of the Labor Movement in Chicago" (*Vorbote,* May 4 and 18, 1887).

There's a birthday today! Whose -? Well, we're going to have to go into this in a bit of detail. Naturally you've heard of the Christian era? And of the Jewish and Mohammedan too? All right then. As you know, these eras have nothing to do with the age of our Earth; they simply represent special passages in life, in the course of history, in the evolution of ideas among individual peoples. When, some hundred years ago, the French people broke the bonds of an antiquated "social order" as it is called, chopped off the predators' long talons to bring about a sense of civilization and proclaimed the Republic, people agreed that an old chapter had come to a close — we're talking about chapters in that book which registers all of mankind's stupid pranks and follies but also its suffering, its struggle for knowledge, progress and freedom — and that a new era had begun. Napoleon, however, thought that the ending to the old chapter was still missing; so he crossed out the new one and continued the old. At the beginning of the Republic in the United States there were two tendencies as well — on the one hand, there were those who felt that July 4, 1776, should mark a new chapter in the history of the world; on the other hand there were those who shared Napoleon's views — that the old chapter hadn't yet come to a close. And that's why our official papers bear not only the Christian date, but also the Republican (the age of the United States). There's still some confusion concerning this point, although the "premature infant" of 1777 has been stone-dead for a very long time.

We believe that **May 1, 1886,** marks the beginning of a new era, and in this sense we are also answering the question posed at the beginning: today is the anniversary of the modern labor movement and the modern struggle for freedom!

One year ago today, the labor movement in this country began to assume form and shape, and four days later, with a mighty surge, it was born! Whoever has understood the task and purpose of the modern labor movement will agree with us that this anniversary is far more important than the anniversaries of all other eras.

The Greek saga tells how Zeus, having become aware of the absence of a strong god, set out to create one. "Mercury," he said, "run over to Helios and tell him to stay put today, tomorrow and the next day; tell him to unhitch the sun horses, and to extinguish his torch, too. I'm going to pay a visit on Amphitryon's wife, to work on an unusually large and warlike god, and to finish him in a single night is impossible." It is much the same with the labor movement; it was not, as some fools believe, created in *one* hour, or in *one* night, or in three nights, or in a year, or even in a dozen years. In a narrower sense, it required a full century to call this "new god" into existence. But this duration has made it all the more imposing, all the stronger and mightier than the old Thunderer's three-night creation. This isn't simply idle boasting. Our birthday child, one year old, has already tested its strength, and has excited and amazed the world! Our best wishes today are combined with the warmly fostered hope that it continues to amass strength and spirit as it has in the past year. . . .

. . . .

In 1868, Congress passed a law which defined a workday as one comprised of e i g h t   h o u r s. A few years later, this example was followed by legislation in Illinois.[1] As far as this law was concerned, agitation advocating the introduction of the eight-hour system was especially successful because the only big capitalists who could have prevented its passage were people who had "made" their money by swindling and cheating as war contractors ⟨Kriegs-Contraktoren⟩. But at that time, these "upright men"—who, by the way, have the whole government machine, including the legislative and judicial branches, in their pockets today—didn't dare flaunt their plunder; the people's indignation, especially that of the veterans, was still too fresh and too intensely directed against them. And thus it was that practically nothing stood in the way of the demagogic eight-hour agitation, and the bills in question were passed with a *whoop and a yell*. We need say no more about this movement, initiated by the workers and then taken in tow and exploited by the politicians, save that people like Anton Hesing, Conrad Folz,[2] and—to keep the list short—the majority

1. The timing of the Illinois law is incorrect here; it was passed in 1867.
2. Anton Hesing (1823-95), the owner of the *Illinois Staats-Zeitung,* and Conrad Folz were prominent German business and political leaders in Chicago.

of the old German mule heads were among its spokesmen and "creators." If the workers had expected very much from this federal and state legislation, they were soon to be disappointed. Naturally the government couldn't possibly enforce the eight-hour system in the employers' shops — it didn't have the right to interfere in a citizen's private business practices to that extent — "but," the argument went, "if the government were to introduce the eight-hour system in all its own shops among all its own employees, then it could be assumed that the factory and mine owners, as well as employers in general would follow this good example." The employers enjoyed a better reputation at that time, for even the smallest child would simply laugh at such naive assumptions today. . . . Thus there resulted nothing from passage of the eight-hour legislation, unless one considers that a number of political loafers managed to raise themselves to positions of influence, to office, and to boodle by scrambling onto the shoulders of the workers they themselves had duped. And these profiteers then declared that the labor question was solved for the rest of eternity. That's also the reason why they react with anger and fury when, twenty years later, someone calls for an eight-hour system or speaks in terms of the labor movement — haven't they "settled" ⟨"gesettelt"⟩ that whole question once and for all?

. . . .

And yet, or so it seems in any case, though the "leaders" of the former eight-hour movement landed in political office — and have since stolen themselves rich — the question itself, no more than the necessity for a solution, did not disappear. How shortsighted to have believed that by pushing aside a few of the movement's spokesmen the movement itself would be pushed aside! Not long thereafter, especially following the big crash in 1873, one began to perceive — to speak figuratively — new labor pains, evidence of the development of the "god" in the process of becoming. This time the appearance no longer assumed the trustworthy, fair character it had donned before, and along with the demand for an eight-hour day there were other demands as well. On a fall evening in 1873, a column comprised of thousands of workers advanced through the streets of Chicago and came to a halt in front of City Hall on the corner of Adams and LaSalle St., where the police had cordoned off the street! Many of the marchers carried signs which conveyed a first impression as to the character and intention of the demonstration. Some of them expressed various versions of the marchers' thoughts — "We demand work or bread!" and others: "A means of providing us with work is the eight-hour day!" Doubtless for the first time in Chicago, the r e d f l a g, carried by the section of the old International, rippled above the column. Having arrived at City Hall, a delegation proceeded to address the city council, which was then in session, instructing the latter as to the unemployed workers' grievances — naturally, this did not have the slightest effect. The police clubbed some of those who hadn't been careful enough to keep a respectable distance — otherwise everything remained as of old. . . .

Many of our readers can probably still remember the incidents which occurred in '77. The crisis which followed the crash of '73 reached its peak in '77. Large numbers of people were unemployed, industry had come to almost a complete standstill, the wages of those with work were low and in many cases not even paid. . . . "Several hundred railroad workers," — thus the newspapers reported one day — "who are employed by the Baltimore & Ohio Railroad in Maryland, walked off the job because they couldn't get their back pay." One read things like that every day in the newspapers but no one suspected what the next several days would bring. It was subsequently reported that the strikers ⟨Streiker⟩ were obstructing traffic; but nobody would have bothered about even this if at the same time Pittsburgh and other eastern cities hadn't reported that the railroad workers there, too, had walked off the job, and had brought traffic to a complete stoppage.

Was it in the air — who knows? The people looked at each other as though a storm were imminent. Who doesn't know that telling look — "I think something's about to happen"? Nobody says anything, feelings are felt and exchanged through looks; each person assumes — without asking himself why — that everyone else feels the same and that speaking is superfluous. About a dozen members of the old International who had recently formed a marksmen's association gathered that night in a saloon on Lake Street and likewise exchanged looks. "In Pittsburgh the militia fired at the strikers; I always said that the workers will be treated like dogs as long as they don't defend themselves like men, as long as they're not armed." Thus one of those present eventually broke the silence. The others agreed and it was decided that the rifles, in any case, should be kept ready. . . .

The first shots had hardly been fired in Pittsburgh when the electric wires from all the eastern cities began to tremble with the news that railroad transport had been discontinued, and that industrial workers had also "hung up their tools." And like a flashfire, whose flaming torrent is urged on by a wild wind, the wage slaves' rebellion spread westward. On the next day, the workers employed on this city's eastern rails had already walked off the job, and shortly thereafter the workers on the western rails followed suit; they were followed by the Southwest Side sawmill and lumberyard workers ⟨Lumberarbeiter⟩, who proceeded from factory to factory. Wherever they went—as though everything had been prearranged—their appearance was seen as a signal to stop working. Then the procession, growing ever mightier, split into several divisions which spread out in different directions. Everything went on peacefully—only now and then, when the divisions weren't made up of many men, did the police intervene, clubbing the unarmed people furiously. On the following morning, the workers in all of the factories (with the exception of Crane's) had gone on strike. In the meantime, the strikers ⟨Streiker⟩ in Pittsburgh had the militia on the run, and when the latter fled into the roundhouse, it was set on fire and burned to the ground. Reports of "riots" came in from other cities, and it is easy to imagine how colossal the excitement was here. What would the next hour bring? was the question which was written on each person's face. The militia was armed and ready, the police had gathered their forces on the South Side and sworn in hundreds of scoundrels and loafers for $2 a day. The present writer found himself nearby Schuttler's Wagon Factory on the morning when the workers there walked off the job. Some twenty policemen were standing on the sidewalk in front of the factory. The workers only had to stand still for a second, or say something, and they were pummeled by billy clubs. Some of the workers thus beaten collapsed, bloody and unconscious; and when several kicks failed to rouse them and send them on their way, they were thrown into a waiting wagon and brought to the police station, where they were then booked. Some 25,000 people showed up at Market Square for the mass rally which the socialists had called for that evening. Speeches were held by A. R. Parsons,[3] Philip van Patten,[4] and others, and it was decided to hold another rally on the following evening, "since tonight's rally will not have received enough publicity." The next morning, poison, fire and flames were spewed by the newspapers. Parsons was arrested and told that his life wouldn't be worth much if he didn't conduct himself peacefully. Raster,[5] who had intended to call upon a delegation of strikers, disappeared as the latter appeared. Throughout the Southwest Side, there were various rows between strikers and police, whereby the latter always got the worse of the deal. Toward evening half the city seemed to be afoot; all of the

3. Albert R. Parsons (1848-87) was at that time the chairman of Chicago's Trade Council. From 1884 to 1886 he was the editor of the anarchist magazine *The Alarm*. He was sentenced in the Haymarket trial and executed in 1887.

4. Philip van Patten was the chairman of the Socialist Labor party.

5. Hermann Raster (1827-91) was the editor of the German-language *Illinois Staats-Zeitung*.

main streets were crowded with masses of people on their way to Market Square, where the rally was to take place. By around 7 o'clock, what must have been a good 75,000 people gathered in Madison, Washington, Canal, Randolph and Lake Streets—but Market Square itself was empty. It was occupied by the police, who had stormed it just as the rally was beginning to form. They tore down the speakers' platform and brutally clubbed Philip van Patten while he insisted on his right of free speech. When it became apparent that the demonstrators weren't going to disperse so quickly, the blue-coated badge carriers let loose with fire. The workers, not being prepared for this, ran to safety. But once they reached Madison or Randolph St., they were prevented from going any further: in the meantime that colossal human mass had gathered, the same which we just estimated to be 75,000 strong.

A hundred policemen held the square against this army! One can imagine that there was many a loud curse among the workers. Some expressed the opinion that they just move in and crush the handful of murderers, that they couldn't let these capitalist murderers rob them of their right to assemble, while others appeasingly added that they shouldn't let themselves be provoked by this shameful violation of the law, since they were not, unfortunately, armed. Still others threatened to take this affair to court, to fire ⟨"firen"⟩ those who had betrayed the Republic and the Constitution. In those days the people still had great confidence in the Constitution. Rather than getting smaller, the crowd grew, since nobody was thinking in terms of going home. The people were determined—they simply didn't know exactly what they should do. After having waited so long in vain for the crowd to scatter, the police opened fire again and then raised the bridges. But it wasn't until about ten o'clock that the "mob" finally dispersed. Having held the field, the police were now cockier, meaner and more brutal than ever. Besides van Patten, who certainly never would have escaped with his life if he hadn't reverted to cunning, many others were horribly clubbed on that evening. "After the battle," Fred Korth[6] was found unconscious in front of the office of the "Vorbote" with a deep head wound exposing his skull.

This behavior on the part of the police surprised the workers. Until then they had always assumed that the police were security officers, whose job was the prevention of crime and the tracking down of criminals; even the organized workers had been on the best of terms with the police.

6. Fred Korth was a member of both the Socialist Labor party and the Cigarmakers Union.

This delusion disappeared now, shoved aside by stark reality. Those who were supposed to uphold the law and call transgressors to account—after all, that's what one assumed their job to be—those same, in the employ of the rich, trod on the laws and the constitution, and clubbed and shot— "in the name of the law"—those others who, as citizens, looked to them for the protection of their rights! These were no longer public security officers; they constituted a herd of soldiers for the big corporations ⟨Corporationen⟩, like the robber-knight's foot soldiers, like the Praetorian bands of ancient Rome; these were the "sluggers" and "bouncers" in the employ of the rich! The workers' eyes were suddenly opened. But what they just barely perceived then would become fully clear in the bright light of the next day, as though they had abruptly been placed upon the royal road to learning. The Furniture Workers Union held a b u s i n e s s meeting on the following day in the Vorwärts Turner Hall. At the same time, not far away, a division of police attacked, and were beaten back by, a group of strikers ⟨Streiker⟩. Furious, and encouraged by the reinforcements they had just received, the brutes burst into the Vorwärts Turner Hall without a word of warning, striking out left and right, clubbing the amazed workers mercilessly. These latter couldn't understand what was happening. The "security officers"—all the wilder for the blood flowing from the head wounds they had caused, or maybe because the clubbing had become too strenuous—drew their revolvers and fired into the crowd of horrified cabinetmakers. Pandemonium broke loose. Nobody in the closed room knew where to go. Pinkerton[7] writes: "The mob (clearly—the mob!) was completely beyond itself; each police blow felled a man—true Spartans! The rabble (the cabinetmakers!), possessed by a wild horror, scrambled up the columns or threw themselves out the windows headfirst—those were the lucky ones! Because those who succeeded in fleeing through the entrance were clubbed down by a group of robust bluecoats!"

Amazingly enough, only one of the cabinetmakers was murdered—his name was Teßmann. He was struck down by a bullet. The number of those wounded was never ascertained, but it cannot have been very low.

We don't intend to moralize about what we've related today, the reader can draw his own conclusions. Suffice it to say that Chicago's workers never viewed the police in the same light as they had prior to this hour. An indication of this can be seen in the fact that the small rifle association

7. Allan Pinkerton, founder of the Pinkerton Detective Agency, wrote a book entitled *Strikers, Communists, Tramps and Detectives,* published in 1878.

This is a contemporary lithograph of the disruption of the meeting of the Furniture Workers Union in the Vorwärts Turner Hall during the great railroad strike of 1877. Notably the caption did not mention that the scene depicted an unprovoked brutal attack by the police that cost one man his life. (*Harper's Weekly*, August 18, 1877; photo Chicago Historical Society, ICHi-14018.)

which we mentioned above could boast over 1,000 members just one year later (Lehr- und Wehr-Verein).[8]

As can easily be imagined, the "preservation of the peace" in the Vorwärts Turner Hall only served to increase the tension—a tension which was now permeated with a sense of animosity. Shortly after this, there was a large clash not far from the Halsted Street viaduct: the police were beaten back, but the militia's 2d Regiment soon appeared on the scene and fired several rounds into the mass of people. Two companies and a further two batteries of federal troops were not far behind. The people, unarmed as always, fled from the approaching muzzles, and "order" prevailed. It was never revealed how many people on both sides were killed or wounded in this confrontation. This encounter broke the *back bone* of the revolt, or whatever the phenomenon should be called. The subsequent reaction was like that which is known to occur after a "colossal fire," and then

8. See the introduction to the section on "Armed Organizations" in this chapter.

everything returned to usual—but the residues of hate and animosity in the violated workers were not soon to disappear.

....

At the close of our last chapter, "order" prevailed over the people's constitutional rights. It was the first successful attempt on the part of capital to disarm the people and surround its palatial plunder with mercenaries (Pinkertons). The importance of this new change was only perceived by a few people; many others underestimated it, and most people simply didn't bother to think about it. And why, by the way, should the law-and-order-abiding citizen t h i n k? Only h e who d o e s n o t t h i n k can possess these bourgeois virtues! But at this point we would like to quote a statement by the most ingenious diplomat and political philosopher history has yet known—we're referring to Machiavelli. In his "Prince," he says: "There is absolutely no parity between the armed and the unarmed (he's talking in terms of the state). It would be unreasonable to expect the armed to submit to the unarmed, or that the unarmed would be secure amidst its armed servants (soldiers, police, military). On the one hand scorn, on the other mistrust: it is impossible that this combination function well. . . . For several centuries, Rome and Sparta have been a r m e d and f r e e. The Swiss are armed and free."

The first consequences of the militia law—and the disarmament of the people which it entailed—were felt in the spring of 1880.[9] As long as the politicians had known that the young labor party[10] had armed backing they had been more or less well behaved; and though they had swindled the labor party in former elections, it had been done with "propriety and decorum." But now they had no reason to fear, and all pretense of respect and consideration was immediately dropped. There have probably been but few instances of more blatant and shameful riggings of elections than those which were committed against the socialist party in the spring of 1880.

In the 6th Ward, the socialist candidate, Baumrucker, had defeated the arch-corruptionist Cullerton, although the latter had won over a mass of "repeaters"[11] who "worked" for him. Defeated him? Well, be that as it may; Cullerton became, or rather remained, alderman, and Baumrucker was left to console himself with the pleasant knowledge that he had

9. Illinois passed a law in 1879 reorganizing the state militia and specifically prohibiting armed groups like the Lehr- und Wehr-Verein from marching in public.

10. The recently organized Socialistic Labor party had won a surprisingly large vote in the Chicago municipal election of 1879.

11. "Repeaters" voted more than once in the same election.

received a majority of the votes. The deceit was carried out with almost unbelievable transparency. Cullerton withheld the results of two of the precincts ⟨Precincte⟩ located along the canal until all of the other precincts ⟨Precincte⟩ in the ward had reported. He then saw that Baumrucker was leading by several hundred votes. Under these circumstances, a common cheat would have thrown in the towel—but not Cullerton. With the composure that comes from much practice, Cullerton proceeded to add as many votes as he needed to those already cast in the two withheld precincts; Baumrucker's lead dwindled to nothing and Cullerton finished with a majority of some 50 votes! An inquiry conducted immediately thereafter by the socialists revealed that the total number of the people in the two precincts ⟨Precincten⟩ in question—including men, women, and children—did not amount to the number of votes which were supposedly cast for the honorable W. Cullerton! Although this fact was mentioned by the "Law and Order Press," it was referred to as *"a good joke on the socialists."*

The socialists chose not to contest the results, since someone they had shortly before brought to court had been acquitted, despite the fact that his guilt had been proved beyond any doubt. A somewhat different strategy was used in the same election in the 14th Ward. The socialist candidate was F. Stauber; his opponent was J. J. McGrath—nominated by John Bühler (Meik's comrade in arms), by the Streetcar Company, and by Republican lowbrows—that crooked politician with a knowledge of all the ropes. After the votes had been counted that night it was clear that Stauber had won by 58 votes, despite the fact that the Streetcar Company had run several large cars throughout the whole day to fetch "quick" voters.

The good citizens' amazement was not slight, however, when several days later a recount of the results revealed that McGrath had posted a victory by 58 votes. A subsequent inquiry discovered that the original entries in the 7th Precinct had been erased and that others had been substituted in their stead: on the spot, a hundred votes cast for Stauber had been changed in favor of McGrath. Some 150 citizens from the precinct signed affidavits to the effect that they had voted for Stauber, though these same only accounted for 58 Stauber votes in the "corrected lists"! Along with the forged lists, these affidavits were presented to the city council so as to prevent McGrath from being declared the winner. In addition, the citizens of the ward organized a torchlight march to City Hall. But this only led the intimidated corruptionaries to put the affair off to another meeting, and then only to see McGrath's friends—the upright Cullerton, the "honest worker" Lawler and his cronies—welcome him among their midsts without hesitation. Not one of the "Law & Order" organs published a harsh word about this blatant obstruction of justice; they all found it fitting that the city council ignored the socialists' victory and, in an insolent violation of the law, a p p o i n t e d a man who everyone knew to be a rogue in his stead.

It is improbable that this boodle band would have dared this bold stroke p r i o r to the passage of militia law; — but now they had nothing more to fear!

The socialists brought charges ⟨Contestverfahren⟩, and had the people responsible for the fraud — the electoral judges and clerks in that precinct — arrested. About a year and some $2,000 later, McGrath was removed from the city council and the boodlers were forced, by court order, to recognize Stauber's victory. The favorable result of this case was due to action taken by Appellate Judge McAllister; had he not intervened, the case would probably have been drawn out for several years. But the proceedings with respect to the criminal charges were dragged along from one date to another; the intention was to wear down the witnesses so they'd tire of the whole thing and stop showing up. But eventually, two full years after charges had been brought, the case came before Judge Gardner. The witnesses' statements were so overwhelming that both electoral judges, Walsh and Gibbs, pleaded guilty to fraud. According to their own testimony, they had taken the voting boxes and electoral documents to Walsh's house, broken the seals and committed the fraud "in the staunch belief that they were acting correctly." This staunch belief could only be explained by the fact that the person who was cheated, and the violated citizens, were socialists! And then came the most unbelievable of all: the upright Judge Gardner acquitted the confessed criminals, "because it has not been proven that the two had acted with criminal intent"!!

Naturally, the workers' anger upon learning of this disgraceful verdict was great; the model judge was burned in effigy ⟨in effigie⟩ in various places, and protest rallies were held, which were in turn attacked by the law and order organs in the usual manner.

With his decision, Judge Gardner had unambiguously stated that politically independent workers had no rights, and that they should spare themselves the trouble of pursuing "legal channels" in their attempts to obtain them. With this decision he gave the political vagabonds of the old parties the right to do as they pleased with socialist votes: to cheat, violate, deprive the socialists of their rights — that would not be considered an obstruction of justice!

Prior to the passage of the militia law, no one ever would have dared such a disgraceful act!

First the people were disarmed, then they were cheated, and when they raised their voice in indignation, they were laughed at!

It is thus no surprise that the socialists, given the circumstances, stopped taking part in elections. And those who until that time had been the most zealous advocates of the ballot, now only shook their heads and said that apparently nothing was being spared to rouse the people to revolution!

Working-Class Cultural Institutions

This section presents typical cultural institutions of the working class, making no claim, however, to discuss them all. Given the scope of the term working-class culture, there are many institutions, such as political parties and unions, which performed cultural functions, although their main purposes were in other areas. Such organizations will not be discussed here. We will limit ourselves instead to cultural institutions in the narrower sense, which fulfilled particular educational tasks (like the Workers Association), which took on a special local cultural significance (like armed organizations), or which served as the main vehicles of working-class culture (like the press). The free schools, which provided an alternative educational opportunity for children, are discussed in Chapter VII in connection with the critique of parochial and public schools. Singing societies and the labor theater are presented in this chapter in the context of the celebrations and commemorations in which they performed.

The Chicago Workers' Association

Founded as early as 1857, the Chicago Workers' Association (Arbeiterverein) represented the German tradition of labor educational societies. Although an occasional communist speaker delivered a lecture before it—or exercised some influence, as did Joseph Weydemeyer in 1860—the association remained solidly in the tradition of artisan republicanism and included middle class and liberal elements in both its goals and membership. It also fought regularly for "German interests." Since it was the most important among the similar as-

sociations founded at this time in other American cities, it assumed the leadership of the loose national organization they formed. After the end of the Civil War it was represented at conventions of the National Labor Union and promoted the first contacts between this body and the International Workingmen's Association.

Nevertheless, its goals were primarily educational and social. This was evident in the Social Workers' Association of the West Side (Sozialer Arbeiterverein der Westseite), one of the branch institutions formed on the model of the central one. The organization on the West Side built the first labor hall in Chicago in 1864. It was designed to accommodate large performances, smaller meetings, and simple social get-togethers. In this regard it preceded the Turner halls which were later built in all parts of the city and which similarly served as centers of German politics, culture, and social life. The Social Workers' Association existed until the 1890s and continued to serve its original purposes.

69. "The New Hall of the West Side Social Workers Association" (*Illinois Staats-Zeitung*, October 13, 1864).

The West Side Social Workers Association has built a new hall, which was made possible by selling shares to German citizens living on the West Side, and especially to its own members. The building is 40 by 70 feet long and 2 stories high. On the ground level, space has been set aside for two stores which are to be rented ⟨verrentet⟩ so as to help the association be able to honor the shares all the sooner. Behind the stores is a spacious room which will be used for association meetings. The actual hall, on the first floor, is 40 by 44 feet long, with very high ceilings, and is extremely light and airy due to the big, stately arched windows.

The association is pleased to have approximately 130 members, all of whom are workers staunchly committed to the goal toward which the association strives—namely to furnish the members with social and political education so they can keep close watch over their rights, in order to insure life, liberty, and the pursuit of happiness for themselves and their children. There are no political charlatans or demagogues in the association who, in order to indulge in their own ambition, pose behind jingoistic phrases as advocates of human rights; there are only men who want justice. That the members are unequivocally in accord about their endeavors and direction can be gathered from the fact that none of them shied away

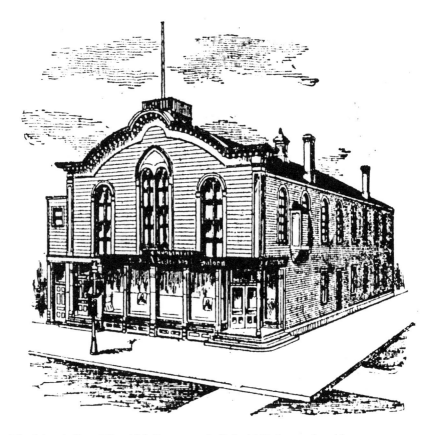

The labor hall on West 12th Street was built in 1864. It was the oldest permanent meeting place owned by Chicago's German workers. (*Der Westen*, September 5, 1897.)

from any sacrifice demanded by the building of the hall, and it is therefore clear that prosperity and success will be the association's due.

On Sunday evenings the hall is to be used for concerts which will begin next Sunday, and on Monday evening the hall is to be inaugurated with a splendid ball. Three cheers for the upright German citizens of the Social Workers Association.

Armed Organizations

German socialists founded the Education and Defense Association (Lehr- und Wehr-Verein) *in 1875 in reaction to election frauds as well as police violence against demonstrations of the unemployed during the depression. Its charter committed it to the following goals: "The association is formed for the purpose of improving the mental and bodily condition of its members, so as to qualify them for the duties of citizens of a Republic. Its members shall therefore obtain . . . a knowledge of our laws and political economy, and shall also be instructed in military and gymnastic exercises." Thus the organization understood itself as a self-defense and educational association and allied itself with the republican traditions of an armed citizenry and militia, particularly as they were represented in America by the Turners but above all as they existed in Switzerland. A popular republican militia was supposed to have been set up in Germany during the Revolution of 1848. Chicago's Lehr- und Wehr-Verein grew considerably in membership after the violence by police against workers during the railroad strike of 1877. In response the Illinois legislature passed a law in 1879 that made such armed groups illegal, while at the same time tightening up the organization of the state militia. This political reaction to the armed organizations of the 1870s was more important than the actual activities of these groups, which in fact limited themselves to training drills, keeping order at meetings, and educating their members.*

Instead of illustrating such activities, the poems reprinted here reflect the self-awareness of the Lehr- und Wehr-Verein and the German-speaking Hunters Association (Jägerverein), which split off from it. The second poem was composed for delivery at the dedication of the flag of the Jägerverein. It illustrates the common tendency of the German-American labor movement to use literary forms for agitational and ceremonial purposes, putting literature first and foremost to practical use in the movement as a means to awaken feelings and emotions and to contribute to the solidarity of its members. The author, Gustav Lyser, was an early spokesman for the romantic and revolutionary tendency in the Chicago labor movement; from 1877 to 1879 he edited the Fackel, *the Sunday edition of the* Chicagoer Arbeiter-Zeitung. *(See the biographical sketches at the end of this volume.) He was a master at using European and American liberal and libertarian traditions for buttressing labor's struggles for civil rights, and at characterizing the two armed organizations as defenders of the inalienable rights codified in the Declaration of Independence and the Constitution.*

70. "Our Dear Police," by Gustav Lyser (*Vorbote,* May 4, 1878).

> They say our dear Chicago police
> Are pretty sore these days,
> It seems the L e h r - u n d We h r - Ve r e i n
> Has led their minds astray.
>
> It t e a c h e s[12] constitutional truths
> For all - not just th'elite,
> And that no one the r i g h t t o a s s e m b l e
> M a y t r a m p l e u n d e r h i s f e e t!
>
> It t e a c h e s what is guaranteed,
> - And read it each man might -
> To l i b e r t y, l i f e, p u r s u i t o f h a p p i n e s s
> We h a v e a c o m m o n r i g h t!
>
> It t e a c h e s, how we must d e f e n d
> 'Gainst tyranny's reckless flood;
> That f r e e d o m much from us d e m a n d s -
> May e'en d e m a n d our b l o o d!
>
> That's why our dear Chicago police
> Are pretty sore these days:
> For such a Lehr- und Wehr-Verein
> Has set their fears ablaze.

71. "Upon Dedicating the Colors of the Chicago Jägerverein on June 15, 1879," by Gustav Lyser (*Fackel,* June 15, 1879).

> T'was here they felled the monarchy, the
>   Stars and Stripes unfurled were flying,
> The people spurred on ever more, the odds
>   all bravely thus defying.
> As people free on land untouched, this
>   was the goal which they all sought,
> So midst the fire of cannon and gun, around
>   the flag they fiercely fought.
> Here was defeated the foe of old, where now
>   a new one's seen to run;

---

12. The verb *to teach* in German is *lehren,* and here it of course relates to the official name of the organization.

Devoid of shame, his methods crude, and
   treason he would hardly shun.
Of this today you must beware, and
   to the flag of freedom true,
If e'er he seek to tread on you, your
   arms must chase the foe from view!
So pledge yourselves to the Republic, and ne'er
   your arms be wrenched away,
For he who is without defense, with
   bondage soon will have to pay!
Labor alone makes all of worth, and
   labor only this shall reap,
No more the lazy parasite, amidst
   the fount of wealth shall steep;
No more shall sons of workers bend, before
   the wealthy tyrant's will,
No more shall hordes of lazy swanks
   in others' anguish find their thrill!
So raise the banner now and swear, by
   strength of arms it to defend,
And every hour of every day, you
   will your service freedom lend.
One day from people's eyes will fall, the
   fold that long has kept them blind,
One day throughout all of the land, their
   weapons will be of one mind!
"More time! more bread!" thus rings the cry
   - advance to victory or death!
And in the end, this sacred war will
   mark the enemy's last breath!
Good hunters all, you'll take a stand, brave
   comrades standing at your side,
You'll prove that only strength and steel, will
   vanquish misery's awful tide!
Faithful always to the flag, bold
   will the volunteer[13] stand by -
And three cheers for those who'll fight,
   it's on our arms we must rely!

13. The German word translated as *volunteer* is *Wehrmann* (wehren = to resist, defend), which calls to mind the Lehr- und Wehr-Verein.

The Labor Press

No institution was more important for Chicago's German-American workers than the Chicagoer Arbeiter-Zeitung *and its Sunday and weekly editions, the* Fackel *and the* Vorbote. *In various forms, this paper existed for a period of fifty years from 1874 to 1924. German labor organizations had attempted to found newspapers in the 1850s and 1860s, but they were short-lived. Only with the development of the Chicago labor movement, in which German workers played so substantial a part, and with the growth of Chicago's German population did a large enough constituency exist to support such a venture on a long-term basis. Competing labor papers representing other political tendencies were founded in later years, but they did not survive. The* Arbeiter-Zeitung *was published by the Socialistic Publishing Association (later the* Chicago Arbeiter-Zeitung *Publishing Company), which was organized on a noncommercial basis following the model of Social-Democratic publishing houses in Germany. The paper even survived the repression after Haymarket, when its offices were raided by the police and its entire staff arrested; it reestablished itself once again in September 1917 after similar raids.*

To be sure, the paper faced constant financial difficulties, except for the vital early years of the 1870s and the first half of the 1880s. The competitive pressure was enormous from German middle-class papers such as the Illinois Staats-Zeitung *and later the* Abendpost, *as well as from the English-language press. Thus throughout its history the* Arbeiter-Zeitung *called on the German workers of Chicago to subscribe, appeals which illuminate the paper's own perception of itself. The paper experienced a particularly severe crisis after 1900, when its former readers changed their reading habits along with their social position and when the maintenance of a distribution network became more expensive as subscribers moved toward the city periphery. The 1903 report of the Publishing Company's delegate assembly is especially impressive for its list of all the organizations which saw their interests represented by the paper. These organizations illuminate the thick network of associations and clubs that helped the paper survive.*

The significance of the Arbeiter-Zeitung *for the German workers of Chicago can be seen by simply listing its manifold functions. It reported in detail on the political, union, and reform movements in*

*the city and the country at large; published announcements of union,
party, and club meetings as well as short accounts of their minutes;
agitated at demonstrations, strikes, boycotts, and elections for labor
interests; maintained contact with developments in Germany; re-
viewed cultural events and theatrical performances; serialized often
demanding and critical historical novels; instructed its readers on
economic, social, cultural, and scientific subjects; and as an institution
organized anniversaries of important events, celebrations, and picnics.
The paper's editors had typically been active as journalists in Germany, and they applied their journalistic and organizational experience in Chicago, where they helped found unions and lead political
initiatives. It is thus no accident that so many of the documents in
this volume were taken from the* Chicagoer Arbeiter-Zeitung.

*The paper was distributed throughout the German neighborhoods.
Hence the* Arbeiter-Zeitung's *readership cannot be adequately measured by the number of its subscribers, since it passed through many
hands and was available in saloons, a fact frequently exploited in
the ads the saloonkeepers put in the paper. The* Arbeiter-Zeitung
*was therefore the most important purveyor of an alternative historical
and social vision within the culture of Chicago's working class, as
well as frequently the only reliable source of information about issues
that directly affected local workers.*

72. "A Few Words to Our Friends" (*Chicagoer Arbeiter-Zeitung*, June 6, 1903).

This number marks the close of the "Chicagoer Arbeiter-Zeitung's"
twenty-sixth year. It could be asked: And just what has been accomplished
in this time? The answer: both little and a lot. A lot, because we have
managed to bring out a radical, independent, German-language labor paper
every day for such a long time in Chicago; little, because there's still so
much to do to bring our goal within reach, the goal of carrying forth the
torch of the revolutionary proletarian movement.

Some readers may shrug their shoulders and think: well, what's so great
about that? several dozen labor papers appear in Germany and Austria.
And this is true enough, but one tends to forget that this kind of paper
has to struggle with completely different, difficult conditions here in America. It's no little trick to get a foothold here, a core, which doesn't evaporate
among the rush of endless unfavorable influences contained in this melting

pot. The following are but a few of these influences: the changes which
the immigrants experience here amidst foreign conditions in their ways of
looking at the world and ways of life. Frequently, those ideals brought
with them are quickly lost on the other side of the ocean. Sometimes it
almost seems as though, in an unguarded moment on the way over, they're
thrown overboard, so that they won't get in the way in the "New World,"
won't serve as ball and chain, won't prevent them from "getting ahead."
Among most of the newly arrived, this "getting ahead" is craved above
all. Few are drawn to the "land of the free"; many more are attracted to
the land of money, of pushiness, of humbug. It isn't long before many
are swimming along with the flotsam, snapping at the bait in front of
them. A few years later you meet them again as second class politicians,
or else they become engrossed in the stifling atmosphere of Teutonic club
life, which is nowhere so pathetically shallow and bogged-down as it is
here. Others reappear as church members, half an eye on God in Heaven,
the other one and a half on "business" ⟨"Busineß"⟩. Above all, there's
no young generation among the German inhabitants with an intellectual
storm and stress in its veins, that wants something more than the dollar-
ideal. The young people prefer sports, the Katzenjammer Kids, Gaston and
Alphonse. Along the mud banks, not against the stream, that is the catch-
word.

Given such conditions, it must be viewed as a glorious deed that a part
of Chicago's German population has shown support for the "Chicagoer
Arbeiter-Zeitung," a paper which has directed its potent weapons against
the everyday slovenliness, the pushiness, the intellectual and political corruption, the stultification and dulling of the mind, and which has issued
the resounding message that humanity, despite all its pathetic complacency,
will not get bogged down in this social mire, but rather march on, the
drums and inspiration of the social revolution, toward our goal: true
solidarity and freedom for all.

Let him who is of this opinion continue to maintain our standards, but
not just that, let him also recruit new readers and friends.

On facing page

These two photographs show the typesetting and printing rooms of the *Chicagoer
Arbeiter-Zeitung.* They appeared in an anniversary issue of the Sunday edition,
Die Fackel, published in 1897. Their poor quality derives from the fact that they
had to be copied from microfilm, since the originals are not available. (*Fackel,*
September 5, 1897.)

Masthead of *Die Fackel*, Sunday edition of the *Chicagoer Arbeiter-Zeitung*. (*Fackel*, May 25, 1879; photo courtesy of the Newberry Library, Chicago.)

On facing page

This advertisement appeared practically unchanged for years. It promoted the daily, weekly, and Sunday editions of the German labor paper. (*Vorbote*, October 12, 1892.)

73. "Delegate Meeting. Lively Interest Is Expressed for the Labor Press"
(*Chicagoer Arbeiter-Zeitung,* October 12, 1903).

Yesterday, at the invitation of its directorate's Agitation Committee, the
"Chicagoer Arbeiter-Zeitung Publishing Company" held a meeting in Wosta's Hall at Lake and Desplaines St. Presided over by Fritz Benthien,
President of the "Chic. Arb.- Ztg. Publ. Co.," the participants were comprised of delegates from all those associations whose interests are closely
affiliated with those of the "Arbeiter-Zeitung." The purpose of the meeting
was to discuss the possibilities of acquiring a larger printing press which
would make the only organ representing the working people's struggle
here in Chicago more competitive.

A three-hour debate ensued, after which it was decided to make plans
for the acquisition of a press, and to have the delegates report to their
respective associations. Another delegate meeting was planned for Sunday,
November 8, at 10 o'clock in Wosta's Hall, where the representatives of
the unions, Turner societies, singing societies, and other organizations
supporting the project will report on the reactions of their respective
groups. They will then start right in on the work to adapt the newspaper —
which has struggled for human rights for 27 years — to modern require-
ments and thus make it more competitive.

The following organizations were represented:

Central Labor Union, by M. Lehn, Abel and E. J. Schwartz.

Brewers and Maltsters Union No. 18, by J. Butzer and F. Jung.

Beer Bottlers Union No. 248, by F. Kraus.

Machinists Union "Equality" No. 366, by Christ. Löffel.

Coopers Union No. 94, by August Hochnapfel.

Bakers Union No. 2, by Hugo Nitz and Jos. Hartmann.

Bartenders and Waiters Union "Allemania," by Louis Panzer and Julius
Meyer.

German Painters Union No. 275, by A. Strampfer, J. Kaiser, Wm. Scharf
and J. Klein.

Chicago Furriers Union, by O. Böttcher and A. Heineke.

Amalg. Woodworkers Union No. 1, Chas. Pueschel and Ernst Huebner.

Carpenters Union No. 242, by Fred Miller and Chas. Neckermann.

Carpenters Union No. 419, by H. Pueschel.

Typographia No. 9, by E. Ebel, Conrad Neff and Wm. Schroeder.

Freedom Lodge No. 336, I.A. of Machinists, by Fr. Waßmann and Gus.
Bloettner.

Social Turnverein, by Frank Kremer.

Englewood Turnverein, by Christ. Loeffel.

Aurora Turnverein, by Leopold Neumann.

Concord Turnverein, by F. Koch.

Almira Turnverein, by E. Liebset.

Advance Turnverein, by O. Weiß.

Progress Turnverein, by Chas. S. Neumann.

Columbia Turnverein, by Fritz Greve.

Oak Turnverein, by Fritz Rethig.

Freedom Turnverein, by S. Schiefelbein.

LaSalle Turnverein, by Fr. Hintz.

Plattdeutsche[14] Main Guild, by J. Hy. Mueller.

Women's Sick and Benefit Club "Progress," by Marie Suhr, Sophie Jacobsen and Marie Isaack.

Debating Club No. 1 of Chicago, by A. Schneider, A. Freymann, Theo Appel and P. Vandree.

Northwest Side Free-Thinking Community, by John Mentzer.

Plattdeutsch Guild No. 1, by Simon Luedemann.

German Singing Society "Freedom," by W. Lehnert, G. Rupprecht, H. Witt and E. D. Deuß.

Socialist Men's Choir, by Fritz Reuter.

Journeyman Butchers Mutual Benefit Society, by Engelken.

Workmen's Sick and Benefit Society Branch No. 49, Otto Papendick and Anton Mahr.

Workmen's Sick and Benefit Society Branch No. 66, Louis Mueller, Oscar Gritschke and Leopold Baer.

Workmen's Sick and Benefit Society Branch No. 101, by Fritz Kalbitz.

In addition, Mr. Aug. Asche and several other board members of the "Chic. Arb.-Ztg. Publ. Co." were present at the meeting.

74. "Are You a Class-Conscious Worker?" (*Chicagoer Arbeiter-Zeitung,* April 21, 1908).

W h y isn't there a copy of the "Chicagoer Arbeiter-Zeitung" in your home? It's the only one which represents your interests.

W h y do you read bourgeois pulp?

D i d these papers ever help you when a w a g e d i s p u t e broke out in your shop or factory?

---

14. *Plattdeutsch* is a regional dialect in northwestern Germany. In this case it is used to designate a lodge whose membership apparently was made up of immigrants from that region.

Or to the contrary, haven't these bourgeois papers always sided, more or less unconditionally, with y o u r   o p p o n e n t s   a n d   e x p l o i t e r s?

Do you w a n t to look like a traitor to your working brothers by lending our common enemies ammunition in the form of subscription money?

Don't you t h i n k that it's high time to rid your home of these bourgeois papers?

If y o u' r e a m a n, you'll look over these questions i m m e d i a t e l y for t h e i r validity and send us your address with an order for the "Chicagoer Arbeiter-Zeitung."

And while you're at it, tell the friend, neighbor or colleague that you meet, too!

Then you'll be a class-conscious worker!

Book Clubs and Lending Libraries

Humanistic and socialist literature was distributed to workers by many organizations, always in close association with similar endeavors by the labor press. The following document illustrates such efforts by the International Working People's Association; but unions, Turner societies, debating clubs, and other neighborhood labor institutions—such as the previously noted Social Workers' Association of the West Side—also established their own libraries. In this way their members could profit from instruction and political education available in books and pamphlets that they otherwise could not afford. The works in such libraries ranged from popular socialist agitational material, through treatises on natural science and reform, to elevated poems and novels, most of them by European and above all German writers. Foreign and domestic newspapers were also available in such libraries. A debating club founded on the Northwest Side in the 1890s subscribed to the following journals besides the Chicagoer Arbeiter-Zeitung *and the* Fackel: *the* Sozialist, *the* Freiheit, *the* Zukunft (all from New York) as well as the Arme Teufel (Detroit). The members of this club were actively involved in the development and maintenance of their collection, as indicated by their numerous discussions about the acquisition of a suitable bookcase in which to store it. The list reprinted below of the works available through the book club of the International Working People's Association illustrates the available socialist literature. This collection was expanded through the works offered in the Zurich* Sozialdemokrat, *which was published* *in exile by the German Socialist Labor party during the period of the repressive Socialist Law. In the summer of 1881 the* Chicagoer Arbeiter-Zeitung *published the* Sozialdemokrat's *list of titles—with 275 entries!*

75. "Socialist Book Sale Agency" (*Chicagoer Arbeiter-Zeitung,* October 27, 1884).

The following titles can be purchased from G. Matzinger and Anton Mirschberger, the librarians at the International Working People's Association, 107 Fifth Avenue, for the prices listed here:

Information concerning the Baden Revolution ....$ .50
A x e l r o d: The Social-Revolutionary Movement in Russia......... .15
B a k o u n i n e: *God and the State*................................... .15
B e b e l, A.: Peasant's War.. .75
—Christianity and Socialism .... .10
—The Woman... .75
—The Era of Mohammedan Culture .... .50
—Our Goals.. .10
B e c k: The Jewish Question .... .30
Leaves and Blossoms from Luther's Writings....................... .10
B l o c k: Parliamentary Practice.................................... .25
The Civil War in France... .10
The Diplomat, A Caricature... .05
D o u a i: *Better Times* .... .10
E n g e l s: From Utopia to Science .... .15
G r e u l i c h: The State... .10
—Karl Fourier .... .15
    The Nihilists .... .05
H a s e n c l e v e r, W.: My Own Experiences....................... .20
H e i n e: A Winter's Tale .... .10
H o ff m a n n: Concerning the Solution to the Social Question ..... .15
J o o s, Dr. W.: Anatomy of the Mass.............................. .75
K a u t s k y: Population Increase.................................... .75
—Ireland.. .30
L a s s a l l e, F.: Court Speeches................................... .25
—Bastiat Schultze .... .35
—Works in three volumes, bound................................. 5.25
    in 41 pamphlets... .10

—Workers' Reader .... .10
L i e b k n e c h t: Knowledge Is Power .... .10
—Concerning Landed Property .... .25
M i r o v i c: Sophia Perowskaja .... .10
M a r x: Capital 3.50
M o s t, J.: Beast of Ownership, 33 pamph 1.00
   single pamphlets .... .05
—The Godly Plague and Religious Epidemic, 33 pamph 1.00
   single pamphlets .... .05
—Tactic against Freedom .... .05
—Petit Bourgeoisie .... .15
—Social Movements in Ancient Rome .... .20
P e t z l e r: Social Architecture, 2 vols 2.00
S a c k: Schools in the Service of Freedom .... .30
S c h r a m m: Basics of National Economics .... .10
Social Democratic Reader .... .15
S t a r k w e a t h e r - W i l s o n: *Socialism* .... .15
S t i e b e l i n g: Reader .... .20
—*People's Reader* .... .20
—Socialism and Darwinism .... .15
V o l l m a r: Isolated State .... .10
—The Devastation of the Woods .... .10
The True Nature of Christianity .... .15
   Struggle and Harmony .... .05
   Song Books .... .20
   Communist Manifesto, 100 pamph. 2.00
   Single pamphlets .... .05
   Communistic Manifesto .... .05

Any socialist titles not listed here can be purchased through us. Groups
and colporteurs in Chicago are entitled to reductions. Those living outside
of Chicago will n o t receive reductions, but all books will be sent w i t h -
o u t   c h a r g e   f o r   p o s t a g e.

The   l i b r a r i a n s   o f   t h e   C h i c a g o   I.W.P.A.

Demonstrations

*In its mass demonstrations the labor movement appealed to a public
much larger than the organized workers that composed it. Whether*

in street demonstrations to support strikes, protest meetings against political corruption, or annual picnics to raise money for the Arbeiter-Zeitung, *the movement had to call upon the solidarity of an audience that varied widely in its commitment to socialist values and in its degree of participation in leftist activities. Thus demonstrations provided an opportunity for the labor movement to present itself publicly and appeal to a wider circle of potential supporters.*

The demonstrations described in the following three documents are included here not so much for their political messages or the occasions which led to them but rather because of their similarity in organizational form and public ritual. Although the dates of these parades mark off a forty-year period from the May demonstration of 1867 to the Labor Day parade of 1903, the three parades all show a notable continuity in set-up, themes, and symbolic forms. The parades obviously served as an occasion for the participating labor organizations to present their images of themselves to the public. In the case of the trade union parades, craft and even guild elements are clearly in the foreground, exemplified by the special costumes of the members and the distinctive craft symbols. Floats were present in all three demonstrations, as were banners typically inscribed with agitational slogans. And, of course, no demonstration or parade would be complete without a band.

The demonstration of 1884 is distinguished from the other two by its radical flavor and its critical stance toward society. That is not surprising, since the demonstration was organized by the International Working People's Association. It counted a significant number of unions among its participants as well. By employing colorful and dramatic satire, the organizers of the parade effectively brought their critical message home to the public.

One should not, however, allow the similarities in the basic symbolic and organizational forms of these demonstrations to obscure the fundamental changes that took place in the second half of the nineteenth century. The Illinois Staats-Zeitung's reporting of the 1867 eight-hour demonstration made a point of describing the German unions and associations in detail as well as justly praising the German contribution to the whole effort. In contrast, little was said about the ethnic composition of the IWPA's demonstration in 1884, except for a reference to the Bohemian and American groups. By the Labor Day parade of 1903 there were not even special sections for particular ethnic groups, despite the fact that some of them were strongly

represented in particular occupations—the Germans were concen-
trated, for example, among the woodworkers, machinists, metal work-
ers, wagonmakers, bakers, and carpenters. The sheer dimensions of
the demonstrations had also fundamentally changed, given the sharp
increase in the organized sector of the work force: over 75,000 union-
ists took part in the Labor Day Parade of 1903, which was also an
indication that this much contested labor holiday had finally become
accepted.

76. The May Day Demonstration of 1867 (*Illinois Staats-Zeitung*, May 2 and 3, 1867).

The Eight-Hour Movement! Magnificent Demonstration Staged by the Workers of Chicago. Mottos and Slogans on the Banners. The Mass Rally. . . .

The Eight-Hour Bill became law yesterday and to celebrate, thousands of local workers set out to the accompaniment of bands, carrying the banners and badges of their trades. The demonstration was grand and impressive.

Forming on Lake Street and the adjoining streets, the procession set out at ten . . . and moved . . . to the lakeshore not far from Harmon Court. More than a mile long, the procession made a deep impression on the thousands of onlookers who had gathered along the streets and especially at the intersections. All along the procession route, the stairways and doorways, even the roofs, were jammed with curious spectators.

The marchers sported an almost countless number of banners, flags, mottos, etc. The following are but a few of the inscriptions: "In God We Trust!" "Eight Hours and No Concession." "To the Advantage of the Coming Generation." "Illinois on the Side of Reform." "United We Stand, Divided We Fall." "Eight Hours, a Legal Day's Work." - "We Respect the Laws of the State." - "The Workers' Millennium."

The marble cutters were represented by a four-horse wagon carrying various monuments and marble products.

The millstone cutters by a four-horse wagon upon which a large millstone was being cut.

The tanners also had a wagon on which two men were working intently on a beam.

The day laborers were represented by a four-horse wagon, on which rode several day laborers with the various tools of their trade.

The Moulders' Union appeared with an eight-horse wagon on which were displayed all the materials, tools, and machinery needed for moulding.

The ship carpenters and caulkers had erected a completely rigged ship on which the caulkers were working.

Next was a delivery wagon with a coffin bearing the inscription "Death and Burial of the Ten-Hour System."

A large wagon carried a steam engine and a drill on which various men were working. Another wagon carried a blacksmith shop in full operation. Still another wagon carried a colossal boiler which was hammered, riveted, and knocked on by a number of workers.

Then another delivery wagon appeared, again with a coffin on which were inscribed the words "Death and Burial of the Chicago Times,"[15] and above the coffin, hanging from a gallows, was a dummy with veiled head.

The fifth division was made up of workers' delegates from Aurora, Amboy, and Centralia, some 500 in number.

We cannot say for sure how many people participated in the procession, but there were several thousand in any case.

A little after noon the procession reached the area along the lake north of Park Row, where the mass rally took place. Mayor J. B. Rice presided, and was the first to speak. After him Mssrs. A. C. Kuykendall, A. C. Trevallick and various others spoke. The rally was highly enthusiastic and unity prevailed.

At about 4 o'clock the various divisions and their bands returned to the city. Later in the evening, to commemorate the day, bonfires were lit in various places.

The German Division in the Eight-Hour Procession

The German Division deserves special mention as one of the grandest and most impressive divisions in yesterday's labor demonstration.

It was commanded by Marshal C. F. Lichtner and his adjutants Gustav Sunshine and John F. Cook. Leading the way was the Great Western Light Guard Band, followed by Mr. Strehlow, standard-bearer of the German Division, with a large German flag.

Next came the German Bricklayers' Association ⟨Bricklegerassociation⟩ 230 men strong, with the organization's insignia—hammer and trowel embroidered in gold on white aprons. The group carried an American flag and a tricolor as well as the association banner which was embroidered with the date of its foundation and appropriate inscription. Next followed

15. There had been a bitter strike by the typographers union against the *Chicago Times* in 1864.

the Union Veterans' Club, 80 men strong, with American flags and banners bearing appropriate mottos. Then came the Union and Aurora Turnverein, some 120 men strong. In their white uniforms and club colors, they offered a magnificent spectacle.

The German Carpenters and Joiners Association, 700 men strong, came next. They were followed by two wagons upon which workers exhibited their various crafts. The first wagon displayed a carpenter's shop where several carpenters were joining doors and sashes, while on the second wagon cabinetmakers were making tables, chairs, bureaus, and sofas. The sides of one of the wagons were draped with canvas on which were drawn a tombstone, a weeping willow, and the words: "10 Hours—Born 1842, Died 1867." The organization also carried a silk flag on which was embroidered a golden eagle with outspread wings.

Next came the German Workers' Association, 173 men strong. Its banner bore the inscription "Progress in Equality and Solidarity."

Behind it there followed a large four-horse wagon displaying a shop where toys and baby carriages were being produced. Two men were busy working at a small anvil, while others worked at a lathe in another corner of the mobile shop. The wagon was adorned with an abundance of baby carriages and toy horses, the products of their labor, as well as with flags and banners. The names of the owners, Mssrs. Westermann and Schoeninger, were attached in front. Behind this a second Westermann-Schoeninger wagon, also garnished with flags and ribbons, carried seven girls in white dresses who were making parts for baby carriages on sewing machines. Above their heads was a banner with the inscription: "The Eight-Hour System Will Be a Benefit for All." A third wagon owned by the same firm carried the motto: "From 12 to 10 and from 10 to 8 Is National Progress."

Bringing up the rear came a wagon representing the gilders, upon which several workers were occupied with pictures and mirrors. It bore a banner with the inscription: "Eight Hours a Legal Day's Work."

The German Division was deservedly welcomed with enthusiastic applause by everyone, and it was, as already pointed out above, the best-ordered and most impressive section of the whole procession.

Many German workers were represented in other divisions as well. Especially the stonecutters in the first Division, more than half of whom were Germans, made a very good impression. The association was 259 men strong. All wore white silk aprons upon which were printed a raised arm holding a hammer, an angle gauge, and a pair of compasses. The officers of this organization wore blue scarves. Then came a wagon drawn by six gray horses on which was displayed the association's banner embroidered with a stonecutter working at a column. One side of the banner had the inscription "We Unite to Protect Ourselves, Not to Hurt Anyone," and on the bottom were written the words "Stonecutter Workers' Association of Chicago." George Washington's picture was on the other side with the inscription "The Father of Our Country," while below were drawn two joined hands and the words "Unity Is Strength." Next followed members of the association and another six-horse wagon. It displayed parts of a gothic column being hewn by several workers. The sides of the wagon were inscribed with the mottos "The Stonecutter Workers," "The Eight-Hour Pioneers," "We Have Them and We Will Hold Fast to Them." Next followed another party of the association and a third four-horse wagon, which on one side carried the inscription "Hail to May 1, 1867, A Day Long to Be Remembered by All Workers." Upon the wagon, stonecutters were busy with hammer and chisel, others held a banner displaying on one side the words "Eight Hours," and a man sitting below in a chair smoking and reading, while on the other side were written the words "Ten Hours" with a man below working on a stone column.

77. The International Working People's Association Organizes a Demonstration and a Picnic (*Chicagoer Arbeiter-Zeitung*, June 30, 1884).

In the past few years, the Weather God has more than once thwarted the communists, why we cannot say. But yesterday he was all the more decent for it: the day was magnificent, a bit warm, but not disagreeably so. And like the weather, not even the smallest cloud darkened the procession and the festival—everywhere one looked, people were being entertained and amused.

A clear sky and cheerful faces—that was the picture which presented itself to anyone visiting Ogden's Grove yesterday. Each person with a bit of feeling was doubtless impressed by the contentment and good will prevalent everywhere, so thoroughly different from the affected festivals of our overfed bourgeoisie.

The overworked proletarian and his modest wife, worn out by worries and cares, can seldom enjoy an hour of amusement, relaxation, and entertainment. At best, this happens but once or twice a year; at worst, not for years on end. But when it does happen, they enjoy this hour thoroughly, though moderately—to the extent that their means allow. But enough of this.

Early yesterday morning, dressed for the occasion, small and large groups of proletarians proceeded to the various gathering points, and from there, in orderly columns and to the accompaniment of music, to the main meeting place at Market Square. At 54 W. Lake St. there was an especial amount of bustling and activity, where dozens of diligent hands were busily completing the decorations on the float. It goes without saying that there was no lack of spectators.

Around 10 o'clock, Market Square began to fill up with people. Group after group arrived, increasing the size of those already assembled. Dozens of red banners and American flags rippled in the gentle breeze, and the crowd, reading the abbreviated slogans on the yet larger number of signs, discussed them with lively interest. The three large floats arrived shortly before 11 o'clock. Their frames were so high that it was not without much effort that they were carried over the bridges. Quickly, Marshals Bluhm and Neebe organized the procession, and at 11 o'clock it got under way. Its makeup was as follows:

1st D i v i s i o n: Meinken's Band, Custom Taylors Union; signs: "Private Capital Is Exploitation"; *"All Workmen Have Identical Interests"*; then came the Typographia No. 9 with its own flag and a red one, as well as the sign: "Workers of the World Unite." The first float was next, representing the Reign of Throne, Altar and Money Bag. Uppermost, seated upon the throne, representing the grace of God, was a dissipated glutton and idiot, a mistress standing next to him as *Rex de facto.* Two monks, representing the domain of the church, stood one step below; to the great irritation of our pious citizenry, they proclaimed the "Holy Word" and spread "Religious Pestilence" and "Priestly Epidemic." The two people portraying the monks played their roles masterfully. On another level, representing the supremacy of money, sat the Jay Goulds, Vanderbilts, Grants and others, while below them the working people were portrayed, enslaved, squirming under the policeman's club in work, need, and misery.

Next came the Lehr- und Wehr-Verein[16] and North Side I.W.P.A. groups.

2nd D i v i s i o n: Carpenters Union with their flag and a sign reading: "Down with Capitalism, Long Live Communism"; the Tanners Union and the Butchers Union, with flags and signs; the second float, portraying Justitia. The tableau portrayed Justitia as being a slave to the money bag, and completely scornful to the propertyless people. Then there was another band, the Bohemian I.W.P.A. groups, as well as the Northwest and Southwest Side I.W.P.A. groups.

16. See the introduction to the section on "Armed Organizations" in this chapter.

3 r d   D i v i s i o n: Choral group, the Singing Section of the Furniture Workers Union with the sign: "Priests Are the Exploiters' Hod Carriers"; the Cigarmakers Progressive Union with the sign: "Exploitation Is Legal Theft"—and the American I.W.P.A. groups.

The 3rd float, representing Brotherhood among Men. The tableau showed the inner affinity and the ultimate brotherhood uniting all people under the protection of the Goddess of Freedom —North Side Socialist Mens' Singing Society, choral group, Metal Workers Union with flag and sign: "Today's Greatest Crime Is Poverty"—the South Side I.W.P.A. groups, and two wagons carrying women and children, representing the womens' struggle for equal rights.

It was an imposing parade. Judging conservatively, some 3,000 people took part. The streets along the procession route were filled with curious onlookers who expressed their feelings of support or indignation quite freely at the sight of these "holy" institutions being mocked. One house on Market Street was decorated very nicely, the motto, "Anarchism Is Freedom," beamed from a window.

Our Comrade Neef distinguished himself by setting up an outstanding representation of the relationship between the capitalist and the wage earner at 58 Clybourn Avenue. A bread basket hanging from a rope drawn diagonally across the street was gradually pulled higher and higher by two capitalists.

Despite the large crowd, the picnic was peaceful and orderly, thanks to the fact that the police were absent. There were but few loafers; these guys are very respectful of the reds.

Comrades Most and Parsons held short speeches throughout the course of the afternoon, and these were received with much applause. It wasn't until midnight that the last people set off for home.

78. The Labor Day Parade of 1903 (*Chicagoer Arbeiter-Zeitung,* September 8, 1903).

Battalions of Workers.—The Largest "Labor Day" Parade Ever Held Here.—Teamsters and Butchers Dominate.

Labor Day in Figures.

Number of participants... 75,347
Duration of the parade .... 4 hours, 7 minutes
Labor Day Parade, 1902 [number of participants]................. 46,654

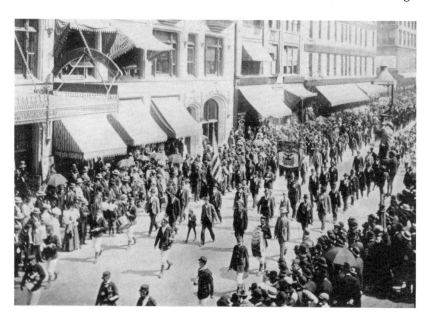

The Carpenters and Joiners Union, one of Chicago's largest unions, had a high proportion of German members. The photo shows the carpenters in the Labor Day parade of 1897. (Chicago Historical Society, ICHi-17258.)

The More Powerful **Unions** Which Took Part Yesterday.

Meat Cutters and Butchers	18,941
Teamsters	17,201
Freight Handlers	4,309
Woodworkers	3,902
Brassworkers ⟨Braßworkers⟩	2,825
Machinists	2,200
Brick Makers	2,016
Metal Workers	1,315
Picture Frame Makers	1,261
Carriage and Wagon Makers	1,171
Iron Molders	1,153
Bakers	1,100
Boxmakers and Sawyers	1,053
Carpenters and Joiners	1,020
Longshoremen	1,005
Women in the parade	2,665

Other Figures.

Number of bands, including the Fife and Drum Corps 107
Number of "floats" 53
Number of carriages...915
Number of horses 6,582

Chicago's organized labor took to the streets yesterday. The 1903 "Labor Day" Parade was the largest ever to take place in the United States. 75,000 workers in rank and file, united to an army at the union's command to show the nonworking minority that the workers constitute a power which is in a position to realize its demands. Never before have Chicago's unions mobilized so many people for a parade. 46,654 people took part in last year's parade. Some 600,000 people must have formed an honor guard to watch the battalions of workers march by. All dressed for the occasion, each union in a different uniform, with flags waving and to the accompaniment of music, thousands of wage earners, the producers of all wealth, appeared on one given day to show their strength. In files of sixteen, taking up the whole width of Michigan Avenue, they marched by the balcony of the Auditorium, where, by invitation of the "Associated Building Trades," the speakers for the afternoon's labor ceremonies and members of the press were already seated. It took four hours and seven minutes for all the participants to pass the spot. The whole affair was conducted orderly; not one unpleasant tone hampered this fine labor celebration, there were no accidents. In contrast to earlier years, where countless floats were to be seen, this year there were only endless masses of people in various uniforms. Everyone was impressed by this crowd of people. Two groups were dominant in the parade. In the rank and file, the United Butchers Unions were represented with 18,941 men, the Teamsters with 17,201. The one group was just four years old, the other not yet two. The younger unions outstripped the old. A conspicuous number of girls took part in the parade. Only the cleaning women and washerwomen were afoot, the other girls—the members of the Retail Clerks Union, the soapmakers, those employed in candy factories—dressed all in white, rode in tallyhoes.[17]

All in all, there were more than 2,500 female workers, or thrice the number which took part last year:

Cleaning women 25
Candymakers ⟨Candymacher⟩..175

17. A coach drawn by four horses.

The butchers made a good impression in their long, white or blue striped aprons, as did the woodworkers, who made an especially strong showing. They proved that the race question poses no problems for them by having a colored person as standard-bearer. The sheep slaughterers carried sticks with long sheep tails on them, the sausagemakers were busy on a float, and threw their products to the crowd as soon as they were finished. Behind them came the brassworkers ⟨Braßworkers⟩, the Kellogg strikers ⟨Streikern⟩ out in front. The Caldwell strikers ⟨Streikern⟩ were also there. "Strike in full force at Caldwells," was the inscription on one of the few signs in evidence this time; "Scabs have no right to Union wages and Union hours" read another. "Labor's second commandment: Honor your agreements and prosper," was the inscription on the "Firemen's" banner. The Stationary Firemen referred to their trade with the following motto: "The only remedy for smoke nuisance Union firemen and good fuel."

The Implement Painters Union No. 987 carried a sign saying that the union had just recently been founded in June, 1903, and the Oleo Workers, dressed completely in white, carried a huge banner with "Peace" inscribed on one side, "Goodwill toward men" on the other. All the waiters were recognizable by the green "badges," and the colored servants, whose very existence here in Chicago is on the line, were identifiable by their white aprons and black hats. The brickmakers, who have never missed a parade, presented an extremely powerful contingent, and made a very flashy impression in their light blue shirts and fedora hats. On the front of their shirts, in white letters, was the local union number. The "International Broth. of Blacksmiths" came next, amongst them their recently organized comrades of the International Harvester Company, the Stove Mounters, who for the first time referred to their label, and the "Candymakers," themselves on the brink of a wage battle—the union has already decided on the strike—stood out in their blue, white and red caps. The Iron Moulders, in their black shirts and brown hats, also made a fine impression, as did the Freight Loaders—with L. J. Curran out in front— in their black shirts and white caps. This column occupied more than six blocks. The Chicago Trades Union Label League appeared with a "Labelwagon." Last year there was much more propaganda for the label than there was this year. The cigarmakers were the only noteworthy exception: their blue label was visible on members' hats as they marched by, and they distributed thousands of cards; and it was impossible for the curious crowd to overlook the banner they carried—some seven feet long—and their float, which consisted of one single huge label. The following signs were also to be seen: "John Drew made by unfair labor," "Geo. W. Childs Cigar made by Children," "Tom Keane made by Trusts." A large trust cigar factory which employs children was represented by various skulls and cast into relief by the wagon that followed, showing a Union Cigar Workshop.

The women cracker packers, who have been locked out by the National Biscuit Co., drove in automobiles and carried a sign which read: "Locked out for Months." They were engaged in an intense propaganda campaign for the Union Label, as were the men of the kneading troughs, the bakers, dressed all in white, whose absence from the bake shops yesterday was felt by thousands of families. It was the same with the "ice men," who marched briskly through the streets yesterday, laughing while they shouted "ice," instead of attending to their work as usual. Behind the bakers came the boxmakers, represented by a large number of members and led by James H. Payne, who founded the union ten years ago. The blacksmiths, in their scarlet shirts, white aprons and varnished caps, were, as always, sensational. A blacksmith shop had been set up on a float, where horseshoes were hammered upon powerfully. The parade's first colored union was represented by the asphalt workers, who marched along with the stockyard people. The hatmakers and pianomakers followed. "We are the striking girls of the Chicago Organ and Supply Co." read the inscription on a tallyho filled with girls. They distributed cards, which clarified the reasons for the strike. The shoemakers had a float which portrayed a chained prisoner whose work was being strictly watched by a guard. The broommakers attracted attention by having made pretty parasols out of the broom straw. The coopers came next, some 1,500 men strong, in handsome suits. The male and female hospital attendants also took part in the parade for the first time, though they rode in carriages. It was noteworthy that the laundry workers were only represented by some 200 people. At least 1,500 had been counted on.

Commemorations: The Paris Commune and Haymarket

In contrast to public demonstrations, the labor movement's annual commemorations were more inwardly directed and contained there-

fore more sharply defined examples of labor's self-image. Occasions for these commemorations were originally provided by important events from the German and European labor movements—above all by the Paris Commune of 1871. After the Haymarket affair the anniversary of the execution of the anarchists became a central annual event for Chicago's German-American labor movement. Originating in the vital and creative years of the 1880s, this tradition increasingly turned into a nostalgic ritual after the turn of the century that was isolated from new developments in the Chicago labor movement.

The celebration of the Paris Commune had a predominantly optimistic tone, despite the Commune's end in the repression of 1871. It was interpreted above all as the precursor of a fundamental restructuring of society, and its main actors were lionized as martyrs for a new historical epoch. This point of view is clearly present in August Spies's commentary on the Commune celebration written for the Chicagoer Arbeiter-Zeitung *in March, 1886. Appropriate to its significance, the Commune was celebrated in a dignified setting with all the means available to the movement, as illustrated by the documents from 1883 reproduced here. Advertised for weeks beforehand in the German labor press, the commemoration took place in the North Side Turner Hall. Three works specifically written for the occasion were presented, including a song sung by the Socialist Singing Society, a play by Wilhelm Ludwig Rosenberg, and a poem by Michael Schwab. Rosenberg's play used the experience of German immigrants in America and thereby tried to relate directly to the audience. (Unfortunately, the text has been lost.) It was performed by a lay acting group similar to the one which had presented Rosenberg's "The Nihilists" the year before, a play that had also been written for the Commune celebration; and the acting group included such prominent Chicago socialists as August Spies, Michael Schwab, and Oskar Neebe. Recited by Rosenberg at the close of the program in 1883, Schwab's poem was written in memory of Karl Marx, who had just died a few days before. In the obligatory address given on such occasions, Dr. Ernst Schmidt—the former mayoral candidate of the Socialist Labor party—also honored Karl Marx and praised his great service to the labor movement. Whether the usual ball that was planned in association with this event actually took place, or whether it was canceled on account of Marx's death, cannot be determined.*

In contrast to the anniversary of the Paris Commune, the commemoration of the execution of the Haymarket victims dealt with so negative an experience that it always took on a solemn and tragic tone. Despite efforts to use artistic and agitational forms like songs, poetry, and eulogy to present the execution of the five men as an arousing warning for the future, the sense that the event marked the end of a particular period of Chicago history came through in the form and content of the commemoration. Thus the elegy was commonly used as the appropriate poetic form for the occasion. This sense of finality was well symbolized by the erection in Waldheim Cemetery of a monument at the graves of the anarchists, exactly one day before Governor Altgeld pardoned the remaining three men who had been imprisoned.

79. "Vive la Commune!" by August Spies (*Reminiszenzen von Aug. Spies*, ed. Mrs. Christine Spies [Chicago, 1888], pp. 133-34).

Vive la Commune!—long live the commune! That was the cry that sounded throughout Paris fifteen years ago, on March 18, 1871, the cry that instantly united thousands around the banner of "freedom, equality, and fraternity," the cry which echoed mightily in the hearts of the oppressed, the cry which, like the trumpet of doom, caused the frightened c r i m i n a l s to flee their soft cushions and elegant palaces! The heroes of March 18, 1871, have in the meantime bled to death; those whom the Versailles stranglers "spared," found their martyrdom in the deadly jaws of New Caledonia, ending in horrible banishment. The mortal frame, from which that liberating flame of pure humanity flared, was destroyed by the desecrators of humanity, but not the magic glimmer which it radiated, not the strength of those golden rays which, like the summer sun which imbues field, meadow and wood with new life, consumed the ice of the human winter and proclaimed the coming of the people's spring. No, that light is still with us; it illuminates the path for all the oppressed people throughout the world, as did once the star which led the Wise Men to Bethlehem and the "savior." But it is not simply still with us; that light of freedom has become a lambent sea of fire, whose molten waves will soon consume the citadel of order. Thus they did not fall in vain, those brave people whose own blood had to still their thirst for freedom, no! And if they could see beyond their graves today and hear the millions who join in the call "Long live the Commune!" they would say: large was the sacrifice, larger yet what has been won!

80. Preview of the Commune Celebration (*Fackel,* March 11, 1883).

A festival seldom offers so much of quality and interest for so little money as does the Commune Celebration which has been organized by the Central Committee. The North Side Socialist Men's Choir will open the celebration with a superb song. The "Red Banner"—that's the name of the song—was written by Heinrich Binder of Detroit, and put to music by C. Majer of the same city. Written just for this occasion, the song has an overwhelming, overpowering effect. The lyrics and composition so capture the socialist inspiration that it in many ways serves to prepare the audience for the powerful proletarian figures which are presented later.

"The Proletarian's Daughter" is a play about life today. Although the play's language is permeated with political resonances, the figures don't part with reality, they have solid ground under their feet, robust, healthy attitudes. The socialist spirit, emphasized by the figures' actions, proves that we're not dealing with any of those caricatures of workers which all too often mar the stage, but rather with men who have understood their class situation. The play starts out in a factory town where a strike has just broken out. The heroine of the play is Maria, a proletarian child with strong moral principles, who gives herself in love to the son of the factory owner, Bensdorf, only to be deceived by him. When Maria realizes what a base character her former lover has, she shoots him down. The jury which is to condemn her ends up by acquitting her, and Maria emigrates to America with her father. From this brief sketch the gentle reader will have gathered that this material lends itself to the most striking scenes, and the author, a renowned socialist writer, understood how to make an effective drama out of it. What's more, this time the play is presented not by amateurs, but by experienced actors.

81. "The Commune Celebration. A Real Folk Festival!" (*Fackel,* March 18, 1883).

On Saturday evening, the North Side Turner Hall was completely filled — the hall as well as the gallery — with visitors who had come to dedicate

---

On facing page

An announcement for the Commune Celebration of 1883. The Commune Celebration was one of the most important anniversaries of organized German workers, and not only in Chicago. (*Chicagoer Arbeiter-Zeitung,* March 15, 1883; photo courtesy of the Newberry Library, Chicago.)

Commune = Feier!

veranstaltet von dem

Central=Comite der sozialistischen Gruppen
von Chicago!

— am —

Samstag, den 17. März 1883

—— in der ——

Nordseite Turn - Halle.

PROGRAMM:

1. Ouverture.
2. „Das rothe Banner", Lied, gedichtet für die Commune = Feier von Heinr. Binder und in Musik gesetzt von Carl Majer, beide in Detroit, vorgetragen mit Orchester=Begleitung vom Sozialistischen Männerchor unter Leitung des Herrn von Oppen.
3. ## Neu!   Neu!   Neu!
Zum ersten Male (für die Commune=Feier verfaßt):

„Die Tochter des Proletariers!!"
Schauspiel in 6 Bildern, dargestellt von der gesammten Ifenstein'schen Theater=Gesellschaft.

Personen des Stückes:

Weiland, ein Fabrik-beiter	Herr Weib	Alfred, dessen Sohn .... Herr Rodenberg
Dessen Frau	Frau Martham	Dr Starf, ein junger Advokat ...... Herr Richard
Heinrich, deren Sohn	Herr Heppner	Ein Arzt .... Herr Kröner
Maria, - Tochter	Frl. v. Trautmann	Reich, Gerichtspräsident .... Herr Richter
Peters, ein Fabrikbeiter	Herr Wachsner	v. Kesselbort, Staatsanwalt .... Herr Hein
Ein Arbeiter	Herr Müh	Der Vorsitzende der Geschworenen...... Herr Heller
Lene, eine Fabrikarbeiterin	Frl Remy	Arbeiter, Gerichtsdiener, Geschworene, Volk.
Lensdorf, ein Fabrikbesitzer	Herr Engel	

Ort der Handlung: Eine deutsche Fabrikstadt. Zeit: Gegenwart.

— Regie: Herr Ferd. Weib. —

Während der Zwischenpausen **Musik=Vorträge** unter Leitung des Herrn v. Oppen.
Nach der Vorstellung: **Marseillaise** (Massen = Gesang).

—— Hierauf: ——

BALL! - BALL!

Anfang präcis 8 Uhr. • • • Eintritt @ Person 25 Cents.
☞ Tickets sind durch die Träger der „Arbeiter-Zeitung", sowie in der Office der letzteren zu haben.

Das Arrangements = Comite.

an evening to the grateful memory of the heroes who died for the cause of humanity. It was evident in the participants' expressions that they hadn't come in pursuit of pleasure. Serious faces with a trace of piety and suppressed enthusiasm for the high cause to which they had also dedicated themselves with great devotion—those were the men and women we met at the celebration, people well aware of its meaning.

Around 9:30 the curtain was raised, and first softly, then gradually working to a crescendo, the splendrous melody of "The Red Banner" resounded throughout the auditorium, a folk song composed by Carl Majer and written by Mr. Heinrich Binder.

The real praise is actually due the "Socialist Men's Choir," which sang the song in a very commendable way, as well as the conductor, Mr. von Oppen. Though a very difficult composition, the recital was perfect, beyond criticism. The insistent calls for more were followed by a da capo.

The premiere performance of "The Proletarian's Daughter" was then staged by the Isenstein Company. We don't want to talk about the play's subject at this point, but rather about the excellent performance which held the spectators in uninterrupted suspense.

Mr. Welb (factory worker) and Miss Remy (his daughter) had the lead roles, and if we say that their—and all the others in the play—portrayals were rendered most masterly, we're not stating too much.

Miss Remy seemed to have been made for the role: graceful, modest, and showing a great dramatic talent which we wouldn't have suspected in her, as we had always only seen her in minor roles. In the third scene of the third act, in which her father repudiates her for her fugitive love affair with the factory owner's son, she acted with an unadulterated emotion which carried the audience along with her; she portrayed the good, but scornfully deceived and unconsolable factory worker's daughter, in a way which must have charmed the author. In the fourth act she was presented a pretty and tasteful bouquet.

As always, Mr. Welb was magnificent. He showed us the character of an uncompromising, intelligent proletarian, thoroughly aware of his class situation and full of animosity for the oppressors. His natural, authentic portrayal of a factory worker frequently drew applause from the audience. The court scene was especially effective; as mentioned above, we will come back to the subject shortly.

Mssrs. Wachsner, Heppner, Engel, Rodenberg, Richard, Kroener, Richter, Grun, Hein and Helfer, as well as Mrs. Markham and Mrs. Mosch, did praiseworthy justice to the roles they played.

The play was received very well, and the author, W. L. Rosenberg,[18] was called out onto the stage after the final curtain. The reaction will encourage the presentation of similar thesis plays as a means of agitation.

Following the play,

C o m r a d e   D r.   E r n s t   S c h m i d t appeared on the stage and held a speech in memory of K a r l   M a r x, recently passed away, the founder of modern socialism. . . . Mr. Rosenberg then recited a poem written by Comrade Mich. Schwab in honor of Karl Marx, and received lively applause.

The whole festival was a success that the socialists can look upon with pride.

82. "In Memory of Karl Marx," by Michael Schwab[19] (*Fackel,* March 18, 1883).

Karl Marx is dead! The tolling of the bell
Our hearts does shock, like lightning's harsh display.
From England's shores the mournful tidings tell,
There where the thinker long and patient lay.
We'd always hoped that he would yet be well,
And would thus see the proud and promised day.
The day when tyrant's fortresses will fall,
The day of freedom and of joy for all.

All you, for whom he faithfully derived,
The path to truth's and science's clear source,
Too early of his genius were deprived.
And those of us still young must mourn the force,
The force his mind has left us to survive,
So great, sublime, did chart the daring course.
Removed for us the riddle's darkest veil,
Revealed to us what future plans entail.

The workingman he offered weapons sure.
In writings deep, their contents full and dense,

18. See the biographical sketches at the end of this volume.
19. See the biographical sketches at the end of this volume.

A mighty arsenal - ideas mature,
And knowledge strong, the hope for our defense;
Courageously we need but now endure,
And with our hordes of troubles we'll dispense.
When all the slaves in all the lands u n i t e,
Then none will bondage know to be his plight.

The teachings which D a s K a p i t a l proclaimed
A new and wondrous world did open wide.
With hope infused we saw ourselves enflamed,
All seekers with their goal it did provide.
And millions came together who exclaimed
The power of his word the people's guide -
The people massed, the men who all produce,
No longer now content with chained abuse.

His fearless words the flames inspired fanned,
With thund'rous pledge the proletariat sounds;
In dearth and death we here united stand,
Confronting danger, courage e'er redounds.
And though by hate and ign'rance we be damned,
The path, the goal, we near with steady bounds.
Mankind's new flag we proud and open fly,
Defeat of malice it shall signify.

This warning loud, our pain shall now drown out.
Together strong, we'll never cease to fight!
Resisting thus, the good and right will rout
The foe, and us to victory incite.
The battle cry must ever be our shout,
The victors will be they who know to smite.
And if the foe's armies we would repel,
Full tilt to weapons! we must be hardshell.

Karl Marx is dead! his teachings, though, alive,
And on they live as rich and ripened fruit.
From him the poorest people will derive
What centuries long they've waited to salute.
And thousand mighty arms are seen to thrive
Upon his word, the sword thrust resolute.
There's motion midst the people - a seething, swirling churn,
The day's already dawning, the tyrants soon will burn.

83. Haymarket Commemorative Celebration. "Chicago's Workers Remember Their Martyrs" *(Vorbote,* November 20, 1907).

All over the world, the eleventh of November marks a day of commemoration for the aware, resolute proletariat. On November 11, 1887, the accursed sentence was carried out, and the best and most zealous champions of the labor movement in Chicago were executed. Capital gave the command, not only in the hopes of dealing anarchy the death blow, but also in an attempt to intimidate the working people who were demanding freedom and bread, so that they would quietly continue to tolerate their chains of bondage. The blow struck deep, the people grumbled, acquiesced to the violence, inspired only with the hope that the day of reckoning would come when thousands of Garys, Bonfields, Schaaks,[20] and other capitalistic mercenaries would try to block the path leading to freedom.

And though the chains can still be heard to jingle, let not the signs deceive. All the whole world over, the proletariat is preparing for the inevitable battle between capital and labor. Everywhere is a seething hate, rage, directed against the atrocities which capital has been committing for millennia, everywhere clouds broadcasting the coming storm.

These clouds were seen last night in Brand's Hall, where a celebration was held commemorating the 20th anniversary of the executions of Spies, Parsons, Lingg, Engel and Fischer, men who died for the people. There were the old faithful followers, those who never despair; there were those upright people who, prosperous for several years, haven't become totally self-centered; there was the old guard, which won't be content until hunger and cold, until the deprivation of rights and heritage have been abolished for all.

They placed a fresh wreath of evergreens on the grave in Waldheim where the innocents lie; they followed the speeches with evident interest, and vowed to inspire the indifferent with a sense of class consciousness until freedom had been won.

It was a good celebration, one worthy of our dead. The hall was well filled; flags representing the Brewers and Maltsters Union No. 18 and the Carpenters Union No. 419 hung from the front wall, and on the tribunal were the statues of Spies and Lingg, adorned in red sashes, along with a picture of the monument in Waldheim. It was already 8:30 when Holl's

20. Judge Gary presided over the Haymarket trial; Bonfield and Schaack were high-ranking police officials. Bonfield ordered a group of two hundred policemen to disperse the protest rally at the Haymarket, where the bomb was thrown.

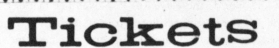

Announcement of the unveiling of the monument to the executed anarchists in
Waldheim Cemetery. (*Vorbote*, May 10, 1893.)

Orchestra played Chopin's funeral march. The chairman, Comrade Joseph Schmidt, then held a speech. . . .

After the applause died down, there was a very good solo for cornet and trombone, and then the music made way for the w o r k e r s i n g e r s. The resolute members of the Debating Club's Singing Section, of the Socialist Men's Singing Society, and of the Bakers' Singing Society—who still always consider it their duty to partake in the commemorative celebrations for the labor movement's 1886-87 victims—took their places. Under the direction of the conductor, Mr. Tamm, they gave a finely intoned, excellent rendition of O. W. Richter's emotional composition, "At the Grave of Our Friends." These w o r k e r singers did themselves an honor, but it is not to the credit of the numerous singers who, though w o r k e r s, were not present yesterday at this sort of celebration. How the women outstrip the men in this respect! The worthy singing section of the Women's Club Progress is always present at this sort of affair. And it should be given credit for the support and effort it displayed yesterday. Its recital of Martin Drescher's inspirational song, "Women's Call to Arms," couldn't have been better.

A musical piece was then presented, and the English speaker, T. P. Quinn, well known for years in the local labor movement, was introduced. Speaking for over an hour, he recounted the whole history of the local labor movement in a factually precise manner, from the '70s up to the scandalous legalized killings, thus granting especially the younger elements an insight into the capitalistic conspiracy of those questionable times. . . .

It was almost 11 o'clock when the speaker finished, and because many of those present had to leave due to insufficient means of transportation, one song and one musical number were dropped, and the German speaker, Comrade Heinrich Bartel,[21] took the floor. Finding it superfluous to once again recount the events of 1886-87, he established parallels between former and present times and launched into a philippic against the uninterested attitude among working people today in an effort to wake them out of their lethargy. This being the right spot, his words were well received. The following is a summary of his speech:

Heinrich Bartel was the last speaker. After a sarcastic introduction, his speech was more or less as follows:

One would almost think that a century had passed, that's how far away that black Friday in the year of 1887 is from today's generation. The descriptions of those events sound like tidings from some bygone era to

---

21. At this time Bartel was editor-in-chief of the *Chicagoer Arbeiter-Zeitung*.

this country's youth, their hearts don't beat in sympathy, and their heads quickly forget what their ears have heard.

As always in the world, so it was in former times: the masses pitted against those men proclaiming new ideas. Had the masses stood behind the accused, no court would have dared hand them over to the hangman. But the masses were in the enemy camp, and that belongs to the curious relationships in this country.

America is a huckster's hovel, a country of self-centered entities, the majority of the people here haven't a trace of altruism. A deceitful tradition has clouded peoples' minds here, has planted the superstition in their heads that freedom and equality reign. Capitalism has poisoned their hearts with greed and envy.

This is one of the reasons for the difficulty the working-class movement has had in taking root here. August Spies and his comrades were also foiled by this obstacle. His last words,[22] spoken at the gallows, have still not been fulfilled. Even in Chicago, there are but few signs of a healthy working-class movement. This fact cannot be hushed. The finest phrases cannot cover it up. The phrase was always the death of every honest endeavor. Thunder and lightning are still a long way off when two good people, but poor musicians, get together somewhere, hold warlike speeches, shake their fists and roll their eyes, until finally they're afraid of themselves. The present does not call for unbounded dreams, no, but rather practical agitational and organizational work.

Wherever one looks in Chicago, the working-class movement is in a bad way. An endless swamp covers the same terrain over which the powerful surf of an emerging radical movement used to crash. The workers are presently being consumed in struggles among themselves. There are at least three radical camps, but all of them seem pretty flimsy, almost barely able to survive. Under which conditions and by what means they keep themselves above water is a very unpleasant story.

There are many who "sympathize," but sympathy is very platonic. Everyone wants to be progressive, but only a precious few would actually think of doing anything for the cause. If someone is absolutely nothing in America, he's "progressive" — and that is also nothing. Ownership-oriented egoists often hide the most malicious hypocrisy and the shrewdest business sense behind the word "progressive."

People's horizons here stop short at their stomach, a feed trough, a bankbook, a house being their highest ideals. And as a result, all our

---

22. "There will come a time when our silence will be more powerful than the voices you strangle today!"

efforts to unionize today are subject to an attitude of ambivalence; for most of the workers, the labor question is one which ultimately boils down to the question of knife and fork.

This should not be the case. The labor question is a cultural question, in the largest sense of the word. From the depths of their misery, countless people direct their yearning and their prayers to the most eternal of the goddesses, to Aphrodite in her unclad beauty, to Athena, the embodiment of wisdom and strength. Here lies one of the worthiest tasks of the working-class movement. Besides struggling for the material, we mustn't lose track of the ideal for a single instant. It is also our duty to capture beauty and art and science. We want to change the world and to appropriate everything which makes life magnificent.

This is the way August Spies conceived of the labor movement, and it was the inspiration of those who were his comrades in suffering.

But we won't be discouraged by the gloom of the present and the grudging progress made by the movement if we refuse to romanticize our true situation away. The spark still glows under the surface; the time will come—despite everything—when the spark will become a blazing flame.

At this point the speaker became profuse, alluding extensively to historical events which confirm his statements, and concluded as follows:

The spirit which transforms institutions is as active today as ever. It lays tunnels, constructs bridges; the galvanic wire and the voltaic cell are sparkling evidence of its genius; like the railroad it stretches out across the country; and in the form of the steamship, it hurries around the world. That is the spirit of work, which will bring about the fall. Each ship which crosses the ocean carries the seed of destruction from country to country; the poison which will wear down the body of today's society hangs from each bale which is shipped. We don't want to predict when the crisis will come. But we know that the awareness which was alive in August Spies and his comrades will one day topple the whole system as it exists today; we know that our anger will one day raise its voice in all countries; we also know that the reign of those in power today will not last an eternity. Our duty is to help shake the foundation of today's mighty structure. Or in other words, to act in the sense of the martyrs of 1887, to act as the executors of their testament.

The orchestra played the "Marseillaise," which has become the international song of freedom among workers, the audience sang along, and with this the commemorative celebration came to a close.

**84. "To the Manes of the 11th of November," by Georg Biedenkapp
(*Fackel,* November 12, 1899).**

> And once again approach the doleful place,
> The cherish'd tomb of our departed brothers;
> Now once again we write a word of grace,
> Anew a hand the wreath of love confers.
> Oh vanguard true, beneath debris and clay,
> Rest here and find decay, full free from dearth -
> Though long to putrefaction fallen prey,
> But still the spirit's present here on earth!
>
> It's not by death immortal men are slain.
> Though deep the grave, they cannot be decried;
> 'Spite malice, hate, deceit and rude disdain,
> The good will win, will never be denied.
> Not from the tomb have ever spoke the dead -
> But even should the flesh be beat asunder,
> The spirit'll shout "To battle!" in its stead -
> The shout of truth, resounding loud like thunder!
>
> Effaced so soon? and is the deed now done?
> O shameless world! which thus so brashly viewed -
> Will Waldheim not a Golgotha become?
> That army brave - the mem'ry not subdued -
> To battle rose, in battle faithful fell.
> And strangl'd by the mercenary horde,
> Our noble victims' highest citadel -
> Toward which, how nobly, human hearts once soared!

Theater and Music

*As the program of the Commune celebration illustrates, music and
theater were essential elements in anniversaries and commemorations.
In fact, it is unthinkable that they would not be included in some
form at every public event organized by the German-American labor
movement. In smaller groups, recitations often replaced the stage
productions that were reserved for the major festivals. Theater and
music had this special place in public events because of their character*

as performances. Since they had to be enacted, they required a communal environment that included a group of actors or singers as well as an audience jointly experiencing and appreciating the performance.

It was not only the labor movement, of course, that used theater and music to sustain itself and build its community. Every type of German association—Turner societies, church groups, regional friendly societies, fraternal organizations—took advantage of popular German musical and theatrical traditions. In 1896, for example, there were at least eighty-seven German singing societies in Chicago. The labor movement clearly tried to incorporate these cultural traditions into its political activities.

Tableaux vivants were part of a popular European theatrical tradition that could be used by small groups without unusual effort or resort to trained actors. The first two documents reprinted here present the tableaux vivants used in the Commune celebration of 1876 and in a picnic held on the occasion of the centennial of the American Declaration of Independence that took place in the same year. The posterlike character of the tableau vivant as it froze one dramatic moment in an event made it especially suitable for symbolically condensing the complexities of a historical process. A revolutionary upheaval like the Commune could be contracted into several "living pictures." As in this case, tableaux vivants were used to celebrate historical events or persons or to expose the exploitative nature of capitalist society—both for the purpose of creating and propagating a distinct working-class cultural tradition. The tableau vivant was clearly similar to other forms of public symbolism: to the portrayals on the floats built by the various crafts for their demonstrations or carnival parades—see also the description of the biting satirical tableau as presented at the Social Turnverein's carnival ball, Document 63—to the musical performances of street ballad and minstrel singing, or to shadowgraphs illuminated by Bengal lights.

With sporadic success, attempts were also made to institutionalize the labor theater in Chicago beyond its occasional use at public events. Following the model of German Social Democracy, Chicago's German-American left resisted the rampant and trivial popular melodramas of the time and offered instead plays, usually with an elevating or political purpose, all in an effort to direct the acknowledged need of workers for entertainment and diversion into the channels provided by the culture of the labor movement. This effort faced unusual obstacles, given the situation of German workers in the U.S., par-

*ticularly because the periodic necessity for ethnic solidarity under-
mined more class-conscious cultural activities. In addition, following
the decline of German immigration after 1890 the supply of artistic
talent dwindled. Thus Chicago's German left turned to the naturalistic
theatrical works of German authors, which were of incomparably
higher quality than the locally produced pieces. The favorite among
these was "The Weavers" (1892) by Gerhart Hauptmann (1862-
1946), a German naturalist writer and playwright who visited the
United States in 1893, and who won the Nobel Prize for literature
in 1912. The play, which deals with an uprising of weavers in the
Silesian textile district in the 1840s, was first performed in Chicago
in the mid-1890s by Milwaukee's German theater company and by
Johann Most's group of lay actors. A labor theater which had been
organized at the Aurora Turner Hall on the Northwest Side, following
the model of the Freie Volksbühne in Berlin, again performed "The
Weavers" in 1900. The review of this production—reprinted here
as Document 87—refrained from criticizing the clearly amateurish
performance of the lay actors group and stressed instead the significance of the play's contents for political agitation. After the turn of
the century, "The Weavers" was even presented in an English version
by a socialist drama club for the workers of the Northwest Side, as
the advertisement from the* Chicago Socialist *illustrates.*

*Music was used to a much greater degree than the theater. It was
a means of expression that could touch the heart and feelings and
awaken on a more elemental level the sense of solidarity and community. Yet, as is argued by the document on the function of music
for workers, the labor movement valued songs—just like theater
pieces—which expressed class-conscious themes and could be used
for agitational purposes. Labor songs scarcely paused to describe the
contemporary social situation, but rather turned their gaze toward
the future and the realization of their vision of a new society. (See,
for example, the section on songs in Chapter VI.) At the same time
singing was granted an almost gymnastic and hygienic function that
helped restore the body and soul after daily labor. A sense for the
extent of the labor singing movement, even as late as 1910, is provided
by a short report on the concert of the Arbeiter Sängerbund of the
Northwest: over 400 singers took part in a festivity organized by an
association that had only existed for thirteen years. The program of
this event, as well as the reporting about it, illustrates how closely*

fused were the ethnic and working-class traditions of the German-American left.

85. Tableau Vivant: The Paris Commune (*Vorbote,* March 25, 1876).

Upon this, all eyes turned to the stage, tensely watching the curtain which hid an episode from the final days of the Commune. The light in the hall gets dimmer and dimmer. The bell rings softly, and the curtain is slowly raised. A common "Ah!" of amazement, an enthusiastic flashing of eyes and a general throbbing among the freedom-loving hearts as the curtain reveals the success of the tableau. On the left, the Commune fighters, and a few feet in front of them, mounted on a horse, General Jeroslas Dombrowsky, struck by a bullet and apparently about to fall back into the arms of his faithful followers; under him a few wounded freedom fighters, and across from them, in blue tunics and red trousers, the executioner's lackeys from Versailles, taking aim at the little group of communists; in the background ruins, and the whole thing bathed in red calcium light— in short, a tableau vivant so delightful and illustrating such a sympathetic motif, that the enthusiastic applause of the 2,500-3,000 people made the huge building tremble. The curtain had to be raised time and again, and time and again the same burning sympathy for the group of workers murdered in May, 1871. The highlight of the evening, it was a means of agitation which won't easily find its way out of the spectators' hearts.

86. Tableau Vivant: The Old World and the New (*Vorbote,* July 8, 1876).

The tableau vivant portraying the Old and the New World was the high point of the festival. Conceived and realized in artistic form by the ideal pair, Turner instructor Gloy and the artist Waidling, the tableau was mounted on a turntable 28 feet high and bathed in the splendor of magnificently produced, colored light. Two worlds were juxtaposed: on the one hand, the present condition of men exploiting men, and on the other the goal of our endeavors: the free, social Republic.

Adorned with fitting costumes, the Old World was represented by the following: on the first level was Enslaved Labor, workers from all sorts of different trades, some in chains, some bursting their chains with yearning, looking out over the ocean toward a ship (Socialism); the two sailors on board carrying signs which read Equality and Justice. On the second level, 7 feet higher, were Poverty and Misery, a grieving woman with her child (Poverty), as well as a woman (Misery) standing in front of an exploiter while he sicked a dog on the wretched figures. On the third level, again 7 feet higher, the Dominion of Money and of the Clergy. Two exploiters sitting on money bags, and above them, blessing their disgraceful business, a priest.

Across from it, separated from the Old World by a screen, was the New World, labor's future. On the first level: Agriculture (a farmer and plough) and Domestic Happiness, the domestic life of liberated humanity, radiating happiness and contentment, released from misery and care. On the next level, 7 feet higher, Industry, Art, and Science as liberated humanity's common property, portrayed by three magnificent women in Greek attire. On the third level, again 7 feet higher, humanity's most cherished possessions and the basic principles upon which the New World is based: Justice and Equality together, portrayed by two women, Justice holding the scales and the sword in her right hand, while Freedom was holding the red banner and the Jacobin cap.

The tableau was a wonderful credit to the performers, especially to Mr. Gloy, and a sheer delight for the spectators. Thousands of spectators broke out in jubilation at the sight of the tableau and could hardly get enough of it. Enthusiastically, they vowed to each other that they would fight for the attainment of the New World just as it was portrayed in the tableau, and if necessary, perish for it.

87. "Free People's Theater: G. Hauptmann's 'Weavers,' with John Most"[23] (*Chicagoer Arbeiter-Zeitung,* February 22, 1900).

In the winter season of 1895, Gerhard Hauptmann's "Weavers" was to be presented for the first time in New York's fashionable ⟨fashionablen⟩ "Irving Place Theater." This premiere was in itself an event for the theatergoers of this eastern metropolis, not only because of the political nature of the play, but also because this Silesian tragedy dealing with starvation was to be presented by an acting company with a reputation for extreme realism. The theater was packed ⟨gepackt⟩ full. Just before the curtain

23. Johann Most, editor of the New York anarchist journal *Die Freiheit*, had assumed the role of spokesman for the German anarchists in the United States upon his immigration in 1882.

was to be raised, there was a general commotion in the theater, followed by applause. Conried, the manager of the theater, hurried onto the stage and asked the actors who had crowded about a peephole in the curtain, "What's going on out there?" — "Most just came in," was the answer. And so it was, as Most couldn't possibly miss the premiere of "The Weavers," and had long in advance reserved himself a seat in the balcony. Arriving that evening, he received a large, unexpected ovation from the audience, proof that Most's presence was considered something very special, and in a sense a public indication of the esteem in which he was held as representative of those political ideas expressed in the play.

The really excellent and realistic presentation of the play was a sensational success, playing every night for four weeks before a sold-out house.

Even the predominant capitalist press had to concede that one seldom finds plays as inherently gripping as "The Weavers" or productions as impressive as was this one. In this sense, the "World," the "New York Herald," and others wrote: "There were only two outstanding theatrical events this season: the German Opera in the Metropolitan Opera House and the Irving Place Theater production of 'The Weavers.'"

The performers held nothing back with respect to realism, and even in the destruction scene in the fourth act, where the revolting weavers assault the factory owner's possessions, the director and propman made sure — irrespective of the cost — that objects doomed to destruction — right down to the vases, knickknacks and flower stems — were all "real." "On that evening," said one of the participants in the premiere, "we must have demolished at least $100 worth of pictures, mirrors, glass and porcelain; later the director toned it down some, otherwise this luxury would have become a little too costly in the course of time. But the realistic effect was attained and thus ensured the smashing success of the performances to come."

Why are we going into all this in such detail? - simply to illustrate what can be achieved when the means and energy are available to put on a political play. At the time, the Chicagoans were also offered a very good presentation of "The Weavers" by the Milwaukee Theater Society, and it was the same with almost all of the permanent German theater companies throughout the country which, latching on to this play, staged more-or-less successful productions in the various big cities.

And everyone who attended will still recollect the presentations staged by Most's amateur troupe. This time the project was planned as a repeat performance by local friends on the occasion of Most's return from his extensive agitational tour across the United States. In San Francisco, on January 28, a staging of "The Weavers" by supporters there, in which "Old Baumert" himself took part, went really well.

In Chicago, a group of Most's admirers who felt they had it in them to temporarily exchange their usual trades for the greater significance of the stage had gotten together to perform "The Weavers" as a drastic means of spreading the play's revolutionary ideas. The project of putting together an ensemble which was equal to the difficult task it had set for itself was surely no trifle, especially if one considers that the participants were children of the people who, until then, had had nothing to do with dramatic presentation. Ultimately, each spectator can judge for himself as to the extent of the presentation's success. Good will can get a lot done, and it was evident that all the participants committed themselves to the project with love and energy. The criteria for a probing critique are in such cases really not applicable. The project's praiseworthy intention alone deserves a friendly review. Essentially, it is a question of the plot and content of the play, not of the people. And these aspects of the play definitely had the desired inflammatory effect. The content is more-or-less common knowledge to everyone who is interested in more than just politics, cards, and his cronies in the local saloon, and it is therefore not necessary to go into detail.

Given last night's nasty weather, the audience in the Aurora Hall, at Milwaukee Ave. and Huron St., was really a good one. One need but consider what a boost so many people probably had to give themselves to leave their warm homes and dare match their shoes against the wild snowdrifts, and the knee-high mud and slush, all those landmarks of the Windy City. Due to the thaw, the intersections along Milwaukee Ave. were completely flooded and almost uncrossable. Lovely conditions for an American city of two million, and almost right in the city center to boot. But there was at least partial compensation in the hall itself: the sight of the considerable throngs of people who had come from the North, South, and West sides to pay a well-deserved tribute to their old "Hannes" and his kind friends who had accepted the risky venture of staging "The Weavers."

And the performance was really very decent, despite the fact that the prompter had to interrupt somewhat noisily from time to time, or that there were small incidents or misunderstandings which occurred while entering and exiting, for these things will have cleared themselves up by the next presentation. Since the author had taken his material from events which had actually happened in the area in the '40s, and his characters straight from the workers' world, the participants didn't have to try and identify with thoroughly foreign or undefinable characters, but rather simply had to be true to the life they know.

Because the number of participants was limited and the means at their disposal were modest, many of the performers had to play two roles, and this is asking quite a bit of amateurs. Given these circumstances, it was also impossible to portray the mass scenes properly. Nevertheless, the scenes in the delivery room of Dreißiger, the factory owner in Peterswaldau, in Scholz Welzel's outdoor restaurant, as well as the revolt in the palace of the exploiter, Dreißiger, and the battle and victory over the *Soldateska*[24] were all lively and graphic, and clearly roused the audience. The scenes where calamity afflicts old Ansorge's house in Kaschbach and old Hilse's little weaving room in Langen-Bielau were also truly moving. The play is so permeated with dreadful and atrocious events, that the spectator who is following the plot with all his heart and soul cannot even find any relief in the jokes and humorous incidents which occur intermittently.

If we were to summarize, we would have to say that every single person fit his role and fulfilled his duty well. Some performers amazed the audience with their magnificent portrayals, and if not all of the performances can be measured according to the same criteria, it is because this role or the other is more or less sharply defined, and the person playing it is thus drawn more into the foreground. As "Old Baumert," John Most was in his element, he lived and breathed his role, and the mask which he chose was also wonderfully fitting. The rendition of the notorious fustian manufacturer, Dreißiger, was adequate, and Paul Vandree's portrayal of the "red" Becker was powerful, as was Peter Schneider's of the reservist, Moritz Jäger. Karl Günther also played the role of the unctuous priest, Pastor Kittelhans, very well. . . . In short, the presentation was a success and the pleasant, private entertainment which followed the performance was something the participants had certainly deserved.

On Sunday, February 25, "The Weavers" will be presented in the Social Turner Hall, which alone will doubtless ensure a full house.

88. Advertisement for "The Weavers" (*Chicago Socialist,* Oct. 25, 1902).

(See p. 284.)

24. Rowdy soldiery.

"THE WEAVERS"

THE GREAT LABOR DRAMA

in five acts, by GERHART HAUPTMANN,

—— will be presented by the ——

Socialist Dramatic Club

—— at ——

WICKER PARK LARGE HALL

Tuesday Eve., October 28th, 1902.

Finely staged, 50 people in cast. Will be concluded with a

GRAND BALL.

"Land of the Noonday Night" and other new labor songs will be sung during the evening

TICKETS 25c. a person, children under six, accompained by parents, free, from 6 to 15 years 15c. Tickets for sale at this office, at the Socialist Temple, 120 S. Western Ave. Curtain will raise promptly at 8 p. m.

Come early if you wish to secure a seat.

89. "The Purpose of Workers' Singing Societies" (*Chicagoer Arbeiter-Zeitung,* August 16, 1899).

If the purpose of the "Association of German Singers" is to train the German male singing societies and to refine them by gradually eliminating tasteless and hollow lyrics and compositions as well as by reinforcing a consciousness of national solidarity among all German tongues, then the purpose of the workers' singing societies can best be summed up by Uhland's[25] verses:

> We are a group determined all, the lightness of sound to sing -
> And from the profundity of the heart, our songs their message bring.
> It's not for money that we sing, and not for vanity trite,
> No, that which us together holds, is sound in all its might."

25. A poet and professor of German literature, Ludwig Uhland (1782-1862) was a prominent German liberal who was a representative to the Frankfurt National Assembly during the Revolution of 1848.

The song's might should hold workers from all regions together and inspire them with the great idea which informs the proletariat. The liveliest speech and the most detailed debate will never be able to evoke the same enthusiasm that a choral group does, when the lyrics and sound, all in unison, ignite the thoughts that lie buried away in people's breasts. Herder thus is correct when he says that in the surge of the song people sense that they have a heart and a soul. In the proper recognition of this oneness of thought, the singing German workers created a singing association which strives, through the might of the sound, to evoke the same feelings in the listeners as those which fill the singers. This is the exceptional power of the song, the praises of which have often been sung, a power to break down the barriers separating people and to unite their feelings in an inner community. Think of the services the song has rendered humanity in the course of the ages! The church hymn is said to carry the enraptured heart heavenwards. Throughout history, songs of freedom inspired people with the goals they conveyed, war songs and battle songs among both cultured and primitive peoples radiated a sense of courage, pushing armies on to daring deeds. Everywhere and at all times music has proven itself to be a powerful and intense ruler of human hearts. The Augustinian monk who reformed and protested against so much, Martin Luther, introduced congregational singing in the church, because he realized what an important confederate it was. Convinced of the power of the song, he exalted this noble art in his well-known eulogy to music, saying that music makes those who are sad happy, gives courage to those who are despondent, discourages the haughty, and subdues the flames of the flesh, of envy and hate. The classic Goethe, too, praises the grandeur of this art. He differentiates between sacred and profane music. While sacred music is fully in keeping with its dignity, the profane song has an inestimable effect on life, an effect which remains the same throughout all times and eras. Without referring to further praises of song, let us state here that the proletariat can and will never find so powerful an ally. Thus it is that all the workers' singing societies propose to enlist the uncontestable power of the song to facilitate the realization and furthering of their goals.

In addition to this goal, other advantages are also derived from cultivating the song. These secondary goals are also described very well by Uhland's verses. He sings:

> "Whether joy or pain,
> All will surface in the song,
> And thus toward heaven strain;

And like a stream, midst wild urges,
Its own bed does create,
In every heart thus fiercely surges
Sound - this wondrous estate."

As pain and suffering, worries and cares, are the working people's constant companions, it should also be recalled that the song sung by sympathetic comrades consoles the burdened heart. The son of labor is excluded or stringently restrained from taking part in the gentle pleasures of the bourgeoisie, and therefore, in most cases, forgoes the sanctimonious talk or severe sermons uttered by the servants of the church, those servants who are in the pay or under the jurisdiction of capitalism. To compensate for this, the workers' singing societies try to ready a dignified funeral ceremony for the deceased comrade by singing a few funeral songs and dirges.

On the other hand, the workers' singing societies seek to embellish family, union, and party festivals by singing fitting songs. Aside from the powerful workingman's song and the song of liberation, the folk and popular song must of course also be taken into consideration. After all, why shouldn't the proletarian sing of nature in all her beauty if he can take pleasure in it? Or is there any reason why the worker should desist from singing about all of life's relations and paths? Clearly the workers will only take that to heart which stems from the heart. Labor songs don't pay lip service to any kind of false patriotism, nor do they serve to idolize the individual. But they do try to glorify the workers' ideal endeavors. To what extent humor should be taken into account depends in most cases on the singers' and listeners' level of education and music appreciation. But whatever borders somehow on the frivolous, or is morally questionable, should in any case be avoided. Unfortunately, many of the societies believe that double entendres or caricatures of the singer are the only ways to entertain their audience. Chairmen and conductors who feel that music appreciation and understanding of art are important should go to pains to distance themselves from anything which goes beyond the limits of respectable humor.

By singing songs which impart the ideas of liberty, equality, and fraternity, the workers' singing societies strive not only to inspire their present supporters and encourage them to renewed action, but rather also to win new supporters through singing about the good cause. It has often enough been the case that a recital or an enthusiastic festive song has proven the turning point in finally winning over those people who had remained aloof from the most comprehensive agitational speeches and continued spoken attempts to enlist them.

Most of the time, however, this recruitment by song is successful only when the well-considered intention is not forgotten, i.e., when one remembers that the workers' singing societies must primarily be accountable to fulfilling a need for art. In the same way that the song can bring about an ethical elevation of the people only by rising to true folk art, so too will it be able to interest and finally recruit most of those who remain aloof from the party only if it is well polished and skillfully executed. The artless, rowdy songs which are sung now and then in different societies will never inspire anybody with the workers' ideas. To refute the hostile claim that the proletariat represents the death of art, societies should ban the tasteless and rowdy songs, and those devoid of content, while encouraging the folk and popular song, and the works by poets inspired with the sense of liberty; only the better composers should be sung, those who put poetry to music, those who grew to maturity midst the ideals of the modern labor movement. When this intention becomes noticeable, and lyrics and compositions correspond to the laws of art, it will little matter who the authors are, because "we honor the Masters with dignity, but art is there for us." In order to succeed in increasing an understanding and appreciation of art, it is above all necessary to pay attention to political songs. Poets singing these songs frequently abuse the basic principles outlined above. It is by no means easy to enlist art to serve the party. That's why it is all the more important to uphold the requirement that the lyrics and composition of the song remain on a high level. Goethe himself called the political song a loathsome song. Let's thus make sure that the majority of our polemical songs aren't detrimental to art!

Large singing festivals conducted in a proper—i.e. artful—manner constitute an important factor in elevating the folk song. In this atmosphere the political battle song, with its resounding chorus, can unfold in all its might. But once again, as far as possible, the entire program should be set up according to the laws of art. The choice of individual pieces to be sung should not be left up to any one singing society, and wherever possible, the pieces which call for the chorus in its entirety should consist of compositions written specifically for this purpose. Performances of this or that Verein displaying the greatest degree of virtuosity should serve to encourage the others to renewed endeavors. Artful singing is furthered by rivalry between the individual societies at these singing festivals. But irrespective of the intention of the workers' singing societies, these singing festivals should be sure to preserve the character of real recitals. Each larger group should therefore have a permanent conductor whose responsibilities would entail putting together the musical program and seeing to all the arrangements pertaining to it. The program for any given festival should be carefully worked out at least half a year prior to its realization, so that each Verein has time enough to prepare and can then offer its very best. Only in this way can a singing festival fulfill its goal of artfully furthering the singing of folk songs.

At this point another purpose of the singing societies should be considered. Most of the proletarian singers have to earn their bread by working in musty, dusty, smoke-filled rooms with insufficient ventilation. These people especially, though all singers in general, can profit from the advantageous effect singing has on the lungs. In this sense, the workers' singing societies also serve a hygienic purpose. According to scientific research, people's respiratory systems utilize considerably more air when they sing than when they normally breathe in and out. And exercising the lungs to their limits also has a very positive effect on the whole body. More intensive inhalation supplies the blood with larger quantities of oxygen which is so necessary for the body. And at the same time, more thorough exhalation also tends to eliminate larger quantities of poisonous and harmful vapors and gasses which the lungs also absorb. It is Dr. Fröhlich's opinion—and we agree with him wholeheartedly—that there is no better way to not only increase the lungs' capacity, but also to effect the most comprehensive cleansing of the lungs than through methodical singing exercises. Through the augmented supply of oxygen in the lungs, they become immune to contagious bacteria, like tuberculosis germs, for instance. The increased oxygen intake also improves the blood. With the poet's words we call to the proletariat: "He whose toil is burning stress, whose face is deathly pale," that person should join a workers' singing society and see to it that his blood is improved. Professors Kronecker and Henricius have called the deep breathing which singing demands "a beneficial heart massage." In addition, Dr. Fröhlich sees a beneficial effect on the digestive organs brought about by the increased activity of the diaphragm and stomach muscles which singing actuates. He consequently recommends that all workers accustomed to sitting and whose digestive organs are impeded by their work also sing regularly for the prevention and cure of frequently occurring congestion and cholestasis. What's more, the erect posture which is required of the singer in order to breathe deeply at the same time constitutes a useful gymnastic exercise, for not only is the spine stretched out, but the entire muscular system of the neck and trunk.

Dr. Fröhlich also claims, as do the societies, that the elasticity of the costicartilage is increased and that the thorax is continually expanded. Thus it is evident that the workers' and all other singing societies serve a hygienic purpose. It is, by the way, also generally accepted that regular singing furthers the bodily well-being and puts one in a good mood. If all the goals of the workers' singing societies are fulfilled, then their great importance will also be generally accepted.

"The People's Song"

90. "The Workers' Association of Singers Holds a Major Concert in Orchestra Hall" (*Fackel*, June 26, 1910).

Wherever fate may cast the German in this large world, his faithful companion is "the German lied." Regardless of where he makes his new home, be it in the wilderness as a pioneer, where he arduously carves out a small bit of Nature for his own; be it on the endless prairie, where by the sweat of his brow he ploughs one furrow at time; be he forced to come to grips with the business of life, now here, later there, continually having to recommence the struggle with existence, his love of the German lied doesn't desert him, for he is born with it.

One of the most powerful cultural factors, even here in America, is the singing of German songs, and nothing serves to bind Germans together like the German male singing societies. The history of these societies is inseparable from the history of the German people and their culture abroad. And thus it is only proper to pay tribute to those special occasions which are distinguished by a concerted effort to cultivate the German lied. In this sense, a fitting opportunity presented itself recently: the Fifth National Singing Festival of the Northwest Workers' Association of Singers.

In this country there is no lack of large, important associations of male singing societies. Some of them are already well established and have frequently illustrated their ability and skill. Others can only take pride in a shorter history. The national singing festivals which are held in a variety of places can help measure their value, their importance, and the quality of their performance.

The Northwest Workers' Association of Singers is perhaps the youngest of those organizations committed to the cultivation of male singing societies, but is nevertheless, as far as the quality of performance is concerned, equal to any of the societies which are already decades old.

The Workers' Association of Singers has been called upon to fulfill a very special mission: to help attain recognition for the German lied among the p e o p l e, and this can only occur through a suitable choice of songs. The motto with which the association introduced the Fifth National Singing Festival indicates how well it has understood its task: "Not t h a t we sing, but rather w h a t we sing will make us free and happy!" The Workers' Association of Singers, remaining true to this motto in the future, is at the same time destined to carry out pioneer work in the field of art. This program, recently presented, clearly shows that the association is resolutely and energetically working against the decline of male singing societies.

We applaud the relatively young organization for its successful activity to date, and we hope that their wreath of laurel will increase from year to year.

The mass concert recently held in Orchestra Hall was—if one wanted to summarize the result in the very briefest terms—a success. But permit us to look more closely at the individual pieces. In so doing, we are assuming that only good work can stand up to—and merits—a stringent critique.

The excellent conductor, Reckzeh, directed both the mass choir and the orchestra, and we can assume that he was also primarily responsible for the compilation of the program, which was thoroughly appropriate. Opening the concert with Littolf's Robespierre Overture and thus establishing just the right atmosphere, the 400-strong mass choir then appeared before the audience and sang Kieserling's "Come, the People's Spring Approaches!" The loud shouts of jubilation which greeted the choir bordered on ovation. The recital was magnificent. The entries were precise and demonstrated how hard the conductor had worked during rehearsals. The most striking passages were thoroughly effective, and the singers avoided the mistake which is unfortunately so often made at these passages, namely that of breaking out into shouting instead of strong, loud singing. The pianissimo passages posed a fitting contrast. The general expression, too, left nothing to be desired. Toward the end, however, the attentive observer could not help noticing that the strain of a summer's singing festival had begun to take its toll on several of the singers' throats. But the extent of this was not such that it effected the performance as a whole.

The two pieces sung by the St. Louis Singers' Association—"On the Beach" and "Child's Lament," by Uthmann—were excellent. At the end of the first song, the tenor showed signs of weakening. The second song was sung in an extremely expressive manner.

The Milwaukee Singers' Association, conducted by Kilian, also selected a composition by Uthmann, "Up to the Light." This was decidedly one of the most worthwhile songs, and the recital was unblemished and well varied. Much time and effort had obviously been spent during rehearsals.

Those pieces sung by the mass choir—"Festive Song" by Ahrenson, "To the New World" by Uthmann, as well as two shorter songs in the first part, one by Uthmann and one by Schau—gave the 400-voice choir another chance to prove its skill. The women's choir, also under the direction of conductor Reckzeh, sang two very worthwhile pieces: "Work Song" by Uthmann, and "Girl's May Song" by Kraunig. The women singers mustered all their skill to do justice to their performance, and they were successful in so doing, so that the rendition was quite fine.

The final number was also the high point: "Arise, My People!" by Bruch. With mass choir, solo, and orchestra, it brought the program to a distinguished close.

The soloists' performances were completely flawless. Mr. Willet sang Latzing's well-known "Czar Lied" with a powerful voice.

Mr. Wedertz played an organ concerto by Guilmant, and Miss Heymar delighted the audience with her polished recital of Bruch's Violin Concerto in G-Moll.

Women and the Labor Movement

The place of women among Chicago's organized German workers was ambivalent. To be sure, on a theoretical level the problem had been solved since August Bebel dealt with it in so thorough and fundamental a way; his book Women and Socialism *was available and widely accepted in Chicago's German labor circles. Yet in actual practice the role of women was disillusioning. In the opinion of many convinced socialists married women belonged in the kitchen and should dedicate themselves exclusively to the family. The overwhelming majority of married German women in working-class families listed their occupation for the census as "at home" or "keeping house." Even though many women contributed to the family income by sewing, washing, cleaning, or keeping boarders, most of them did so when they were on their own and had to earn money after their husands had left them, became disabled, or died.*

Women were of course not excluded from the labor movement, but they were given functions considered appropriate and proper for their social role as the caring wife and mother. They took part in essentially auxiliary, supportive, and social activities either on an ad hoc basis, when Christmas bazaars and celebrations, collections of money, or picnics had to be organized, or on a more permanent basis in singing and benevolent societies reserved exclusively for women. Women appeared then in the labor movement as both organizers and participants on such "appropriate" occasions—and mostly in the presence of the whole family.

Many a working woman fought against such discrimination. In the late 1870s, for example, a women's section of the Socialist Labor party was organized in Chicago. During this same period the following open letter appeared, demanding that women be able to march in the upcoming eight-hour demonstration on July 4, 1879, rather than, as usual, being put on display while riding in wagons and on floats. The S.L.P. accepted this demand, and for the first time in Chicago working women—120 strong—took an active part in a demonstration, as the report from the Chicagoer Arbeiter-Zeitung *noted. Later, women's unions were a part of the demonstrations, as in the Labor Day parade of 1903. Their members were predominantly unmarried girls and young women.*

Within families there were clearly disputes between husbands and wives about the desirability of social involvement for women. In a letter to the editor, a working woman complained that even politically active men would not allow their wives to participate in benevolent societies, while they expected of them an everyday solidarity as an indispensable source of support for their work and political activities. In the last two documents a woman rejected the insults of a middle-class German paper against working-class families; and Ludwig Lessen, a poet and journalist active in Germany, poetically expressed his high regard for the courage and trust of the working-class wife.

91. "Submitted by a Reader: To Chicago's Working Women" (*Chicagoer Arbeiter-Zeitung,* June 26, 1879).

The 4th of July is approaching and with it the large demonstration for the eight-hour normal workday. Working people should use the planned demonstration to express their demand for a reduction and regulation of working hours. But don't women belong to the people, too? If they in fact do, then they too have an interest in the introduction of the eight-hour system and thus an interest in the planned demonstration. If the men demand a regulation of working hours for reasons of expedience and in the name of justice, t h e w o m e n d e m a n d t h e s a m e i n t h e n a m e of t h e f a m i l y !

The Socialist Labor party demands equality among all people, and thus demands equality for women among men, too. And that's why, in the name of their human rights and in the name of the family, women must also take part in the demonstration favoring the eight-hour workday, for this question is of great importance to them.

The Socialist Labor party can and will not disapprove of women taking active part in the demonstration, but rather will have to welcome it. It is unimaginable that any large people's movement be limited to half of the people—to the men. If a people's party wants to be powerful and victorious, it has to call upon all of the people. History throughout the ages has taught that any question of national importance is only recognized as such and solved when it becomes so vast that it—contrary to general tradition— inspires the female sex for its cause and encourages women to play an active role in its unfolding. In every revolution in France, the noblest and best women struggled for the cause of freedom. The same happened in Poland and is presently happening in Russia. The labor movement in Chicago is ripe to challenge the female sex, which is greatly concerned, to become independently active for their rights. Or do the socialists also feel that mothers and daughters of the people are entitled to less than the fathers and sons? Should women desist from taking part in the demonstration because it isn't fashionable? How paltry this would be! Let's make it fashionable that women are treated equally and that they act on their own behalf in questions which concern their most sacred interests!

New, unique things shouldn't be measured according to old standards which are foreign to them. Today's social movement requires its own standards. The women would like to take part in the demonstration in large numbers and thus show the ruling classes how seriously the people consider the eight-hour workday, to show them how deeply socialism has taken root among the people, how important the tenet of equality for all people is, and that the professional politicians who until now have enjoyed their lot are ruined, because the people are acting on their own and making their own decisions, and are thus unpredictable. In addition, we would like to recall a promise that Mr. Grottkau made to women in his speech at last year's big picnic: "The time will come, and it seems not so very far away now, when in the name of liberty, humanity, and the family, the idea of equality will move everything with a human countenance, the women of the proletariat not excluded, to independently appear on the stage of public life.

"The Social Democracy cannot exclude half of humanity from agitating for its own liberation; the old prejudices chaining women to the narrow confines of their households like slaves must disappear. Women must raise their voices with the men in protest against the dominant violation of the proletariat by capital and especially against the disenfranchisement of their sex." When the women shouted their agreement, the speaker answered as follows: "At the next large demonstration, the Labor party will also give women's equality its due by giving women the opportunity to take part alongside the men in the struggle for the emancipation of the oppressed and disenfranchised." And now, just before the large party demonstration, many women and female workers would take part and express, through their personal participation in the demonstration, their hate for today's scandalous system of exploitation and their sympathy for socialism, as well as their interest in a normal eight-hour workday. If they were so requested by the people responsible for making arrangements for the demonstration, the women would participate in the parade in very large numbers, and they will have to regard their exclusion from demonstrating as a deprivation of their rights.

A strong showing of women participants in the demonstration would be the most effective way of foiling the pitiful twaddle spewed by the capitalistic press about alleged communist plans to take advantage of the 4th of July to commit murderous and larcenous deeds. Unfortunately, there are many men who are more womanly than the women; having read the trash in the newspaper, these "heroes" would prefer to keep their own cowardice company at home, to wait and see what the drift is on the 4th of July and what the papers have to report about it on the fifth, before they perhaps decide to participate on the sixth. Such men could learn from the women's example and be reminded of their duty.

If female advocates of temperance can do so much for a crazy cause, shouldn't the wives and daughters of socialists do as much for their interests and a good cause? Even the church, which is known not to generally accept equal rights for women, doesn't exclude them from its processions.

There should be but one condition: "ladies in coaches" should not be tolerated in the parade. On the contrary, it would be commendable if all female participants exercised the greatest simplicity in choosing their wardrobes, perhaps with a small red bow to be worn on the left shoulder as an insignia. Up until now, women were always gratuitously "tolerated" as a kind of secondary issue, as "baggage." They didn't have to pay for anything, nor did the men have to sacrifice 25 cents for them; at picnics and other festivities, the Labor party opened its doors to all the women of Chicago free of charge; because: "women are just half-people and as such duty-free"!

But that's not the way it will be on the 4th of July. Everyone who participates in the parade will be able to enter free of charge, but those who come later, just for the entertainment, can pay. So the women have to pay also, and rightly so, for otherwise the festivities would have to be free for everyone. Why? Well, because each man—old or young, poor or rich—who is for the eight-hour day should be in the parade, and whoever is healthy and can walk and just the same doesn't participate in the parade without very good reasons for missing it, that person doesn't have any business sniffing around the festival site. Whoever is not with us is against us. Whoever is for us should be in the parade and comes to the festivities free of charge. Whoever is against us—we don't want their company later anyway.

If, as has previously been the case, women didn't have to pay, it would be inconsistent to accept money from anyone, and this would be ridiculous. Even the women who can't participate in the parade—and there are many of them—and whose husbands enter free of charge because they took part in the parade, these will also pay their 25 cents. Women want equal rights and are all too willing to accept equal responsibilities as well. And to the question of whether many women will be able to get away, we say: all women and girls who are otherwise employed outside of their houses can get away and take part in the parade. And there are lots of these.

All those women who can spend several hours in church, who walk alongside the parade, who stand and wait for hours on street corners to see the parade, all of these can participate themselves. And as to protection for the women, an arrangement could be worked out with the armed organizations so that the parade's wings be comprised of men in uniform. The socialists lack nothing for an imposing 4th of July demonstration save the good will, the enthusiasm, and the agitation of the female sex for their cause.

We request Chicago's women to continue to express themselves apropos of this question, and we hope that they will partake with enthusiasm in the 4th of July demonstration. Let us roll out the banner applauding the sanctity of the family, in whose name we demand the eight-hour day!

For many women and girls,

Mrs. Ida Bensoll,
Mrs. Katharina Rinker,
Mrs. Auguste Grottkau

92. Letter to the Editor from Mrs. M. B. concerning Women's Mutual Benefit Societies (*Chicagoer Arbeiter-Zeitung,* April 15, 1887).

Distinguished Editors,

As a member of the Women's Mutual Benefit Society, Lassalle No. 1, I've often heard it asked: Why are there so few working women in these kinds of societies? You don't have to go too far to find the answer: quite simply, they're not allowed to join, their husbands won't have it! Hard to believe and yet true. A man, a worker, himself a member of a union or society, which indirectly as well as directly serve the same cause, prevents his wife from taking part. I myself know women who would think rationally enough to decide to dedicate themselves to such a noble cause: but women must first get permission from their Herr Husbands. Her mate, however, knows how to convince her to forget it; he tells her how indecorous it would be for a woman to attend a meeting, tells her that she really belongs in the kitchen, doing the housework, etc.; in a word, nothing can come of it. And this is not right! Each worker whose thoughts are in the right place should encourage his wife to join such a society, for women's societies can only achieve something of magnitude if they become strong. And that's why you who read this should shake yourselves out of your lassitude; you've waited too long as it is. A city like Chicago should show other cities in the union what women together can achieve.

Mrs. M. B.

93. "The Worker's Wife": Letter to the Editor from Mrs. Fanny Adler (*Fackel,* April 10, 1887).

To the Editors of the "Fackel."

Chicago's "German Intelligentsia Paper," which goes by the name of the "Freie Presse,"[26] printed an article bearing the above title on the 7th of the month which so writhes with base and mean statements that I cannot help but permit myself the use of these columns to draw attention to the rubbish printed in Michaelis's paper, for the benefit of all those workers who haven't had a chance to see it. It is interesting to see how that individual, whose ethical and moral principles are so notoriously corrupted, who always pretends to be such a friend to workers and tries to peddle subscriptions among them, how this man drags the worker's family life—the sole and most sanctified thing the worker has—through

26. "Free Press."

the mud in such a loathsome manner that it would cause the crudest and most reprobate of men to blush.

In the above-mentioned issue of the "Fr. Presse," its "highly moral" editor published a letter which was allegedly submitted by "the wife of a worker," which he supposedly took from a New York paper. But this "submitted letter" was construed in an editorial office, which is why neither the authoress nor the New York paper is named. But I don't want to go into this fictitious letter, exactly because it is fictitious; I only want to address the conclusions which Michaelis, the "worker's friend," draws from it.

He writes:

Should a l l women think like the one who submitted the above letter (that workers should refrain from striking u n d e r a l l c i r c u m s t a n c e s and be content with their situation, F. Adler's note), it would represent a tremendous counterbalance to the men's blindness.

"The so-called labor press has long since seen to it that the women have also been infected by the anarchistic plague. The misery visited on workers' families by this horrid, shameful garbage, which defiles, mocks, and distorts everything, is inexpressible. The first strategy employed by the anarchistic poison, and which is exploited with ever-increasing deviltry, is reference to immorality, which is discussed in the vilest imaginable way. These odious newspaper scoundrels have recognized that the women's natural shame is the largest obstacle to their plan to spread their bestial, destructive teaching, and that's why special attention is focused on revealing and cultivating the most outrageous moral breaches. Having once broken down the women's shame, their task is easy: then the women are just the way they're supposed to be to understand anarchism—furies and hyenas. The extent to which the local inflammatory press has succeeded can be seen if one takes a look at the way such working-class families live, those families which acquire their 'intellectual nourishment' from this mud. I n t h e s e f a m i l i e s, w h i c h c a n b a r e l y l a y c l a i m t o t h e n a m e, b e c a u s e t h e i r m e m b e r s f e e d f r o m t h e s a m e p o t s a n d g u z z l e f r o m t h e s a m e b e e r m u g s, y o u d o n' t h e a r a s i n g l e w o r d b u t w h i c h w o u l d b e t r a y t h e r a w e s t a t t i-t u d e s, c o m p l e t e l y d e v o i d o f h i g h e r, h u m a n s e n t i-m e n t s. W h e n t h e y f i n d t h e m s e l v e s w i t h o u t a n y t h i n g e l s e t o e a t a n d d r i n k, t h e b a s i s f o r t h e i r m u s i n g s i s b l o o d t h i r s t y h a t e d i r e c t e d a g a i n s t e v e r y o n e w h o s e a p p e a r a n c e i s n' t d e s t i t u t e l i k e t h e i r s, a n d w h e n t h e y w a n t t o e n j o y t h e m s e l v e s 'q u i e t l y,' t h e n t h e y i n d u l g e in reading about the immoral practices flaunted with beastial pleasure in their 'family paper.' Should need have finally driven the husband to look for work, the neighboring women brood the whole day long over the 'Arbeiter-Zeitung,' stuffing their chaotic heads full with jingoism, while only understanding the vulgarity. And then at night when their husbands have returned from the hated work, they 'debate' the question as to how the world is to be improved. Each day they reintoxicate themselves with the poison, and just as sure as the slave to opium will, this unhappy brood, with which we can hardly sympathize, degenerates, and if they are prevented from directly falling into a life of crime, it is only due, in the best of cases, to cowardice."

The readers of this newspaper, the workers and their families, will be justifiably scandalized when they read of how such a dirty paper has the audacity to invade the purity of their home and expose it to the scorn of "public opinion"; but what's more, it is the invention of an utterly callous person who wouldn't hesitate to use the filthiest invention if it served his purpose in the fight for a dollar. - But I do ask every resident of Chicago, man or woman, who has ever read the "Arbeiter-Zeitung," to ask themselves if they can recall ever having come across such language, ever having been offered such "intellectual nourishment" in this paper—a paper which is so very maligned by Michaelis because of his insane sense of competition—which even vaguely approximated the language of the pitiful scribbler Michaelis, even when it was a question of discussing "delicate topics," or of branding disgraceful acts committed by the capitalists and monopolists against the workers. Phooey on such a low person, and thrice phooey on such a topic which has the audacity to defile the worker and his family in such a crude way.

Workers and workers' wives, mark well the scoundrel who dares talk about you like this!

Mrs. Fanny Adler

Chicago, April 8, 1887.

94. "The Proletarian's Wife," by Ludwig Lessen (*Fackel*, September 15, 1896).

> Oh spare me, please, you people prim,
> So cautious and upright!
> I want to spend my life with him,

I know for what I fight.
To him I'll give all that I can,
A woman free to a free man.
My fate be bound to his!

I didn't braid roses in my hair,
The morning we were wed,
And we weren't tied by some priest's prayer -
T'was mis'ry and lack of bread.
We did not seek amusement droll,
But were called by the one high goal:
The people's golden day.

All burdens with him I will share,
And let them never cease!
This thorny path o'er which we dare
Grants hardly any peace.
When choosing him t'was well I knew,
The bonds which us together drew,
Are those we seek to burst!

His woman am I. His woman is free!
She doesn't court favor or grace.
And at his side, should fate decree,
The battle we'll embrace.
To die with him I'd ne'er abhor -
For death is rich, it's life that's poor,
And boundless is our love!

VI. LITERATURE

As in Germany, the labor press in Chicago was the movement's most significant literary institution as well as the most important means of literary publication. In its emphasis on information, agitation, education, and entertainment, the newspaper itself was a characteristic example of a written culture that translated the claims of the Enlightenment into political terms—it intended to combine the formation of political consciousness and group solidarity with both the entertainment and the "higher" education of the workingman. The way these different intentions were put into practice may be illustrated by a brief look at the layouts of Vorbote and Fackel (the weekly and Sunday editions of the Chicagoer Arbeiter-Zeitung).

On the front page the random news of everyday life and events (the raw material of history) was contrasted with—and indirectly commented on by—poems which expressed a political faith in the inevitable and progressive development of history. Some pages later—under the rubric "Workers' Affairs"—poems or short dramatic sketches were occasionally printed which may have been recited or performed at some working-class celebration or festivity. The feuilleton section, on the other hand, was clearly dominated by prose—reports on new discoveries in science, an essay on social history or cultural criticism, and the inevitable roman de feuilleton. Despite the abundance of pulp and schmaltz fiction—sentimental novels of dear old home and fatherland, adventure, cloak-and-dagger novels from Ganghofer to Gerstäcker—the feuilleton of the Fackel nevertheless maintained a comparatively high intellectual and literary standard. Between 1880 and 1910 the paper introduced its working-class audience to the most important representatives of the European and American "progressive" bourgeois novel (Howells, Norris, Hugo, Daudet, Zola, Turgenev, Gorki) as well as to contemporary German and European literature. This, of course, says much about the cultural idealism of the editors, yet it also shows a certain lack of creative commitment or original talent. For reasons which are not entirely clear, the German *working class in Chicago and elsewhere left prose fiction to the bourgeoisie—in any case its role within the communicative system of working-class literature was insignificant.*

Song, poem, sketch, and drama were therefore the most important forms of working-class literary production. It can be no accident that, other than fiction (aiming predominantly at private consumption), these are genres rooted in collective modes of production and reception—in the oral tradition of rural or artisan communities, in recital, performance, and ritual.

The newspaper, therefore, was not only part of the written culture, it also functioned as the medium of exchange between the written culture and the community that used it in politics or festivities. For the literature of German workers in Chicago was pragmatic and functional: a literature made for use. It was produced for a clearly defined audience; it originated from, or referred to, concrete historical events or contexts; in its many songs and its didactic and battle poems it confirmed group solidarity and socialist articles of faith. The subjective element (the expression of subjective feeling, of individual experience—the whole range of private existence) was rigorously excluded. By ritualistically repeating symbolic gestures of defiance or by creating model stereotypes of proletarian existence, it combined ideological firmness with the appeal for a collective identity. In the many allegorical nature poems (whose images of cyclical renewal connote the inevitable coming of the spring of revolution) and in quasi-religious mystery plays at Christmas, Easter, or Pentecost, collective voices proclaimed the message of a Sacred History of socialist redemption. When, as in this case, working-class literature used the established conventions of a Christian folk literature to express its new socialist gospel, it both continued and radically reinterpreted mature literary and cultural traditions. Well-versed in the literary heritage of the German classics and the Vormärz—most of all in Schiller, Freiligrath, Heine—the poets, songwriters, and dramatists of Chicago's German working class used well-known literary conventions and models for their own pragmatic purposes. Perhaps the phenomenon can best be described as a process of cultural appropriation which manifested itself as parody and burlesque, or in the travesty of established forms and widely known models of literary history.

In all this the literature of German workers in Chicago was not essentially different from the literature of the early working-class movement in Germany. This can be partially explained by the fact that many working-class writers who had fled from Bismarck's Socialist Law to the United States simply continued their work there, while keeping open the channels of communication with the fatherland. More important, however, is the functional character of German working-class literature, which made its geographic and cultural transplantation comparatively easy—its disregard of formal innovation, its emphasis on reusing the received tradition, the internationalism of themes and motifs, the stress on the didactic and argumentative over the subjective—all this made such literature almost independent from the particularities of a specific locality. But the new social and cultural environment also exerted its influence, of course. The predilection of Anglo-American workers to parody culturally sacrosanct texts—the Decalogue, the catechism, the Declaration of Independence—enlarged the spectrum of conventions available to German working-class writers in Chicago.

Whether the circle of these writers is more or less identical with the circle of journalists, editors, and agitators that maintained the working-class press is not entirely clear, even though we can say with some assurance that anyone who considered himself a writer of or for the German working class in Chicago was affiliated, at one time or other, with the Chicagoer Arbeiter-Zeitung. *In any case, without the institution and the staff of the labor press there would not have been any working-class literature. The editors of the German labor press did not only fulfill their everyday journalistic routine, they also—especially in the 1880s—organized unions, tirelessly spoke and campaigned on behalf of socialism, wrote reportages, poems, plays, and—on occasion—also acted in, and directed, their own theatrical productions. They had come to Chicago as refugees from Bismarck's Germany, or with the explicit mission from their party in Germany to run the German-American working-class press and to propagate socialism among German immigrant workers. Most of them had been journalists, editors, or writers in Germany or Austria; they brought with them a knowledge of the German classics as well as of traditions of early working-class literature in Germany. They not only stayed in contact with what was going on in the "fatherland"—politically, socially, culturally—but some of them returned there after Bismarck's Socialist Law had been suspended in 1890. Therefore, the vitality of German working-class literature in Chicago depended on a regeneration through the steady influx of members of the working-class intellectual elite. When they stopped coming— as was increasingly the case after the turn of the century—the continuity of this literature, even its very existence, was threatened, first, because the small intellectual elite that had been sustaining it was aging and slowly dying out, and, second, because the new generation of those born in America increasingly lost interest. The second generation sought to express its political and aesthetic consciousness in other, more "American," forms and ways.*

Contrafacture, Travesty, and Satire

These forms were frequently used in working-class literature because they demanded the presentation of antithetical positions about any given type of subject. They also called forth the most aggressive descriptions of both contemporary society and the condition of workers. Satire offered the best opportunity for immediate literary commentary on events, while contrafacture was most suited for frontal attacks on accepted social values. To varying degrees both forms accentuated the distance of the working class from the dominant society and made more concrete labor's alternative set of values and ideals.

Labor writers used the literary traditions of both German and American culture. The first two documents reprinted here clearly take over the tradition of the travesty of religious texts widely used in the nineteenth-century American labor movement. The use of that literary form illustrates how overcoming puritanical Christian values appeared to be an indispensable precondition for the success of the American labor movement, in contrast to Germany where the state was seen as the critical opponent. By utilizing available literary forms— while at the same time transposing and transforming the content and values of the ideological context in which they were used—labor intellectuals both placed themselves within the established literary tradition and gave it a radical and subversive function. One of the best examples of this literary reconstitution was the repeated rewriting of the American Declaration of Independence by German-American socialists. (See, for example, Chapter VII, Document 121.)

The first two documents—both contrafactures of the Ten Commandments—are subtly different. Taken from the newspaper of the furniture workers union, the earlier describes the capitalist economic system as exploitative, on the basis of its work relations, and formulates a stance of fundamental opposition to the dominant society. In contrast, the second document directs criticism inward, using the general formulation "Thou shalt not" to construct a new list of commandments which set up the values of the labor movement as the accepted norm and condemn behavior which does not conform. In this case one can speak of the complete appropriation and reconstitution of the religious form.

The fundamentally didactic intention of working-class literature is expressed even more strongly in the fictional diary of a capitalist during a strike against his firm. The document turns the usual experiential perspective of workers upside down by taking the position of the entrepreneur; his subjective "I" implies that his view of the strike is being reported. Yet, in comical contrast to the private character of a genuine diary, the real author sets up negative signals, such as the selfish motives of the entrepreneur or the slandering of labor, which are designed to point out to workers the necessity of class solidarity during decisive confrontations like strikes.

The next poetic work has to be understood both as part of the German literary tradition and as originating in the concrete experience of immigrant workers in America. Opening with the first verse of the well-known German lied "Be always loyal, true and brave," Conrad Conzett could assume that his readers knew the remainder of the song and then proceed to set up a diametrically opposite message in his own text. Whereas in the song loyalty and honesty are praised as the highest virtues of an upright and moral way of life, Conzett unmasks social success as the result of unscrupulous deception and cynical renunciation of the very principles upheld in the original lied. (Conzett was an important labor leader and editor of the Vorbote; *see the biographical sketches at the end of this volume.) Conzett was not alone in writing this kind of literature. For another excellent example see Gustav Lyser's satirical one-act play, "Congress for the Muddling Up of the Labor Question in New York," written on the occasion of the congressional hearings on the "Condition of Capital and Labor" held after the great railroad strike of 1877.*[1]

1. This play has been published in *Labor History,* Vol. 20, No. 1 (Winter, 1979), under the title "A Forgotten Piece of Working-Class Literature: Gustav Lyser's Satire of the Hewitt Hearing of 1878" by Heinz Ickstadt and Hartmut Keil.

95. "Ten Commandments for Workers" (*Möbel-Arbeiter-Journal,* September 25, 1885).

1. Thou shalt have no other Bosses ⟨Boß⟩ before Me.

2. Thou shalt make unto thee no comfort, or any likeness of anything which is advantageous to thee in heaven above or which is in the earth beneath. Thou shalt bow down to Me, and idolize Me and serve Me, for I am the Lord, thy Boss ⟨Boß⟩, and am an angry and jealous Boss ⟨Boß⟩ and will have no mercy with thee, but rather will force thee to honor My commandments.

3. Thou shalt not use the name of thy Boss ⟨Boß⟩ in vain, or I thy Boss will give you the sack ⟨dir den Sack geben⟩ for having done so.

4. Remember that thou shalt labor from sunrise to sundown, eleven hours each day, six days a week, with all thy spirit, and that thou shalt do all that I, thy Boss ⟨Boß⟩, demand of thee; but on the seventh thou shalt remain within thy gates, and shalt not amuse thyself in any way, so that thou canst rest and gain strength, courage and force, and serve Me again on Monday.

5. Honor thy Boss ⟨Boß⟩ and thy Foreman, that thy days may be few and evil; for I will vomit thee out of My mouth and will cast thee from My view, when thou becomest old and fragile and thou shalt then spend the rest of thy days in the house which is called the poorhouse.

6. Thou shalt not walk on the paths of evil, midst heathens and sinners which are called labor unions ⟨Arbeiter-Unions⟩; for they are an outrage before the Lord, thy Boss ⟨Boß⟩.

7. Thou shalt not bear false witness against Me or Mine, though I may cut thy wages from ten to fifteen percent. Be content that I, in My grace and in My endless mercy, allow thee to work for Me, though I pay thee 90 cents a day and advise thee the half of it to save.

8. Thou shalt go hungry and thirsty, naked and cold, if it so pleases the Lord thy Boss ⟨Boß⟩. Thou shalt receive thy wages so that I may earn golden shekels and silver shekels, and that I may build My house, clothe Myself in purple and fine cloth, and fill My stables with fiery horses.

9. Thou shalt not come into contact with others or hold meetings. Thou shalt not confer with others as to thy own well-being, or grumble about cuts in thy pay. Thou shalt also not read newspapers, that I may keep thee in ignorance and stupidity all the days of thy life.

10. Thou shalt not covet thy Boss's ⟨Bosses⟩ money, nor His ease, nor His conveniences, nor anything which is His. Thou shalt not covet thy Foreman's wages, though he earn 3 dollars each day to thy one. Thou shalt

object to nothing, for I shall rule over thee and order thee, and I shall keep thee in servitude all the days of thy life till thy death, and then, for all I care, thou canst go to Sheol.

96. "Twelve Commandments for Union Members" (*Vorbote*, March 25, 1891).

Workers—whether organized or not—still make many mistakes which prevent them from forming any sort of bonds among themselves. Even in many existing organizations, these mistakes are responsible for preventing further development; frequently they contribute to completely ruining an association. But if these mistakes are to be corrected, all workers seriously willing to stand up for their vital interests must consider the fulfillment of the following twelve tasks their most important duty:

1. You should not think that striking is a union's only function, but rather you must always bear in mind that it also has other tasks to fulfill.

2. You should not think that a union is worthless just because your ideas aren't immediately, or not always, accepted.

3. You should not expect your wages to increase substantially just because you've been paying your union dues for a while.

4. You should not imagine that high wages can be attained with low union dues, as large gains are rarely won with little sacrifice.

5. You should not think, "the meeting can get along without me," because if every worker were to think that way—which is, unfortunately, frequently the case—the unions would be in a very bad way.

6. You should not sneak away from a meeting too soon.

7. You should not talk too much and about everything at meetings. Remember that even the most beautiful musical pieces have to have pauses.

8. You should not buy capitalistic newspapers while workers' papers are fighting for their existence.

9. You should not call yourself a "union member" if you don't subscribe to at least one workers' paper, and more than one if possible.

10. You should not forget that workers' papers should be passed on after they've been read so others can also read them. Workers' papers are too valuable to be used for wrapping things up in, especially if they haven't been read yet.

11. You should not disregard books or writings which can enlighten you as to your social relations and show you the way to improving your class situation in favor of reading fictitious stories—frequently pretty

stupid fictions! Social science, if understood by the workers, will substantially improve their social relations.

12. You should not — forget the above.

Yes, if all workers would remember these points, take them to heart and act in strict accordance to them, it would be easy to form good and strong organizations; and good and strong organizations would make it possible to successfully resist the storms brewing on the economic horizon and heading your way.

97. "The Strike. From a Capitalist's Diary" (*Chicagoer Arbeiter-Zeitung,* February 1, 1899).

January 2

The pack of workers is getting greedier with each passing week. Just last week I had to equip the machines with new protective gear because some stupid oaf had three fingers chewed off his right hand. Today the pack demanded another pay raise and discontinuance of the piecework system. I wouldn't even mind granting the former request, but absolutely not the latter! No, never! I'd sooner close the whole shop! - Thank God the government finally came up with the prison bill! If it only wouldn't take so damned long! A few years behind bars on bread and water would serve that red incendiary right! That rabble-rousing Social Democratic agitator, going around seducing all the others, I'll have to can him first. But I will absolutely not give in to anything!

January 3

Today they sent their so-called "commission" to my office again; they trampled all over my good carpets from Brussels with their filthy boots. But I immediately told them that there was no way I was going to negotiate with a commission; whoever didn't like it at my place could see where the carpenter had left a hole in the wall. To which they replied that if this was my last word concerning their just requests, they would pass it on to their colleagues. I told them to do just that; but inside I was boiling over with anger and rage at the fact that I had to lower myself to deal with these creatures at all; these creatures whose salutations I ignored as, leaning back in my landau, I slipped by them while they slowly and drunkenly skulked along the street with swaying stride! . . . All right then! Let's put it to a test of strength, my good workers! . . .

January 4

Save a few apprentices, nobody showed up to work today! So the union dares spite me! Let's just see who's the strongest! . . .

January 5

These damned apprentices are good for absolutely nothing! They can't even work a lathe. A purely mechanical operation. I tried to insert the support myself, but got all jammed up in it. Go ahead and strike! Don't worry, I'll find workers all right! The new workers will get a pay raise, but not you—I don't let anyone tell me what to do! My agents are already looking around in lots of industrial cities. Free beer and cigarettes at the recruitment headquarters should do the trick. In two days my shop will be running as though nothing had ever happened.

January 6

Now of all times Bonily and Co. have to have their joiners benches. They want to remind me that they were supposed to have been delivered yesterday, and let me know of the fine stipulated in the contract.

January 7

What am I supposed to do now? Another telegram. The joiners benches have to be finished by the day after tomorrow at the latest. Where am I supposed to get workers? The other factories have declined the offer to make the joiners benches, because they're afraid of an uprising in their shops, too. I didn't get a wink of sleep all night.

January 8

If only I had granted their requests. I'm going to try to renegotiate with the commission. I'll grant everything, put everyone back to work, everyone except those damned rabble-rousing reds!

January 9

Today the negotiations were resumed. I had to grin and bear it, though I had to bite my tongue when, for the sake of propriety, I not only had to offer these plebs a chair but also my good cigars. But this pack is proud! My cigars were curtly, though politely declined, and it was clear that they didn't want any gifts from me. With a distinguished smile and a shrug of the shoulders, I snapped the case shut and placed it back on top of my iron strongbox. We didn't reach an agreement today. These workers' skulls are thick. Would anyone fifty years ago have thought that the factory owner would have to negotiate with the people who are dependent on him for their bread and wages? Times are changing at an unbelievable rate!

January 10

Thank God! Eleven "nonstrikers" arrived today from the country. That puts an end to my humiliation, I can cut off the hateful negotiations and will be able to deliver the machines in three to four days!

January 11

This pack of country workers that I've picked up off the street and that's now filled up my factory—new ones also came—are simply too stupid and lazy! They haven't the vaguest idea how to mount the files or forge a length of steel. Today they ruined more tools and wrecked more material than the others did in half a year. I wish the others were here in my shop, those men whose honest faces I know. This shady mob, slithering around with bowed backs, gives me the creeps, makes me nervous! I've already warned my gatekeeper to keep an eye out that nobody walks off the grounds with a tool or something. This sort of security measure wasn't necessary when my old people were there. If only the prison bill were already law, it would end these strikes once and for all! With the people I have here now, my shop may as well be empty!

January 12

Today something happened which really gratified me and relieved my burdened and irritated heart. The main rabble-rousers were sentenced to 2 and 3 months in prison for violating paragraph 153 of the penal code. They have to start serving time immediately. Recently they tried to prevent the "nonstrikers" I've brought in from coming to work for me. But ours is a constitutional system, where the police do their duty. Maybe the others will knuckle under now that the main ringleaders are behind bars.

January 13

I'd pull my hair out if any grew on my polished skull. The machines aren't ready. They're barely half done, and now I'm going to have to pay the 2,000 Mark fine stipulated in the contract. These sluggards, these bunglers, loafers—and all here in my shop. Today I'm going to throw the whole lot out. If this goes on for another fourteen days, I'm ruined, bankrupt. I wrote the "commission" again. I'm ready to throw myself at their mercy and disgrace myself. I have no choice, otherwise I may as well pack everything up and join the beggars.

January 14

How small I felt today vis-à-vis my workers. My face must have shown plainly how desperate I was. I listened again to all their demands, which now also include the immediate release of all the recently hired nonstrikers;

I asked them to make a few notes for me, as I'd need two days to think it over.

January 15

I wracked my brain over this affair all day and all night. The conditions they've given me are pretty tough, considering how working conditions used to be, when I could manage things as I pleased. But as they say, any port in a storm. I'll just have to drink my cup of bile. Not counting future pay raises, the strike has cost me some 10,000 Marks. I'll have to work awfully hard to make it up. Tomorrow I'll dismiss the provisional personnel. It'll be my only satisfaction in this whole affair, finally getting rid of this rabble; somehow I didn't feel like master in my own shop anymore. Tomorrow I'll have to air my defeat publicly.

January 16

The commission has left. I granted all their demands and signed a statement saying that I would honor the conditions. Midst much grumping and coarse remarks, I also cleared the shop of the "nonstrikers." At their insistence, I had to pay them their wages — right down to the last penny — through the end of the week, as had been agreed to. A quick tour of the factory was more than enough to show what enormous amounts of materials had been wasted in the past few days. Big piles of burnt steel and broken pieces of cast iron had been stacked up in the corners behind tin plates. That's what you get when you hire unskilled labor. But oh what a shameful feeling to be pressured by the very people who are dependent on you for their living. This foul plague. Whoever wants to fight against the epidemic should first have the antidote. This mob's red fury should be beaten out of them with a whip. Like they say, if you're not just parrying, always give the whip free rein.

January 17

Today they came back to work. The files and wheels took up their old, industrious melody again, the big flywheels and hammers clanking and humming. I was too embarrassed to go down and exchange a friendly word with the people who had forced my hand. From the window of my apartment, I watched them arrive, clothed in their thin jackets and shirts; a few of them looked up to the window where, hidden behind the curtains, I was watching them; I almost had the feeling that the set of their pale lips indicated a sense of pride and victory. . . . But maybe I just imagined it, and it was just the reflection from the two big lanterns at the factory entrance.

98. "The Rich Man to His Son," by Conrad Conzett (*Vorbote,* April 17, 1875).

Be always loyal, true and brave,
When choices few there be:
And never swindles too much crave,
If profits you can't see.

Always the poor your help please lend,
To lose their pennies saved.
It is by theft, you can depend,
The road to fame is paved.

They say that love's the sweetest thought,
And oft the heart makes mild;
So love her well, but marry not,
The poor man's fairest child.

And oh! that stuff they conscience call -
Get rid of it right now;
It is a thing can make you crawl,
But riches won't allow.

And ign'rance cultivate where you can,
Ensuring your power and might.
The masses forever will plod without plan,
And then you can dupe them but right!

The Father in Heaven you've also to keep
From getting in your way;
For when the priest talks to his sheep,
It's just so they'll obey.

And sink your snout, Son, deep inside
The people's vital sap -
Your money gives you the right to bestride
The people that you've tapped.

You've only, Son, my advice to take,
And watch your money grow.
Then let the people work till they break,
They'll nothing for it show.

In this world you'll remain a king,
The poor they'll remain slaves.
It's money has the purest ring,
The honest are but knaves.

The Reinterpretation of Middle-Class Christian Holidays

While taking pains to create its own tradition of celebrations and anniversaries, the labor movement was confronted with the weighty heritage of the Christian liturgical calendar, which fundamentally determined how workers conceived of the right order and proper celebration of holidays. For simple practical reasons, therefore, the culture of the labor movement could not simply ignore this strongest of cultural traditions, but rather had to contend with it directly. Its goal was the reinterpretation of Christian symbolism and the explanation of Christian holidays in a way that would make them immediately available for the expression of labor's world view and conception of history.

When it came to secular holidays like New Year's a relatively small shift in emphasis was needed in middle-class custom. If unlimited optimism prevailed amidst toasts to success, health, and happiness, then authors like the Detroit anarchist Robert Reitzel used the occasion to critically take stock of society and to refer, with a pessimistic undertone, to the realities of the established order. The execution of the Chicago anarchists in November, 1887, and the imminent centennial of the French Revolution led Reitzel to the laconic and resigned conclusion that bourgeois society granted a certain "fool's freedom" to the labor movement and its culture so long as it did not threaten the established order, but the powers that be would never let the reins of power be taken from them. (On Reitzel see the biographical sketches at the end of this volume.)

When they reinterpreted the Christian tradition and its holidays in their commentaries and articles, the intellectuals of the labor movement called upon the communistic tradition of early Christianity, whereas in their poetry they tended to make use of the symbolism of redemption. Just as August Spies could extol the Bible as the most significant legacy for a just and humane society in his conversational pieces written from prison, so too could Robert Reitzel in a com-

mentary reprinted here compare the sufferings of the Haymarket victims to the passion of Jesus. In the following poems composed on the occasion of the most important Christian holidays—Easter, Pentecost, and Christmas—the utopia of a just society takes the place of religious transcendence. No longer is man to simply suffer and endure and wait for the divine mercy of redemption in another world, but rather he is himself to create a humane society in the here and now by means of a "powerful blow" (Reitzel). The resurrection hopes of Easter have not yet been fulfilled—"He still sleeps" (Drescher). And the Holy Ghost no longer announces its pentecostal message in the churches, but rather amidst the wonders of bountiful Nature. Men should build their new and free "Kingdom of Man" on its model. (See the biographical sketch on Drescher at the end of this volume.)

99. "New Year's, 1888," by Robert Reitzel (*Fackel,* January 1, 1888).

> It was like always,
>   Was just the same;
> We all were upright,
>   And very tame.
>
> Courageous we were -
>   In saloons well filled;
> And bravely watched,
>   While others were killed.
>
> For now, we said,
>   We must keep cheer!
> And grimly ordered
>   Another beer.
>
> Our advice to the people,
>   Was very exact -
> The hangman, however,
>   Knew how to a c t.
>
> *   *   *
>
> We console ourselves, just another year,
> But then you'll be shocked to see,
> For we will make it historically clear,
> That soon it's a century!

And all the while the police will allow
The Bastille storming to praise,
We'll fire our guns and make our vows,
And drone out the Marseillaise.

The shawms of peace, we'll let them resound,
It's here our abil'ty excels;
We blink back tears, without a sound,
Not good for anything else.

That's right, we'll wait another year,
We're gathering wisdom galore -
And if the future's not quite clear,
Well, we'll just wait a little more.

100. "Jerusalem and Chicago" (*Der arme Teufel,* **October 30, 1886).**

I have often said: scorn not the Bible! It's a book which reflects the human spirit and the human heart—that spiteful and despondent thing— as well as Dante's description of hell or Shakespeare's tragedies. The sound of plaintive longing which traverses the centuries is also found in the Bible, and if the Old Testament is a book of "Kings," the New Testament is a book of "Revolution."

Whether you view Chicago's eight condemned men as legitimate representatives of a new world view, or whether you see them as fanatics pursuing a misconceived notion of justice, you have to think of that curious trial, related in relatively similar terms in the Four Gospels, of the Jewish boy named Jesus who laid claim to heaven and earth.

What Jesus preached was complete anarchism; because even though he counseled a patient passivity toward the government, all of his statements with respect to this topic express a scornful nonacceptance of profane authority. The basic tone is always present: there is only o n e Father for all of us, we only have o n e Lord in Heaven; and when he spoke the proud phrase—"My Father and I are one"—he proclaimed himself the representative, the embodiment of this anarchistic movement which was directed against the entire civilization of those times. Even stronger were his attacks on the Jewish state religion and its priestly representatives, so strong that we have borrowed from that Jewish youth some of the sharpest expressions of outrage against hypocrisy, religious lip service, and the arrogant priesthood. Thus Jesus died not only as a revolutionary speaking out against Rome's "legitimate" supremacy, but he was also condemned by the high priests who had deliberated "about Jesus, that they kill him."

Didn't the degenerate and hypocritical religion of our present America also sit in judgment on the sinners in Chicago? Weren't the Pharisees also represented in that jury, and the Sadducees as well, those "free thinkers" of the stamp of Ingersoll,[2] who rejected immortality because they found it so much more convenient, but who along w i t h immortality also rejected every ideal endeavor, and who also, by the way, were seeing to their stomachs and their pocketbooks?

When Judas saw that Jesus was doomed to die, he repented and gave back the blood money and hung himself. Unfortunately, our Judases don't have as much sense of honor! And how many hundreds of times do we meet the cowardly Peter these days, who is perhaps crying bitterly inside himself, but who in the presence of people abnegates himself and swears: "I don't know this man"?!

And doesn't the pious and loyal mob still cry out to the governor and his power to pardon today: we want Barrabas; let the thieves and murderers free, as many as you want, but these must die?!

And haven't the eight men in Chicago answered to charges of anarchism, of political demagoguery, of preaching revolution, with the same pride as did the Son of Man: "Thou sayest"!

And finally the judge. Mr. Gary is doubtless a good Christian and knows his New Testament very well: is it possible that the similarity between his position and that of his colleague of some 2,000 years ago, Pilate, hasn't occurred to him? When Pilate pronounced judgment "he took water, and washed his hands before the multitude, saying: I am innocent of the blood of this just person." Just the same, that was a noble confession of his own weakness. Judge Gary, however, chose to carry out the exoneration quietly, to himself; but when he pronounced judgment, he literally broke down, tears flooded from his eyes, and consciousness fled him.

Who was guilty in Jerusalem? Was it the man who, his head bloody and full of wounds, responded to the contempt of his enemies with the noble words: "Father, forgive them, for they know not what they do"? Or was it not much more the frenzied church mob and Rome's proud prefect, who let himself be forced into sanctioning a horrible breach of justice by p u b l i c o p i n i o n? - Where did the guilt lie in Chicago? Did it lie with those eight men, who with bold, bright eyes were able to face death — an apparently shameful death — in the light of their convictions?

2. Robert Green Ingersoll (1833-99), lawyer and lecturer, was known as "the great agnostic."

O r was it not much rather to be found in that broken
man who sat in judgment of the condemned?

Jerusalem — Chicago — the same tragedy, the same actors, the same violation of a sense of justice! Only the latter was carried out in modern
Chicago in a much cruder way than in ancient Jerusalem. At least the
representatives of the law in Jerusalem engaged in a mock battle with
public opinion. In Chicago, public opinion spoke from the mouth of the
judge and more or less told the jurors to "crucify." In Jerusalem the crowd
was aware of its responsibility, "his blood be on us and on our children,"
cried the people. In America, however, the church mob, and the mercenary
and mercantile slaves saddled their twofold scapegoat, God and State,
with the murder. But the story of Judas, the story of Rome, they speak
and bear witness, and as long as injustice triumphs, so too will Doomsday
continue to be repeated throughout human history.

101. "Easter Hope" (*Vorbote,* April 18, 1906).

> Smiling, youthful springtime bloom,
> Softly springtime's bells are sounding -
> What are lights and sounds expounding?
> That the Lord has left the tomb?
>
> Yes, a Savior has been born!
> Youthful King who's known as "Springtime,"
> Loud his praises all do chime,
> Everywhere his hues adorn.
>
> But that herald of such worth,
> Who the darkness of the grave
> Fled, and toward the light did stave,
> For the sinners here on earth -
>
> Oh, his slumber still is deep,
> Under stones, so dead and cold,
> All his faithful, tears untold,
> Hoping life's reward to reap -
>
> Crucified each day once more -
> Daily to the grave he's sent,
> By the people smug, content,
> Now as in those days of yore.

Alone the poor they wish and wait,
Yearning that he reappear -
Full of longing, full of fear,
Waiting for a better fate.

All this Easter signifies:
Breezes rushing through the heart -
Grievances will then depart,
When the people choose to rise!

Courage growing now, oh dreamer!
Come, oh novel Easter fest -
Come, oh freedom's valiant quest -
Come, the only t r u e redeemer!

102. "Pentecost," by Martin Drescher (*Vorbote,* June 6, 1906).

Pilgrims of pent'cost so devout,
Enter your greying house of stone!
O u r song from the fields we'll shout,
From the peaks and woods intone.

There, midst springtime's glowing youth,
We will praise the holy ghost,
Showing us the path to truth,
Midst a worldly, surging host;

Which with voices mass'd regales,
And to us of freedom sings,
Which to e'en the lowest dales,
Summer's lustrous cool air brings;

Calling loud: "The time is now!
Spread your glory through the world,
Sigh, that others soon allow
Freedom's flag to fly unfurled."

103. "Christmas," by Robert Reitzel (*Chicagoer Arbeiter-Zeitung,* December 23, 1899).

Christmas, Christmas! Christ is born,
    Satan chained,
    We've regained
The Garden, which from us was shorn.

"Peace on Earth, good will to men!"
  Heaven expounds -
  Church bells resound,
And still many sigh: when? when?

Do you light up houses poor,
  Heavenly glow?
  Come and bestow
Your gold on the angry and the sore!

To the oppressed they preach of peace!
  Audacious gall -
  While we fall
Spilling our blood, with no release?

Should we still to the fairy tale cleave?
  Suffer the slum,
  Our time will come,
When new worlds our cares will relieve?

Christmas, Christmas, evening bells ring,
  As such it must go!
  A powerful blow -
That is the Savior of which I sing.

Reportage and Editorial

In accordance with its goals of enlightening its audience and criticizing contemporary society, Chicago's German labor press highly valued reportage and editorial. Both journalistic forms complemented each other, since they often took up the same subject from different points of view. While reportage uncovered a contemporary abuse, often letting the reader hear in the first person the opinions of those directly involved, the editorial took up the whole set of circumstances, analyzing them on the basis of the principles of the movement. The high standard of this political literature is striking, as is the quality of the essays on scientific, social, political, and cultural themes which regularly appeared in the Fackel.

Like the preceding literary documents, the article "Thanksgiving" challenges the justification of a middle-class Christian holiday. As the article sheds a revealing light on the condition of poor working-class families, it exposes "Thanksgiving Day" as the exclusive province of the well-fed and established. In this piece a highly dramatized and emotionalized structure of dialogue serves as a didactic medium for political enlightenment. Repeatedly employed during the early 1880s by the Chicagoer Arbeiter-Zeitung, such democratic reporting "from below" can be seen as a precursor of the widely used "muck-raking" style of journalism that appeared ten years later. In his editorial on Christmas August Spies transposes a news article's implicit recognition of the class character of Christian celebrations into a verbally polished and intellectually acute political indictment.

Published in 1884, like Spies's editorial, the understated report on the joint suicide of a married couple is, as befits its subject, free of all sensationalism and cheap effects. During the 1880s reports on the suicides of workers became more frequent in Chicago's German labor press. The papers saw in this development a gruesome but unerring index of the existential needs of immigrant workers, who, in extreme and hopeless cases, were driven to this final act. Even though the statistical significance of these suicides cannot be determined, there is nevertheless substantiation for an especially high rate of suicide for German immigrants in New York City. And, not infrequently, the records of the German Society of Chicago contain cases of needy widows whose husbands had taken their own lives.

104. "Thanksgiving midst the Unhappy 'Liberated' People and the Happy Captives" (*Vorbote*, December 3, 1884).

"Bread!" cried a four-year-old girl.

"Yes, we want our bread!" echoed four other children's voices.

A boy said, "Oh, you should have seen the huge turkey that Jim's mother pushed into her oven! It was a real beauty, and my mouth started to water when I thought about one of the wings! Say, Ma," he continued, his voice getting louder, "don't you even have a chicken—don't you have any meat for us at all?"

"Chicken! Meat!" the children's voices began to shout anew. "But first give us our bread!"

The mother bent her face, crimson from the strain of her work, lower over the washtub where she was working. Her fourteen-year-old daughter was standing next to her at an ironing board, her ghostly thin naked arms wielding the iron, her weak little legs occasionally trembling under the strain of her work. She looked up to her mother with a melancholy air.

"Be still, my little ones!" the mother said, a large tear falling into the soapy water. "Be still. Don't worry, you'll get something. Learn patience - - -"

"Patience, patience?" the boy yelled. "Jim doesn't have to be patient when he's hungry. Jim's got a turkey and I—I at least want my bread! - - -"

"Yes, bread! Bread!" were the cries.

The young ironer now raised her little head with its thin, transparent little face.

"Charley," she said chidingly, "what's gotten into you, working your little sisters up like that?! Don't you know that the fine lady on Dearborn Ave. was out when I brought her wash yesterday, and that's why I didn't bring home any money? I was there again today, but she didn't have any time to see me. - As soon as I've finished these towels I'll bring 'em over to the barber, and then there'll be tons of money - - - Just be quiet, Charley, you know that Mama can't wash as quickly as usual since she burned her hand! How do you expect to see chickens and turkeys in our kitchen, especially now when Pa's out of work. Go on and play with the little ones and soon you'll get something good to eat!"

Ashamed, Charley crept away. The mother averted her face to hide her tears. -

A reporter from the "Arbeiter-Zeitung" happened to witness this sad scene; he was out looking for stories for today's edition, and he made this study in life and suffering on the ground floor of a house on Wells Street, not far from the bridge. The newspaper man approached the woman and started up a conversation.

"It breaks my heart," she said, "to have to see this misery. My husband had been out of work since September, and so he began to drink out of anxiety and desperation. They sent him to the Bridewell[3]—so he can work for the city while in the meantime we are slowly but surely on our way to starvation - - -"

"Yes, we're hungry, we want bread!" the children cried.

Nellie, the pitiful creature at the ironing board, went to them in the corner. "Look at that beautiful fire," she said. "Hundreds, thousands of poor children don't even have that, and they don't complain! Can't you just wait until I've finished the towels for the barber! - - -"

The writer and his colleague from an American paper glanced at each

---

3. The local prison or workhouse.

other. Reading each other's look, each placed a small coin in the hungry children's hands before they continued on their way. There was much rejoicing, and the poor washerwoman with the burned hand cast a glance full of emotion at the two departing strangers, who apologetically said—"You know, like the fine lady of Dearborn St., the barber might not be home either, and then the little ones would really have to starve."

Wesson Street.

A narrow, dirty street, the houses dilapidated, trembling at every gust of wind, the windows broken, makeshift paper repairs covering the holes, the stairs worn, walls filthy.

Crossing the street, the reporters greeted a man leaning in the door of his house.

Their greeting was answered with a curse.

The people from the newspaper stopped. "What do you want?" they asked. "We're not responsible for your misery, even if our jackets are better than yours. We're reporters and - - -"

"Reporters?!"

The man burst into raving laughter. And with a blow from his fist, he banged open the door to his rooms. "Take a look at our Thanksgiving dinner ⟨Danksagungsdinner⟩!" he said.

The room was desolate and almost completely empty. A small fire was burning in the oven. At the table was seated a woman who must once have been pretty. She looked at them, frightened and sad. A nursing child hung from her breast, its visage deathly pale, its hands balled tightly around the source that was supposed to furnish it with life, nourishment.

In front of the mother was a bowl of hot water, in which she was softening some hard bread—that was her and her children's Thanksgiving dinner.

We only had a quick look at the room. "Shut the door!" the occupants shouted. - "We're freezing!"

But the man threw his hat into the air and roared: "*Vive la Commune!*"

105. "Tired of Living. A German Husband and Wife Hang Themselves" (*Vorbote*, March 26, 1884).

In the mortuary of the County Hospital, laid out next to each other on a cold marble slab, are the corpses of a man and a woman, united in death as they had been in life. A thin, strong cord fastened around the throat of each tells the story of their death much more eloquently than can any human tongue.

It is not known when the unhappy couple committed suicide. But it seems that it occurred on Saturday, or at the latest on Sunday morning, though they weren't discovered until last night. In any case, the couple had carefully considered everything and made the most extensive preparations in advance. The man was approximately forty years old, 5' 8" tall, thin, of dark complexion. The woman was six years younger, 5 feet tall and of slightly lighter complexion.

Not much is known about the couple. Mrs. Broderich, the landlady at 119 Hubbard Street, has related the following about the discovery of the suicides. Her husband, James Broderich, is a night watchman, and could thus hardly notice that the two occupants hadn't been seen for the past few days. But Mrs. Broderich, because she hadn't seen them leave the house since Friday night, went to see why yesterday. The storm door was locked from the inside, the windows were not only shut tight but also covered with paper so that it was impossible to see inside. Accompanied by a neighbor, Mrs. Broderich took courage and broke in a window. Not a sound was to be heard. The neighbor pushed the paper aside, but then suddenly jumped back and shouted: "Be careful. He's shaking his fist at you." The two women left to wait for Mr. Broderich. As soon as he came home, they all went to the window. Peering through, Broderich saw the man hanging in the doorframe, his feet brushing the floor, motionless, dead. He hurried to the door and broke it open. A new shock awaited him: across from the man, fastened to the wall, hung the woman, likewise cold and dead.

Both were dressed in their best things and carefully groomed. The woman, whose hair was neatly done, was wearing a smart kerchief. The man had dressed himself neatly and polished his boots. They were hanging across from one another. The hooks had been nailed in for this purpose. They had probably hanged themselves like this so that they could see themselves in death, and lend each other courage and determination. How terrible the determination, how grim the desperation must have been to have led them to this fateful pose! Their feet brushed the floor. A mere stretching of their limbs would have raised their heads enough to save them from strangling to death.

In the large, comfortably furnished room, there was evidence that the suicides had been carefully thought out and prepared: the fine bed sheets, clothes, curtains, woolen blankets, etc., everything which could possibly be put to use had been cut to pieces. Even a washline had been cut up, the pieces scattered about. Neither one of the people seems to have hesitated. They carried out their plan in the most deliberate manner.

Papers found in the apartment of the deceased reveal the following about the couple's personality and life: their names were Friedrich Wilhelm and Augusta Wilhelmina Alberta Jagow, widow of a certain Marter. They had only been married for about a year. A marriage license issued in Leipzig is dated March 20, 1883, a wedding certificate dated March 27. The couple arrived in New York from Germany on October 10, and proceeded here without stopping over. From October 13 to January 19, 1884, they lived at the residence of a Mrs. Anna Henkel, where they payed $10 a month. Then they moved into two rooms at the back of Mrs. Broderich's house, where they payed $6.50. The rent had been paid in advance and the next installment would have been due tomorrow. But only five cents were found in the rooms.

It can be ascertained from Jagow's papers that he was born on September 15, 1844, in Writzen, Spreewald, in the Province of Brandenburg, and that he was recruited to the 7th Brandenburger Infantry Regiment No. 60 on June 29, 1866. He served until September 26, 1868, at which time he was put on half-pay as a reservist. In this capacity he took part in the war against France, fighting with his regiment in battles at Gravelotte, Rogent, Le Roy, and in sorties and outpost engagements during the sieges of Metz and Verdun. He received numerous medals.

He was a paperhanger by trade, and had hoped to find work in abundance in America; but in this he was bitterly disappointed. Faced with this relentless misery, and perhaps starvation, the couple must have come to the desperate conclusion that it would be more agreeable to take their own lives than deliver themselves over to slow murder. Neither one of them spoke English. Everyone who knew them had good things to say about them and described them as having been honest, upright people.

106. "Merry Christmas!" (*Chicagoer Arbeiter-Zeitung,* December 24, 1884).

". . . Peace on earth, good will to men." - According to the well-known legend about the birth of humanity's savior, the celestial hosts proclaimed these words to the peoples of the earth almost 2,000 years ago; and they are about as credible as our modern Adventists, who have already prophesied the end of the world so many times, but whose calculations, as they recently confessed, have been wildly wide of the mark just as often.

As far as the latter are concerned, who modestly concede that "to err is human," one can make allowances; but for the former, who proclaimed their message of peace from the celestial heights so many years ago, not to have excused themselves for their stupidity even once—let us state it clearly once and for all: they are humbugs, humbugs whose audacity could only stand up to that of our American politicians.

"Peace on earth!" How these words must sound to the people whose throats have been cut by Christian Brotherhood! What merriment the "Merry Christmas!" must evoke in the hearts of the homeless, the half-starved and half-frozen who are forced to slink to this or that police station ⟨Polizeistation⟩ tonight, in the hearts of millions of proletarian children, for whom Santa Claus—but enough.

"Merry Christmases" only exist for the rich. Not because Providence so decrees, but rather because that's the way the rich want it, and they've set things up according to their wishes. If they just relied on Santa—like the proletariat—then everybody's lot would be the same. If workers only wanted it enough, they could be in a position to celebrate Christmas next year like it's never been celebrated before.

Nothing would be easier. They would simply have to emphatically declare that they are no longer workers, but rather people; they would simply have to take possession of that which they've v o l u n t a r i l y re-nounced until now. But if this simply isn't what they want, if they're so content with their present position, then they'd do well to keep their complaints to themselves, then they'd do well—for lack of anything better— to let the "angels" sing them their little songs of peace forever. Because those who will not listen to reason cannot be helped.

But then the children of the proletariat should join in on the refrains of all of the angels' songs of peace: "Cursed be our cruel parents."

Workers, don't you want to celebrate Christmas, the "pagan" midwinter festival, the festival of the winter solstice, as free and happy people in the future - - -? It's up to you!

A. S.

Occasional Political Poetry

This form of literary treatment of significant as well as ephemeral political and social events was such a widely used vehicle for social criticism that it cannot simply be seen as the special instrument of intellectuals within Chicago's German-American labor movement alone. More or less successful verses were composed for every occasion—whether for the countless social events organized by clubs, or to support striking workers (see the satirical poem—Chapter IV, Document 57—about Bruschke, the furniture manufacturer whose business was struck), or by readers of the labor press who sent a poem instead of an argumentative letter. The function of these poems for ventilating anger and protest against abuses is clear. Didactic and enlightening elements naturally predominated in this poetry because it tried to make workers conscious of the class character of publicly well known events.

Only a few of the qualitatively better poems have been selected from the wealth of material for presentation here. On the occasion of the coming elections in 1877 Gustav Lyser so thoroughly transposed the meaning of a slogan propagated by the two major parties— "Don't throw your vote away!"—that one could only be true to its appeal by voting for the labor party. An unknown author, though probably Lyser, also turned his biting sarcasm on his own socialist party: In order to castigate its unscrupulous political dance with the Greenback party, he uses the well-known philosophical fable of Buridan's ass. Attributed to the fourteenth-century French philosopher Jean Buridan, this fable refers to an ass who, placed between two bundles of hay, cannot decide for one or the other and dies of starvation—a warning to man to make use of his free will. In his poem W. L. Rosenberg depicts a symbol of state power that others besides the Chicago German working class perceived as a conscious provocation and a glorification of indiscriminate police brutality. The monument to the police killed by the Haymarket bomb was repeatedly destroyed and just as doggedly put up again; finally after the unrest during the 1968 Democratic convention and the anti-Vietnam protest movement, it had to be exiled from its pedestal in Haymarket Square to the courtyard of the central police headquarters in order to protect it against further attacks.

In varying ways two poems composed after 1900 take up the subject of the unequal distribution of the fruits of labor. Martin Drescher attacks Labor Day, in obvious contrast to the 1st of May, which the international working class had established in other coun-

tries as the genuine workers' holiday. He sees Labor Day as something bestowed from above that hides the real relations of power and property in America. On the other hand, "Flamingo"—the pseudonym that Drescher occasionally used when writing in the Chicagoer Arbeiter-Zeitung—*takes a meeting of the National Civic Federation in the home of Mrs. Potter-Palmer as the occasion for satirically dissecting the irreconcilable styles of high society and the working class and for revealing the unbridgeable gap between them. The* Chicagoer Arbeiter-Zeitung *had already evaluated the meeting as an attempt to "lull the workers into a peaceful mood," characterizing this "so-called conciliatory effort of the entrepreneurs" as a "swindle that stinks to high heaven." The sum of it all from the fictional visitor reads: "Never again to Mrs. Potter-Palmer's place!" The poem reminds one of a corresponding scene in Upton Sinclair's novel* The Jungle, *in which the protagonist, the immigrant Jurgis who frequently finds himself out of work, casts a revealing look at the mansion of a rich Chicago businessman.*

107. "Cast Not Your Votes Away!" by Gustav Lyser (*Vorbote,* November 10, 1877).

> In recent days was calmly said
> A great word which you should espouse,
> And just this word we'd like to spread
> From town to town, from house to house!
> You need but follow what they tell,
> And wonders will be brought to play,
> Elections near, let us all yell:
> "Cast not your votes away!"
>
> Too long now we have borne the weight
> Of cocky enemy's heavy hand,
> But now's the time to force the gate,
> Though tough the battle, tougher our stand!
> Let stormy waves above us thunder,
> We'll boldly sail right through the spray,
> The enemy's cunning will shamefully blunder,
> Never cast your vote away!

And if by Democrats refined,
Or by Republicans mistreated,
Election over, you will find:
You've once again been smartly cheated!
For only you yourselves can free,
It's Justice your sole protégé,
And in its service always be,
Never cast your vote away!

So onward now! The banners fly,
And boldly freedom's path we'll clear,
Our enemies we will defy,
When armed with weapons they appear!
Whether victorious, whether we fall,
Our enemies we will waylay;
Bravely fighting, shouting to all:
"Cast you not your votes away!"

108. "An Old Song Which Is Always New, or: **Greenback-Ticket** or Socialist Workers-Ticket?" (*Vorbote,* March 23, 1878).

On his left and his right a bale of hay,
The donkey midst the two -
To which side he should finally stray,
He simply hadn't a clue.

To and fro, 'twas thus he swayed,
With a nibble and sometimes a sniff,
Till finally - thanks to his thorough dismay -
He starved, and dropped, quite stiff.

And just like then, so too today,
In keeping with customs serene:
The righteous hard to the left do stay,
The donkeys in between.

And those who still to both sides turn,
Like whores, who're trying to vend,
The same as Buridan's ass, will earn
A wretched, hideous end.

109. "The Shameful Monument at Chicago's Haymarket (which, in the meantime, has been torn down)," by Wilhelm L. Rosenberg (from *An der Weltenwende* by Wilhelm L. Rosenberg [Cleveland, 1910]).

Thus mounted on a pedestal
In lofty dignity,
A mercenary, full of gall,
Is "Order's" referee.

While on his brow, a somber hate
For freedom and its feats,
With ox-like gloom he stares irate
Across all public streets.

On haughty lips, drawn back in scorn:
"Such powers do I serve,
Instead of revolution's storm,
It's peace I will preserve.

"Peace in the name of a state secure,
Peace in the name of God,
The peace to keep a system pure,
Which long has been a fraud.

"I am the savior of this site,
'Gainst thieves' and pirates' gall;
Such is the reason for my might -
All brigands to forestall.

"As long as you look up to me,
Though raging, here I'll stand.
While laughing at you, full of glee,
With mean and massive hand.

"I am the heart of capital,
Revenge's instrument;
Those who to sacred causes crawl
Will feel my ravishment.

"Whoever seeks to shake the frame
Of 'Order's' fundament -
Capital's fury him will tame
And with the state's consent!"

Such are the words from the pedestal,
As heard throughout the land,
And while they ring, on thousands fall
A fierce and shameful brand.

A nation's shame, in polished stone,
Immortal, cruel and mute -
And next to Lincoln, Washington,
Is glorified - a brute!

110. "Labor Day," by Martin Drescher (*Vorbote,* September 5, 1906).

It's Labor Day - a swelling, joyful tide
Our hearts does lift; in spirit we see all
Of those whose strength the world's welfare provides,
In fields of green, in decorated halls,
The day that they themselves alone have chose,
A people free, they step back from their task.
And then they rest, and then their souls repose,
While finding spots where untapped strengths still bask.

Thus in their work, true wages of their trade,
They have agreed these hours to enjoy,
And goods which they themselves for all have made,
Provisions rife for every girl and boy.
They all are working men, with brawn or brain,
The day's events saw each man give his best,
And brimming o'er with pride and strength again,
Each sees himself the founder of this fest.

And thus we dream - oh, yes! There is no doubt -
Ignore we would the pictures others see:
In Sunday best the worker walks about,
On Labor Day may have some hours free,
But really free this man is not, his time
Is not his own. And if this seems the case,
It's only 'cause officials high, sublime,
Have chose the slaves with this one day to grace.

And just as Labor Day in days of old
To Mammon bowed - is how it is today.
The well-fed pharisees will try to hold,
The people's children ignorant, their prey.
And still successful is the clever plan,
But don't despair - for freedom's arms are near!
A day will come when each and every man,
The blinds removed, his own fest loud will cheer!

111. "The Potter-Palmer Swindle," by "Flamingo" (*Fackel,* January 20, 1907).

So tell me, Jim, how did it go
When to Miss Potter-Palmer's you went?
For sure there was fun in an endless flow,
Not to mention choice whiskey to set you aglow,
And grub you just couldn't resent!

Not at all, Joe, you're far from the mark,
From the outset nothing went right.
Arriving too early, alone in the dark,
The doors being closed I crept 'round the park,
And froze from the chill of the night.

But surely, Jim, when the doors opened wide,
The cold you quickly forgot.
And Miss Potter-Palmer, your smiling guide,
Bade you enter and so that your shivers subside,
Brought you drink and food steaming hot.

Oh, really, Joe, you can't mean that;
Not a word we spoke all the time.
And when in her parlor I casually spat,
She looked at me in a manner whereat
You'd have thought I'd committed a crime!

Agreed now, Jim, it's hard to believe,
But then on the other hand,
Among such fine people you can't be naive,
Amidst so much wealth each guest has to cleave
To an image advantageously grand.

Among such fine people, oh no no!
This nonsense just never stops.
There staked through the house, high and low,
For heaven's sake, what do you know -
A poorly disguised group of cops!

And the speeches, Jim, how did they ring?
Were they spoken loud and true?
Did the words bear the anger and staunchly bring
The union man's pride and the union man's sting
To the light where they found their due?

The speeches - oh Joe, don't make me moan!
Of these you won't want to learn.
The scoundrel Belmont and the traitor Stone[4]
Purred like kittens in the friendliest of tones,
Till my stomach was ready to turn!

I'll tell you, Joe, as this be the case,
If my judgment you will permit:
Never again to Miss Potter-Palmer's place!
Never again accept capitalist grace!
For they'll always just treat us like sh - rimp!

Songs

*The especially high value placed on labor songs was already referred
to in association with commemorations and workers' singing societies
(see Chapter V, Theater and Music). Probably no other literary form
was so independent of particular geographical and political contexts
as songs; thus there were practically no limits on copying or ex-
changing them, even between those who otherwise fought over basic
principles. Even the ocean did not constitute an insurmountable
barrier to the transfer of songs between the German and the German-
American labor movements, and the exchange went in both directions.*

4. August Belmont (1853-1924), a banker from New York, was president of the National
Civic Federation. Warren S. Stone (1860-1925) was the leader of the International Brotherhood of Locomotive Engineers.

All well-known German labor songs, whether by Georg Herwegh, Jakob Audorf, Johann Most, or others, were sung in America. In 1883 the Chicagoer Arbeiter-Zeitung *published all the working-class songs appearing in the "Socialist Song Portfolio," in order to make them available and known to a wider public. Conversely, songs from the pens of German-American authors were included in collections published in the United States but also distributed in Germany, particularly during the years of the Socialist Law — 1878 to 1890 — when such publications were illegal.*

Compositional talent was nonetheless scarce in the German-American labor movement. An exception was Carl Sahm, whose "Song of the Commune" is reproduced here. Sahm was active in New York as a musical director and composer for the movement, and thus one may assume that he wrote his own score for this song. (See the biographical sketches at the end of this volume.) More frequently, new texts were added to well-known melodies, as in "Beyond the Grey Wat'ry Desert" and "Demonstration Song." Both were sung to the tune of the "Marseillaise," and thus obtained an additional international dimension. The texts of all these songs are distinguished by a certain abstractness of expression and a universal symbolism, both of which facilitated their wide distribution as mentioned previously. Nevertheless, the song "Beyond the Grey Wat'ry Desert" contains an interesting reinterpretation of the passage of a ship, traditionally freighted with images of immigration, liberty, and democracy: Here the crossing is made in the ship Revolution, *which lands on the coast of a new earth, namely a socialist society. Ferdinand Freiligrath (1810-76) wrote the text in 1846. However, only four out of seven stanzas of the poem entitled "Vor der Fahrt" (Before the Crossing) were selected and sung by German-American socialists, presumably because they were more topical with reference to the socialist vision. Interestingly enough, the name of the author was not given, probably because everyone in the radical German-American community was thoroughly familiar with it. (Also see the tableau vivant in Document 86 in which a ship is employed as a symbol of socialism.) Similarly, all these songs express a hopeful expectation for the future, whether with images of the battle which must precede the new order or with the symbols of a rosy dawn and red flags.*

112. "Beyond the Grey Wat'ry Desert" (F. A. Sorge Collection, New York Public Library).

(To the tune of the "Marseillaise")

1.

Beyond the dark grey wat'ry desert,
The future opens wide its arms!
An emerald coast so bright, alert,
:,: America with all its charms! :,:
So let the waves high o'er us thunder,
Let threaten us sandbar and reef,
For in this ship is our belief,
Courageous men aren't thrown asunder!
Let's go, then, plunge right in! Let's go, then, lend a hand!
:,: Cast off! Cast off! Bold through the storm!
Seek land and find your land! :,:

2.

Oh trusty vessel! Right on keel
Thus brazenly cut through the flood!
Black the masts, and black the steel!
:,: And the pennants are red, like blood! :,:
The sails are brown from fire and steam,
From beneath the tarp guns blaze,
Protecting thus the cause we praise,
And the unsheathed sword is our beam!
Let's go, then, etc.

3.

Amazed, you ask: what is its name?
The answer ever loud and strong:
In Austria or Prussia the same
:,: The ship is called "Revolution"! :,:
It is the only ferry true,
Into the sea, then, pirates great!
Into the sea and capsize the state,
That rotten galley and all its crew.
Let's go, then, etc.

4.

Oh day so proud, the people's ship
The battle 'gainst deceit has won!
Having reached the end of its trip,
:,: Came to rest in the long sought sun! :,:
A beach brand new, its emerald frame,
Where freedom and justice reign,
Where none are the poor who groan in their chain,
Where shepherd and flock are the same.
Let's go then, etc.

113. "The Song of the Commune," by Carl Sahm (1876) (*Fackel*, March 18, 1883).

I.

A storm it was, which furiously raged,
When in the month of March,
Your swords prepared a war to wage,
Your hearts toward freedom arched.
It sounded clear, like Roland's horn,[5]
A call from the oppressed,
And on the hopes of millions borne,
You battled on the crest.
And loud and fine the song is heard,
To furthest Baltic dune,
Inspired by freedom, onward spurred:
The song of the Commune!

II.

Satory's plain[6] thus caused to drop
So many a comrade bold.
There was rejoicing: what a crop!
The harvest'll be threefold!
The Vatican, too, was full of cheer,
The robes then writhed with glee,

5. This is a reference to the French epic *Chanson de Roland* written about 1100. Roland was to sound his horn "Olifant" as a call for help. When he finally made up his mind, the "call" came too late.

6. Satory, a military camp southwest of Versailles, was used as a prison for many Communards after the defeat of the Paris Commune. Several leaders were executed there.

While thinking freedom wouldn't appear,
For maybe a century!
Awake, you champions, be hard as steel;
To injustice they are immune -
And ten times stronger our voices peal
The song of the Commune!

III.

You island dwellers, full of spite,
All staring at the sea,
Not knowing where the waves unite,
Or where the Savior be -
We all can feel you in your pain,
Your wounds they burn as ours,
The final ground we will attain,
United, full of power.
The France of old is not yet dead,
The plan's still being hewn,
Just one more blow - all chains we'll shed,
With the song of the Commune!

IV.

So soon the day, in radiance spun,
In glory bathed will dawn;
When France receives the very sons,
Who once from her shores had gone.
She's calling now: come! help us form
The Republic of the free.
Already striving the world to reform,
United we always will be.
And furnishing all a haven secure,
As strong as an August monsoon.
Now everyone's singing in voices pure
The song of the Commune!

114. "Song of Fraternity" (*Chicagoer Bäcker-Zeitung,* **December 31, 1888**).

Raise high the flag and with it for'd,
We'll all be close behind!
And save whatever will accord

Our march from misery's grind!
Too long now have our tears made damp
The workers' granite bread;
With protests pealing, break your camp,
And raise our banner red!

The bourgeoisie is at the pump
And sucking at our blood;
So weak from hunger, workers slump,
Their children inherit the mud.
Too long now from us have you squeezed
The anguished cry of dread:
Now with conviction we are seized
For our flag is rippling red!

Let's go! You see the flame's been fanned,
The iron's glowing white;
So let's set off across the land,
Forge freedom with our might!
See how the flames from west to east,
Still burning brightly spread;
Our steps not faltering in the least,
Because our flag is red!

Now march together closely bound,
Yes, each and every man!
Where is the foe our strength'd confound,
And who can foil our plan?
There's not a one our army'll quit,
Though death we may yet wed!
So onward now, we won't remit,
Because our flag is red!

115. "Demonstration Song," by Martin Drescher (*Vorbote,* May 22, 1907).

(To the tune of the "Marseillaise")

In numberless and stretching columns,
We forge our way through dust and squall,
And thus the world aware becomes,
We are united one and all.

That to our brothers we do hold,
This is the message we proclaim;
Despite deception, callous, cold,
We won't lose track of our great aim.
Though malice will connive,
United here we stand;
The workers' army's on the watch,
To thwart the enemy's hand.

Still peaceful we our steps pursue,
Not yet we seek the battle sites.
We want no more than what's our due:
The brothers' uncontested rights.
But should we see a half-dug grave
Thus meant for justice's radiant light,
Then you with bitter wrath we'll brave -
The workers' army, furious, will fight.
Though malice will connive,
United here we stand;
The workers' army's on the watch,
To thwart the enemy's hand.

It's long enough, with voices meek,
We've cowered frail before the strong;
But now's the time for us to speak,
And raging, tell you that you're wrong.
All you who working men despise,
Though proud you be, let you take heed:
Expect him not to crawl and plead,
When you outrageous crimes devise.
Though malice will connive,
United here we stand;
The workers' army's on the watch,
To thwart the enemy's hand.

Narrative Prose

Working-class culture had a peculiarly ambivalent relationship to the novel and short story. On the one hand, socially critical fiction was highly regarded, and reference was made, for example, to the influence of Harriet Beecher Stowe's Uncle Tom's Cabin *on the abolition of slavery. But, in its effort to found its own tradition of prose literature, Chicago's German labor movement had to reach back to the few labor novels by German writers, because of the lack of talented German-American writers. Thus August Otto-Walster's well-known work* Am Webstuhl der Zeit *was serialized in various German labor papers in America, and in 1889 a thoroughly revised version appeared for the first time in the* Chicagoer Arbeiter-Zeitung. *This was one year before the author returned to Germany after fourteen years of journalistic activity in the U.S.*

Sophisticated European bourgeois literature was also reprinted in order to fill the pages of the daily Arbeiter-Zeitung, *the weekly* Vorbote, *and above all the* Fackel, *the Sunday edition in which so much space was given over to prose fiction. Also found there was a wide offering of entertainment literature which could claim no special affinity to the working class. Frequently built around the old German village, local color novels were printed along with the tales of German authors like Robert Schweichel and Otto Ruppius, who still treated regional folk experience. Adventure tales by Friedrich Gerstäcker and Balduin Möllhausen appeared—melodramatic trivialities announced as "sensational novels" and detective stories—that partly took place in aristocratic and courtly circles and in which ideological perspectives remained completely in the background.*

The fictional world of these novels and tales was either Europe or an American fantasy world completely divorced from reality, as in Gerstäcker's works. The reality of America was dealt with sporadically in novels, and more often in short stories, as in the tale by Ludwig Geißler excerpted here, which takes as its theme the experience of emigration and the pursuit of a career in the U.S. Geißler takes advantage of sentimental and melodramatic elements in contemporary entertainment literature in order to more surely achieve his didactic purposes. He wants, for example, to discredit the false myth of success sanctioned by America's puritanical values and prove instead that honesty, decency, and industry no longer represent the prerequisites of occupational and social advancement in America, but rather real hindrances. (See the biographical sketch at the end of this volume.)

116. "With Industry and Thrift," by L. A. Geißler (*Fackel,* September 28, 1879).

[Franz Berger, industrious and reliable, had just married Bertha Reuter when he was promoted to the position of manager of a furniture factory in a large German city—presumably Berlin, though the name is never specified. Settled in his new position, he is assured a good income. Johann Mauser, an unskilled, low-level employee in the firm, asks Franz to make him a market porter. The latter complies.

So much for the first part of the story, which takes place in Germany. To a great extent falling back on clichés of personal fortune and getting ahead, this first part does not offer any detailed description of the milieu, and contributes little to the theme of this volume.]

Several years passed. Mrs. Reuter, having taken gentle leave of this world, slumbered peacefully under the earth. Bertha Berger had gone out of mourning for her beloved mother. She was happy and in love with her husband, who was generally appreciated by all; she was happy within the small circle of close friends—she was happy, overjoyed, with the lively little boy kicking on her lap. The furniture factory where Franz Berger was manager was doing splendidly, and the firm's chief shareholder made no secret of the fact that this was primarily due to the young man's prudence and industry. He expressed his appreciation through lavish Christmas presents. A rich American who owned a big furniture factory in New York also noticed Franz Berger and made him generous offers to come and work for him. Around this time, Johann Mauser, who had remained at his position as market porter, came into an inheritance of six thousand talers. He immediately gave up his position and squandered all the money in less than three months. There was just enough left over to pay his way to America, after which no more was heard of him.

When Bertha found herself rocking both a little girl and a little boy on her lap, Berger's situation changed. The firm's chief shareholder died, and the other owners wanted to retire from business, so the firm was sold. The new owner was himself a joiner by trade, a real lucky fellow who had suddenly won a big, popular lottery and was smart enough to invest the money immediately in a sure and profitable business. Because, as already mentioned, he himself was a joiner, a change in Berger's position was imminent. He remembered the American, wrote to him, and was happy to learn that he was still of the same mind. Berger accepted the highly paid position of manager, and took his wife and children to New York.

The first two years in the American metropolis passed in perfect hap-

piness. The charming family lived affluently. They soon had a large circle
of acquaintances, and Bertha's bright laughter mixed with her two children's joyful cries and the voices of the cheerful guests. And all the while
Berger never lost track of the future; the figures in his bank book were
soon able to show three zeros.

Then the crash came.

The rich factory owner went bankrupt, the factory was closed, Berger
lost his job.

The banks suspended payments, Berger lost his savings.

These were hard blows, but the upright couple didn't despair. Trusting
to their knowledge, their ability, their reciprocal love, they decided to
begin again from scratch. The maidservant had to be let go, the furniture
that wasn't essential was sold at half its value, and the family moved into
a small apartment with two rooms and a kitchen. Berger was prepared to
work in any joiner's shop or furniture factory—in vain! Bertha planned
to give piano lessons, and put ads in several newspapers—in vain!

And the sum resulting from the furniture they had sold got smaller and
smaller, the prospects gloomier and gloomier. Their little girl got sick;
together, father and mother guarded over their dearly beloved little child
jealously, waging a battle over her with death. The girl gradually recovered,
then her father took ill. He had a burning fever.

We find the family again in a small attic room on the fifth floor of a
tenement house. In the corner there is a shabby bed, the fireplace shelters
an empty brazier, a pot and a pan, and on the crude table there are a
bowl and several plates. Next to the bed is a simple wooden box.

Sitting at a small window on the only chair, Franz Berger, convalescent,
sighs as he looks out over the roofs and chimneys. He is pale and haggard,
and his hair has thinned considerably. Supporting a tired head in his right
hand, he loosely holds an old newspaper in his left.

The children are playing with little stones on the floor. Their clothing
is very meager, but clean. The little girl gets up and calls: "Father, I'm
hungry." The boy also stops playing and calls: "Father, I'm very hungry.
We haven't had anything to eat all day."

A pained groan forces its way from Berger's breast. He hits his forehead
with his fist. Then he turns back to the room and says with a dull voice:
"Be patient, children, be patient! Mama's gone to get something to eat."
Then he picks up the newspaper again and takes a look at it. He is attracted
by an article entitled: "Our self-made men." The article mentions a rich

man from California who just bought the large furniture factory which had been closed so long "for a song." Seven or eight years ago John Mousre came over from Europe with nothing; now he's a millionaire and the chances are good that he will play an important role in the future.

"Yet another proof," the article concluded, "how far one can get in this country with i n d u s t r y a n d t h r i f t!"

"With industry and thrift!" Berger sighs and stares off grimly. "There was really no lack of industry and thrift in my case. Do unfortunate people have to be ridiculed by this rubbish, on top of everything else?" He pauses, then continues: "I'll go there as soon as Bertha gets back. The new owner, the one who got rich with industry and thrift, won't turn down the former manager; even if he offers me the crudest and worst paid work."

Steps became audible, Bertha was back. She was no longer the cheerful, graceful being whose light laughter could be heard from far off. Her face still showed signs of her former beauty; but misery and worry age people quickly. These worry lines were printed on her forehead and cheeks, her lips were painfully pursed, and her lively step had become slow and burdened.

"Mama, Mama, we're starving!" cried the children as they rushed to greet her.

"All right, all right!" she said as she placed her basket on the table and took out a loaf of bread. She cut off a piece for each of the children. Then she went to Franz and, laying a hand on his shoulder, said softly:

"It was useless again, I couldn't arrange anything. I pawned my wedding ring. It was the last thing." Franz groaned deeply, but Bertha threw herself on his chest and began to cry.

Berger told his wife about what he had read in the newspaper the children had brought up with them from the street, and Bertha felt new hope stir in her breast. After he ate a bit of bread, Franz left the house, his legs swaying. When he arrived at the factory, work there was in full swing. The whole building had been freshly scrubbed and painted. John Mousre, Esq., wasn't on the premises, but Berger inquired as to his private address. His apartment was on Fifth Avenue. Berger wearily started out, and finally arrived in front of the elegant brownstone building.

He rang the bell.

A Negro in rich livery opened the door, and when he saw the pale and impoverished man standing there in front of him he thought he was a beggar and was about to close the door again. But in the meantime Berger had gotten his foot in the door so it couldn't close.

An unusual commotion was caused in the fine house by the Negro's angry words and Berger's assurances that he wasn't there to beg, but rather to speak with Mr. Mousre about work.

At this point a head smelling of pomade poked out the side door and asked what was going on. In a flash, Franz was at his side; removing his hat and bowing politely, he put forward his request. Amazed, the gentleman looked him up and down, then asked: "Isn't your name Berger?"

Franz answered in the affirmative, upon which the gentleman nodded his head and said: "Come in!"

Berger followed the gentleman into a room and remained standing at the door. But his host dropped back into the fauteuil he had just left. Beside him, on a table, were an opened bottle of champagne and a tray heaped with caviar and other delicacies. The Havana cigars the gentleman was smoking filled the room with a pleasant odor.

John Mousre, Esq., was a man in his mid-thirties. His wide face was red with wine, the tips of his red moustache were turned up, not a single strand out of place; his Vandyke beard was just as manicured. Originally red, his hair was now chestnut brown, skillfully groomed with countless, orderly little curls. A lorgnette set in gold was posed on the red, somewhat thick nose. His suit was extremely elegant, but too conspicuous. A heavy gold chain disappeared into his watch pocket, diamond buttons sparkled from the front and cuffs of his shirt and precious rings adorned his beefy fingers.

John Mousre pointed to a chair and, addressing his guest in German, said: "Have a seat!"

Amazed, Berger sat down. The voice sounded familiar; he thought he had seen the face somewhere before, too, only he couldn't remember where.

"You've changed, Berger," the rich man continued. "You're not doing so well, from the looks of it. Yes, yes, the crash!—Ho ho! That's the way it is if you don't have foresight. And how's the cheerful Frau Bertha? She's still alive, isn't she? What?"

"Thank you, yes. She's as well as circumstances permit. But you seem to know everything about me, Mr. Mau—aha!" He broke off suddenly, as it dawned on him.

"Huh, huh? Do you recognize me now? Oh yes, I've anglicized ⟨englisirt⟩ my name, it's more distinguished ⟨distinguischter⟩ this way. I guess I've changed, too, what? but in my favor. Ha ha! With industry and thrift you can really get ahead in this country. But come closer! Have a glass of wine, and tell me what's happened." The rich man rang a nearby bell; it gave a clear sound, and the Negro immediately entered the room respectfully. "Another glass and a few bottles!" the millionaire ordered. The servant disappeared.

Berger, still completely confused, drew closer. It didn't make any sense. Mauser, the awkward oaf, the crazy squanderer, the epitome of slackness and foul stupidity — Mauser had become a millionaire through prudence, industry and thrift, and now sat here, the Lord and Master, upon whose whim Berger's whole existence depended? It just didn't make any sense!

While these thoughts buzzed through his head, the Negro entered with what had been requested; on a sign from his employer he uncorked a bottle and filled a glass. He then placed it before Berger respectfully and departed again.

"So, now we're alone. Drink up, now! To Frau Bertha! She was a wonderful, cheerful woman, and always kind to me. You were always good to me also. I don't forget things like that, and I'll take care of you. So tell me now what happened!"

Berger gave a simple account of his story.

"Hm, hm! That's bad! Damned bad luck, but also a lack of prudence! You people don't have the right way of looking at things, the right — a — sperpective! But drink up! drink up!"

"Thank you, Mister Mauser. But I'm still a bit weak from my illness, haven't eaten very much today, either. Too much to drink won't agree with me, I'm afraid."

"Well, as far as food is concerned, you can catch up right now!" He pushed the tray covered with delicacies to Berger. "Go to it, otherwise I'll really get mad."

Berger, who was really very hungry, feasted on the fine foods, thus also being able to do better justice to the champagne.

Mauser continued the conversation again. "So, you'd like to come to work for me, what? I'll tell you something. I know you like the back of my hand. I know that you have a solid understanding of the business, and that you're upright and honest, too. I'll engage ⟨ingähdschen⟩ you as manager. But times are hard. What do you expect ⟨expektiren⟩ for wages?"

"You're very right. Times are hard, and I'm forced to be modest."

"How much were you earning before the crash?"

"Three thousand dollars."

"Three - thousand - dollars? - No surprise the factory went bankrupt. And the workers were presumably paid in kind — much too much? Ha ha! Times are better now. Supply is incomparably higher than demand, and workers can be had cheap. I'll tell you something. I'll give you 75 dollars a month. You content with that?"

"I have to be," said Berger, who felt, as they say, like a great weight had just been lifted from his mind. "But," he continued, "my terrible situation requires that I ask for a small advance."

"No sirree! There won't be any loans. But let's be noble, what? I'll give you a token for Frau Bertha." He pulled out his wallet and handed Berger a fifty dollar bill.

Berger reached for it hesitantly; but then he thought of his wife and children and quickly pocketed the bill.

"You are herewith engaged ⟨ingähdscht.⟩ Consider this, ah, a handsel!" Mauser laughed at his presumably successful pun. "You begin tomorrow. You will sign a contract stating that you will give me three months notice before leaving. You'll hire the necessary workers, and—one more thing!— as cheap as possible. Thrift is the soul of business."

"Thrift; yes, be thrifty at the workers' expense, the workers who make you rich," Berger wanted to say. But he thought of his wife and children and kept it to himself.

In the meantime, Mauser had been helping himself freely to the champagne, and the effect was noticeable. He kept pressing Berger, who would have liked nothing better than to leave, to drink to him. He offered him one of his fine Havanas, and then he mellowed and began to talk about former times in Germany, and then finally, completely intoxicated, he told of his path to riches.

After arriving in New York, he had found lodging with a Methodist minister. His job was easy. The old man was a widower and lived alone. Mauser got dinner for the two of them from the refectory, tidied up the rooms and cleaned the clothes. He had spent more than a year with the minister, and in that time had gradually become so familiar with the old man's phrases that he could finally recite them himself with ease. The minister died, the congregation buried him, and since Mauser claimed that he had back pay coming to him, he was given the minister's wardrobe. He was prudently quiet about the fact that he had managed to put 60 dollars aside.

He went to Philadelphia, where he read in a newspaper that a German Methodist congregation in a small city was looking for a pastor. He possessed the insolence to go there dressed in the clothes of his former employer. He held a trial sermon, using the phrases he had learned in New York, and—was hired.

He was exceedingly pleased with this. He collected several books of sermons and learned a number of sayings by heart; when Sundays came along, he could be seen thundering away at the pulpit, really giving his faithful flock hell. But the very best was when he visited the women during the week while their husbands were at work in order to exchange spiritual words with them. Words of love and tenderness (Christian, be it understood) flowed from his lips, and once in a while, from his pious eyes, there could be seen a very secular twinkle. The best that was in the house was naturally proffered the pastor, and he stuffed his little tummy. Oh, his was a most pious work; this pastor with his singing and his squeezing, with his caresses and the kiss of Christian charity—and he indulged in the latter so zealously that it wasn't long before the husbands began to get grumpy and suspicious. And one day the devoted pastor disappeared. Nobody knew where—and in the same night, the radiant young wife of a wealthy merchant disappeared, and with her, a few thousand dollars.

Billing and cooing over each other, the two of them lived in a hotel in St. Louis until the bulk of the money had been squandered. And then, the last 200 dollars stashed securely in his pocket, Reverend Mauser cleared out and headed west. As a deposit against the unpaid bill, he left the hotel proprietor the pastor's collar and the remorseful young woman, rudely awakened from her dream of love.

In Omaha, a shrewd band of gamblers managed to take him for every cent of his own stolen fortune. Completely cleaned out—but one experience the richer for it—he offered the crooks his services, and was taken on as a "touter." He was especially effective in this capacity. He conducted so many unsuspecting strangers to the gamblers that the incoming money, which they shared with him honestly, accumulated with increasing abundance. But now he had become more wary. He took care of his money. And when one day a vigilance ⟨Vigilanz⟩ committee was formed to put an end to the audacious activities of all the crooks, he suddenly disappeared again, and again with a very pretty little sum.

In Leadville he used the crooked money to open a saloon, and in this way was able to rob the people l e g a l l y, though on occasion illegally, as well. One day a trusting soul came to him, someone who "wanted to see the elephant," and gave him 10,000 dollars for safekeeping. The following night he was brought back, already stiff, with three knife wounds in his body. Mauser forgot about the substantial sum, and didn't remember it again until he had already invested it in silver mine stocks in San Francisco.

"Fools have all the luck" is an old and time-tested saying. He followed in the footsteps of experienced stock exchange swindlers and did just as they. He bought stocks or surplus, whatever he could scrape together once it had been forced low enough—and then, as soon as it had been manipulated this way and that to its desired height, sold immediately.

N o n   o l e t, money doesn't stink, even if it's been dredged up from the deepest morass. His millions made John Mousre, Esq., a highly respected man, and to cloak himself yet more in the nimbus of respectability, he decided to get into a legitimate industrial business. Thus he came to New York and bought, as we have seen, the big furniture factory for a song.

The noble man recounted all this in his intoxication, then lay his head on his arms and fell asleep on the table. With an intense sense of disgust, Berger quietly got up and left the house, the Negro accompanying him respectfully.

Outside on the street he took the fifty dollar bill from his pocket, looked at it, then pocketed it again. "Sold!" he cried, "body and soul sold to the devil! - Ha ha ha! - With prudence, industry and thrift! - And I have to serve this worthless blackguard, have to invest all my knowledge, all my strength, to squeeze whatever I can from the poor workers to make the rich man yet richer! Oh, what's the use! I've sold myself to him for my wife and children, and now I'm his. - Ha ha ha! Long live industry and thrift!"

VII. WORKING-CLASS CULTURE AND THE DOMINANT CULTURE

Conflict with the Established Norms and Values

German-American workers had to overcome both cultural and social obstacles in their struggle to establish themselves in Chicago. Even if one assumes that German immigrants were welcomed and easily assimilated into American society, fundamental cultural differences repeatedly made themselves felt in social and political conflicts. From the middle of the nineteenth century to World War I the same contentious issues arose again and again: the way the Germans spent their leisure time, the teaching of the German language in the public schools, and particularly the German disregard of the norms of Sabbatarians and temperance advocates. Immigrant workers, moreover, had the concentrated power of the established political institutions against them when they organized radical unions and labor parties. In fighting the initiatives of foreign-born workers, the dominant forces in society often consciously aroused nativist feelings among the American-born against the alien character of foreign cultures as a way of discrediting a labor movement whose membership was overwhelmingly made up of immigrants.

In jeopardy as both foreigners and radicals, the members of the German-American left often came to a harsh judgment of American society, and their writings commonly have a bitter tone. The first document in this section was written by August Spies from prison after he had been condemned to death during the Haymarket Affair (and it is strongly colored by his personal fate). Spies uses the arrest of the Haymarket anarchists — which in his opinion had been agreed upon beforehand — and their disputed trial as an occasion to confirm Heinrich Heine's judgment of America as a "monstrous prison of liberty." The poem "The Moor Can Go!" by W. Feinkorn expresses disillusionment over the fact that immigrants were welcome so long as they helped build up the country and win the Civil War for the North; but when massive immigration had begun again they were seen as a foreign menace and greeted with "Go back home across the sea!"

When it came to defending their right to drink beer in public, the Germans could unite, despite their various social and political differences, as well as build powerful alliances with other ethnic groups. From the time of the notorious "Lager Beer Riots" of 1855, the Germans successfully resisted temperance movements, fighting in the name of personal freedom and civil rights under the leadership of the energetic Saloonkeepers Association. The call to a mass demonstration in 1910, which is reprinted here, attacks the attempt of temperance advocates to enforce their puritanical values on others as a violation of the rights of the majority: "The so-called foreigners and their immediate family represent 75% of Chicago's entire population."

Despite moments of unity in the defense of civil liberties, the labor movement and the German-American middle class had irreconcilable views on religion. Broad sections of Chicago's work force were alienated from the churches, and the German-American labor press never tired of exposing the contradiction between Christian preaching and practice. An example is the fictional account of the experiences of a recently arrived immigrant worker from a staunch Christian home with the symbolic name of "Zacharias Gottlieb" (Zachary Godloving), who was refused entrance to churches of both the middle class and the rich. Clearly church attendance was limited to people of the proper status. In the end Zacharias spends his free time outdoors enjoying nature and reading the Fackel (the Sunday edition of the Chicagoer Arbeiter-Zeitung) and "good books."

The centennial of the Declaration of Independence in 1876 provided an opportunity to propose an alternative to the dominant values of American society. While throughout the country the centennial was celebrated as a confirmation of the ideals of the Declaration of Independence, the Labor party of Illinois pointed out how these ideals had been perverted and betrayed. The party utilized the form of the Declaration to communicate its message, and in this way symbolically assumed the cloak of the American radical democratic tradition. Nevertheless it filled the form with new contents, calling for the further development of America into a "social republic."

117. "Confabulation. Written in Prison," by August Spies (*Reminiszenzen von August Spies,* ed. Christine Spies [Chicago, 1888], pp. 138-41).

September 26, 1886

". . . Shall I"—wrote Heinrich Heine in 1830—"go to America, to that dreadful prison of liberty, where the invisible chains would weigh more heavily upon me than the visible ones at home, and where the most revolting of all tyrants, the mob, exercises its raw power! You know what I think of this godforsaken land that once I loved, before I knew it. . . . You good German farmers! Go to America! Everyone there is equal, equally uncouth . . . with, of course, the exception of several million slaves. . . . The brutality used in dealing with the latter is more than just shocking. . . . And at the same time these Americans make such a big fuss about their Christianity and are the most zealous of churchgoers. They acquired this hypocrisy from the British, who, by the way, bequeathed to them their very worst characteristics. Profane utility is their actual religion, and money is their God, the one almighty God. Of course it is possible that there be noble spirits there, quietly bemoaning the general selfishness and injustice. But should they try to fight it, they could expect nothing less than a martyrdom which would confound all European attempts to understand it. I believe it was in New York where a Protestant preacher was so outraged about the way the black people were being mistreated that he married his own daughter to a free Negro to spite the horrible prejudice. As soon as this true Christian deed became publicly known, the people stormed the preacher's house, and only by fleeing was he able to escape death; but his house was demolished, and the preacher's daughter, the hapless victim, was taken by the mob and forced to suffer its fury. She was finished, i.e., she was stripped stark naked, painted with tar, rolled around in the feathers of a mattress which had been torn open for the occasion, and, thus tarred and feathered, was dragged through the town and ridiculed. . . ."[1]

Yes, Heine is right to call this Canaan of the rich mob a "dreadful prison of liberty"! Dickens, who was so passionately enthused for the Republic of the United States, spoke of this mob in even more caustic terms after he had gotten to know the country in person. And as is well known, the mob never quite forgave the great writer for this. Besides its brutality and boorishness, the mob is also obsessed with an unbelievable vanity.

1. Heinrich Heine, *Ludwig Börne. Eine Denkschrift,* in Manfred Windfuhr, ed. *Heinrich Heine. Historisch-kritische Gesamtausgabe der Werke,* Vol. 11 (Hamburg, 1978), pp. 37-38.

Incidents like those described by Heine are still common today and create little or no stir among the populace. And they only occur less frequently where the Germans have had an impact on public life. The Germans have lent Anglo-American crudeness a somewhat more—let us call it conciliatory—character.

The events which followed the monopolistic Praetorian Guard's unsuccessful act of violence on May 4 are still fresh in everyone's memory. Poorly guised, the mammon-mob's crudity was revealed in its unadulterated form. A passionate barbarity and despotism reveled in the sight of their defenseless victim, and each new triumph of bestial brutality was met with wild applause like in the amphitheaters of ancient Rome. Ha! that was real gratification for the mob, for the sanctimonious hypocrites! Law, civilization, Christianity—?

Bah! . . . Allah is a moneybags, and law, civilization and Christianity his prophets!

Allah, the moneybags, was in trouble. Prophets, help! shouted the "Citizens Association." And they helped. . . .

It's probably not commonly known that the officials placed on the stage by the political directors and elected by "the people" are only puppets in the hands of a higher, self-constituted power. But it is true. In this city there is an intimate network among big capitalists; it goes by the name of the "Citizens Association," and is actually a sort of senate, the high authority in our community. It was the "C.A." that gave Bonfield, the man with the Mephistophelean face, the order to break up the meeting at the Haymarket. The mayor was against it. But he must be still when his superior, the "C.A.," speaks. It was the latter's unmistakable intention to have the so-called leaders and speakers of the revolutionary labor movement murdered on that evening. One of the witnesses swore to having wrenched a pistol out of the hand of a secret policeman, a pistol which was aimed at one of the speakers. But it's more probable that this shot, seemingly fired by the crowd, was to have been the signal for the other 200 policemen to open fire. . . . And then, as though by an act of benign Providence, the historical bomb was thrown, spreading death and confusion midst the ranks of murderous attackers. . . . True, seven human lives were destroyed, many people were wounded—but hundreds were thus saved from a brutal death. Where today there are three or four widows who mourn their fallen husbands, we would perhaps have counted a hundred of them, maybe more. . . .

In accordance with our laws, Bonfield should have been arrested immediately and charged with murder. But in this case—we're assuming that it is impossible to bribe or otherwise influence our judicial system—Bonfield could have betrayed his superiors! And thus it was that the leading parties among the latter called a secret meeting the following morning at the break of dawn, and what was decided has since run its course successfully. Grinnell[2] and Bonfield were enlisted to carry out the decisions, and the newspapers were also brought into the conspiracy. The latter concealed the facts and in their stead publicized the story of a conspiracy of the anarchists, who as such had nothing to do with the meeting in question. That's how the atmosphere was created, and as we've since witnessed, with great success. The readers' hair stood on end when they read the horrible fairy tales, and, instead of bringing the criminals to account, directed all of their grief and hate against the victims of that skillfully contrived conspiracy. "Stop the thief!" cried the Citizens Association in order to divert suspicion away from itself; and Bonfield, the actual thief, appeared on the scene as the one who had apprehended the thief.

On the night of May 4, while Brothers Spies, Schwab, and Fielden were sitting in the Central Station dungeon, several members of the Citizens Association gathered in one of the side offices. After a period of brief deliberation, they agreed upon a plan. The newspapers had already primed public opinion, now the police were to seek out a number of "honest, reliable men" from among their protégés—from among the ranks of criminals; these would in turn recruit other kindred elements, and get rid of the four arrested men—or in any case A. Spies, the most hated of them all—by lynching ⟨Lynch-verfahrens⟩ them that very night. "By due process," they concluded, "we've nothing on them."

It was then that the well-known lawyer, W. D.,[3] appeared. "Given the tension that's presently afoot," he objected, "this plan would be more than just a daring venture . . . and why risk it? We'll hang them in the name of the law; the necessary steps have already been taken. I've already spoken with G. and B. . . . We more than anyone else have to cultivate a respect for the law."

What W. D. . . . meant by "the necessary steps" has come to light in the course of the trial through testimony by Thompson, Gilmer, and a few detectives, as well as by Seliger, Waller, etc., those spineless creatures bribed with "Citizens Association" money. Capt. Schaack's role was only that of go-between. Thompson received a lucrative position in Marshall Field's business. . . . The "jury" was comprised of people who were in the

2. Julius S. Grinnell was the district attorney in the Haymarket trial.
3. Probably a reference to Wirt Dexter.

employ of members of the "Citizens Association," i.e., who later came under their "moral" guidance. *Ma Foi!*[4] D. . . . knew what he was talking about when he said, "We'll hang them in the name of the law." He had already worked it all out with Grinnell!

Yes, Heine, you were right—you won't find a more brutal mob or a lower band of hypocrites than those in that "dreadful prison of liberty," America!

118. "The Moor Can Go!" by W. Feinkorn (*Fackel,* January 30, 1887).

(For Nativists ⟨Nativisten⟩ and Their Friends)

T'was once this land was bleak and sore—
Though no one knows it anymore—
And then the goddess Freedom came,
Said, "Yes, this place shall bear my name!"
All those oppressed from every shore,
Did shout with joy, a loud furor:
"It's here reigns freedom's guarantee,
Come one, come all! Across the sea!"

T'was thus they flocked, still more and more,
Devoting work to freedom's store.
And with them brought goods most refined:
A healthy body, healthy mind;
From forest dark, from vast prairie,
So loud was heard their melody:
"It's here reigns freedom's guarantee,
Come one, come all! Across the sea!"

And in the course of time there grew,
A people strong, with life and thew.
Where earlier but rock and sand,
There sparkled cultivated land;
And trade upon this land did show'r,
A rich renown, great pride and power;
T'was there reigned freedom's guarantee,
And many came across the sea.

---

4. "By God!"

Despite the words of nativist scorn —
"All those who on these shores weren't born,
Full citizens will never be,
Because this land belongs to me" —
Was many a foreigner's daring son,
Who fought and died for the Union;
"Unity," shouting, "will always be
In freedom's land from sea to sea!"

Thus with the danger put aside,
Anew was built with steady stride;
The country's wealthy production,
Brought wages that were not to shun.
And art and science helped make space
For even nativistic ⟨Nativisten⟩ grace;
And they loved freedom's guarantee,
And many came across the sea.

Then all began to speculate,
Producing fast, a race with fate;
Till balance 'tween supply/demand —
While mis'ry grew — got out of hand.
And now they're closing everywhere,
They shout, while others, helpless, stare —
"Though here be freedom's guarantee,
Do not, oh please, come 'cross the sea!"

"Just like 'China', we'll begin,
And won't let any strangers in —
Unless they pay five thousand cash,
Though that might be a little rash —
For they might eat up all our food,
The situation would be rude . . .
Though here be freedom's guarantee,
Do not, oh please, come 'cross the sea!"

"If English you can't read and write,
Your citizenship forget you might;
And if your knowledge not be 'nough,
About elections ⟨electionirt⟩ and such stuff,

The ballot box you'll never know,
And that, my friends, is pretty low!
It's here reigns freedom's guarantee,
So go back home across the sea!"

119. "Guardianship Not Necessary" (*Chicagoer Arbeiter-Zeitung,* March
23, 1910).

(*See p. 355.*)

Guardianship not Necessary.
The Foreigner is not Beneath the "American."
**His Education and Cultivation compared to the Virtues of those, who
want to be better.**
A Battle for Freedom.

The so-called foreigners and their immediate family represent **75% of
Chicago's total population,** while the alleged natives make up less than
25%. Nor can it be denied that the immigrants and their children have
played a very large role in making Chicago one of the largest and richest
cities on the face of the earth. They therefore have every right to demand
that they be granted the same consideration for their customs and practices
as is the weaker element. As they are loyal and law-abiding citizens, and
adhere to the Constitution as well as the principles of our government,
they do not feel obliged to accommodate themselves to the **religious,
social or other prejudices** which a portion of those people stemming from
New England brought with them.

They are in no way less cultivated than their American fellow citizens.
Many of them are highly educated or highly skilled in all arts and useful
crafts. It is extremely presumptuous to refer to these citizens in terms of
a crude, ignorant and dangerous mob. They certainly don't need to be
illuminated and led by the neighboring minions, or by the sectarian clergy
and its following of eccentric women.

But, from behind the mask of paternal legislation, this is exactly what
is being attempted. They seek to infringe upon the harmless, sociable
habits of the overwhelming majority in our city and to prevent us, **within
our own four walls,** the pleasure of indulging moderately in mild stimulants.
While preserving the empty form of a republic, they seek to totally destroy
the individual's freedom.

Nowhere has a tyrant or despot ever dared treat his subjects the way

Keine Vormundschaft vonnöthen.

Der Ausländer steht nicht unter dem „Amerikaner".

Seine Bildung und Gesittung verglichen mit den Tugenden Derer, die besser sein wollen.

Eine Schlacht für die Freiheit.

Die sogenannten Ausländer und ihre unmittelbaren Abkömmlinge stellen

75% zu der Gesammteinwohnerschaft Chicagos,

während die angeblichen Eingeborenen weniger als 25% ausmachen. Auch kann nicht geleugnet werden, daß die Eingewanderten und ihre Kinder sehr viel dazu beigetragen haben, daß Chicago eine der größten und reichsten Städte auf Erden geworden ist. Sie können deshalb mit Fug und Recht für ihre Sitten und Gewohnheiten dieselbe Rücksicht beanspruchen, wie das schwächere Element. Während sie treue und gesetzliebende Bürger sind und der Verfassung sowie überhaupt den Grundsätzen unserer Regierung anhängen, fühlen sie sich nicht verpflichtet, sich auch die

religiösen, gesellschaftlichen oder sonstigen Vorurtheile

eines Theiles der aus New England stammenden Leute anzueignen. Ihre Gesittung ist in keiner Hinsicht minderwertig im Vergleiche mit der ihrer amerikanischen Mitbürger. Viele von ihnen sind hochgebildet oder zeichnen sich durch Fertigkeit in allen Künsten und nützlichen Gewerben aus. Solche Bürger als einen rohen, unwissenden und gefährlichen Mob anzusprechen, ist im höchsten Grade anmaßend. Ganz gewiß bedürfen sie nicht der Orientirung und Führung durch die umgewohnenden Flurenbreter oder durch die Seelengeistlichkeit und ihre Gefolgschaft überspannter Weiber.

Doch nichts Geringeres wird unter der Maske väterlicher Gesetzgebung versucht. Es soll in die harmlosen geselligen Gewohnheiten der überwiegenden Mehrheit in unserer Stadt eingegriffen und es soll uns verwehrt werden,

in unseren eigenen vier Pfählen

milde Anregungsmittel mäßig zu genießen. Mit Beibehaltung der leeren Form eines Volksstaates soll die Freiheit des Einzelnen gänzlich vernichtet werden.

Kein Tyrann oder Despot hat jemals seine Unterthanen so zu behandeln gewagt, wie die Sittenverbesserer eigener Schöpfung sie behandeln wollen. Sie schildern uns als Trunkenbolde, die sich in der Gosse wälzen, sie nennen unsere Vereinskränzchen Faßstreiche des Teufels, sie geben zu glauben vor, daß wir unsere eigenen Kinder zum Laster und Verbrechen erziehen, und sie behaupten in ihrer angeborenen Beschiedenheit, daß sie von der Vorsehung beauftragt worden sind, und unsern Beistand zu leisten und uns arme Idioten gegen uns selbst zu schützen. Wir sollen ihnen womöglich noch kniesällig für ihre selbstlose Güte danken.

Doch sind wir leider undankbar genug, ihre Vormundschaft abzulehnen. Nach unserer Ansicht würde es viel mehr angebracht sein, wenn diese Generalpächter der Jugend und Sittlichkeit sich ihrer eigenen Herde wildmeten. Warum donnern sie nicht gegen den Rassenselbstmord; die mit Hilfe gerichtlicher Scheidungen vollzogenen Probeheirathen; die scheußliche Massenabschlachtung der Arbeiter an den Eisenbahnen, in den Fabriken und Gruben — diesen ärgsten Schandfleck der amerikanischen Zivilisation —; gegen die schmachvolle Häufigkeit von Mord und Todtschlag hierzulande; die amtliche und außeramtliche Bubelei; die ständige Zunahme von Fälschungen und Unterschleifen in den höchsten Kreisen, oder gegen die unersättliche und aller Gesetze spottende Habgier der amerikanischen Geldfürsten? Wenn ihre Moralbegriffe von den unseren verschieden sind, so brauchen wir uns dessen nicht zu schämen, sondern können ihnen im Gegentheile stolz darauf sein.

Es steht übrigens ganz im Einklange mit ihren Moralbegriffen, daß sie ihre Absichten unter falschen Vorwänden zu verstecken suchen. Sie sagen dem Publikum, daß ihr Kampf lediglich dem „Saloon" gilt, während Sie in Wahrheit ein Gesetz befürworten, das — wenn es vom Volke gutgeheißen werden sollte — den Verkauf und die Abtieferung von Wein, Bier und Branntwein in der ganzen Stadt Chicago vollständig verbieten würde. — Kein Gast- oder Speisehaus, kein Verein oder Klub, ja nicht einmal der einzelne Privatmann wäre von diesem Verbote ausgenommen. Nur durch Schliche, saute Vorwände und Lügen könnte der freie Amerikaner sich eine Flasche Bier verschaffen, um sie im eigenen Hause zu trinken. Oder freilich sind Schliche, saute Vorwände und Lügen den Sittenverbesserern nicht anstößig. Diese Kardinaltugenden werden ganz allgemein in jedem Staate und in jeder Ortschaft geübt und verziehen, wo der Segen der Prohibition eingezogen ist.

Vielleicht ist die Gefahr nicht groß, daß

Chicago „trocken gelegt"

wird, obwohl es niemals gute Taktik ist, allzu vertrauensselig zu sein. Wenn sich jedoch die Stadt Chicago damit begnügt, die Prohibitionisten eben nur zu schlagen, so werden sie sich unzweifelhaft ermuthigt fühlen,

ein Staats-Prohibitionsgesetz

zu verlangen. — Die meisten Counties im Staate Illinois außerhalb Cook Countys sind bereits „Anti-Saloon Territory". Unter diesen bedauerlichen Umständen ließe sich, eine kleine liberale Mehrheit in Chicago sehr leicht durch die Prohibitionsmehrheit im ganzen Staate überwinden.

Aus diesem Grunde — wenn aus keinem anderen — müssen die Prohibitionisten hiervorzit von den Liberalen nicht allein geschlagen, sondern vollständig erdrückt werden—und das wird zum größten Theile von den unwissenden Ausländern besorgt werden müssen.

Wir fordern daher alle Mitglieder unserer Vereine auf, sofern sie Simmberechtigt und in die Wählerlisten eingeschrieben sind, sich am

fünsten April

an ihre Stimmplätze zu begeben und auch alle ihre freisinnigen Freunde und Bekannten auf die Wichtigkeit dieser Wahl aufmerksam zu machen. Es gilt diesmal keinen kleinen Stimmgettel, sondern den den Wählern unterbreitete Frage wird am Fuße des gewöhnlichen Stimmgettels stehen und sollte nicht übersehen werden.

Macht bei der Abstimmung keinen Fehler, durch den Eure Stimme für ungültig erklärt werden könnte!

Schreibt nicht Yes oder No,

sondern kreuzt folgendermaßen Ä:

| Shall This City Become Anti-Saloon Territory? | YES |
| | NO X |

Wir hoffen und erwarten, daß die Mitglieder der verbündeten Vereine ihre Freiheit so kräftig vertheidigen werden, daß sie in Zukunft nicht wieder bedroht wird.

United Societies for Local Self-Government.

the self-made moral do-gooders want to treat us. They describe us as drunkards who wallow in the gutter, they label our club gatherings devil's snares, they claim to believe that we bring our children up to vice and crime, and, in their native-born modesty, they maintain that in lending us support and protecting us, poor idiots, from ourselves, t h e y are doing the work of Providence. Perhaps we should fall to our knees and thank them for their selfless kindness.

Unfortunately, though, we are so ungrateful that we are rejecting their guardianship. In our opinion, it would be far more appropriate if these favored tenants in virtue's palace dedicated themselves to their own flocks. Why don't they thunder against race suicide; against trial marriages, which are made possible with the help of legalized divorce; against the horrible mass slaughter of workers on the railroads, in the factories and mines — the most shameful blemish American civilization has to offer; against the disgraceful frequency of murder and bloodshed witnessed in this country; against official and unofficial boodle ⟨Budelei⟩; the continual increase of forgery and fraud in the highest circles; or against America's monied aristocracy's insatiable greed which mocks all the laws? If their idea of morality is other than ours, we don't need to be ashamed, but rather to the contrary, we can be proud of it. . . .

That they try to hide their intentions behind false pretexts is, by the way, thoroughly in keeping with their idea of morality. They tell the public that their battle is directed solely against the saloon, but in fact they are advocating a law which — if it should be sanctioned by the people — would completely prohibit the sale and delivery of wine, beer and liquor in Chicago. No restaurant or eating house, no society or club, not even the private citizen would be excepted from this law. The only way the free American could get a bottle of beer to drink in the confines of his own home would be by way of tricks, dirty pretexts and lies. But the moral do-gooders don't, of course, have anything against tricks, dirty pretexts or lies. These cardinal virtues are generally practiced and forgiven in each state and in each town where prohibition's blessing has been bestowed.

There is perhaps but little danger that **Chicago might be "drained dry,"** but just the same, it is never a good strategy to be too optimistic. However, if the city of Chicago is satisfied with just beating the prohibitionists ⟨Prohibitionisten⟩, there is no question but that they will be encouraged to demand **a state-wide prohibition law.** — Not counting Cook County, most of the counties in the state of Illinois are already "anti-saloon territory." Given these lamentable circumstances, a s m a l l liberal majority in Chicago could easily be overcome by the state's prohibition majority.

If for no other reason, this is why the prohibitionists ⟨Prohibitionisten⟩ in Chicago must not simply be defeated by the liberals, they must be completely crushed—and in large part, this will have to be accomplished by the uninformed foreigners.

We are thus calling to all members of our societies who are entitled to vote and already registered to go to the voting locations on **April 5,** and to call the attention of all their liberal friends and acquaintances to the importance of this election. This time, instead of little ballots, the question submitted to the voters will be at the bottom of the normal ballot and should not be overlooked.

Be careful not to make any mistakes by which your votes could be declared invalid!

Don't write Yes or No, but rather make a mark like this:

Shall This City Become Anti-Saloon Territory?

	YES	
	NO	X

We hope and expect that the members of the united societies will defend their freedom so staunchly, that they'll never be threatened again in the future.

United Societies for Local Self-Government.

120. "Sunday Observations" (*Fackel,* September 14, 1884).

As is generally known, Christian love and brotherhood have not made much ground here. Even in its earliest phases, so-called equality was a chimera in the Christian Church. It never occured to the so-called apostles that there was anything unjust about the crudest form of slavery predominant at the time. Their writings are devoid of any proud feelings of independence. Each line in the New Testament preaches the gospel of blissful servitude. The "servants and handmaidens" are told that it is theirs to obey—first of all, of course, God and Jesus, but then the secular authorities and their masters, too. Much has already been written about the way Christianity treats all people equally. Everyone is equal before the "Lord" in his temple. But, dear reader, it is very possible that, after weeks without work and pay, you might have to pawn your best clothes. Now, if you just happened to be religiously inclined and wanted to go spend your Sunday in some church to hear the "Gospel," which, as is well known, "preaches to the poor" . . . you might be in for a surprise!

Just listen!

Zacharias Gottlieb was born in a small German village. As fate had it, he was wrenched from his hometown and deposited in the Garden City of Chicago. Gottlieb had been brought up according to the "faith of his elders"; he was a pious man who believed in the teachings of the Bible. After much trouble, he succeeded in finding work at a building site as a hod carrier. Sunday morning saw him afoot, shuffling along the big city streets. His clothes were worn and mended, but clean and well-kept. He looked at everything he saw with the curious, rather slow-witted eyes of someone from a village who is gradually getting to know the big city. Gottlieb had not yet been paid. All his cash, which he was carrying on him, amounted to 10 cents. His stroll brought him to a so-called elegant neighborhood. Bells were chiming from the steeple of a so-called house of God. This was a church reserved for elegant society. Coaches thundered up, one after another. The dolled-up contents of these horse-drawn vehicles got out, their dainty little hands holding finely bound prayer books which were richly engraved in gold. Wealthy little ninnies, their noses turned up, strutted past Gottlieb, their Brother in Christ. As for Gottlieb, he was completely amazed by the ever-unfolding splendor; his mouth fell open and his eyes bulged. With his face, tanned from outdoor work, his rough and calloused hands, his worn clothes of cheap material, his scuffed boots and the old German military cap he was wearing, Gottlieb offered a striking contrast to the elegantly manicured congregation. The women and girls were covered with jewelry, and their male escorts, flawlessly dressed, measured the "nervy" stranger with looks of outrage as he pulled a threadbare prayer book from his pocket and prepared to follow the others into the church. Opening the door and seeing all the pious, rich people seated in their places, Gottlieb was overcome by misgivings. It seemed completely weird to him. He hung back, not daring to go forward, undecided if he should leave.

His doubts didn't last long. A sexton descended upon him, gesticulating and speaking furiously; for Gottlieb, a greenhorn ⟨Grünhorn⟩ who didn't understand much English, the sexton's tirade was like a book of seven seals. But finally the man of order took him by the arm and led him to the street. This, however, was understandable.

The sermon that day in church had to do with the topic: "How a worker can live on 12½ cents a day." The pious gentleman, who received $10,000 a year for serving the Lord, proved beyond any doubt that every wage cut was an act which would please God, as it would help put an end to the gluttony among the "lower" folk. For these people, who should be happy that "the Lord God" had promised them a place in heaven at all, water and bread constituted a healthy and sufficient diet. Each and every exploiter was seen to be a person working for the good of humanity. The congregation was very pleased with the pastor's words and drove home contentedly. Zacharias Gottlieb, who hadn't the vaguest idea what had happened to him, quickly stole out of the elegant neighborhood and landed at the doorstep of another "house of the Lord." Just as he was about to enter, the doorkeeper shouted: "Ticket, Sir!" Gottlieb hadn't been in America very long, but he knew what a ticket was. He even had had a few on him. Surprised, he looked up to the man, a German-American, who explained that the privilege to watch the church circus would cost him 25 cents. Having only 10 cents in his pocket, Zacharias Gottlieb had to renounce the pleasure of hearing "the Lord's word" here, too, even though it didn't look quite so distinguished. The simple, pious man proceeded on his way. Not long thereafter, he came to a building; melodies could be heard from within, and he knew that they could only be church hymns. Gottlieb tried his luck a third time. As he entered the chapel, the song came to a close. A man with a very red nose and restless eyes showed the seeker of the Lord to a seat, upon which Gottlieb then sat, his soldier's cap in his hand. Sitting in the pews were conspicuously dressed girls, whose heavily made-up faces betrayed their business. They had either come out of curiosity, or in the hopes of finding clients. "Honest" girls, driven there by bigoted mothers or a neglected education, were also to be seen, sitting next to elderly matrons with puritanical looks. The male portion of the "devout" was comprised of a few shop boys with vapid personalities and hypocritical looks, who sought to win the favor of their bosses—sacred stock exchange sharks, exploiters, bordello owners—by this show of zealous piety; drunken, wretched figures, driven into the arms of the church by a hangover brought on from an overindulgence in schnapps, figures who, time and again, had solemnly sworn off alcohol forever; others had come to take a look—finally—at the place and the show that was being presented; and lastly, though but few, there were the simpleminded, but truly devout people. The man with the red nose opened the proceedings. He told of his life, what a scamp he had been, how he had frequently slept in the gutter, how he had been saved. This man had been hired by the pious organization to serve as a frightful example; there was one condition: "If you want to wet your whistle, don't do it like the heathens, who sit around in saloons causing trouble for everyone, but rather do it piously in the quiet of your own little room; if it's good kümmel, it's delicious and delightful when drunk on the sly."

Gottlieb, who understood almost no English, pricked up his ears at this.

The man got more and more enthusiastic, more and more zealous. His audience also became quite emotional when he began to give touching descriptions of the seductive effects of all the drinks he knew; it was a lengthy list. Shouts of: *"Oh Jesus! That's right! Hurrah for Christ! O God!"* inarticulate noises, sighs, sobs, moans—a colorful, chaotic cacophony. Gottlieb thought he had strayed into a madhouse. The woman next to him, heavily painted with a wide-rimmed hat, her former beauty faded, edged closer and closer to the poor German greenhorn ⟨Grünhorn⟩, who was immune to the general elation. Beads of sweat trickled down his forehead; glancing toward the door out of the corner of his eye, he rocked to and fro. Suddenly there was a loud scream. Zacharias Gottlieb's neighbor threw herself to the floor and began to writhe at his feet, all the while gasping out the words, "Oh Lord! Oh Lord!" Someone struck up a pious, triumphant song on the little organ, a song celebrating "the soul's salvation." The congregation seemed to be comprised of crazies, not rational beings. Gottlieb gathered all his strength, and in three bounds was out of the chapel. He wasn't, however, to go to church again for quite a while. Somewhat later, Zacharias Gottlieb became a very reasonable person, and now he spends his Sunday mornings out-of-doors, or reading the "Fackel" and other good literature. These latter are of course not exactly pious.

121. "Declaration of Independence" (F. A. Sorge Collection, New York Public Library).

When in the course of human events, it becomes necessary for the members of one class of people to dissolve the political and social bands which have connected them with the others, in order to assume among their fellow citizens the separate and equal station to which the Laws of Nature entitle them, a decent respect to the opinions of mankind requires that they should declare the causes which impel them to the separation.

We hold these truths to be self-evident: that all men are created equal; that they are endowed by their Creator with certain unalienable Rights, that among these are L i f e, L i b e r t y and the **full proceeds of their Labor.** That to secure these rights, Governments are instituted by Men, deriving their just powers from the consent of the governed, that whenever any Form of Government or System of Production becomes destructive of these ends, it is the Right of the Majority of the People to alter or to abolish it, and to institute a new Government and a new System, laying their foundations on such principles and organizing their powers in such form, as to them shall seem most likely to effect their Safety and Happiness. Prudence, indeed, will dictate that Governments and Systems long established should not be changed for light and transient causes; and accordingly general experience has shown that mankind are more disposed to suffer, while evils are sufferable, than to right themselves by abolishing the governmental forms to which they are accustomed. But when a long train of abuses and usurpations, pursuing invariably the same Object, evinces a design to reduce the Majority of the People under absolute, exploitative Despotism, it is the right of the majority of the people, it is their duty, to throw off such Government and such System, and to provide new Guards for their future security. Such has been the patient sufferance of the Producing Classes of all Lands; and such is now the necessity which constrains them to alter the former System of Exploitation. The cultural history of this country, and especially the history of the capitalistic system of production, is a history of repeated injuries and usurpations, all having the direct object of establishing and solidifying an absolute Tyranny of the Rich over the Poor, the Propertied over the Unpropertied. To prove this, let us submit the following charges against the Bearers of the Ruling System, the Aristocracy of Capital, to the judgment of a candid world.

They have used the right of the "United States Congress to dispose of public domain" in order to place the rich in illegal possession of the best of that public domain, to raise the price of land through all artificial and manipulative means so as to make it impossible for the people to ever attain i n d e p e n d e n c e. They have built their railroads on government land at government expense, and have used these railroads for the sole purpose of robbing producers and consumers alike through arbitrary freight rates. All of their property constitutes a plundering of the people; the people are forced to bear all burdens and pay all taxes, while they claim all rights for themselves.

They have made the legislative process their paid servant, and degraded the general electoral process, making it into a fig leaf for their despotism.

They brought the last civil war on our country to abolish black slavery, but left wage slavery as it was, while augmenting its ever-increasing cruelty.

Through their contemptible greed, they rent the most sacred bond among working people—the family—by introducing child and female labor, thus bringing women and children into competition with the head of the family. Thousands and thousands of prematurely murdered women and children litter the industrial battlefield and weigh on their conscience. Their blood decries heaven! Their addiction to exploitation has robbed the worker of at least half his life, and today—on the 100th anniversary of the Republic—a large percentage of the workers is without work and has thus been handed over to slow starvation. They define themselves through their attitude toward the social misery which is everywhere dominant: devoid of all human feeling, they are only concerned with amassing property, with proclaiming themselves absolute rulers over the u n p r o p - e r t i e d people, and with forcing them into submission as quickly as possible.

But the absence of planned production and the mass misery which it brings about, as well as the social and political servitude imposed on the people, will be eliminated for all time when all of the people unite in a **"social republic,"** and when they take possession of all m e a n s o f p r o - d u c t i o n and all m e a n s o f t r a n s p o r t a t i o n, when l a n d has become i n d i v i s i b l e p u b l i c p r o p e r t y, and when production is planned and carried out by the s t a t e and regulated according to the reasonable n e e d s o f t h e p e o p l e.

We, the Socialists assembled here today, therefore solemnly publish and declare, that we absolve each and all allegiance to the political parties in power, and that independent of them, we will work toward our great goal: the Abolition of the present System of Production, and the Establishment of the true People's Republic based on Socialism—peacefully, if we can, violently, if forced!

C h i c a g o, July 4, 1876

Conflicts with the Police and Courts

Conflicts between the Chicago police and the German-American left run like a red thread through the history of the city's labor movement. They began with the attack on the Vorwärts Turner Hall in 1877 and continued through the Haymarket tragedy of 1886 to the two interrelated incidents during 1891 in the Vorwärts Turner Hall and Greif's Hall, which are documented here. (On the incident of 1877 see Chapter V, Document 68; on Greif's Hall see Chapter IV, Document 48.) From the course of the events and the tone of the news reporting about them it is clear how heavily laden these confrontations were with the legacy of the conflicts between the police and the anarchists. Clearly the anarchists and their sympathizers had been followed and spied upon since 1886.

Although the physical force applied by the police when invading

Greif's Hall should not be played down, it is the symbolic character of these events that is particularly striking. The absence of the American flag in the meeting at the Vorwärts Turner Hall was of profound significance, the pretext, in fact, for the intervention of the police. The police demanded that it be raised as a symbol of the acceptance of American institutions, and the Chicago press interpreted the flag incident as a defeat for the anarchists and thus as a symbolic victory. Similarly, the police seized flags during the incident in Greif's Hall shortly afterwards and presented a red flag as evidence of insurrectionary motives for the interrupted meeting, while prudently keeping quiet about the union flags they also had in their possession.

During the subsequent court trial the judge took special note of the conflicting value systems symbolized by the flags in justifying the decision against the labor leaders. He referred to the French Revolution, the Paris Commune of 1871, and to the Haymarket Affair in 1886. The incident ended with the effort of established authorities to minimize its significance and excuse the police, which was grist for the mill of the labor press as it constantly pointed out the obvious violations of basic constitutional rights. After much delay those arrested were judicially exonerated. In a city with a largely foreign-born working class the battles over the flags clearly took on symbolic meaning as part of a struggle for the allegiance of the labor force.

122. "Another Failure! A Second Provocation Is Thwarted by the Workers' Constraint" (*Vorbote,* November 18, 1891).

"The Star Spangled Banner, the American flag, was dragged through the mud by t h o s e who have power behind them, but not the law—and now it no longer belongs here! We have no desire to stand under this flag because it has been prostituted by those who are supposed to defend it. But here, standing under our flag, I declare that the man who threw the Haymarket bomb was right in attempting to protect the liberties of speech and assembly that are guaranteed by the Constitution. The Garys and Grinnells were the ones who dragged the flag through the gutter and the mud."

It was this thoroughly justified critique of "flag-waving" on the part of the "law and order mob" which incited the very same to an angry outburst last night during the mass meeting in the Vorwärts Turner Hall. If the meeting's officers hadn't suspected this sort of outburst, if cool heads hadn't prevailed, if they hadn't been able to maintain order through their emphatic appeals to those present, it could well have ended in a terrible bloodbath.

These words were pronounced by Henry Weißmann, the editor of the "Bakers' Journal," in his speech commemorating the heroes—Spies, Parsons, Fischer, Engel and Lingg—who were ignominiously murdered on November 11, 1887, by the capitalist class under the guise of the law.

The huge Vorwärts Turner Hall was completely filled, right down to the last seat in the furthest corner of the gallery. Nor was there any extra standing room; even the stairs were covered with men and women who had come to commemorate their fallen champions in a manner worthy of the occasion.

The Vorwärts Turner Hall hadn't housed such a large, enthusiastic, and at the same time orderly gathering for years. A wide range of nationalities were represented, as well as almost all social standings. One saw merchants, clerks, and artists alongside men with calloused hands who work all day long at hammers, saws or planes. It was an imposing meeting, one well suited to remind the ruling class that its power won't last forever, and that the sense of disgrace which these villainous murderers have instilled in the people is approaching calamitous levels.

Weißmann's words, quoted at the beginning, were met with thunderous applause.

At that point, several men pushed their way through the crowd to the stage, stopping next to the reporters' table. One of them—it was Inspector Hubbard—interrupted the speaker, stating that he wouldn't tolerate that kind of "insult" ⟨Insultierung⟩ to the American flag, and that he would clear the hall if the American flag were not unfurled on the stage along with the others.

The whole house was on the brink of pandemonium. Everyone was on their feet; men and women alike stood on their chairs to get a better look at what was going on. There were many calls from the audience to throw the hecklers out, but Schmiedinger, the chairman, and Weißmann himself managed to quiet the angry crowd. Then they asked the heckler who he was, and when he had identified himself, Weißmann showed him that the "red, white and blue" was hanging from the hall's ceiling. And the ceiling is, in fact, completely draped with these colors. At the same time, the meetings' officers considered how a row brought on by the insulted citizens' and workers' sense of outrage would necessarily entail horrible consequences in the packed hall.

Some two hundred policemen were supposed to have been at the meeting, their clubs and guns ready for action; they weren't in uniform, but rather in plain clothes, and this situation would have increased the confusion considerably.

Nevertheless, the two hundred "champions of order" would simply have been overwhelmed by the huge crowd. The officers further considered that at least a quarter of those present were women, girls, and children, and they realized that if the meeting were actually broken up, it would doubtless result in a serious clash between police and citizens.

For all of these reasons, they considered it wisest to give in, and to put off to a later date the question of whether some police scoundrel has the right to disturb a peaceful meeting and invent regulations as to the decorations. Thus they had the "Stars and Stripes" brought in and, to the loud applause of the crowd, placed in a corner on the left side of the stage.

Hubbard said he was satisfied, and Weißmann continued his speech. The police avoided any further disturbance.

It is understandable that today the capitalistic press is hounding the citizens and workers from yesterday's mass meeting with all its might for having had the courage to both uphold the flag representing the right to revolution—which was made sacred by the Declaration of Independence of the United States of America—and to protest the murder and imposed servitude of the masses.

The following are only the headings of the stories which writhe with distortion and malicious misrepresentation. The "Tribune"—the same paper which once recommended poisoning the "tramps" with strychnine—is carrying these headings:

Made to honor the flag. - Police Force Chicago Anarchists to Hoist the National Colors. - Over the Emblems of Red. - The Stars and Stripes Given a prominent Place at the Meeting. - Inspector Hubbard's Ultimatum. - He Warns the Assemblage That on Further Insult He will clear the Hall.

The "Times"—the same paper which once recommended throwing hand grenades at the striking seamen—writes:

Greeted with Hisses. - Forced Display of the American Flag at the Anarchists Memorial Meeting. - Incendiary Speech Interrupted by Inspector Hubbard's Distasteful Command. - West Twelfth Street Turner Hall Filled with a Turbulent Crowd of 2000 People. - The Dead Leaders Eulogized in Fiery Symbol and Speech, the Use of Bombs being freely advocated.

The "News" is carrying these stories:

Dishonor the Flag! - Anarchists Offer an Insult. - Inspector Hubbard and a

*Squad of Police Compel the Committee to Exhibit the Stars and Stripes. - The
Meeting at Turner Hall.*

The "Herald" has this to say:

*Reds on the Rampage - Hold an Incendiary Meeting. - Twelfth Street Turner
Hall the Scene of an Assembly That Rivaled the Days before the Haymarket.
Forced to Raise the American Flag.*

Hemp's darling paper, the "Inter-Ocean," incites thus:

*Hisses for the Flag. - Inspector Hubbard Cows an Anarchist Gathering. -
Forced to Show the Flag. Speakers Praise the Hanged Anarchists as Martyrs.
- The Inspector and his Men Enforce Order and Respect for the Stars and Stripes.*

Hemp's "German News-Nigger" ⟨Preßnigger⟩, Jojo Bombastus Thunder
Sheet, lies in his campaign paper ⟨Päper⟩ known as the "National News":
Anarchist Festival. - The Police are F o r c e d to Intervene.

The scab paper ⟨Scabblatt⟩, with poorly guised gloating, writes: "In
Keeping with the Old Style. - The Police Force the Anarchists in the
Vorwärts Turner Hall to Raise the National Flag."

It is also worth noting that Police Inspector Hubbard, who tried to
sabotage the meeting in the Vorwärts Turner Hall yesterday, has been
promoted to Assistant Chief of Police. This promotion—and the pay raise
it entails—apparently caused him to "do a little e x t r a for his money."

123. "Outrageous! Defenseless Workers Assaulted by Police. Hundreds of Dollars Worth of Union Property Destroyed. 23 Members of the Socialistic Publishing Society and the Painters Union Arrested. Bail set at $17,000. Forceful Measures Being Taken to Expiate the Crime." (*Vorbote,* November 18, 1891).

The police committed an outrageous assault yesterday on the "Socialistic
Publishing Society" and the "Painters Union" at 54 W. Lake St. The members
of the Painters Union meet there every Thursday, and the Soc. P. Soc. holds
business meetings there once every three months.

Yesterday was to have been like any other Thursday. But these unsuspecting workers hadn't counted on Police Inspector Lewis from the Desplaines Street Station. It was around 8:30 when the hall was suddenly
stormed by a gang of policemen and detectives.

The intruders acted like madmen, swinging clubs and revolvers at the
guests standing peacefully at the bar. They pushed their way to the door,
where Thomas Greif, the owner of the house, was standing. Here they
brutally demanded entry.

Greif told them that the agitation meeting announced the night before in the Vorwärts Turner Hall was not being held on his premises, and that only members of the Painter Union and Soc. Publ. Soc. would be permitted entry. Upon which he was grabbed by the shoulders, thrown out of the way, and in no time at all, the police had broken down the door.

Then they stormed up the steps and forced their way into the hall on the second floor. Exactly eighteen people were present: sixteen members of the "Socialist Publishing Society," which had rented the hall yesterday for its monthly business meeting, and 2 employees of that society (Mssr. Schultze and Skowronski), both of whom had received written invitations from the secretary of the S.P.S.

Swinging their clubs and creating a huge ruckus, some 50 policemen descended upon those 18 men in the hall. *"Search them!"* the captain commanded, and four policemen threw themselves on each of those present.

Then they broke open the cabinets and lockers, smashed the glass doors of the wardrobes, pulled the Wagonmakers Union's $250 silk flag out of one of them, ripped it into pieces, and—stole the pieces.

"Bring them to the station!" ordered another police officer, and everyone was dragged off to the Desplaines St. Station. Mr. Schultze, the editor of the "Arbeiter-Zeitung," was quickly released after identifying himself, but the other 17 weren't released until $1,000 bail had been posted for each. Thomas Greif posted bail.

The hearings began this morning at the Desplaines St. Station with Judge Woodmann presiding. The men have been charged—though charges were not brought until t h i s   m o r n i n g—with "disorderly conduct" and "resisting arrest."

The names of those arrested are as follows:

Wittemeier, Pfeiffer, Braunswarth, Palm, Urban, Rütter, Segebarth, Kastner, Carl Heinke, Fr. Heinke, Skowronski, Kaune, Behrens, Heck, Benthin, A. Schmidt.

Witnesses for the prosecution—i.e., a group of detectives ⟨Detektives⟩ and policemen who took part in the assault—testified this morning. The essence of their testimony was that the detectives ⟨Detektives⟩ had heard people in Greif's saloon cussing the police and the mayor. They swore zealously and without blinking an eye that the defendants were holding a meeting and that there was a chairman; but in reality the meeting had not even begun when it was brutally broken up by the police.

The prosecution produced the scraps from some red flags which had been lying around the hall for years, as well as a few society sashes; the remains of the union flags which they stole, however, were not produced. The police seem to want to "get rid of them once and for all," and the Wagonmakers Union would do well to obtain a *"search warrant"* and have the police stations ⟨Stationen⟩ checked out.

The witnesses for the defense are to testify this afternoon.

By tomorrow, in any case, we should be able to print an extensive report about the hearings.

It is also worth noting that the policemen, after having destroyed the middle hall in Greif's building, stormed to the top floor like uniformed robbers, where Carl Fritz was presiding over the weekly business meeting of the German Branch No. 160 of the Painters and Decorators of America.

Yesterday's meeting was poorly attended. Only about 20 members took part, and only union business was on the agenda. Like a herd of stampeding cattle, the "heroes of order" disrupted these peaceful workers too. When the union chairman objected that the union had been incorporated according to the laws of the state, and that they had a legal right to hold their weekly meeting, the "commander" answered with a crude "Shut up!" Shouting "Keep your arms raised!" the police pressed in upon the defenseless workers with swinging clubs; the workers were surrounded, frisked like common criminals, and dragged downstairs to the saloon — but not however, until the police had also demolished much in this hall, ripped up a few union flags, and destroyed several union charters.

The "German Painters Union" belongs not only to the "American Federation of Labor," but also to the Building Trades Council here in Chicago and to the "Central Labor Union." Organized workers will and must demand that the most extensive amends be made for the assault, damage, and abuse at the hands of Chicago's police.

The "Socialistic Publishing Society," an incorporated business, will naturally demand the most thorough amends for the violent, malicious harassment of their business, as well as for the people who were taken into custody.

124. "The Talk of the Day. The Exact Wording of the Great Decision. Based on a Lie. Hypocrisy Revealed in City Hall. - Indignation among Those Present. Forceful Resolutions. Huge Mass Meeting in the Social Turner Hall" (*Vorbote,* **December 16, 1891**).

The following is the decision as read verbatim by Judge Woodmann. His decision is the talk of the day:

"Before I address the actual case, I would like to express my appreciation to the attorneys for the able way they presented the facts. By so doing, they helped me considerably in arriving at a just and impartial decision. It is not always agreeable to pass judgment on so many legal questions in a court with limited jurisdiction. But there is always one basic principle: 'Do your duty regardless of the consequences!' It is first of all necessary to come back to the meeting which was held in the Vorwärts Turner Hall on Wednesday, November 11. At this meeting, Weißmann spoke — Robespierre's apostle, the defender of those people who cold-bloodedly murdered the Archbishop while he was being held prisoner in Paris in 1871, the man who approves of the murder of Madame Roland, whose last words, as she ascended the scaffold, were: 'Freedom, oh freedom, what crimes are committed in your name!' Such a man is Weißmann — wildly inflammatory. The defendants would sit at his feet and accept each of his words as Gospel. At said meeting, this man advocated dragging our nation's flag through the mud, and when Inspector Hubbard interrupted him, he announced that the meeting was adjourned until Monday evening at Greif's hall, a place with a reputation for fostering anarchy. After hearing the defendants swear that they had been present at the meeting in the Turner hall, I was convinced that testimony pertaining to the meeting was admissible, and a further reason for the police to be on guard in regards to the meeting at Greif's hall.

"Has the counsel for the defense forgotten the 1886 Haymarket riot? Has he forgotten the widows and orphans of the brave policemen, five of whom rest peacefully in their graves, while another 15 to 20 will carry their wounds with them for the rest of their lives? Has he forgotten that this was the result of the former administration's lenient policies, which invited the horrible catastrophe?

"If anarchist meetings and parades adorned with red flags had been repressed at the time, many otherwise honorable men would not have been taken from their friends, and many a wife and child would have been spared the shame of having to see their loved ones end up at the scaffold.

"A significant fact should be noted with respect to these arrests: although they took place just a stone's throw away from where the Haymarket bomb fell, they didn't come to blows. This proves that the police acted without prejudice, though in the staunch belief that these people belonged to the dangerous group of anarchists.

"As far as proof of disorderly conduct is concerned, the remarks of the people gathered in the saloon, remarks such as — 'Hang the mayor!' 'Hang the police!' 'Shall we mix it up?' 'We'll hold our meeting just to spite the police!' — were aimed at disturbing the peace. The same people who uttered these remarks went upstairs to the meeting. And one mustn't forget the notice in the 'Arbeiter-Zeitung' from the 12th of this month, listing Weißmann as one of the speakers to discuss a revolutionary topic. It was thus not referred to as an 'Arbeiter Zeitung' shareholders' meeting, but rather in connection with a revolutionary meeting. According to the charter of the corporation, a quarterly meeting shouldn't have taken place prior to December.

"The police have been faulted with having destroyed property within the building. But one could just as easily hold Gen. Sherman responsible for the actions of some of his men during his 'march to the sea'[5] as place blame on Police Chief McClaughry and Inspector Lewis in this case.

"According to the law, the city council has the right to issue orders to the police and to prevent and repress all disorderly meetings; under the circumstances, the police procedure was clearly justified.

"Does anyone doubt for a moment that if the anarchists were of a majority in our city, those people in positions of responsibility would be the very first to suffer, 'in the name of freedom'? Earlier experiences prepare us for the future. An ounce of precaution is more valuable than a pound of cure. These anarchists, or 'reds,' have shown their bloody hands in various instances. There may be certain excuses for such organizations in Europe, but not under our form of government. The citizens' right to assemble — in the interest of their work or for other purposes — is not being cast into question here. I myself would be the last person to oppose the notion that our sympathies must rest with those who work with their hands and brains. But from the moment I was called on to take the helm in arctic waters or under the burning sun of the equator, my principle was always: Do your duty!

"Considering Weißmann's speeches at Waldheim and in the Vorwärts Turn Hall, and considering the relocation of the meeting to Greif's hall and the notices referring to it, I find the defendants

5. In the fall of 1864 General William Tecumseh Sherman led his army from Tennessee to Savannah on the coast of Georgia. Of decisive significance for the ultimate victory of the Union, the "March to the Sea" was also notorious for the wholesale destruction it left in its path.

guilty of Paragraph 2222 of the statutory regulation in question, which reads as follows:

" 'Whosoever causes unseemly noise, a riot, a disturbance, a breach of the peace, on the streets or anywhere else in the city, or who aids and contributes to such, and all those who gather together with illegal intentions or with the intention of disturbing citizens or travelers, will be fined not less than $1 and not more than $100.'

"Of the 150 to 200 people present, 22 were arrested. Some of these were in the possession of revolvers, others made threatening statements. I am fining the leaders of the society the highest amount prescribed by the regulation, and the others $10 each."

Education and the Public School System

During the 1860s, as the largest ethnic group in Chicago, the Germans were able to institute the teaching of the German language in the public schools—much to the anger of other nationalities who were not granted this privilege. In alliance with other liberal and free-thinking elements of the German population, the German-American labor movement in Chicago struggled to maintain German instruction in the public schools, particularly in the late 1880s and early 1890s when a nativistic political mood in the state threatened it. The labor movement worked just as strongly, however, for the improvement and expansion of the whole system, goals which put it at odds with the Catholic and conservative Lutheran churches which maintained substantial parochial school systems in competition with the public schools.

The following documents present typical ideas of the German-American labor movement about a sound school system. In 1880 the socialist alderman Frank A. Stauber laid his proposals for educational reform before the Citizens Association, a powerful public interest lobby group. (For Stauber's role in the collection for flood victims in 1883 see Chapter IV, Documents 49-54.) He pushed strongly for enforcement of the truancy laws, since they offered the only legal administrative means to fight child labor at the time. Generally his proposals were informed by the educational ideals of the German pedagogue Froebel; thus he calls for kindergartens, vo-

*cational schools, improved training of teachers, and instruction in
foreign languages. In contrast to the nativists, who often wanted to
limit the right to vote to those competent in English, he wanted to
make voting dependent on literacy in any foreign language used in
Chicago, certainly an appropriate solution for a city of immigrants.*

*When it came to the issue of German instruction in the schools,
the labor movement found itself opposing religious and nationalistic
elements of Chicago's German middle-class community, who wanted
the schools to propagate their values. The second document illustrates
this conflict, as well as the labor movement's opposition to the dilution, even the vulgarization, of German culture by those who wanted
to make it more palatable to children raised in the United States.
Like the German Social Democrats, Chicago's German socialists
considered themselves the true heirs of the German classical tradition.*

*In order to better meet this claim German socialists in Chicago
established special Sunday schools, often in cooperation with freethinkers. Such schools were common in other cities with large German
populations. Difficult to maintain, these schools were most successful
in the period after the Haymarket Affair of 1886, when official
repression put the whole radical labor movement in jeopardy. In the
late 1880s such "free schools" were founded in the various districts
of the city, and well-known labor leaders taught in them, such as
Jens L. Christensen and Paul Grottkau, editors of the* Chicagoer
Arbeiter-Zeitung. *Curriculum materials were developed and a newspaper was set up to preserve the unity and quality of these schools.
The report from Chicago to the* New Yorker Volks-Zeitung *reprinted
here describes the main subjects in the curriculum—the physical
sciences, history, geography, biology, social science, and natural history based on the teachings of Darwin. Although the "free schools"
ultimately could not maintain themselves, they were nevertheless
pioneers in educational methods and curriculum, some of whose
innovations were taken up in the public schools.*

125. "Our Educational System. Memorandum from Alderman Frank A. Stauber to the Citizens Association of Chicago" (*Chicagoer Arbeiter-Zeitung*, March 27, 1880).

Memorandum concerning compulsory education in public institutions
for education, with comments on high schools, normal schools, specialized
and elementary instruction.

Compulsory education, as understood by the writer, does not necessarily mean corrective training, but rather has much more to do with the possibility for all children growing up in the state to be exposed to the kind and extent of education which would best be suited to the development of their own natural aptitudes, and which would give them a basis for becoming good people and good citizens. If the term "compulsory" is offensive, the writer would also be content with some other term designating the same meaning. The goal of this sort of general education can, to a greater or lesser degree, be attained through the following means:

1. A law against truancy which should be enforced by the proper authorities.

2. A law making the right to vote dependent upon the ability to read at least one of the languages spoken in Chicago.

3. Rewards for those teachers who bring uneducated children to school and succeed in seeing to their pupils' regular attendance.

4. An attempt to make the schools attractive for the children through the introduction of kindergartens and Fränkel schools[6] which teach with activity methods.

Point 1. A law against truancy should provide for punishing, through imprisonment and fine, those parents who prevent their children from attending school regularly for at least nine months a year and over a period of at least six or seven consecutive years; furthermore, police officers and school principals or members of the school committee should be authorized by the latter to keep an eye on pupils who are truant or who are idle while in school, and to see to it that they attend classes regularly; furthermore, there should be precautionary measures to ensure that children under fourteen are not employed as wage earners in industrial establishments. Finally, for communities which do not provide sufficient schooling and educational materials for all school-age children, the law should provide the means of forcing them to do so, either by severe punishment, or by having the state correct the inadequacies at community cost. England now has such laws, and they have existed in Switzerland for years.

Point 2. A law similar to the one mentioned above already exists in Massachusetts, and wherever it has been enforced it has contributed considerably to raising the general educational level among the state's inhab-

6. The name of Fränkel does not seem to make sense here. It should probably stand for Froebel, the pedagogue who initiated substantial educational reforms.

itants. To ensure the faithful administration of this law, it should provide for the severe punishment of registration officers and election judges who neglect their duties as stipulated by the law. That a state is thus justified to protect its institutions by demanding a certain degree of education from its voters is surely evident.

Point 3. A law of this kind already exists in England. More than anyone else, teachers can help take the necessary steps to encourage regular attendance among the children in their districts. Educational authorities who can't be bothered with providing classes for all of the children in their districts should be relieved of their positions and replaced by others.

Point 4. In all kindergartens which are worthy of the name, attendance is perfect, because the children find the schools so attractive. Kindergartens are the best means of preventing truancy and of developing the child's natural aptitudes in such a way so as to guarantee that serious study will become, and remain, an agreeable habit for the rest of the child's life. The results seen in St. Louis, where kindergartens were introduced into the public school system, offer the best proof in this respect. It is a fact, which is confirmed by all good kindergartens, that children who have attended t h e s e need no other elementary education before their seventh year, since they outstrip all other elementary school children. It is actually a waste of time, or a farce, to send children to school before they have turned eight years old, because the natural preconditions for grasping abstract subjects of instruction are only found in the rarest of cases. On the other hand, this same time spent in a kindergarten contributes inestimably to the development of the senses, the free use of language, spontaneous activity, and observation, all of which facilitate the process of understanding these abstract subjects. The same holds true for the Fränkel schools, where approximately half of each school day or half of each school week is used for teaching through activity methods, thus constituting a sort of continuation of the kindergarten system for children ranging from 8 to 14. Half of the time presently being used in elementary and grammar schools ⟨Grammar-Schulen⟩ could be put to better advantage if it were used as it is in kindergarten, for higher subjects like singing, gymnastics, drawing, sculpting, reciting, acting, visual instruction, knitting, etc., whereby hand, arm, eye and the whole body is exercised, and whereby habitual loafing becomes impossible.

Because schools which teach through activity methods don't exist at all in America, and there are only very few in Germany, good kindergarten teachers should be encouraged to seek training which would enable them to become principals of such schools. Of course each elementary school teacher should also study kindergarten methods. Teachers must learn to use their time—their actual capital—sparingly, and if they can learn this, lessons in all subjects will be appealing to the pupils. Instruction conducted on an impersonal, businesslike basis must go, and teachers' salaries must be raised. Children who are educated in this way will love school, and will ask their parents not to take them out of school before they've reached high school. High school and grammar school ⟨Grammar-Schulen⟩ rooms will gradually become as full as those of the elementary schools, until the number of high schools will have to be increased, and the higher level of education among the masses will be recompense for the high costs of education.

The state should therefore revise the laws pertaining to its schools and

1. Introduce kindergartens in all public schools, and insist that they also be introduced in all private and parochial schools.

2. Fix the school age for children at eight years old, and convert all afternoon classes in elementary and grammar schools to the Fränkel method of teaching through activity. All crafts should be taught in these afternoon classes ⟨Grammarklassen⟩.

3. Discontinue classes in Latin and Greek in all high schools, and teach modern languages in their stead; the classical languages should only be taught in extra hours.

4. Normal schools should concentrate solely on the science of education, including kindergarten and training for administrative positions in schools which teach through activity. Only those pupils who have completed high school should be accepted. Teachers should only be required to have a diploma from a state or municipal normal school ⟨Normalschule⟩.

5. A retirement system for all teachers in the state, contingent upon 25 years of uninterrupted professional service.

As soon as the Citizen's [*sic*] Association becomes seriously interested in presenting these plans to the state legislature, the writer will lend it a helping hand by supplying the names of books and persons best able to offer the most helpful and extensive information about these reforms.

Permit the writer to conclude with a few remarks about the study of German. Today, instruction in one or more foreign languages is an essential factor in any rational curriculum; instead of an exhaustive argument concerning this position, let it suffice here to say that all true pedagogues are convinced that the knowledge of at least one foreign language is necessary for a fluent and correct use of one's mother tongue. Latin and Greek, as they are presently taught in high schools, cannot serve this purpose; but instruction in some other foreign language, if conducted reasonably, can.

Let's assume that German or French is the second language, and that it is being explained by comparing it to the native language. Experience acquired over long periods of time has shown that it is much easier to learn this country's language when it is taught along with one of the other two—provided that instruction begins in the kindergarten or the school teaching through activity, where the normal method of alternate prompting and repetition is used—than when the native language is taught alone. After a few years of having exercised speaking two languages (and it would be just as easy to add a third), it would be a simple step to learn to read and write them in the preschools and grammar schools if half the teachers were well versed in both. Andrew Rickoff, a school superintendent in Cleveland, O., and one of America's leading pedagogues, would be happy to explain to you how this can occur i n l e s s t i m e than that which is presently wasted in learning one language. It would be the wish of the person presently submitting this proposal that German be the second language. The great use to which German could be put in practical life recommends it as such. To begin learning a foreign language i n h i g h s c h o o l a l o n e is more than just vain—it's a waste of time and energy.

Should you desire further information on this topic, know that I would be pleased to place myself at your disposal.

Frank A. Stauber.

126. "German Instruction" (*Chicagoer Arbeiter-Zeitung,* October 31, 1900).

It needn't be especially emphasized here that the "Chicagoer Arbeiter-Zeitung" is committed not only to the preservation of German language instruction in the public school system, but also to its improvement. Just as we welcome each educational means by which the intelligence of the people is raised, so too do we welcome an enriching of this intelligence — notwithstanding our international character—in German classes. It is, in fact, exactly this character which assumes a familiarity with the cultures of all peoples; for true education has never been inimical to the realization that the people have to unite in a fraternal bond opposing their common oppressors if they want to free themselves from the latter's despotism.

But this is also why we have to clearly distance ourselves from the German chauvinism which, in its disagreeable manner, is spreading throughout the movement to maintain German classes in our schools. This boisterous patriotism not only often cloaks a creeping political ambition, it also carries a narrow-minded, pseudonationalism in its wake, one which is hostile to culture, and which, in regards to the question of national education, aims not to further, but rather to confine. Contrary to our way of looking at the question, the representatives of this tendency do not see education and knowledge as a means of freeing the people from their bonds of servitude, but rather see the schools as a means of preparing young people to tolerate, or even more, to worship these bonds. They want the schools to train pupils to be good, i.e., tolerant subjects who are sure not to miss church.

When, for instance, Pastor Heldmann shows enthusiasm for German classes, his support of these endeavors has absolutely nothing to do with our understanding of the importance of German language instruction. We don't care in the least if there is a decline in the number of German churchgoers. We are the last people in the world who would want to do the shavelings any favors in this respect; we want to do it as little as we expect them to be open to our ideas. One shouldn't try to deny opposites which go together like fire and water.

If we look at these sanctimonious and patriotic advocates of German classes a little more closely it becomes very clear that we are dealing with people who otherwise have little to say for national education. Just ask them what they would select from German literature for the school curriculum. One would be amazed at the ignorance and the furtive, reactionary craving reflected in the responses. The intellectual and literary level of these answers would perhaps approach "The Gartenlaube," "From the Rock to the Sea," "Book for Everyone," etc.[7] They would probably say that "Watch along the Rhine" or "Hail to Thee in Victor's Laurels"[8] were true pearls of German literature, though unfortunately there were a few names herein which good Germans could only utter with just indignation. Among these would be Heinrich Heine, Herwegh, Gottfried August Bürger, all of Young Germany,[9] early Goethe, early Freiligrath, and a whole slew of other names offensive to a sense of piety and patriotism.

7. The references are to German journals offering light entertainment to families.
8. These are two German nationalistic songs.
9. Young Germany was a literary circle of liberal nationalists that emerged after the failed revolution of 1830. They advocated a unified German state based on democratic political principles and cultural and intellectual liberty.

127. "The Socialist Sunday School in Chicago. Its History. Its Curriculum. Its Effectiveness" (Sunday edition of the *New Yorker Volks-Zeitung*, July 28, 1889).

The socialist Sunday school movement was mounted a good year ago. An article in the *Arbeiter-Zeitung* pointed out that even people who didn't want to have anything to do with religion were nevertheless sending their children to Sunday schools run by priests—"to get rid of them for a few hours" or "so they won't hang around out on the streets"—and that it was thus time to offer such parents' children an alternative to the priestly institutions of stultification. In this sense, it suggested Sunday schools which would teach the natural sciences and cultural history instead of religion, and which would thus prevent the coming generation from being systematically robbed of its ability to think and inundated with religious superstition.

As regards the external structure and the curriculum of our schools, both arise—or to a large extent in any case—from the goals they have set. They were founded on the one hand to keep the children away from religious Sunday schools, and on the other also to help make them into people who will understand the world in which they live and thus be capable of taking part in forming the future in a reasonable manner. But in order for children to learn to understand their own world, a knowledge of world history is above all necessary—not, of course, that "world history" which deals exclusively, or almost exclusively, with the princes and their wars, where the people are only important in that they serve as cannon fodder, but rather the true world history which is concerned with the people, with their suffering and their achievements. Our history lessons thus begin with the period where today's civilized nations begin to make their appearance. We talk to the children about the state of communistic affairs which reigned among all of these peoples; we show them how private property gradually developed, how class differences, the monarchy, militarism, the legal system, the tax system, the parliamentary system, etc., etc., came about; we talk not only about the structure of these institutions, but also about the way they have developed right up to the present day. We trace these developments step by step, and show how they were connected with the given economic conditions.

In this way the children are brought to a point where they understand how present institutions have come into being, where they can judge which of them have been beneficial and which detrimental for the well-being of humanity, and where they thus become aware of the direction in which they must work if they want to strive toward the betterment of mankind.

We purposefully avoid saying anything about socialism. We are convinced that children schooled in this way will automatically find the right path. Nevertheless, each week the English-language newspapers here carry articles, sometimes even illustrated with pictures, claiming that we teach the children how to make dynamite bombs and tell them that they're supposed to kill the capitalists and the police. In its lies, the local English-language press balks at nothing when it comes to pinning something on the wicked socialists ("anarchists").

The second principal area of study taught in our schools is natural science, particularly geology and biology. Lessons in these fields serve above all to give the children an idea of the way the world came into being, and of the life forms found on it. It is perhaps superfluous to mention that these classes are based on Darwin's theories. But as these theories alone would be too abstract for children, we combine them with the history of the earth's crust, as well as with zoological and botanical descriptions. Thus we start with the beginning of the earth—according to the theories of Kant and Laplace—and then discuss the various periods in the earth's development, as well as the animal and plant life peculiar to each one. While so doing, we show that, and how, the life forms evolved from one period to another, until they finally found their culmination in "creation's crown," *homo sapiens*. This latter is then accompanied along his various adventures through primaeval times, through the Stone and Bronze Age to the Iron Age, where world history begins. And from there, we trace man's path into the present.

Even if it's taught in the most popular way, this type of class naturally requires a certain intellectual maturity on the part of the pupils. And for this reason, we only begin with children who have reached their twelfth year. Younger pupils are prepared through visual instruction and the like; in addition, we sing little songs with them, either for one or two voices. And with the very youngest, we practice Fröbel's kindergarten methods.

In this way all of the children are provided for, and they are thoroughly pleased with their classes, as the rapid increase in attendance proves.

For those who leave our schools to begin work in a trade, we want to found a "Youth Club" in the near future, so that our teachers can remain in contact with their former pupils. In this setting, lectures on contemporary political questions will also be held.

The Dilution of German Culture in America

By the 1890s Chicago's substantial German community was over half a century old. Enlarged by several massive waves of immigration, its social composition, generational structure, and cultural orientation were so diverse that unifying interests had been reduced to a minimum, and it was difficult to speak of a common identity. Now and then — during the periodic fights against temperance and for German instruction in the public schools — the Germans of Chicago had achieved a political unity, but it disappeared thereafter. In the last decade of the century German traditions were further called into question by second-generation German-Americans who grew up with American institutions and were attracted to American ways, thus becoming alienated from the traditions of their parents. Naturally, the process of acculturation, which proceeded so quickly and with apparent ease, caused considerable anxiety among German-American leaders, particularly those engaged in preserving German cultural and educational traditions. The German-American left with the labor press as its mouthpiece was a part of this group.

It is no coincidence that the three articles from the Vorbote *and the* Chicagoer Arbeiter-Zeitung *reprinted here were written in the 1890s, as the debate about the future of German culture in America increased in intensity. The author of the article "German Culture" reports on the current state of German disunity, attributing it first of all to the considerable class divisions within the group. He also holds the materialistic upward striving of the German middle class responsible for the dilution of German culture in the schools, theater, press, and social clubs, while finding the German labor press to be the only bulwark against this trend.*

The two subsequent documents take up the decline of traditional German culture, using its most important vehicle, the German language, as their example. The authors found the wide usage of American idioms and forms of speech by German-Americans to be an indication of the contamination and corruption of the German language and tradition. The officials responsible for German instruction in the public schools were accused of being incapable of using the language properly and of promoting easy but mediocre German literature instead of the classics. "Flamingo" satirically shows how low the teaching of the German classics threatened to fall by his humorous rewriting of a text by Schiller to make it more accessible to German-American students.

128. "German Culture"[10] (*Vorbote,* **March 13, 1895**).

"It is a fact that German culture here in Chicago—its schools, its press, its theater—is suffering from the multiplicity of interests which bind the Germans to the most varied societies. Can this apparently continuously growing fragmentation be stopped, and if so, how?" In order to properly answer this question—posed by the North American Turner Association—it is above all necessary to clarify the term "German culture."

The "multiplicity of interests which bind the Germans to the most varied societies" would tend to indicate that one can no longer speak in terms of a unified German culture, one which is motivated by common interests. The variety of interests, which divides any nation into many nations, also makes itself apparent in Chicago's German cultural life. We are familiar with a German culture which knows how to finance the building of a Schiller monument by selling shares, which takes advantage of fortune-tellers and other useful people, which understands perfectly how to combine the virtues of the most rabid republican with the most submissive, expiring royalism and veneration of Bismarck. And we know another German culture, which rallies round the country's labor press, one for which the German people's heroes and singers of freedom have not given their lives in vain, and which seeks to preserve the valuable legacy which the men of German science have bequeathed unto the world.

And midst that German culture in pursuit of the money bag and that which prizes labor and science, there is yet a third German culture roaming about, one which, although it makes desperate attempts to gain a voice in the camp of the prominent, nevertheless finds itself less able, with each passing day, to resist those forces which are pulling it toward the unpropertied masses, who are arming themselves for the class struggle. Which of these different German cultures are we talking about?

That of the prominent people, whose interests are so basically different from those of the workers, or the one which—besides heritage and language—has nothing in common with that Teutomaniac hermaphrodite cross between bourgeoisie and proletariat?

People are united through their material and intellectual interests. In the capitalistic world, the latter are pushed into the background by the

10. "*Deutschtum.*"

former. The intellectual interest which c o u l d a f f i l i a t e the Germans in this country—their language—no longer serves to connect them. Because language is the means by which expression is lent to thought, but where, as everywhere in modern society, conflicts of interests collide so harshly, the images and reflexes of these conflicts must consequently collide with one another as well. And collisions are neither symptoms nor elements of harmony.

These conflicting material interests, which divide German culture into various camps of battling interest groups, make themselves apparent in all areas, and not least in those areas describing the education of our youth, the theater, and the press. Bourgeois Germans send their children to private schools, whose doors are shut to the children of the poor. Religious Germans send their offspring to parochial schools, which are not attended by the children of the educated and liberal-minded. In the public schools, however, the German language is taught in such a manner that its effect more nearly approximates torture than an act of benevolence. Here is where German culture—by bringing pressure to bear on the heads of the schools, and above all, the school committees—would have an opportunity to effect a change. To achieve this, there exists at present but one means: practical politics. But when politics comes into play, material interests again step to the foreground, and break down unilingual German culture into its social components.

The theater fares no better. As a rule, p r o m i n e n t Germans lack the necessary education, and the poor lack the necessary money to make a sacrifice for the German stage. As for the press, there is no medium which so acutely defines the conflicts of interest. On the one hand the labor press, continually struggling for its survival, on the other the now overly opulent press of the bombasts and the royalists and Bismarck-infatuated Jacobins. The German law-and-order press does not suffer from this "fragmentation" of "German culture"; to the contrary, it prospers from this fragmentation. Which also explains the nauseating flattering of the German societies in the papers of the respectable. The exuberant nonsense about the societies is the bait capitalist newspaper publishers use to fish for the dollars of society members, and the endearing vanity and boastfulness of many society elders only lends powerful support to their "noble" efforts. In contrast, the labor press addresses the intelligence of the masses, and disdains taking human weakness as a means of exploitation.

And now our answer to the above question: The fragmentation of German culture can only be prevented by drawing those interests into the foreground which would offset the social and economic class conflicts within German culture. But since a stunt like this is impossible in modern society, we will have no other choice but to let matters run their course, until the victory of socialism makes possible tomorrow what is impossible today.

129. "German in America" (*Vorbote,* July 18, 1894).

The following is an excerpt from an article which appeared in the "Frankfurter Zeitung" about the way Germans living in the United States care for the German language:

"I've already barked ⟨gebellt⟩ three times, and nobody's answered." That's the way a German-American addressed me last summer when, having completed a convivial reporter's trip, I finally landed at the door of my host, a busy Milwaukee doctor, at midnight. At first I thought the stranger had been bitten by a mad dog. But his demeanor was too composed for that, so I lay a consoling hand on his shoulder and said: "I'll open up; but—what do you say, as a fellow countryman, would you bark first?" He didn't seem to understand the purpose of this request, but he nevertheless nodded, and, while I waited for him to start barking, he raised his right arm and—rang the doorbell. At the same time, having followed his hand with my eyes, I saw a little plaque inscribed in both German and English: *"Nightbell."* I finally realized what the good man had meant by "barking" ⟨"bellen"⟩.

This little nocturnal adventure is an amusing illustration of the lamentable fact that the large majority of German immigrants in America have neglected their native tongue. It has, in fact, been almost completely cast off, and along with it, all its native peculiarities and customs. And indeed, this happens much quicker among Germans than among other nationalities. It is well known that this fact cannot be denied, and those who are not favorably inclined toward us are extremely pleased to be able to reproach us for it from time to time, as does Max O'rell [*sic*] in his book, "Brother Jonathan and His Country." After praising the Irish immigrants in America enthusiastically for the fact that their offspring remain Irish to the third and fourth generation, he states: "What a contrast to the Germans one encounters in America! They forget their language, their children never learn it, their fatherland is judged severely. Wherever the German settles, he becomes a native. He doesn't colonize, but rather immediately assumes the customs, faith, and language of his new fatherland; in Africa he becomes a Negro!"

Well bellowed! But just the same, this Frenchman, normally very acute, is going too far—despite the frenzied Chancellor Leist and the way he administers his office, which—with respect to his good person—justifies the conclusion. Above all, O'rell is forgetting that the Irish who come to America need not learn a foreign language, and that's why they cannot neglect their own. Though granted, it is true that the Irish in America have much more of a clannish spirit than the Germans. Otherwise, being in a minority, they wouldn't be able to have the say in almost all local administrations, wouldn't be able to govern the country, as it were.

But let's concentrate on the language. Those who emigrate to America to practice a trade must necessarily learn English if they don't want to quickly find themselves at a great disadvantage. This in itself is difficult enough for many Germans, and by the time they've finally learned English, their German is already, to a greater or lesser degree, vulgarized, interspersed with English terms. You won't find a single German-American who says "Straßenbahnwagen" instead of *"car,"* because the latter word is much shorter. And then you have immigrants from all over Germany; one person talks in terms of the "Schlachter," another of the "Metzger," yet another of the "Fleischer."[11] To avoid confusion, even when Germans are speaking among themselves, they simply say *"butcher."* The word *"plumber"* (Bleigießer, Spengler, Klempner) is used for the same reasons. And there are many more, some of which force their way into written German, too, as a look at German-American newspapers quickly confirms.

The problem is yet augmented when less-educated people attach German endings to English verbs (setteln, mooven, driven, etc.), and—what is even worse—when they mistranslate English words. The word of comparison, for instance, *"like,"* is translated as "gleich," which is correct. But what follows is not correct: "to like" is translated as "gleichen."[12] The German who has come to America for the first time can't believe his ears when he is asked: "Do you resemble [gleichen] potatoes?" Once I visited a German farm in the state of Wisconsin, and while I was there, the daughter's engagement was being celebrated. I couldn't help but say a few cordial words about the really splendid bride and groom. Upon which the father lit up and spoke the standard words, "They've resembled ⟨geglichen⟩ each other for so long now, it's time they married." In Pennsylvania, where the German language has survived for two hundred years, one hears completely different things. There, for instance, a farmer's son addressed his father:

11. *Schlachter, Metzger,* and *Fleischer* are regional variations for the word butcher.
12. *Gleichen* means to resemble, to be equal to.

"Der Ox is over die Fence gejumbt und hat's Corn verdamnished." (The ox jumped over the fence and damaged the corn.)

It would, in fact, be no great loss if this kind of German were to disappear completely; or in any case, it's not worth teaching it to children who have been born in America, especially since they lean more toward English anyway. At best, they struggle along with *"Dutch"* for their parents' sake, and when the latter die, the subscriptions to German-language newspapers are canceled, the German Bible is locked up in the closet with the rest of the family relics, and the process of assimilation is complete.

More-educated people — unless they foolishly renounce their origins and speak only English — keep their German as pure as possible, and see to it that their children learn it before English, letting them more or less pick up English later from contacts with the domestic help, neighbors, and fellow pupils. But once this happens, English can easily supplant German again, and not every immigrant is as impressive when talking to his children about their native language as is the German-American doctor and writer, Friedr. Carl Castelhun — originally from Worms, now living in San Francisco:

> Guard the German language,
> Praise the German phrase;
> Out of which our fathers,
> And their spirits gaze;
> Which the world with so much
> Greatness has instilled,
> Which the heart so often
> With its beauty thrilled.
>
> That which Lessing thought of,
> That which Goethe said,
> Always will be present,
> Always will be read.
> When my thoughts to Schiller,
> Quickens my heart's pace:
> Far too poor's the world
> Schiller to replace!
>
> Value, children, always,
> This land where we live,
> But the German language,
> So much has to give.

> Don't forget the homeland,
> Guard it from distress;
> E'en your great grandchildren
> Shall its charm possess!

130. "How Can We Save Our Classical Writers? A Word of Warning to Schiller's Successors in America," by "Flamingo" (*Chicagoer Arbeiter-Zeitung*, February 20, 1897).

Heartrending is the lament heard from German-American school "men" about their charges' aversion to the German language and German literature.

The good gentlemen—who, with a refreshing sense of humor, refer to themselves as youth's preceptors—would certainly overcome this aversion if they directed all their energies toward the works of the Moderns; works which, naturally, have been led astray by the wicked Frenchman, Zola, and which dare sprinkle their vile poison on all that is sacred: on marriage, property, and—hard to believe—even on the paternal system of government. Unfortunately, however, the armies of little boys and girls who can only derive pure pleasure from dime novels ⟨Dime-Novelle⟩ have even turned away from the great writers, who, though long since decayed, have been expressly recognized by the authorities—even if somewhat unwillingly from time to time—as classical poets; poets who have secured the upright German people the honorific reputation of being a people of poets and thinkers for all time, a reputation which can't be stolen by any socialist law, by any police spy trials, nor by any Brüsewitz.

The proud hope of being able to create a particular German-American line of poets, as rich in talent as in character, and of being able to evoke a patriotic enthusiasm among the younger generation—if not yet mature, then coming of age—seems to have but meager chances of being realized. Despite the classical endeavors of both the upright rhymester Kastelhuhn, with his poetic warning to Wilhelm Busch's[13] ripest creations: "'Midst the anarchistic crew, / Count me not, I beg of you," as well as Chicago's corpulent bard of the roast, Alexander Seebaum, with his noble efforts to collect the traditional jokes of the forefathers in his sham paper which caters to corny humor—they simply can't completely replace the old

---

13. A painter and poet, Wilhelm Busch (1832-1908) was probably the most popular satirical humorist of his time.

classical poets. The question as to how we can save our classical poets remains open, as does the incomparably more important one: how can we save the German-American schoolmaster, who, even if not as successful as his glorified, all-German colleague who won the battle of Sadowa[14] with Moltke's kind support, has nevertheless—to borrow from the delightful language of Berlin liberalism—engaged all his unestimable energies, just like the victor in the dear fatherland, in trying to sow respect for these original roots of divine cosmic order in receptive hearts on the other side of the sea.

In the midst of this quandary—it sounds fantastic, but it's true just the same—a pious servant of the "Lord," bearing the unpretentious name of Zimmermann,[15] has indicated the only possible path to salvation. We, the people of Chicago, should feel special pride in being able to watch this multifaceted champion of God; for he is ours as much as the man with the splendid lackey's head, the fearless Wash. Hesing,[16] who shys away from nothing, not even the certain prospect of being immortally stamped with the label of ridiculous.

Unbiased in his cheerful judgment by any knowledge, Reverend Zimmermann has written a little book on literature in a German which cannot but evoke the purest delight in all children of German parents who have had the benefit of seeing the world's rather somber light from the vantage of America's sacred shores.

Thoroughly undaunted, Mr. Zimmermann ignores the lamentable rules of our pedantic language. He blithely bestows literary citizenship on expressions wondrously derived from English and German—expressions like those which tend to spice up the talk in Randolph Street beer halls— thus making his somewhat monotonous dish digestible for the readers' stomachs, which are accustomed to a diet of candy and whiskey.

Why not follow this example! Why not adapt the German classical poets to the mentality and visions of young German-Americans! Why not Americanize our great poets!

When the youth of German parents in America opens up—I almost

14. The battle of Königgratz (Sadowa in English) took place during the Austro-Prussian War on July 3, 1866, when under the leadership of General von Moltke the Prussians scored the decisive victory of the war.

15. Dr. G. A. Zimmermann (1850-1903) was minister of the St. Johannes Parish and superintendent of German instruction in the Chicago school system. He published several readers on German literature for high schools and colleges as well as histories of German and German-American literature.

16. Washington Hesing was the editor of the *Illinois Staats-Zeitung.*

wrote "his" — Schiller, and finds Hector's moving poem of farewell to Andromache on the first page, there's no question but that he'll shrug his shoulders and close the book again.

What is he, whose heart goes out for the only valid ideal in the land of the brave ⟨Braven⟩ and the free, the God of Gods, Mammon, what is he supposed to do with the "old Greek guys"?! What does Jay Gould's[17] roguish admirer care about Hector's dumb, honest bravery, or of Achille's grim fury which is totally inapplicable in business?!

How different he'd react if the following were to be found:

Hermann's Farewell.

Antonie:
Is it true that Hermann really plans
There to travel, where with unwashed hands
Indians his lovely throat will cut?
Who, pray tell, will bend to pour me wine,
Buy me Rippspers,[18] take me out to dine,
If in forests beasts should on him sup?

Hermann:
Beloved dear, do stop these blasted tears!
A longing hot, oh, my poor heart now sears;
To light out for New York, for this I yearn.
Thus fleeing from the formless faithful horde,
Soon now o'er a million I will firmly lord,
To the Panke's[19] banks then I'll return.

Antonie:
Ne'er again the Panke you will know,
In the chest your suit I'll have to stow,
And your top hat's form will sag and wilt;
There you'll go where German is not spoke,
Where the Mormons mean can but provoke,
And your love midst wild men be kilt.

Hermann:
All my debts, and all my silly ticks,
I will seek to lose 'mongst Yankee cliques,

17. Jay Gould was a notorious American financier during the Gilded Age.
18. A favorite among Berlin gourmets. (Footnote as in the original text.)
19. Sweet? smelling rivulet? near Berlin. (Footnote as in the original text.)

But my Toni I will keep.
Hark! conductors' curses from the train,
Here's my bag, from nagging now abstain,
Know that Hermann's love will never sleep!

Thus adapted and—why not say it right out loud—improved, Schiller would certainly find his way to the hearts of German-Americans.

So go to it, you in the United States of sun and fun, passion and fashion, aching and quaking, thieves and reprieves, rhyme like crazy by the sweat of your brows! Throw yourselves into the German classical poets, revise them, make them useful for today's youth! To the extent that my work on the "Decline of Intelligence, With Special Emphasis on Feature Articles in the Illinois Staats-Zeitung" permits me the free time—a work which would actually demand a lifetime's energies—I, too, am going to work in this direction; and indeed, I plan to shine as a local patriot: given the bankruptcies we've seen in the past few months, and the achievements of Chicago's city administration, I have chosen one of Schiller's early dramas: "The Robbers."

Flamingo.

Self-Evaluation and a Look Ahead

The assessment by the labor press of the experience of German workers in America remained contradictory, and it changed over the course of the years with the development of American society and the altered position of German workers within it. When the Chicagoer Arbeiter-Zeitung *took up the question of upward mobility in 1879, it came to the conclusion that the immigrants' hopes of moving up were increasingly contradicted by the reality of working-class life in industrial Chicago. Following the depression of the 1870s this assessment was probably shared by the considerable number of German immigrants who helped build a vital and aggressive labor movement in the city—one of the most significant in American history. The conversation reprinted here from a book by Alfred Kolb illustrates a different mood among German workers around the turn of the century after the radical political impetus of the 1880s had failed: the workers in the discussion are apolitical and uncertain how to judge their own situation in Chicago.*

The four other documents illuminate the situation of the labor movement in the first two decades of the twentieth century. Obviously, numerous children of working-class families had taken advantage of the opportunity offered by the public school system to be trained for middle-class jobs. As recently as 1889 an editorial of the Deutsch-Amerikanische Bäcker-Zeitung, *which was published in Chicago, had considered this development impossible, since poverty was inherited and passed on "from father to son, and from son to the grandchildren." This upward social movement of a large number of German workers and particularly their children helps explain the relative decline of the German element in the Chicago labor movement.*

After the turn of the century German organizations and German working-class culture were no longer at the center of the labor movement, but were relegated more and more to its periphery. Even the children of German workers who remained in the working class left the declining traditional trades of their fathers and entered expanding and prosperous new sectors of the economy, such as the electrical, machine-tool, and automobile industries. Because of the heterogeneity of the work force in such industries (compared to many of the old ethnically dominated crafts), the German language and culture could not provide the basis for organizing unions. Too many of the German-Americans born in Chicago did not know enough German anyway. Clearly, English had to be the main language for labor organizing among second-generation Germans, since it was the only language that could establish communication between the various immigrant groups.

Understandably, written and oral expressions of German working-class culture, as well as the organizations that maintained it, declined as the immigrant generation died out and German language competence receded. Nevertheless, the social and cultural forms and traditions introduced by the German-American labor movement were incorporated into a heritage drawn upon in the twentieth century by workers of varied ethnic background—for example, the use of picnics for the cause of labor as well as for leisure, the appropriation of traditional literary forms for agitational and educational purposes, and the visual and symbolic enactment of class conflict and social revolution, as in the "pyramid of exploitation" taken up by the Industrial Workers of the World (all of these being things that do not lend themselves to being documented in an anthology of German-language sources). The pessimism of some of the following documents derives from their authors' recognition that the experience of class remained closely bound up with the varieties of ethnic experience, particularly for the "new immigrants" arriving after the turn of the century, while many of the "old immigrants" including the Germans had already become integrated into a new multi-ethnic American working class, assuming a new national and cultural identity in the process.

And yet this clearly discernible tendency toward integration should not let us forget that German immigrant workers remained a sizeable element in the American working class and labor movement through World War I. As Adolf Dreifuss, the Chicago-based secretary of the German language group in the Socialist party, reminds us in the last document, older German immigrant workers who had arrived in the 1880s as well as those who came after the turn of the century still were not familiar enough with the English language so that a real need remained for a German language organization, which was founded at a surprisingly late date, i.e., in 1913. In Dreifuss's opinion, German labor leaders had for years stubbornly held to the illusion that to Americanize the party was equal to the total abrogation of the German language. Although Germans indeed represented neither the leadership nor the majority of the party's membership any longer, they, like other nationalities in the labor movement, still clung to their cultural traditions for all practical purposes. Thus they, too, merited foreign-language organization and agitation. In one significant way, however, the situation had changed: German workers no longer outnumbered other nationalities—in the summer of 1916 the German language group had only about 4,800 members—which meant that they were now on a par with other groups; even so Dreifuss still claimed that because of their older tradition they still could make a special contribution to the American labor movement.

131. "Commemorative Writ to the Chicago Central Labor Union," by August Nuber (*Fackel*, June 19, 1910).

(Commemorative writ of the Northwest Workers' Singing Association)

The site of the huge construction project, which is to become the station of the Northwestern Railroad on Chicago's West Side, once looked very different. It was neither beautiful, charming, nor attractive. Year in, year out, the dirt gathered in huge piles, especially on Lake St.; ugly, horrendous, grey-black junk shops interspersed between factories, other business offices, workers' saloons and meeting halls. Suspiciously idyllic, a row of pitiful, wretched houses adorned Clinton from Randolph to Washington streets; the huts were all crowded together, like a column of parading soldiers — they were all shrines to Venus. All of this splendor and magnificence is now gone. And yet nowhere else in the entire city was so closely connected to the progressive labor movement as was just this spot. When the powerful eight-hour movement shook the city in 1885-1886, West Lake and Randolph streets witnessed by far the most labor meetings. Masses of workers thronged here on that fateful May 4, 1886; most of the meetings on behalf of the victims of May 4 were held here; the progressive German workers gathered here and mourned in impotent pain following the catastrophe on November 11, 1887; here is where the police raided the meeting hall where peaceful workers were holding their meetings in 1891, where they arrested and dragged off a number of the workers, where they destroyed union property, tore up union banners, and for which they were later harshly reprimanded in court; here is where, some years later, many progressive German societies gathered in various halls to work together under the name of the "Socialistic Federation"; and even if this association's success did not last, its debates nevertheless played a large role in forming future developments. This is where, during its heyday, the central body of the German unions in Chicago was found, the Central Labor Union!

How it was known, hated, respected, feared and loved throughout the country — this organization which, unwept and unsung, passed away last year. Let's for once forget all the disappointments, the thwarted hopes, the betrayal and the persecution, and consider the way the Central Labor Union spread such powerful, deeply felt agitation in 1885-1886. As far as artisans were concerned, the C.L.U. organized all German-speaking workers with whom it came in contact; and it was just as successful with large numbers of unskilled workers. It was especially successful with three hardworking trades: the butchers, bakers and brewers! Even though the former butchers union was dissolved, it exists today in another form. And remember how incredibly hard people worked to strengthen the brewers' and bakers' organizations. How shamelessly the brewers were exploited, having to work endlessly long days, as were the bakers, who were even forced to lodge with their employers. And though so many things were not changed in these trades — and though in many respects conditions are still so bad — so many changes in these trades were nevertheless brought about, such great progress was made. And that was exactly the C.L.U.'s main contribution: when, after May 4, the reaction set in, the C.L.U.

continued to lend support to individual unions which had been weakened, and thus encouraging the debilitated troops, helping them get through the critical period. Assuming official posts and serving in delegations and committees free of charge, the C.L.U. thus stood up for the equal rights of the less talented, and this is what progress among workers is all about; and this was present in the C.L.U. And the time came when the flame of enthusiasm once again flared up; whose heart doesn't begin to race when thinking back to that night in July, 1894, when the union declared a sympathy strike on behalf of the Pullman and railroad strikers? and the subsequent meetings, full of young people, with their burning, tempestuous longing for freedom, and the general enthusiasm which reigned in the halls along West Lake and Randolph streets? One day, when the history of the North American labor movement is written, there will be a chapter entitled, "Chicago in the Last Two Decades of the 19th Century." And in that chapter, there will be a section on the C.L.U., maybe even reference to that historical spot occupied by the train station. In the C.L.U.'s heyday metal workers and workers in the building trades comprised the real foundation. Though all the unions had intelligent people in the central bodies, the cigarmakers, furniture and metal workers probably formed the elite. Later, in the '90s, the situation changed to a great extent.

And then the younger unions began to make themselves felt.

One circumstance which caused the German unions huge problems around the time of the worst reaction was a lack of people who were in sufficient command of the English language. Thus, when questions of strikes, label propaganda ⟨Label-Propaganda⟩, or other union-related issues arose, it was difficult to represent the German position to Anglo-American unions. The masses of backward workers almost always hinder the honest fellow worker from coming out in meetings and saying what's bothering him. He's mocked, ridiculed, and consequently intimidated. Moreover, public speaking isn't something which comes naturally, and a very, very large amount of practice is necessary before one can parry skillfully and logically in a foreign language! Now, we have to be tolerant of these backward workers because of their ignorance. But even formerly, it was these smooth-tongued smart alecks—always adept at shirking work, be it "delegation and committee work which isn't paid, or other kinds of difficult agitational work"—who often hurt the cause. It was also always interesting to observe how so often, after years of laborious and unrelenting work and energy on the part of the progressive element, when success finally seemed at hand—when success had to be at hand—some smart aleck would jump in right at the moment of triumph, someone who had contributed absolutely nothing; and the backward people cheered him joyously: "Look, here comes the victorious hero!" This, too, must be taken into consideration if we want to discuss the activity of the C.L.U. What's more, we must also consider those elements which always then appear, when their own organization has difficulties and grievances, elements which never comprehend that a central body can only be successful if the delegates are above all committed to general causes. . . .

I wouldn't at this point presume to unequivocally judge the causes which led to the dissolution of the C.L.U. These words are about the selfless work done by the progressive elements at the time of the C.L.U.'s heyday, about the reaction, and about the time when the organization's existence was more apparent than real! Some may have become renegades, some complacent bourgeois; and some little swank may talk disparagingly about that serious, grand period, the period of Chicago's battle and strife; endless errors may well have been committed, there may have been terrible battles within the organization, but we should nevertheless be elevated by the awareness that "there were once selfless, sacrificing men of conviction in the C.L.U., whose achievements were magnificent."

It is to these men, who were once so active and who still sympathize with the cause, that we would like to dedicate a friendly word: to the missing, to those who had to leave, to the deceased and the ruined—to each one of you an immortal wreath!!!

132. "Pessimism and the Labor Movement" (*Fackel,* May 24, 1908).

Not only is the number of pessimists in the labor movement much larger than is generally assumed, but this number is also growing, especially among the Germans, and at a rate which is staggering. Where have they gone, all of those who, years ago, so zealously contributed to the foundation and expansion of the workers' new class movement? Many have in the meantime become totally acclimated to a bourgeois existence; at best only a very few remain in touch with the organization by still reading one or two radical newspapers.

Looking back, one finds that this distancing became more and more popular in the course of time. Whereas formerly, people used to stick to the movement for an average of ten years, later you had to be content if you were lucky enough to see your so-called comrades occasionally over a period of five years! Today, as a rule, a comrade's activity doesn't last more than two years!

Sometimes we meet some of those who have disappeared in a saloon, and if we ask them about their indifferent behavior, they pretend to be either completely head over heels for unions or completely uninterested in them. Their excuses—if they even deign to make excuses—reveal a pessimism which is extremely unworthy and contemptible.

Whoever wants to appear especially impressive declares that he'll be there in the thick of it "if it ever gets going." The others scold like fishwives about diverse people who are active in the labor movement, and are quick to identify these people with the movement at large, with its endeavors, with the whole historical position of the proletariat as a social class. According to their opinion, each person who is connected to the labor parties is corrupt, the movement is "for the birds," the goals not realizable, humanity is just a bunch of crazy fools, etc.

And what is at the bottom of this desperate and bitter attitude? A lack of patience, and more, a lack of any real degree of courage to sacrifice, a courage which can only be evidenced in the most unshakable perseverance, and above all the lack of an ability to judge the general world and social situation, the human resources at our disposal, and the reasons which make the reorganization we strive for irrefutable.

Complaints concerning the human resources at our disposal are, when considered reasonably, completely unfounded. Whoever shares our view of the world must know that the people living today, coming out of society utterly consumed by egoism and ground up, as it were, between the grindstones of master and slave, have no choice but to be the way they are.

It's exactly this poor quality of today's people that should inspire the comrades—if that they really are—to remain true to the cause, never to desert, never to become depressed because of a momentary lack of apparent success.

To march along with the large crowd in the moment of triumph, to add one more voice to the general shout of victory, this demands neither artistry nor courage. True courage means not giving up the struggle, means uncompromisingly holding to principles which have been recognized as right.

It is true that those who are involved in political life and thought are persecuted, fought, denied, cursed and offended at every step and from all sides; their lives are made so disagreeable that they begin to question if it's worth living at all. But what do these difficulties—which, as already said, represent the natural, if rotten, fruit of the existing system—have to do with the revolutionary idea? T h a t is what we serve, not those

people who, regardless of whether they fancy themselves to be our comrades or not, make every day and every hour of our lives bitter. Should
the best of us bow to these others, who are ultimately more to be pitied
than hated? This would be a crime against the cause, or in any case the
most shameful disgrace.

Pessimism in the movement is responsible for more harm than all of
our enemies put together. Especially the caustic, poisonous pessimists.
Though these parasites have little or no interest in the working-class
movement, they nevertheless read our papers and sniff about here and
there—only, of course, in the hopes of getting information about disa-
greements and, like true devils, deriving pleasure from whatever difficulties
they might come up with. These people are not content to sit sulking in
the corner, oh no, they go out of their way to indulge in their favorite
pastime: they systematically destroy every other person's enthusiasm for
the cause. They complain about everything which was formerly sacred to
them until finally their friends and acquaintances also become obsessed
with the demon pessimism.

If these people would only stop to think seriously about the terrible
effect their comportment has, if they would skim back through the pages
of the book of their own life until they came to the chapter which described
those grand and enthusiastic hours when they, too, worked for an ideal,
then perhaps they'd be happy to give up their ruinous pessimism.

Pessimism is a distinguished, and of course, poisonous plant; it is only
appropriate for lifelong misanthropes; workers are treading along the wrong
path if they follow the example of the enemies of their class and turn to
pessimism. To be a pessimistic worker is synonymous with losing faith in
oneself, with barricading all paths to oneself. Let's look up and forward!
Let our souls be happy and full of optimism, and we will accomplish great
things.

133. Conversation among German Workers in Chicago (Alfred Kolb, *Als Arbeiter in Amerika* [Chicago, 1909], pp. 91-95).

Our evening diversion jumped from descriptions of their travels to other
experiences the raconteurs had had—their arrival in Chicago, the difficulties posed by the language, their first attempts to find work, the high
cost of living, etc. They also talked about childhood memories, about
their families, about military service—the latter was the favorite. In this
way, it was impossible to avoid comparisons between then and now,

between this side of the ocean and the other; and America was by no means always given precedence. "The only law here is money." - "Whoever's rich can do whatever he wants here without having to worry about being punished." - "Sometimes people still talk about an 'honest man' at home, but here there's only s m a r t ⟨Smarte⟩ and d u m b ⟨Dumbe⟩."

Remarks like these are not unusual. Social reform in Germany, the advantages of our health, accident, and disability insurance, our factory inspection carried out by officials with unblemished hands, all of these things were fully appreciated. In contrast to American officials, this last advantage, the uprightness of ours, was especially emphasized. One evening a young Saxon, the son of wealthy parents, complained that he had been declared fit for military service by a doctor at the consulate, and what's more, had been jumped on pretty hard because he had made a cash offer to free him from service; he had been ridiculed and told that he should have known better: the doctor was no Yankee, but rather had been sent by our Kaiser, and h e didn't send anyone with itchy fingers.

I don't recall having heard anything disrespectful about our Kaiser from Germans. Just the opposite: "Now there's someone who's still a m a n! If he could only do as he pleased, he'd take the breath away from the damned big mouths here!" This more or less corresponded to the feeling, expressed in many remarks, revealing a burning national pride. And the Yankees, too, — you could sense it clearly — when talking about "the Kaiser," with his strong personality, seemed to admire him in inverse proportion to their attempts not to show it.

If once in a while their cursing about America and the American became too abusive, the Americans began to boil over. "Hey! If you really had it so much better back there where you came from, what the hell did you come over here to us for? We didn't call for you, goddam!" Now this was a complicated question, and what our good countrymen answered, after their fashion, was sometimes pretty muddled. And no wonder: even intelligent people have come up empty when trying to explain why people emigrate. Nero's preceptor, Seneca, had already found three motives: political, economic, and personal. The religious motive was added later. And ultimately, all of them explain nothing other than the fact that the shoes back in the homeland are beginning to pinch. The only question is where to go? - and whether the cobbler's any better there.

Sitting at our stove, there was no agreement on this topic. One fact that was most often cited as a main advantage in America, and the praises of which I always had to hear in the above-mentioned charming terms, was that you could insult the President of the Republic without being punished for it. This fact then tended to be followed up by reference to freedom of speech in America in general, and safety from being charged with slandering royalty in specific. What's more, not much fuss was made about differentiating between Republic and republicanism. And why should there be? "Liberty enlightens the world" is written on the giant bronze lady who, a torch in her raised right hand, adorns the entrance to New York ⟨Neuyorker⟩ Harbor. The catch to this freedom, however, is noticed soon enough by those in America who don't have a checkbook. But then I also remember one evening, when someone wanted to link a weariness of Europe with a pressing need for freedom, and in this sense referred to the fact—as such correct—that far fewer French emigrated than Germans, Russians, Italians, etc. What was the reason for this? he asked. Quite simply because France was a Republic. When confronted with the objection that the handful of German cantons in Switzerland, which is also a republic, represent more emigrants than in all of France, the good man unfortunately just got crude. -

"One day, in our village back home," began another, "a letter came from Chicago. It was at the time of the World's Fair. The letter went on about the high wages here, about how a simple hod carrier could earn 9 Marks in 10 hours, how people ate meat three times a day, wore fine clothes and how workers got together at night with their boss ⟨Boß⟩ over a drink. The news shook the village like a bomb. Everyone would have been happy to drop everything on the spot and head off to the wonderland, America. Oh yeah, what a wonder! Wages are good here, true enough; but the letter didn't say anything about how long you can go without bread between jobs. We didn't find out about that until we got h e r e. If I had it to do over again today, I'd think twice before leaving home."

"But just the same, you wouldn't want to go back, right?" someone else threw in.

"Well, why not?"

"Because you couldn't last three weeks over there anymore. You'd get mad, go back to sleeping in the corner, eating boiled potatoes and herring. Oh no, my friend, we're better off now. Aside from good wages and a good living. Just think how different our relationship to the boss ⟨Boß⟩ is today. Do the likes of us have to take our hats off to him? It'd never even occur to him. We're just as good as him, on the street and in the saloon, everywhere. Nobody looks down on the manual worker; and the pen pusher isn't treated like a lord here, either. And that's the way it should be! Do you guys know the little story about the student who took a walk through the fields and watched the farmers ploughing? And got into a conversation with them. And when they saw how soft and smooth his hands were, they asked him if he wasn't used to working. 'I beg your pardon,' he protested, 'I work with my head!' And then they laughed at him and said their oxen worked with their heads, too."

Most of us laughed, too, although it was hard to imagine that they didn't already know the silly story. But it flattered the pride of their calloused hands and was often told again with remarkable pleasure.

There was no lack of contradiction, either. "They're just lazy jokers," began an older, well-paid locksmith. "Whoever isn't just a bag of rags will make something of himself here. T h a t' s w h y I came over. You say that wages are better here. You might just be right. But what're you worrying about wages for: you've got to become your own boss ⟨Boß⟩ if you want to get on. But t h o s e days are over in America. I tried it myself a couple of times. The last time as an innkeeper. Me and my late wife, we'd saved ourselves a nice little sum. Within a year everything was gone. No, you can forget it nowadays; for every o n e who gets rich, there are ten who go broke. And it's getting worse each year." -

For the Yankees who were present, this sort of thing was grist for their mills. "And whose fault is it, anyway, that it's getting worse and worse?" they shouted. "Who else if not the quarter-million European starvelings who come over every year and take up all the jobs. High time for some sort of law against this rabble. Stay home, why don't you, we don't need you. You work like snails anyway. . . ."

Such jingoistic ⟨jingoistische⟩ insolence incited the Germans' self-consciousness and loosened their tongues, thus leading to endless wrangling. The bitterest judgments about America stemmed either from those who had just arrived, or from those who had already been here for a long time. Some of them claimed that they'd like nothing better than to go home tomorrow, if only they had the money for passage. Those who so spoke did not, of course, consider how much quicker and easier they could now save money for the voyage home than had previously been the case when trying to save money for immigration.

134. "What Should the Worker's Child Become?" (*Fackel,* January 2, 1910).

At first glance, the question seems superfluous. If the parents have been waiting impatiently for their children to finally go out and earn something, what else should they become but workers. As soon as the boys and girls have finished school, they are immediately sent off to the factory, the office, the store, etc. Whether they are sent here or there is not a decision they make themselves; it simply depends on where there happens to be a vacancy, where they can earn a few dollars each week. Where dire need immediately forces the children into a position offering the best wages, it would really be a bad joke to begin thinking about what workers' children should become. Given the circumstances, they have to thank their lucky stars if they find any kind of work where the conditions are more or less tolerable.

But there are other workers whose means allow for such considerations. Workers with higher wages, with permanent, secure jobs, could in fact permit themselves the luxury of thinking about what their children should become. For they could grant them, even if only with much difficulty, somewhat more latitude as far as a livelihood is concerned.

But then the rigid class-conscious comrades come along and bluntly declare: "It's nothing but sinful arrogance, nothing but bourgeois class prejudice, if you let your children be something else. They should be workers, they should pride themselves in remaining true to their class. If you let your children desert the ranks, you're betraying your own class interests!" And it might even be that some parents who have ambitious plans somewhere in their hearts abandon them with bad consciences.

Dear parents, you who want the best for your children, don't let yourselves be misled by this sort of noise. It is nothing more than a senseless exaggeration of class consciousness. We needn't be so mean that we ask each and every one of these noisemakers: "Shouldn't you yourself be deeply grateful that your present position has distanced you from the wretched misery of the proletariat?" For they really s h o u l d be grateful for it. Nor do we want to find out if they aren't spending everything so that at least their son can attend a better school—for in fact, they should be doing that, too. Instead of this, we want to calmly refute a senseless argument for what it is—senseless.

Now we must also add that it is a fine thing for workers to take pride in feeling like workers. But let's be completely honest: is the individual worker really always proud of his class position? when he's reprimanded by his master, when he's put out on the street by his landlord, scorned by the rich and considered only half a person by the intellectual? When his wife scolds him because of his meager wages, when his children don't have shoes, and he himself has no winter coat? The answer: each time the individual worker is humiliated, each time he must go without, he feels the misery of the proletarian existence too sharply to be able to pride himself in belonging to the ranks of the disenfranchised. The only real opportunity for him to experience class pride, and where he should experience it, is when, midst roaring multitudes, he feels himself one with thousands of others, when he is prepared to vanquish this wretched fate, when he feels himself among the masses of his comrades in misery, when he feels that together they constitute a power which wants to—and could—build a new world.

And should the children, too, have to relive all the degradation of the proletariat, even though it might be possible to let them begin on a higher level of living? No and no again! Children should be able to do more and do it better than their parents; so, if there's any way to swing it, see to it that they are better armed with knowledge and energy. If you are only unskilled workers, your children should be skilled workers; if you were only journeymen locksmiths and maids, then let your boys be technicians and your girls trained nurses and teachers, if you can find a way. The young people want to come forth, and they should come forth, in every sense of the phrase.

And where, in all the world, is it written that a better position will cause them to lose their feelings for their class? Bring them up with the great ideals of a liberated and elevated mankind—and they, with more knowledge and secure in their independence, will be more valuable fighters than those who vegetate in misery and silent resentment. A stance toward socialism is not contingent upon position, it is contingent upon conviction, upon a belief in the future of humanity.

135. "The German Language Group of the Socialist Party," by Adolf Dreifuss (*Fackel*, September 3, 1916).

For some socialist parties, most notably in Austria and the United States, the question of nationality is a sore spot. In the United States, however, it is less a question of nationality than of language, and the problem assumes a different form than in other places. . . . Here in America, national groups have no desire to shake the foundations of the state's political unity. Nor do they inhabit areas set aside just for themselves: everywhere they live interspersed throughout the entire population. They recognize English as the official and colloquial language, they attempt to learn and make use of it to the best of their abilities. Soon they are sufficiently familiar with the language to find and hold down jobs, i.e., to be able to understand the technical terms related to the job in question. They also learn to buy things in the national language, gradually "picking up" enough English so they can no longer, as the saying goes, be "sold." But in most cases, this is as far as they go. Only a few learn enough to be able to read English-language newspapers without difficulty. It is very rare that, in addition to newspapers, foreigners feel called upon to read, let alone study, English-language literature. And they rarely take part in public life - unless, that is, they become politicians, who are richly rewarded for swaying and "delivering" their fellow countrymen's votes to one side or another.

This is not surprising. Given today's education, the average person must be praised for even partially mastering elements of a foreign language. And once the indispensable amount has been acquired, the will to go on from there seems paralyzed. People claim they can "learn" no more. If their economic circumstances are by this time more or less secure, they find social gratification in all sorts of clubs and societies made up of fellow countrymen — singing societies, Turner societies, skat clubs, sickness and mutual benefit societies, etc. The merit of such institutions is beyond doubt. But the result is an even greater immersion in the language, mores and customs of the homeland. People believe they understand enough English to support themselves and their families and that everything else can be taken care of via their native language. With the exception, of course, of participating in public life, though they don't worry too much about this. . . .

In all of these societies and clubs, and outside of them as well, one can find plenty of workers who think and feel socialistically and who make no bones about it. But they shy away from English-speaking organizations. Feeling insecure when it comes to speaking English, they can listen, but cannot speak up. And then there is the fact that they have no agitational basis. Their friends and acquaintances are — to exemplify our own case — German, speak but little English and do not want to join English-speaking clubs. It is true that many Germans belong to English-speaking socialist branches. We are not, however, talking about these people, but rather about those who do avoid them because of language barriers.

But where there's a will there's a way, and foreign-language branches were organized throughout the entire land. Party branches were formed among Germans, Jews, Bohemians, Russians, Hungarians, Italians, etc.

It was like this for many years. These branches agitated in their districts, doing all they could. But their efforts were necessarily limited. . . . These branches were good; but once founded, it was absolutely imperative that they establish contact with one another in order to profit from all the means and energies available.

Thus the language groups emerged.

The Finnish language group was the first. . . . Today, the following language groups exist, all connected with the Socialist party: Finnish, Southern Slavic, Italian, Scandinavian, Hungarian, Bohemian, Jewish, German, Slovakian, Lithuanian, and Latvian. All told, they account for about one third of the party's members. . . .

The German language group is one of the most recent. It was established in March, 1913. The necessity for a German language group within the Socialist party had already existed for a long time when, on December 28, 1912, at the convention of the German branches in New Castle, Pa., the resolution was passed to found one. The German socialists identified so strongly with the party as a whole that, in an effort to help further the actual movement, they had been neglecting propagandistic efforts among their own fellow countrymen. Many old comrades remembered the time when Germans had gone to great lengths to make the party American, and the pleasure which was derived from hearing a newly recruited *American* comrade address a *German* audience in *English,* thus giving the impression that the movement had become an English-speaking one. But finally it was generally conceded that conditions had thoroughly changed, that the English-American movement had outstripped its German parentage, that many Germans—even German workers who had been active in socialist organizations in Germany—had no access to the movement here or felt completely estranged from it. Most people further realized that agitation capable of winning over German-speaking people—newly arrived immigrants as well as those already living here—could only be attained by means of a *strong language group.* Indeed, it was also recognized that only a language group would enable German experience and staunchness of principle—indisputable traits, not because we are better, but rather because literature and tradition are older and deeper with us—to exert a greater influence on the movement as a whole.

The *founding* of the German language group occurred psychologically at the right moment: just long enough prior to the outbreak of the world war so as to be strong enough to meet the challenges arising in the wake of this catastrophe.

These challenges were extraordinarily large. Those who did not find themselves in the middle of the turbulence cannot imagine the confusion and alarm in the German party branches in America after August 4, 1914. Opinions clashed, and those who were not firm left the party. This can be seen in the fluctuating membership figures, though these can also be attributed in part to the extensive unemployment of the times. . . . It is worth noting that despite the confusion caused by the war and despite unemployment in the most critical phases, membership in the German language group never receded to what it had been at the beginning of 1913; to the contrary, it remained consistently a good deal higher.

These are results which underscore the effectiveness of the young German language group, results which could only be attained through independent, systematic attempts to inform and enlighten. Comrade Kollontay, commissioned by the German language group to conduct an extensive agitational tour through the United States from October, 1915, to the end of February, 1916, played a very important role in clarifying the situation.

The large number of organizational and agitational tours conducted by the German language group in its brief three years' existence attest to its unremitting agitational activity. Sometimes stepping in for two or more tours, the speakers included: comrades Jos. Ameringer (Milwaukee), Heinrich Bartel (Milwaukee), Max Bedacht (San Francisco), Jos. Beregszaszy (Detroit), Martin Bunge (Milwaukee), Adolf Dreifuss (Chicago), Jos. Jodlbauer (Cleveland), Jul. Koettgen (New York), Fritz Krueger (New York), Carl Minkley (Milwaukee), Jos. Mosler (New York), Philipp Scheidemann (Berlin), Emil Seidel (Milwaukee), F. Speer (New York), Ernst Untermann (Milwaukee), Carl Vogt (Lawrence, Mass.), Bruno Wagner (New York), and the comrades Alexandra Kollontay (Berlin) and Marie McDonald (New York).

In the next few days Otto Sattler (N.Y.) is to begin a tour until election day which will take him from the East to the Midwest. Somewhat later he will be followed by Max Bedacht (San Francisco) for the West and Fritz Krueger (N.Y.) for the East. Jul. Koettgen, presently active in New England, will also continue until election day.

And if the war hadn't placed a stumbling block in our path we would have had a delegate from the German Reichstag and Rosa Luxemburg at our side for the upcoming elections.

The German language group has already published a large number of leaflets, among them two for women, which are being distributed among the individual branches through the zeal of our comrades. Just off the press is a special election leaflet entitled: "Hughes or Wilson?" Another leaflet deals with the contemporary issue of "Armament Robbery" and another warns: "Workers, Think of the Future!"

In addition, the German language group solved a long-standing problem by printing a series of German-American brochures. Our "Socialist Workers' Library" already comprises eight volumes, among which is a historical work of lasting value: Hermann Schlüter's "The International in America," a history of the labor movement in the United States from the outset of the Civil War to 1880, with special emphasis on the activities of the International Workingmen's Association on American soil.

Due to a dearth of appropriate material, most German-speaking workers in this country take no pleasure in reading any more. The German language group's "Socialist Workers' Library" is meant to—and hopefully will—restore these pleasures, a service which in itself would make our efforts worthwhile, for reading this literature means knowledge, and—"knowledge is power."

BIOGRAPHICAL SKETCHES

ANNEKE, Fritz (1817-72)   Born in Dortmund, Anneke served as an officer in the Prussian army. Together with his wife, Mathilde Franziska, he took part in the Baden Revolution of 1848. Both he and his wife traveled via Switzerland to the U.S. Anneke first worked as a day laborer for the railroad in Illinois, and was then active among German liberals in Milwaukee, primarily as a journalist. He contributed to various German-American newspapers, including the *Anzeiger des Westens,* and was correspondent for the *Augsburger Allgemeine Zeitung.* In the 1850s he lived for a time in Newark, New Jersey, where he edited the *Newarker Zeitung.* An ardent Republican, he served as a colonel in the Civil War, commanding the 35th Regiment of Wisconsin. He was later active in Chicago; his last position was as agent of the German Society there.

CONZETT, Conrad (1843-97)   Born in Switzerland, Conzett was trained as a printer. After a sojourn in Leipzig beginning in 1867, he immigrated to the United States in 1869. He was a member of the First International, co-founder and chairman of the German printers union of Chicago in 1873, and in the following year was a founding member of the Labor party of Illinois. Shortly after the founding of the Chicago *Vorbote* in 1874, he became its editor and owner. In 1876 he was a delegate to the founding conference in Philadelphia of the Workingmen's party of the United States. Having returned to Europe, Conzett became active in the Swiss labor movement. In 1882 he assumed direction of the Swiss Co-operative Printing Association and Volksbuchhandlung Hottingen-Zurich. Conzett took his own life in 1897.

DRESCHER, Martin (1863-1920)   Born in Wittstock, Brandenburg, Drescher studied in Breslau, Berlin, and Göttingen. After immigrating to the U.S. in 1891, he at first had to make his way as a tramp; he then became active in the German-American labor movement as a journalist. From 1898 to 1900, following Robert Reitzel's death, Drescher edited his paper *Der arme Teufel;* he then worked on the *Chicagoer Arbeiter-Zeitung*—for a time as editor-in-chief—where he published many of his poems, some of them under the pseudonym "Flamingo." Drescher later distanced himself from the labor movement. His works include *Gedichte,* 1909; and *Vom Sturm gepeitscht. Skizzen und Geschichten aus einem Zigeunerleben,* 1913.

GEIßLER, Ludwig (?-?)   A German socialist, Geißler lived in New Orleans. In 1876 he published the radical magazine, *Der Hammer.* In the early 1880s he contributed short stories and other work to the *feuilleton* section of the *Fackel,* the Sunday edition of the *Chicagoer Arbeiter-Zeitung.* Geißler took part in a communistic colony in Covington, Louisiana. In 1891 — obviously in response to Edward Bellamy's *Looking Backward*—he published his utopian work, *Looking Beyond.*

GROTTKAU, Paul (1846-98)   Grottkau was born into a noble family in Cottbus, Brandenburg. Instead of studying architecture, he took up practical training as a mason in Berlin, where he came into contact with the labor movement. By 1871 he was already on the executive board of the Allgemeiner Deutscher Arbeiterverein, and at this time he organized the masons and edited their union newspaper, the *Grundstein.* Grottkau served several prison terms, and before fleeing to the U.S. in 1878 was on the editorial staff of the *Berliner Freie Presse.* In Chicago he edited the *Vorbote* and the *Chicagoer Arbeiter-Zeitung,* but left his position in 1884 when irreconcilable differences arose between himself and the anarchists. Appreciated for his brilliant speeches, Grottkau went to Milwaukee and worked as an editor. He was arrested there and brought to trial during the May disturbances in 1886. Later he worked again in Chicago as well as in San Francisco as an editor, and made extensive trips as an organizer for the American Federation of Labor. He died in Milwaukee in 1898 while on an agitation tour for the Social Democratic party.

LESSEN, Ludwig (= Louis Salomon) (1873-1943)   Lessen studied history, philosophy, and literature. In 1896-97 he was on the editorial staff of the *Volksblatt* in Halle. From 1900 to 1919 he was in charge of *Die Neue Welt,* after which he joined the editorial staff in the *Vorwärts* publishing house. In 1933 he was prohibited from practicing his profession. Lessen took his own life in 1943. His works include *Fackeln der Zeit,* poems, 1904; and *Aus Tag und Tiefe,* poems, 1911.

LYSER, Gustav (1841-1909)   Lyser was born in Dresden. His parents — both of them artists—acquainted him with the Vormärz literary tradition. When he was thirty years old, he was on the editorial staff of the Braunschweig *Volksfreund.* Barred from the Sozialdemokratische Arbeiterpartei in 1873, Lyser emigrated to New York. There he worked in his profession as a printer before soon becoming editor of the *Social-Democrat.* Shortly thereafter he became co-editor of the *Sozialist* in Milwaukee, and in 1876 represented the Milwaukee socialists at the founding conference in Philadelphia of the Workingmen's party of the United States. In Chicago from the late 1870s onward, he was on the editorial staff of the *Fackel;* during this time he also produced a wealth of poems. Lyser later returned to Milwaukee. After another halfhearted commitment to the labor movement in Chicago in the early 1890s, Lyser apparently distanced himself from it permanently.

REITZEL, Robert (1849-98) One of the most talented among the radical German-American writers, Reitzel emigrated in 1870 and soon became the minister of a German reformist congregation in Washington, D.C. While still in Washington, he gave up his profession and aligned himself with the freethinkers. Later he went to Detroit. There he founded the paper *Der arme Teufel,* which he edited and wrote—for the most part alone—from 1884 until his death in 1898. Reitzel was closely associated with the Chicago anarchists, to whom he lent his unconditional support. After their executions in 1887, he gave the funeral address, and also spoke at radical gatherings. His works include *Der arme Teufel,* 1884-98; *Des Armen Teufel gesammelte Schriften,* 1913; and *Abenteuer eines Grünen,* 1909.

ROSENBERG, Wilhelm Ludwig (1850-193?) Rosenberg studied the natural sciences, medicine, philology, and philosophy. After receiving his doctoral degree, he taught Latin for several years. In the mid-1870s, he began writing for the Social Democratic press, including *Die Neue Welt.* In 1880, threatened with arrest, he fled from Frankfurt on the Main to America. At first he was a teacher in Boston, but in 1881 he assumed editorial duties at the *Chicagoer Arbeiter-Zeitung.* In 1884 he was called to New York to be secretary for the Socialist Labor party, and in this capacity was co-editor of the party organ, *Der Sozialist.* In 1889 Rosenberg was removed from his position, after which he worked as a journalist in Cincinnati. His last position there was on the editorial staff of the *Cincinnatier Tageblatt.* Around the turn of the century he founded a school for retarded children in Cleveland. His last publication, in 1928, was a contribution to the *New Yorker Volkszeitung.* His works include: *Die Nihilisten,* drama, 1882; *Vor der Wahlschlacht,* comedy, 1887; *Crumbleton,* drama, 1898; *An der Weltenwende,* poems, 1910; and *Krieg dem Kriege,* poems, 1915.

SAHM, Carl (1821-83) Sahm studied music in Paris. A political refugee, he emigrated to New York in 1853, where he gave music lessons and conducted singing societies. He composed over three hundred pieces for men's choirs, forty solo pieces, duets, a comical opera, operas for children, and a few longer works. He also wrote the texts to many of his own compositions.

SCHILLER, Josef (Seff) (1846-97) While still a child, Schiller had to earn his living in a factory. In 1869 he co-founded the first Social Democratic organization in Bohemia (Liberec), and was active in the socialist labor movement as an agitator, organizer, poet, and journalist until his death. In 1896 he emigrated to the U.S., where, having retired to the country, he died one year later. The only surviving copies of some of Schiller's poems are in his own hand; many were lost. His works include *Gedichte,* 1890; *Ausgewählte Gedichte,* 1885; *Blätter und Blüten aus dem Kranze meiner Erinnerungen,* 1890/91; and *Selbstbefreiung,* a play written for a festival (which was performed in 1883), 1889.

SCHWAB, Michael (1853-98)   Born in Kitringen, Franconia, Schwab was orphaned at an early age. After leaving high school prematurely, he was trained as a bookbinder. In 1872 he joined the Sozialdemokratische Arbeiterpartei. From 1874 to 1879 he traveled through Europe as a journeyman, and then emigrated to the United States in 1880. After another year of travel in the West, Schwab found a position on the *Chicagoer Arbeiter-Zeitung* in 1881, where he worked as a translator, reporter, and editor. In 1886, following the Haymarket bombing, he was arrested and sentenced to death, but his sentence was commuted to life imprisonment. In 1893, together with Neebe and Fielden, Schwab was pardoned, after which he continued his activity in the Chicago labor movement until his death.

SEIDEL, Robert (1850-1933)   Although he grew up in a poor family, Seidel was nevertheless able to become a master weaver. He took part in the founding congress of the Sozialdemokratische Arbeiterpartei in Eisenach in 1869. In the late 1870s he emigrated to Switzerland to avoid being drafted into the army. In Zurich he attended the teachers college and the university. Seidel became a schoolteacher, then taught at the polytechnic institute, and finally became a university professor. From 1890 to 1898 he was the business manager of the official paper for the unions and the Social Democratic party in Switzerland. His works include, among others, *Aus Kampfgewühl und Einsamkeit,* poems, 1895.

SPIES, August (1855-87)   Born in Landeck, Hesse, Spies attended the polytechnic institute in Kassel. In 1872, after his father died, Spies decided to emigrate to the U.S. In New York, and shortly afterwards in Chicago, he learned the upholstery trade, and went into business for himself in 1876. In the same year, his mother and siblings followed him to the U.S. In 1875, via the Labor party of Illinois, Spies came into contact with socialism for the first time, and two years later joined the new Socialist Labor party. He was a candidate for public office several times. In 1880 Spies became manager of the *Chicagoer Arbeiter-Zeitung,* and when Grottkau left in the fall of 1884, Spies became editor-in-chief. In 1883, he was a delegate at the congress of the International Working People's Association in Pittsburgh. In 1886, following the Haymarket bombing, he was arrested and sentenced to death; he was hanged on November 11, 1887.

STAUBER, Frank (1848- ?)   Born in Switzerland, Stauber came to Chicago as a young man in 1867. He first worked as a tinsmith, and three years later opened a hardware store on the Northwest Side. In the late 1870s he made a name as a Socialist Labor party candidate for alderman. In 1878 he was elected to the city council, and again in 1880, though this time only after contesting the election on grounds of electoral fraud. After 1886 Stauber worked for the commutation of the death sentences against the anarchists, and in 1886 he was the United Labor party's nominee for the post of county treasurer. Stauber was active in party politics until after the turn of the century, but he distanced himself from the Socialist Labor party, becoming active in the Democratic party instead.

SUGGESTIONS FOR FURTHER READING

AVRICH, PAUL. *The Haymarket Tragedy* (Princeton, 1984).

BUHLE, MARI JO. *Women and American Socialism, 1870-1920* (Urbana, Ill., 1981).

CONZEN, KATHLEEN NEILS. "Germans." In *Harvard Encyclopedia of American Ethnic Groups* (Cambridge, Mass., 1964), pp. 405-25.

DAVID, HENRY. *History of the Haymarket Affair* (New York, 1958).

FONER, PHILIP, ed. *The Autobiographies of the Haymarket Martyrs* (New York, 1969).

GUTMAN, HERBERT G. *Work, Culture & Society in Industrializing America* (New York, 1977).

HOFMEISTER, RUDOLF. *The Germans of Chicago* (Champaign, Ill., 1976).

HOLLI, MELVIN G. "The Great War Sinks Chicago's German *Kultur*." In *Ethnic Chicago,* rev. and expanded ed., edited by Melvin G. Holli and Peter d'A. Jones (Grand Rapids, Mich., 1984).

JENTZ, JOHN B. "Bread and Labor: Chicago's German Bakers Organize." *Chicago History* (Summer, 1983).

JENTZ, JOHN B., and HARTMUT KEIL. "From Immigrants to Urban Workers: Chicago's German Poor in the Gilded Age and Progressive Era, 1883-1908." *Vierteljahrschrift für Sozial- und Wirtschaftsgeschichte,* Bd. 68, Heft 1 (1981).

KEIL, HARTMUT. "German Working-Class Radicalism in the United States from the 1870s to World War I." In *"Struggle a Hard Battle": Essays on Working-Class Immigrants,* edited by Dirk Hoerder (DeKalb, Ill., 1986).

KEIL, HARTMUT. "Einwandererviertel und amerikanische Gesellschaft. Zur Integration deutscher Einwanderer in die städtisch-industrielle Umwelt des ausgehenden 19. Jahrhunderts am Beispiel Chicagos." *Archiv für Sozialgeschichte,* Bd. 24 (1984).

KEIL, HARTMUT, ed. *Arbeitswelt und Lebensweise deutscher Arbeiter in Chicago von 1850 bis zum Ersten Weltkrieg. Amerikastudien/American Studies,* Bd. 29 Heft 2 (1984); special edition on the Chicago Project.

KEIL, HARTMUT, and HEINZ ICKSTADT. "Elemente einer deutschen Arbeiterkultur in Chicago zwischen 1880 und 1890." *Geschichte und Gesellschaft,* 5. Jg. Heft 1 (1979).

KEIL, HARTMUT, and JOHN B. JENTZ, eds. *German Workers in Industrial Chicago, 1850-1910: A Comparative Perspective.* (DeKalb, Ill., 1983).

KÖLLMANN, WOLFGANG, and PETER MARSCHALCK. "German Emigration to the United States," trans. Thomas C. Childers, *Perspectives in American History,* 7 (1973).

LIDTKE, VERNON. *The Alternative Culture* (New York, 1985).

PIERCE, BESSIE LOUISE. *History of Chicago,* 3 vols. (New York, 1937-57).

POORE, CAROL J. *German-American Socialist Literature 1865-1900* (Bern and Frankfurt, 1982).

RITTER, GERHARD A., ed. *Workers' Culture. Journal of Contemporary History,* vol. 13, no. 2 (1978); special issue.

Friedrich A. Sorge's Labor Movement in the United States: A History of the American Working Class from Colonial Times to 1890, edited by Philip S. Foner and Brewster Chamberlin (Westport, Conn., 1977).

TOWNSEND, ANDREW JACKE. *The Germans of Chicago* (Chicago, 1932).

WALKER, MACK. *Germany and the Emigration 1816-1885* (Cambridge, Mass., 1964).

INDEX

Page numbers in italics refer to introductions, those in roman type refer to documents.